INTERFIGURAL READINGS OF THE GOSPEL OF JOHN

EARLY CHRISTIANITY AND ITS LITERATURE

Shelly Matthews, General Editor

Editorial Board:
Jennifer A. Glancy
Joseph A. Marchal
Anders Runesson
Janet Spittler
Matthew Thiessen

Number 26

INTERFIGURAL READINGS OF THE GOSPEL OF JOHN

Ingrid Rosa Kitzberger

Atlanta

Copyright © 2019 by Ingrid Rosa Kitzberger

All rights reserved. No part of this work may be reproduced or transmitted in any form or by any means, electronic or mechanical, including photocopying and recording, or by means of any information storage or retrieval system, except as may be expressly permitted by the 1976 Copyright Act or in writing from the publisher. Requests for permission should be addressed in writing to the Rights and Permissions Office, SBL Press, 825 Houston Mill Road, Atlanta, GA 30329 USA.

Library of Congress Cataloging-in-Publication Data

Names: Kitzberger, Ingrid R., author.
Title: Interfigural readings of the Gospel of John / by Ingrid Rosa Kitzberger.
Description: Atlanta : SBL Press, 2019. | Series: Early Christianity and its literature; 26 | Includes bibliographical references and index.
Identifiers: LCCN 2019032650 (print) | LCCN 2019032651 (ebook) | ISBN 9781628372533 (paperback) | ISBN 9780884144014 (hardcover) | ISBN 9780884144021 (ebook)
Subjects: LCSH: Bible. John—Criticism, interpretation, etc. | Bible. Gospels—Criticism, interpretation, etc. | Intertextuality in the Bible.
Classification: LCC BS2615.52 .K5675 2019 (print) | LCC BS2615.52 (ebook) | DDC 226.5/066—dc23
LC record available at https://lccn.loc.gov/2019032650
LC ebook record available at https://lccn.loc.gov/2019032651

Contents

Acknowledgments vii
Abbreviations xi

Foreword
A Call to Personal, Transformative, Autobiographical Criticism:
Reflections on the Work of Ingrid Rosa Kitzberger
  Fernando F. Segovia 1

Introduction 27

Part 1. Reading Strategies

"How Can This Be?" (John 3:9): A Feminist-Theological
Rereading of the Gospel of John 43

How Can You Read John?! The Pains and Pleasures of Reading
the Fourth Gospel 67

Part 2. Reading Characters in John, the Synoptics, and the Hebrew Bible

Mary of Bethany and Mary of Magdala—Two Female Characters
in the Johannine Passion Narrative: A Feminist, Narrative-Critical
Reader Response 81

Stabat Mater? Rebirth at the Foot of the Cross 107

The Three Marys and the Fourfold Gospel 127

Aging and Birthing: Open-Ended Stories and a Hermeneutics of Promise..........141

Part 3. Characterization and Gender

Untying Lazarus—A Sisters' Task? Revisioning Gender and Characterization in John 11 167

Transcending Gender Boundaries in John..........179

Part 4. Characters in John and My Self-Text

"The Truth Will Make You Free" (John 8:32): The Power of the Personal Voice and Readings of/from the Gospel of John 219

Reading and Rereading the Samaritan Woman's Story: Characterization and Social Location..........237

Flowing Identities..........249

Part 5. Teaching Strategies

Models of Discipleship and Teaching Strategies: Learning from John..........269

A Response: Where from and Where To?
Francis J. Moloney, SDB 281

Bibliography..........291
Ancient Sources Index..........307
Modern Authors Index..........316
Subject Index..........320

Acknowledgments

Without the encouragement of many people, colleagues and students, this volume would not be. Since my work was published in diverse places, on three continents, it has not always been accessible to interested readers. On the other hand, there has been interest in reading papers I presented at various conferences that have remained unpublished. I thank all those who suggested and supported my decision to compile a collected volume.

I especially thank David G. Horrell from the University of Exeter, the series editor, and the editorial board members of Early Christianity and Its Literature for graciously accepting my proposal and for their encouraging positive responses, practical help, and suggestions for revising my original plan. Without Horrell's patient and faithful support through the various stages, this volume would not have taken the shape it has. Thus, he also guaranteed the smooth transition to the new series editor shortly before manuscript submission. I thank Shelly Matthews from Brite Divinity School at Texas Christian University for her kind reception of my newborn.

Bob Buller and Nicole Tilford from SBL Press have been the most encouraging and patient supporters, too, from the very first to the final stages. It was Buller's great response to my initial contact presenting my idea for this volume that put me on track. Tilford, and later Heather McMurray, provided precious practical help with the details of getting the volume published. I am most grateful to all three of them, who give such a kind face to SBL Press.

Fernando F. Segovia (Vanderbilt University, Nashville) and Francis J. Moloney, SDB (University of Divinity, Melbourne) have been a great source of support, in many ways, in this multidimensional process of compiling such a volume. I graciously thank them for sharing their editorial expertise, besides their encouragement at various stages in my professional career and their unfailing friendship, regardless of the tide being in or out. It was, therefore, very special and a great joy to meet both again, after many years, on Austrian home ground, at the International Meeting of the Society of Biblical Literature in Vienna in 2014. I am most grateful for their kind willingness to write the foreword and response. Due to their own locations in the United States and Australia, respectively, and my own in between, in Europe, the global, intercontinental perspective of this volume is underscored.

The essays included here would not have come into being without numerous colleagues, men and women from around the globe, whom I encountered and worked with beginning in the early 1990s, with whom I shared exciting discussions at conferences on both sides of the Atlantic and cooperated on various projects. I am grateful for and to all of them, too many to be named individually here. However, some are mentioned in the introduction and in the essays, including footnotes, as well as in the publications referred to in this volume.

Besides my colleagues, my special gratitude is extended to my students at different universities from whom I have learned as much as they might have learned from me. My students at the Graduate Theological Union in Berkeley, however, have a very special place in my heart as well as in my scholarly career. The invitation extended to me by the Jesuit School of Theology to teach as visiting professor of New Testament in the academic year 2001–2002 turned out to be the most wonderful experience, which provided the unique opportunity to work with students from across the world and very different cultural and religious backgrounds. These were truly transformative encounters in the global village classrooms on Holy Hill.

I gratefully acknowledge reprint permission granted by the following publishers (in chronological order of publication):

Cambridge University Press and the Society for New Testament Studies for "Mary of Bethany and Mary of Magdala—Two Female Characters in the Johannine Passion Narrative: A Feminist, Narrative-Critical Reader Response," *NTS* 41 (1995): 564–86.

Scholars Press (now SBL Press) for "'How Can This Be?' (John 3:9): A Feminist-Theological Re-reading of the Gospel of John," in *Literary and Social Readings of the Fourth Gospel*, vol. 2 of *"What Is John?,"* ed. Fernando F. Segovia, SymS 7 (Atlanta: Scholars Press, 1998), 19–41.

Lumen-ISEDET for "Aging and Birthing: Open-Ended Stories and a Hermeneutics of Promise," in *Los caminos inexhauribles de la Palabra: Relecturas creativas en la Biblia y de la Biblia; Homenaje a J. Severino Croatto*, ed. Guillermo Hansen (Buenos Aires: Lumen-ISEDET, 2000), 387–411.

Deo Publishing (now Blandford Forum, UK) for "Flowing Identities," in *Autobiographical Biblical Criticism: Between Text and Self*, ed. Ingrid Rosa Kitzberger (Leiden: Deo, 2002), 79–96.

Bloomsbury Publishing for "Transcending Gender Boundaries in John," in *A Feminist Companion to John*, ed. Amy-Jill Levine with Marianne Blickenstaff (Sheffield: Sheffield Academic, 2003), 1:172–206.

Brill Academic Publishers for "Stabat Mater? Re-birth at the Foot of the Cross," in *Biblical Interpretation*, Jubilee Volume 11.3.4, *Texts, Currents, Hermeneutics*, ed. J. Cheryl Exum (Leiden: Brill, 2003), 468–87.

Due to the profound changes in the publishing business, besides different style sheets and various computers I or volume editors worked with, every single chapter included in this volume had to be retyped, just as one colleague had prophetically foreseen. Thanks to him for encouraging me to "go gently" when facing such a challenge. It was a unique experience to be my own secretary, reconnected to my former selves at the time of the original writings and their respective contexts. I have grateful memories of all those who shared these with me.

Abbreviations

AARSR	American Academy of Religion Studies in Religion Series
AB	Anchor Bible
ABRL	Anchor Bible Reference Library
Ann.	Tacitus, *Annales*
Ant.	Josephus, *Jewish Antiquities*
ATD	Das Alte Testament Deutsch
BETL	Bibliotheca Ephemeridum Theologicarum Lovaniensum
BibInt	*Biblical Interpretation: A Journal of Contemporary Approaches*
BibInt	Biblical Interpretation Series
B&L	The Bible & Liberation
BLS	Bible and Literature Series
BN	*Biblische Notizen*
BTB	*Biblical Theology Bulletin*
BZ	*Biblische Zeitschrift*
CBQ	*Catholic Biblical Quarterly*
CC	*Cultural Critique*
ConBNT	Coniectanea Biblica. New Testament
DA	Die Altertumswissenschaft
EdF	Erträge der Forschung
EJL	Early Judaism and Its Literature
ETL	*Ephemerides Theologicae Lovanienses*
FCB	Feminist Companion to the Bible
FFNT	Foundations and Facets. New Testament
GBS	Guides to Biblical Scholarship
GCT	Gender, Culture, Theory
Haer.	Irenaeus, *Adversus haereses*
JAAR	*Journal of the American Academy of Religion*
JBL	*Journal of Biblical Literature*
JJS	*Journal of Jewish Studies*
JR	*Journal of Religion*

JSNT	*Journal for the Study of the New Testament*
JSNTSup	Journal for the Study of the New Testament Supplement Series
JSOT	*Journal for the Study of the Old Testament*
JSOTSup	Journal for the Study of the Old Testament Supplement Series
KST	Kohlhammer Studienbücher Theologie
LXX	Septuagint
Neot	*Neotestamentica*
NLH	*New Literary History: A Journal of History and Interpretation*
NovT	*Novum Testamentum*
NovTSup	Supplements to Novum Testamentum
NRSV	New Revised Standard Version
NTS	*New Testament Studies*
NTTS	New Testament Tools and Studies
ÖEH	Ökumenische Existenz heute
PR	*Psychoanalytic Review*
QD	Questiones Diputatae
RSV	Revised Standard Version
RT	*Revista de Teologia*
RTT	Research in Text Theory
SBABNT	Stuttgarter Biblische Aufsatzbände: Neues Testament
SBLDS	Society of Biblical Literature Dissertation Series
SBLSP	*Society of Biblical Literature Seminar Papers*
SBS	Stuttgarter Bibelstudien
SemeiaSt	Semeia Studies
SFSHJ	South Florida Studies in the History of Judaism
Sir	Sirach
SNTSMS	Society for New Testament Studies Monograph Series
SNTW	Studies of the New Testament and Its World
SWR	Studies in Women and Religion
SymS	Society of Biblical Literature Symposium Series
Tib.	Suetonius, *Tiberius*
TS	*Theological Studies*
UTB	Uni-Taschenbücher
WUNT	Wissenschaftliche Untersuchungen zum Neuen Testament
ZSNT	Zacchaeus Studies: New Testament
ZTK	*Zeitschrift für Theologie und Kirche*

Foreword
A Call to Personal, Transformative, Autobiographical Criticism: Reflections on the Work of Ingrid Rosa Kitzberger

Fernando F. Segovia

I distinctly recall the context in which I met Ingrid Rosa Kitzberger. Not precisely so, I would have to say, but rather in general terms. It was as part of the General Meeting of the Society for New Testament Studies at some point in the early 1990s. At that time I was well into my tenure as professor of New Testament and Early Christianity at Vanderbilt University, while she was a Lise Meitner Research Fellow at the University of Münster in pursuit of her *Habilitationschrift*. Since then, our paths would cross many times over, across the world, not only within the confines of these annual gatherings of the Society for New Testament Studies but also in meetings of the Society of Biblical Literature, annual and international alike. Now, twenty-five years later, they cross yet again, this time only in discursive fashion, by way of this volume, a collection of her studies brought out by SBL Press. She asked, in effect, whether I would be willing to write a foreword for the volume, and this invitation I accepted without hesitation. Indeed, it is a task that I undertake with a keen sense of gratitude.

That initial acquaintance of ours within the context of the Society for New Testament Studies proves essential, I believe, for an appropriate understanding and appreciation of Dr. Kitzberger's work in general and the present collection of essays in particular. In fact, she herself uses throughout the framework of professional meetings, including those of the Society for New Testament Studies, as a marker for her own academic-intellectual development. For this introduction to her work, I shall proceed in three steps. I shall begin with a twofold reflection on the Society for New Testament Studies: its ethos as a learned society, on the one hand, which I shall develop by way of annual program, historical origins, and social-cultural orientation; and our particular site of encounter as a formal component of the Society, on the other hand, which I shall unfold in terms of its peculiar, even unique, bent within the Society. From there I shall proceed to trace the development of Dr. Kitzberger's critical stance by following her own observations in this regard. I shall conclude with a reflection on the present state of affairs in the field, twenty-five years later, with both the Society for New Testament Studies and Dr. Kitzberger in mind. The result, it is my hope, will be a mapping of the wherefrom and the whereto of Dr. Kitzberger's life as a biblical critic.

The Context of the Society for New Testament Studies

The Ethos of the Society for New Testament Studies

Program

First, then, I begin with a word about the structural arrangements of time and offerings of the Society as reflected in the program of the General Meetings. For quite some time now, and certainly for as long as I have been associated with the Society for New Testament Studies, the annual gatherings of the Society have followed a stable structure, revolving around a set of three full days of meetings. This structure has involved, on the one hand, a number of recurring organizational features: morning prayers, business meetings, and the presidential address. On the other hand, the structure has also included a number of time allocations for presentations each day: an early morning session, a late morning session, and a mid-afternoon session. Taking up the early morning session as well as the mid-afternoon session, a number of general presentations are offered: some of these, the main papers, are designed as plenary addresses; the rest, the short main papers, encompass a variety of presentations offered at the same time. During the late morning session, a wide number of seminar groups—hovering around fifteen in all—take place concurrently.

These seminar groups, which to my mind represent the backbone of the meetings, are submitted to and approved by the committee of the Society for a set period of time, usually lasting a term of five years. Some take up a specific topic of inquiry, lasting for a limited number of terms. Others pursue general, traditional areas of research, extending term after term without interruption. The seminar groups function, therefore, along the lines of a task force, to which members subscribe during registration and which they then attend for the duration of the meeting, three sessions in all. Such attendance, I should note, is by no means mandatory; members registered for any one seminar group can attend sessions of other seminar groups.

It was as part of one such seminar group, one devoted to a specific and timely topic, that our paths came together for the first time and on a systematic basis thereafter over a period of years. In terms of the Society for New Testament Studies and its ethos as a learned society, this site of encounter was a most unusual endeavor indeed. Its critical parameters, objectives, and discussions differed sharply from those at work in all other seminar groups.

Origins

Second, I continue with a word on the institutional foundations of the Society as conveyed by its historical origins.[1] The Society for New Testament Studies was formally founded in September 1938 at Carey Hall, Selly Oak, Birmingham, United Kingdom. Such roots are worth recalling. These are to be found in the missionary movement of the Christian churches throughout the world during the course of the nineteenth century. In fact, the desire for the creation of such a society was first expressed within the context of the World Conference on Faith and Order held at Edinburgh in 1937, among a group of scholars of the New Testament in attendance. The Society for New Testament Studies is thus ultimately related to the Faith and Order Movement, which in turn comes out of the womb of the World Missionary Conference of 1910 at Edinburgh.[2] The untoward competition of the churches in the mission fields of the world throughout the preceding

---

1. For such background, I rely on the following recollections of the history of the Society, both to be found on its website: William R. Telford, "SNTS, Its Origins, and Robin L. McWilson's Contribution to the Society" (address given on the occasion of the Ninetieth Birthday Celebrations for Prof. Robin L. McWilson at the University of Saint Andrews, February 18, 2006, https://tinyurl.com/SBL4523a); and G. H. Boobyer, "The Early History of Studiorum Novi Testamenti Societas," *Bulletin of New Testament Studies* 1 (1950): 7–10.

2. For the Faith and Order Movement, I am indebted to the following pieces: Mary Tanner, "What Is Faith and Order?," World Council of Churches, August 1, 2009, https://tinyurl.com/SBL4523c; Thomas J. Ferguson, "Faith and Order Movement Turns 100," Episcopal Church, October 18, 2010, https://tinyurl.com/SBL4523d.

century was increasingly viewed as scandalous for its message and detrimental to its credibility. Consequently, this conference of 1910 was called to focus on cooperation, laying aside controversial and divisive issues for the occasion and giving rise thereby to the modern ecumenical movement.

After the conference, driven by the realization that unity would come about only if there were agreement in faith and the conviction that such unity was feasible, an initiative was launched to go beyond the goal of cooperation, to move toward mutual understanding and earnest dialogue among the churches. The result was a call for a global conference on matters of faith and order, which, after much consultation, led to the First World Conference on Faith and Order, which took place at Lausanne, Switzerland, in 1927. The agenda was fourfold: the call for unity, the nature of the church, the common confession of the faith, and the ministry and sacraments. This agenda continued, in one way or another, in all subsequent World Conferences on Faith and Order, beginning with the second one, held at Edinburgh in August 1937.

It was on this occasion, therefore, that a number of New Testament scholars, about ten or so, gathered together, led by Professor J. de Zwaan of Leiden University, to discuss the launching of a learned society for the study of the New Testament. Most hailed from the United Kingdom, but there was representation from Continental Europe as well. Given the interest expressed in such a venture, plans were made to invite more scholars to participate in this project, and a decision was taken to meet again at Selly Oak in September 1938.

That is indeed what happened. At Birmingham, after further discussion, the following actions took place: a proposal to launch a society "for the furtherance of our New Testament Studies" was made by Professor C. H. Dodd, then holder of the Norris-Hulse Chair at Cambridge; the motion was carried unanimously, bringing the Society into being; and the process of preparation toward a First General Meeting—to take place September 20–22, 1939, at Birmingham—was put into place. This inaugural gathering, however, would not come to be until years later, given the earlier declaration of war by the United Kingdom that September and the outbreak of World War II. It would thus not be until after the utter devastation of the war, on March 26–28, 1947, that the Society—with a total of thirty-eight members in attendance—finally came together for the first time at Christ Church, Oxford University.

In the light of this historical trajectory, it is quite appropriate to bring together for critical analysis the material and discursive dimensions behind the institutional foundations of the Society. Such juxtaposition involves, on the one hand, the holding of a World Conference on Faith and Order, growing out of the missionary movement, attended by the founding members of the Society; on the other hand, the launching of a learned society of biblical scholarship, devoted to the study of the New Testament, undertaken by this group of scholars. In point of fact, the ecclesial and ecumenical dimensions of the Faith and Order Movement can be readily perceived at work in such a move. The proposed joint and open study of the Christian Scriptures among the biblical scholars of Europe through the creation of a learned society can be readily construed as a way of advancing this vision of unity and ecumenicity. Such dimensions may be seen at work in the Society in a variety of ways.

In terms of practice, first, the program adopted for the First General Meeting of 1939 was to open with a worship session on the part of the membership. I have no doubt that such a service did take place at the 1947 meeting, and I know for a fact that such a liturgical practice has remained in effect through the present. In fact, what one finds today is a threefold series of worship services. These take place as the initial event of each day and are conducted each day in a different official language of the Society.

Further, in terms of objective, the proposed joint and open study of the New Testament could be readily reinterpreted as a contribution toward a vision of reconstruction, reconciliation, and redirection for Europe, in the face of a wasted, divided, and exhausted continent. This was indeed a Europe overwhelmed by material and cultural ruin, riven by a struggle just concluded against the onslaught of fascist ideology and a struggle in the offing against the expansion of Communist ideology, and crisscrossed by massive waves of displaced groups and populations looking for a new home. Such a view of the Society, I well recall, was actually conveyed to me during a General Meeting, but, alas, my memory of the details of this occasion—the where, the who, the why—is but a trace at this point.[3]

In terms of orientation, last, a driving focus of the proceedings throughout has been religious-theological in character. Here, however, a fundamental distinction is imperative. Such has been the case, and continues to be so, not at the level of the agent of study, the realm of interpreters and interpretations, but rather at the level of the object of study, the realm

---

3. My instinct tells me that it was a conversation with John Painter, professor of New Testament at the University of Canberra, Australia, that supplied such information.

of the texts and contexts of Christian antiquity. Very little light has been cast, let alone shed, on the religious-theological backgrounds and orientations of the members of the Society and the effects of such convictions and contexts on the task of interpretation.

In this respect, too, the unusual nature of the seminar group in which our paths first crossed and subsequently collaborated is beyond question. In this site of encounter, a space was opened, theoretically and methodologically, for the emergence of the religious-theological focus of inquiry at the level of interpreters and interpretation, namely, the domain of the agent of study.

Orientation

Third, I end with a word about the academic-intellectual parameters of the Society as embodied in its orientation toward the field of studies. The historical trajectory outlined above reveals a number of other material and discursive features of the Society. To begin with, the Society for New Testament Studies came to life as a decidedly European organization, with a heavy base in the United Kingdom but also with an open door to Continental scholars. With the passing of time, and certainly by the time that I joined, the Society for New Testament Studies had turned into an organization of the Global North, given the incorporation of a growing number of scholars from the world of English-speaking North America as well as from the world of the British Commonwealth, such as Australia and New Zealand as well as South Africa. Representatives from the Global South were few and far between, more often than not by way of invited guests. Moreover, the Society for New Testament Studies functioned from the beginning as an elite organization. Membership was reserved for established scholars, at both the senior and the middle rank: members not only had to satisfy the publication equivalent of a German *Habilitationsschrift* but also had to obtain the backing of two standing members of the Society by way of letters of recommendation. Last, the Society for New Testament Studies came to life as a learned society grounded in and committed to the pursuit of philological-historical scholarship. It embodied and advanced the academic-scholarly ideals, approaches, and objectives of biblical criticism as conceptualized and formulated in the long-standing grand model of scientific historical criticism.

This portrayal of the Society was still very much in evidence forty years later, when I joined its ranks in the late 1980s. I was nominated for and elected to membership in 1987 and attended my first meeting as a member in 1988, which was the Forty-Second General Meeting of the Society for New Testament Studies and took place at the University of Cambridge. It was overwhelmingly a gathering of the Global North, mostly male in membership. In fact, it was only that year that the Society had its first female president, Professor Morna D. Hooker of Cambridge University. It was also decidedly senior in constitution. The Society controlled and marginalized the presence and contribution of beginning scholars and graduate students by relegating them to the category of guests, limited in number and subject to approval. It was distinctly wedded as well to the principles of scientific historicism. On the one hand, with regard to texts and contexts, empiricism, determinacy, and stability ruled; on the other hand, with respect to interpreters and interpretation, reconstruction, objectivity, and impartiality were the norm. This was still very much the era of historical-theological inquiry: the historical-contextual analysis of Christian antiquity with a focus on religious-theological formations and backgrounds, positions and conflicts, in texts and contexts.

Even here, however, the winds of major theoretical and methodological developments taking place in the field of studies—and across the entire spectrum of the academy—since the mid-1970s were beginning to make themselves felt, if ever so slightly. The seminar group wherein our paths crossed and collaborated was, without question, a salient site of such developments. In no way did it fit the traditional historical-contextual and religious-theological task of scientific historical biblical criticism, rendering it thereby as a most unusual endeavor indeed within the academic-intellectual ambit of the Society. In retrospect now, some thirty years later, this seminar group stands as unique, for no other such group along these lines, taking up in sustained and systematic fashion theoretical and methodological innovations, has emerged since then. Such were, then, the peculiar circumstances in which Dr. Kitzberger and I met and worked for a number of years and in which her work began to take a different turn altogether.

Site of Encounter

What was this space?[4] It was a seminar group focused on the problematic of readers and reading in biblical criticism, started and cochaired by Pro-

---

4. For this information, I am indebted, beyond my own recollections, to written electronic communications with Professor James Voelz of Concordia Lutheran Semi-

fessors Bernard C. Lategan of Stellenbosch University in South Africa and Edgar V. McKnight of Furman University in Greenville, South Carolina, from 1985 to 1989, and cochaired by Bernard C. Lategan and James W. Voelz of Concordia Lutheran Seminary in the United States from 1990 to 1999. The seminar was first approved in 1985, under the name The Role of the Reader in the Interpretation of the New Testament, and renamed Hermeneutics and the Biblical Text in 1993. The seminar began with the Thirty-Ninth General Meeting of the Society in Trondheim, Norway, in 1985 and concluded with the Fifty-Third General Meeting in Pretoria, South Africa, in 1999. Among its regular participants over the years were such figures as Edgar V. McKnight and Elizabeth Struthers Malbon, Bas M. E. van Iersel and Sjef van Tilborg, Detlev Dormeyer and Wolfgang Schenk, Robert M. Fowler and Stephen Moore, Willem Vorster and Francis Watson. My own attendance began upon admission to the Society in 1988, while that of Dr. Kitzberger started two years later, on the invitation of Professor Detlev Dormeyer, whom she worked with then at the University of Münster. This seminar group reflected the growth of one particular methodological-theoretical development in the field during the late 1970s and into the 1980s, namely, the rise of literary biblical criticism. This new grand model of interpretation, which paralleled that of sociocultural criticism, focused on the dynamics and mechanics of the text as text. As such, it would come to encompass a variety of directions, drawing on different movements within the field of literary studies—structuralism, narratology, reader response, rhetorics, psychoanalysis, deconstruction.

At this point in time, the seminar pursued the question of reading as brought to the fore by narrative criticism and reader response, doing so along largely formalist lines, such as intratextual reader constructs and historical reader constructs. At the time of its conclusion, the seminar had begun to entertain the question of the real reader, the flesh-and-blood reader, with its attendant questions of social location and perspectival agenda. In so doing, it was reflecting and intersecting with the rise of ideological criticism in the field, with its focus on differential relations of power in society and culture. However, a decision was taken by the cochairs not to seek renewal. Two factors played a large part in such a decision: a perceptible trend of declining attendance and the fact of much

---

nary and Stephen Moore of Drew University, both of whom were active participants in the life of the seminar group.

too long a trajectory for a pointed rather than a general task force within the program.

In retrospect, that such a seminar group was accepted in the first place within the resolutely historical-theological context of the Society for New Testament Studies was indeed an amazing feat. That it was renewed not just for a second term but also for a third one is even more incredible. Perhaps a renewal in terms of full-fledged ideological criticism would have proved impossible. In any case, it was the last of its kind, for nothing akin to it, nothing that reflects the complex and conflicted developments of the field since then, has found its way into the program in the course of the years that have elapsed since its folding. Dr. Kitzberger joined this group as a scholar formed in the historicist-theological model but would eventually be profoundly transformed by the readings and discussions of this seminar and beyond. Indeed, this collection of essays captures such a turn of events, such a different impulse in her life and her work.

Transformation: A Critical Trajectory

Toward the end of the seminar group, Dr. Kitzberger produced three edited collections of essays, all related in one way or another to the problematic of reading and readers. The first of these, *The Personal Voice in Biblical Interpretation*, came out immediately prior to its conclusion.[5] The other two, *Transformative Encounters: Jesus and Women Re-viewed* and *Autobiographical Biblical Criticism*, appeared shortly afterward.[6] For all three volumes she contributed a general introduction and a topical study. The introductions provide highly informative and insightful information not only about the collections themselves, their respective parameters and objectives, but also about the volumes as a set, the contextual and critical relations among them.

The introductions thus provide much information about the professional and academic settings within which the volumes, individually as well as collectively, were forged, given the emphasis placed throughout—as previously noted—on the pivotal role played by annual conventions and program units of learned societies. They reveal, first of all, the close

---

    5. Ingrid Rosa Kitzberger, ed., *The Personal Voice in Biblical Interpretation* (London: Routledge, 1999).
    6. Ingrid Rosa Kitzberger, ed., *Transformative Encounters: Jesus and Women Re-viewed*, BibInt 43 (Leiden: Brill, 2000); Kitzberger, ed., *Autobiographical Biblical Criticism: Between Text and Self* (Leiden: Deo, 2002).

interaction at work between such cultural production on her part and the social-cultural context of the seminar group within the Society for New Testament Studies. Such information includes the trajectory of her formal relationship to the Society: first, her election to full membership in 1995, at the Forty-Ninth General Meeting of the Society in Prague, the Czech Republic; and, second, her attendance as a guest for a number of years already, beginning in 1987 with the Forty-First General Meeting of the Society in Göttingen on the invitation by Professor Eugen Ruckstuhl from the University of Lucerne, Switzerland. The introductions reveal, in addition, an expanding connection between this cultural production and the social-cultural context of the Society of Biblical Literature by way of increasing participation in the work of its Annual Meetings. In what follows I use these introductions to trace the path of her academic-intellectual development over the course of these years.

Personal Criticism

In the introduction to *The Personal Voice in Biblical Interpretation*, Kitzberger pinpoints the driving aim of the volume.[7] The time has come, she states, to foreground the voice of the critic in interpretation, after having lain "muted and suppressed"—though by no means inactive, for its presence was always in play—for so long under the model of scientific historicism. This first project she traces to a variety of developments. Two of these have to do with the approach of reader response: the move toward the construct of the real reader and the concomitant focus on the social location of such readers. Here she points to the work of several members of the Society for New Testament Studies seminar along these lines and refers most particularly to a presentation of mine on cultural studies at the International Meeting of the Society of Biblical Literature of 1995 in Budapest. Two other developments involve publication projects: the beginning of autobiographical criticism in biblical criticism and the existence of a project on the voice of the critic in classical scholarship.[8] The latter, under consideration for publication by Routledge at the time, she learned about

---

7. Kitzberger, *Personal Voice in Biblical Interpretation*, 8.
8. Jeffrey L. Staley, *Reading with a Passion: Rhetoric, Autobiography, and the American West in the Gospel of John* (New York: Continuum, 1995); Judith P. Hallett and Thomas Van Nortwick, eds., *Compromising Traditions: The Personal Voice in Classical Scholarship* (London: Routledge, 1997).

while in Budapest, in a conversation with the editorial assistant in charge of the project. It is there that the idea of the volume was hatched, leading to a formal launching in 1996 and culminating in publication in 1999.

This insertion of the personal voice, Kitzberger argues, bears weighty consequences for the understanding and practice of criticism. This it does both in terms of the plurality of individual critics and the plurality of reader positions within individual critics. With regard to the plurality of critics, the insertion of the personal voice is said to alter the dynamics and mechanics of interpretation. With regard to the plurality of readers in critics, such insertion is viewed as raising the highly complex and conflicted problematic of identity.

How does the intromission of the personal voice affect the mode of interpretation? Kitzberger points to three such ways. First, such foregrounding affects the status and role of the critic directly. In opting for self-exposure and eschewing the traditional persona of anonymity, the critic not only renders oneself vulnerable but also reveals how critical reading is ultimately grounded in ordinary reading, tearing aside the traditional binomial in this regard. Second, it has an impact on the character of any interpretation advanced. Criticism is now viewed as intertextual in nature, the result of a dynamic encounter between text and reader, through which meaning is produced. As such, criticism is further seen as yielding a panoply of readings of any text, insofar as neither text nor reader is autonomous. Criticism, moreover, is regarded as creative in character, for the dynamic encounters in question do not follow any particular rules of engagement, leading to a wide range of genres instead. As such, criticism is further seen as encompassing a variety of possible readings of any text, insofar as neither text nor reader is autonomous. Last, such foregrounding affects the process of interpretation itself. In opting for self-disclosure, the critic is forced to claim the reading advanced as one's own as well as reflect on the effects that such a reading may have on others, highlighting thereby the ethical dimension at the core of all criticism.

How does the irruption of the personal voice introduce the question of identity? Kitzberger mentions three ramifications. To begin with, the voice introduced is not single and bounded but rather multidimensional, like the texts themselves, so that no one reading, no one dynamic encounter between text and reader, involves the voice of the critic in its entirety. Real readers encompass within themselves a plurality of readers at all times. In addition, such a voice is by no means determinate and stable but rather fleeting and relational, so that it is in constant flux. Real readers represent a number of readers over time. Finally, the voice introduced is not natural and self-evident but rather a rhetorical construct, so that any one reading presupposes a choice in the what and how of communication on the part of the reader. Real readers, therefore, construct themselves in different ways at different times for different purposes.

Such external as well as internal plurality of critics leads, according to Kitzberger, to two highly significant and most welcomed results for criticism. On the one hand, criticism emerges as a "symphony of voices" in ever-expanding fashion:[9] the participants in the project engage in dynamic encounters with texts, unique in each case; then, readers of the volume engage in dynamic encounters of their own with the interpretations offered, similarly unique in each case; and so on, as the circle of interpretations, dynamic encounters, grows and widens ever more. On the other hand, criticism emerges as a "democratic enterprise," as interpretation is tied to dynamic encounters throughout and as the personal voice is identified in all such encounters. In this exercise the ideal becomes to speak with one's own voice and to listen to the voices of others, so that "equality, justice, and respect" prevail.[10] It should go without saying that in all these aspects of the project—be it the driving aim expressed, the weighty consequences outlined, or the welcomed results portrayed—the influence of the seminar group, its discussions and its readings, on Kitzberger and her work is unmistakable, far reaching and wide ranging.

Transformative Criticism

The introduction to *Transformative Encounters* does not explicitly relate this project on re-viewing Jesus and women to the first one on personal voice; implicitly, however, the connections are manifold and manifest. Four such links can be readily discerned. The first involves the matter of editorial timing—the conceptualization, formulation, and development of the projects. The second has to do with the question of theoretical framework—the view of criticism as an encounter in both projects. The third concerns the matter of methodological perspective—the focus on women and the adoption of feminist criticism as object and lens of criticism, respectively. The

---

9. Kitzberger, *Personal Voice in Biblical Interpretation*, 10.
10. Kitzberger, *Personal Voice in Biblical Interpretation*, 10.

fourth involves the question of methodological approach—the close relation at work between personal criticism and transformative criticism.

With regard to editorial timing, the launching of this volume is traced to the same year as the other, 1996, so that both projects were begun and pursued alongside each other. In this second project, the role of professional conventions and consultations in its development is more keenly highlighted: its trajectory is said to comprise two General Meetings of the Society for New Testament Studies (1997 in Birmingham and 1998 in Copenhagen) as well as three Annual Meetings of the Society of Biblical Literature (1996 in New Orleans, 1997 in San Francisco, and 1998 in Orlando). The project on personal voice found its way to publication in 1999, one year earlier than this one on transformative encounters, no doubt as a result of its more ambitious scope.

With respect to theoretical framework, both projects revolve around the notion of a critical encounter involving critics and texts. The idea of a "symphony of voices," cast as a key consequence of the project on personal voice, whereby participants engaged in dynamic encounters of various sorts, comes across in this project as well, though by way of a different metaphorization. In this project on re-viewing Jesus and women, the professional venues and discussions comprehended by the process of composition are described as "gardens of transformative encounters, in virtual and real reality," where participants are likewise said to have engaged in a variety of transformative encounters, in which "many different and charming plants grow from the seed, in as many varieties as the soil they sprang from."[11]

With respect to methodological perspective, the first project points forward, indirectly, to the second. The introduction to the volume on personal voice refers in passing to a long-standing commitment to feminist biblical interpretation. This observation was made in the course of the exchange with the editorial assistant of Routledge cited earlier, during the International Meeting of the Society of Biblical Literature in Budapest.[12] Such interest in women and feminist criticism, however, did not find its way into that project, formally or materially. Thus, the volume had but three women among the contributors. Similarly, no critic, male or female, wrote on a topic having to do with women or feminism—with one exception. Such interest did, however, become a primary focus of attention in the project on

---

11. Kitzberger, *Transformative Encounters*, 3.
12. Kitzberger, *Personal Voice in Biblical Interpretation*, 9.

transformative encounters, as its goal of re-viewing the interaction between Jesus and women reveals. Now, the one exception in question is the study by Kitzberger herself, who proves significant in another way as well.

With regard to methodological approach, the first project again points forward to this second one, though now quite directly so. A marked concurrence in critical approach can be readily discerned. In effect, at the heart of Kitzberger's exercise in personal voice criticism lies the element of transformation central to the second volume. In fact, this study very much points forward to the third project on autobiographical criticism as well.

That contribution certainly represents an example of personal voice criticism, as both title ("Border Crossing and Meeting Jesus at the Well") and subtitle ("An Autobiographical Re-reading of the Samaritan Woman's Story in John 4:1–44") indicate. The result is a dynamic encounter with the text: "Entering John's story-world from my own story-world," she declares, "and entering my own story-world from John's story-world, both have been informed and transformed intertextually." At the same time, the contribution looks beyond to the projects on transformative and autobiographical criticism as well. On the one hand, Kitzberger undergoes a transformative encounter with the woman of Samaria, crossing borders and meeting Jesus anew by way of this character. On the other hand, she undertakes this transformative encounter on a distinctly autobiographical key, with copious recollection of places and events, persons and experiences, in her life, all activated by the story of this woman of Samaria. What ensues, she argues, is that "a new story has emerged which is no longer one or the other, but both, a story of mixture and otherness."

Thus, in effect, in the exercise of personal criticism, Kitzberger is already integrating and performing transformative as well as autobiographical reading. All three projects may be seen, therefore, as coming together at the same time in Kitzberger's program of research. It is no wonder, therefore, that the connections among all three are manifest and multiple.

This second project on re-viewing the interaction between Jesus and women advances, it should be noted, a complex notion of transformative encounter. It is complex, yielding a fourfold field of attention with corresponding sets of approaches. The first two dimensions deal with the past. The first level addresses the transformative encounters that take place between Jesus and women in the gospels. It is concerned with the world of the text and has recourse to a variety of literary approaches. A second level focuses on transformative encounters between Jesus and women within the temporal-historical and social-cultural context of Palestine and the

Mediterranean. Its concern is with the world behind the text, and it appeals to a number of historical as well as sociocultural methods. The other two dimensions address the present. A third level involves the transformative encounters that occur between texts and interpreters, as the latter analyze the encounters between Jesus and women. The fourth level refers to the transformative encounters that develop among interpreters in the process of their collaborative work on the encounters between Jesus and women. These focus on the world in front of the text and represent actualizations of the texts. In both diversity is the aim and the rule: whether as a result of different critical approaches brought to bear on the texts or as a consequence of the different faces and voices brought together by a global and inclusive roster of participants. Such dimensions of transformation, one should add, are viewed as by no means self-standing and mutually exclusive but rather as interrelated and border crossing.

What is sought in the end is a re-viewing of the interaction between Jesus and women "by asking new questions, addressing new issues, realizing new contexts, and challenging what has so far been taken for granted, including one's own stance in biblical scholarship."[13] Further, as in the case of the first project, what such re-viewing seeks is an "awakening of the imagination"[14] on the part of the readers of the volume. These are invited to take up the task and move forward with their own multidimensional transformative encounters, in order to re-view "our present world and our relations, inside and outside academia."[15] This last point introduces, as in the first project as well, the question of ethical interpretation: all must be held accountable for their interpretations and "the worlds created out of them."[16] What this entails, however, remains undeveloped.

Autobiographical Criticism

In the introduction to *Autobiographical Biblical Criticism*, Kitzberger pointedly addresses the relationship of this third volume to the first one on personal voice, but not to the second one on transformative encounters. With regard to the former, personal criticism, she does so materially as well as discursively. From a material perspective, she recounts how the

---

13. Kitzberger, *Transformative Encounters*, 2.
14. Kitzberger, *Transformative Encounters*, 9.
15. Kitzberger, *Transformative Encounters*, 9.
16. Kitzberger, *Transformative Encounters*, 9.

genesis of this project flowed directly from that first project, and here again the recurrent marker of professional gatherings and consultations plays a key role. From a discursive perspective, she explains the difference between the two projects by distinguishing between criticism in the style of the personal voice and criticism in the form of the autobiographical voice. With regard to the latter, transformative criticism, there is no formal focus on women or feminist criticism. Nevertheless, two indirect links are present. At the heart of autobiography, she argues, lies the problematic of identity, the politics of identity involved in the construction of a self. This the contributors are said to engage by attending to the constitutive markers of identity, among which that of gender is listed. Further, in her own study for the volume, "Flowing Identities," such a focus does play a role in her own process of autobiographical construction.

The volume is even more keenly tied than the other two to the element of professional conventions and consultations. It is thus said to have emerged out of a session sponsored by the program unit Semiotics and Exegesis at the 2000 Annual Meeting of the Society of Biblical Literature in Nashville. This session, she adds, had been put together, as is often the case, at the previous Annual Meeting of 1999, and hence just after the publication of *The Personal Voice*. It bore the title "What Is Critical about Autobiographical Criticism? Methods and Ethics of Personal Voice," and its goal was "to keep alive and to continue the discourse and practice of *The Personal Voice in Biblical Interpretation*."[17] The format was designed not along the lines of a panel discussion on the volume but rather in terms of paper presentations that would take up the topic in question from a variety of perspectives. Kitzberger recalls the occasion in exalted terms: "On November 19, 2000, an emerging new interpretive community assembled … to bring real life back to Scripture and Scripture back to life, to experiment within the open space between text and self."[18] The volume thus brings together the presentations from that session, now developed as full-fledged studies, while incorporating a number of studies of a similar nature either originally given in other contexts or expressly solicited for the publication.

The project is said to follow a different path, a "most personal and intimate variant" thereof,[19] in advancing the discourse and practice of the

---

17. Kitzberger, *Autobiographical Biblical Criticism*, 3.
18. Kitzberger, *Autobiographical Biblical Criticism*, 3.
19. Kitzberger, *Autobiographical Biblical Criticism*, 5.

personal voice. In effect, Kitzberger now describes personal criticism as an umbrella model of interpretation, within which three variations may be found. This grand model represents, to my mind, a variant of reader-response criticism, in itself a critical approach within the grand model of literary biblical criticism. It is reader response with a focus on real readers. The three variations identified are as follows: readings that focus on real readers, readings that foreground the social location of real readers, and readings that integrate the personal lives, the autobiographies, of real readers. This third volume represents, therefore, a shift from the first variation, with its focus on the personal voice of real readers, to the third, with its focus on the autobiography of real readers—the bringing together in conversation by critics of the texts of the Bible and the texts of their lives.

Whereas in the first project Kitzberger concentrates on the consequences of the personal voice for criticism, here she emphasizes the academic-intellectual background of autobiographical criticism—and thus, ultimately, of the model of personal criticism as a whole. In so doing, she relies on a classic work from the heyday of reader response in the 1970s, David Bleich's *Subjective Criticism*.[20] This background is captured in terms of a shift in cultural paradigm alongside a shift in ethical practice. The former involves a change from objectivism to subjectivism in the academic-intellectual world at large, a development that, writing in 1978, Bleich saw as tied to the narrative of modernity and at work since the 1920s and 1930s. The latter involves a change from removed knowledge to engaged knowledge, a development revolving around the place assigned to ethics in such pursuit.

Autobiographical criticism is said to embody the cultural shift. It, too, follows the introduction of personal experience, of the subject, in the critical experience and analysis of the object, so that objectification is problematized and the objective is approached, in turn, as a construction of the subjective. Autobiographical criticism is further said to reflect the ethical shift. It also follows the incorporation of personal involvement, of the critic, in the critical experience and analysis of the object, so that distantiation is problematized and knowledge is viewed instead as no longer standing apart from personal responsibility but rather as demanding "relationship, responsibility, and commitment" on the part of the critic.

---

20. David Bleich, *Subjective Criticism* (Baltimore: Johns Hopkins University Press, 1978).

In this subjective and ethical mode of knowledge and criticism, therefore, the critic is aware of a choice among interpretations, assumes responsibility for such a choice and its consequences for others, and enters into dialogue with critics who have chosen otherwise. What is said here by way of background, it should be noted, was expressed by way of consequences regarding the mode of interpretation in *The Personal Voice*. Autobiographical criticism joins a well-established critical tradition, therefore, though at a much later time, and undergoes a drastic change in its dynamics and mechanics as a result.

The first two volumes included a direct invitation to readers to continue the process of critical encounter initiated in the respective projects. In this way the symphony of voices and the transformative gardens envisioned by those volumes would be appropriated and extended. The present volume is no exception. Such a desideratum for the projects on personal voice and transformative encounters comes to expression as well in this project on autobiographical criticism. It constitutes, borrowing from Bleich, "an invitation to you, dear readers, to enter into dialogue with us and 'create a new community of interest.'"[21] The result is now provided a different metaphorization: this invitation is "to learn and enjoy the pleasures of a different alphabet and of the reading process that results from it."[22]

Looking Back: A Critical Reflection

What transpired in the course of the six years in question at the turn of the century, from the gestation of the first two collections in 1996 to the appearance of the third in 2002, I would describe as a veritable burst of cultural production on the part of Dr. Kitzberger. What I should like to offer at this point, upon the publication of the present collection of essays, is a twofold reflection on this body of work as well as on the Society for New Testament Studies as its point of origins. This reflection I undertake from the point of view of the present state of affairs in the field of studies. It is, therefore, a looking back in the light of my perception of what has come to transpire since, and thus a critical assessment with the benefit of hindsight. My aim in so doing is to capture the importance of such work

---

21. Kitzberger, *Autobiographical Biblical Criticism*, 5, citing Bleich, *Subjective Criticism*.
22. Kitzberger, *Autobiographical Biblical Criticism*, 5.

using the concomitant trajectory of the Society for New Testament Studies as backdrop and contrast.

The Path of Kitzberger

Taken as a whole, the volumes reflect, from within the focus on reading and readers brought to bear by narrative criticism and reader-response criticism, the movement toward the problematic of real readers—the role of extratextual rather than intratextual readers, beyond the historical and intended first readers. Such a movement toward the flesh-and-blood reader was pursued in terms of context and agenda, social-cultural location and ideological-political perspective. In the case of these volumes, I would make two points, one with regard to the construct of the real reader and the other with respect to the configuration of this construct.

First, the work of Kitzberger tilts decidedly toward a construct of the real reader as an individual figure rather than as a social entity, a member of a group identity formation, howsoever defined. Such emphasis is clear throughout the project: from the initial activation of the personal voice, through the subsequent focus on transformative encounters, to the final invocation of autobiographical narrative. It is the individual reader who undergoes an encounter with the text in interpretation. At the same time, the reader as a social entity is certainly not forgotten. All individual exercises in criticism are called on to enter conversation with one another as part of a larger enterprise—a symphony, a garden, a community—of reading, a collaboration envisioned as ongoing and expansive.

Second, the approach of Kitzberger leans decidedly as well toward a configuration of the construct in terms of context rather than agenda. This emphasis is similarly evident throughout: from the initial notion of a dynamic encounter, through the subsequent vision of a profound transformation, to the final activation of real-life experience. It is the context of the individual reader that undergoes a process of change brought about through an encounter with the text in interpretation. Nevertheless, the ideological-political perspective is by no means bypassed. On the one hand, all such exercises in reading are envisioned as self-consciously ethical, whereby readers take responsibility for their interpretations as well as for the consequences thereof, in conversation with others. On the other hand, such a vision of conversation is construed as global and inclusive, bringing together readers from all areas of the world as well as from all the different formations of group identity.

Such work represents, to my mind, a high point in the trajectory of reader-oriented criticism. It is a call for awakening and engaging the voices and lives of readers in the task of interpretation and thus for showing how any work of criticism is indelibly and irretrievably subjective in character. In the process of interpretation, therefore, a text cannot be divorced from a reader, and a reader cannot be divorced from a text. In the face of the long hold and trajectory of objectivism and impartiality in the field, therefore, this is a contrarian call for acknowledging and exposing the constructive character of all reading and all criticism.

It is indeed a high point in terms of quantity, given the production of three volumes one after the other along these lines. It is no less a high point in terms of quality. It is a project well done: well conceived and well argued throughout, well developed by way of many and diverse contributors, and well oriented, given its demand for collaborative work, ever expanding, and for moral responsibility, ever attentive to matters of justice and liberation. Consequently, the name of Kitzberger, more so perhaps than any other name, will always be associated with this particular methodological-theoretical development in the field.

What would have happened in the time since, one can ask, had she been able to continue her work of research and publication? That is an intriguing but ultimately unanswerable question. What did ensue in the field was a steady pursuit of the construct of the critic as a social entity as well as a steady configuration of this construct in terms of agenda. Such emphasis yielded a twofold and interrelated representation of the critic as embodying a variety of social-cultural formations and as engaging a complex and conflictive set of differential relations of power. It is possible that Kitzberger would have continued with her focus on individual critics and their personal contexts. It is also possible that she could have moved toward greater emphasis on critics as social entities, with attention to their social-cultural formations and their political-ideological relations of power, especially given her long-standing adherence to feminist criticism.

What is certain is that her work stands as a pointed reminder that the individual reader—the personal voice, the transforming self, the autobiographical voice—cannot be forgotten in the problematic of readers and reading in the interpretation. Real readers are individual figures and social entities at once. One should not approach the one dimension without proper attention to the other. How to do so is the question, given the need such attention requires, if I may so put it, to matters personal-psychological as well as to matters social-cultural.

The Path of the Society for New Testament Studies

What happened within the Society for New Testament Studies, one can ask, over this same period of time? What path has it followed since the turn of the century: from the cessation of the seminar group on the role of the reader in interpretation, through the undertaking of this threefold project on the reception of the text by real readers, to the heightened attention bestowed on the reception of the text in social-cultural formations as well as on the deployment of ideological-political perspectives involving unequal relations of power in society and culture? This question is, alas, altogether answerable. The Society has stood, by and large, unchanged.

This can be readily established by revisiting its distinctive characteristics as outlined earlier. With regard to models of interpretation, the Society has remained committed, by and large, to analysis of the text at the level of production and thus to the study of the context of antiquity; as such, it has remained tied as well to the use of scientific historical criticism. During this period of time, no alternative critical option is to be found in its set of program groups: no seminar on any dimension regarding the reception of the text in modernity and postmodernity, none revolving around any variation of ideological criticism, and none on any aspect of either its own academic-scholarly trajectory or its relation to the course of historiography. With regard to organizational structure, the Society has steadfastly held on to its status as an elite learned society. The restriction of membership to senior scholars with an established trajectory has continued, as has the integration of scholars outside this circle by way of the category of guests, subject to invitation by approval of the committee and limited in the number of invitations extended. With regard to membership, the Society has preserved its composition as a mostly male, mostly senior, and thoroughly European and Euro-American organization.

Yet recently the winds of change made themselves felt again, and now much more sharply so. This time, it was not as a result of theoretical and methodological developments in the field of studies, not directly anyway, despite the proliferation and intensification of such developments. In this regard, by way of contrast, the Society of Biblical Literature has always proved far more receptive and far more proactive. This time, rather, it was the realization of a worrisome demographic phenomenon. This situation came to the fore at the Seventy-First General Meeting of the Society for New Testament Studies in 2016 in Montreal. In her presidential report at the first business meeting, the outgoing president, Judith M. Lieu, Lady

Margaret's Professor of Divinity at the Faculty of Divinity of the University of Cambridge, highlighted a peculiar trend facing the Society, calling for critical reflection on the part of the membership.[23]

For the last four years, from 2013 to 2016, she pointed out, the number of members leaving the Society, by way of death or resignation, had exceeded the number admitted. In the face of this demographic decline, she posed a fundamental question for reflection: "Why would a person want to be a part of the Society for New Testament Studies?" In so doing, she identified four issues for consideration: (1) the crucial role of the membership in nominations, with a need for balance between the desire for upholding elite standards and the desire for adopting an "inviting, forward-thinking" attitude; (2) the imbalance in gender, throughout all levels of the Society, described as more pronounced than in the field at large and as not in keeping with the need to model "good practice"; (3) the possibility that other contemporary interests at work in the discipline are not being adequately integrated; and (4) the imperative role of the membership in promoting the goal of international scholarship. It was an extraordinary intervention. On the one hand, the question advanced was at once existential and radical: in the past, no one in their right mind would have thought of making membership in the Society a problematic. On the other hand, the issues identified went straight to the heart of the problem and the character of the Society: the tradition of elitism, the lack of diversity in faces and voices (gender), the lack of diversity in critical approaches, and the character of the Society as an organization of the North Atlantic.

Clearly troubled by the evident and progressive decline in members, Lieu took it on herself to urge the Society, with utmost diplomacy, to revisit and reconsider its tenets and practices. To be sure, the question raised was one long posed by a good number of its members and would-be members: Why would anyone wish to belong to and take part in the work of this learned society? Again, revealing her sense of urgency, Lieu followed this report with an open letter to the membership later that year, attached to the minutes.[24] Both the fundamental question and the attendant issues were amplified therein. With regard to the former, Lieu gave

---

23. Studiorum Novi Testamenti Societas, "The Seventy-First General Meeting: Minutes," https://tinyurl.com/SBL4523e.

24. Studiorum Novi Testamenti Societas, *SNTS Newsletter* (October–November 2016), https://tinyurl.com/SBL4523f.

it a different turn, more along the lines of identity than of existence. Thus, she suggested, all members—whether concerned with the drop in numbers or not—would do well to ask themselves what is it that makes the Society different and whether the Society is living up to its commitment to serve as "*the* international professional society for our field." It was a strategic appeal to elitism with change in mind. With regard to the issues, she adopted a more pointed yet affirming and reassuring approach. It was a strategic appeal to living up to ideals and commitments. Throughout, utmost tact was in display.

With regard to the first point, the elitist character of the Society, Lieu conveys the sense of the membership at large: "The majority feeling seems to be that we want to continue with our high expectations of members, but not that we want to be seen as actively exclusive." Consequently, she urges members to be actively inclusive, serving as advocates for the Society by presenting it as attractive and useful to all those deemed as potential members. In terms of the second point, the dearth of women, she emphasizes the comparative element and the need for modeling and leading in good practice: "The percentage of women members is lower than that of women in Departments of Theology and/or Religion in a number of our well-represented countries, and the percentage of proposals for new members who are women continue to be low. Why is this?" Such a situation she presents to the members as an obstacle to membership and participation—"This can sometimes color the perception we offer of ourselves."

In terms of the third point, the critical bent of the Society, Lieu identifies the absence of other critical frameworks and methods as among the most problematic: "I am aware that this may be one aspect of the Society that is most debated: what sort of approaches do we, or do we not, want to sponsor?" Here she calls on members to be more proactive in the creation of seminars—"especially in areas not currently covered.... With regard to the last point, the envisioned scope of the Society," she recalls the implications of membership: "Membership is a privilege, and also a commitment." Such commitment, she reminds the members, implies support for international scholarship, especially through the work of a project, launched in 2011, precisely to expand the scope of the membership and the program, involving international initiatives. Such initiatives were designed to promote such scholarship and recruit new members by establishing formal links—under the direction of a secretary and by way of liaison committees—in Africa, Asia and the Pacific, and Latin America and the Caribbean—plus Eastern Europe.

That the intervention had a substantial impact on the Society is without question. In the letter appended to the minutes, Lieu already attests to such a reaction: feedback from the membership had come to her and other members of the committee, and more such feedback was invited. Later on, in early 2017, the committee decided to undertake a formal survey of the membership on all such concerns by way of an expansive and pointed commentary. An initial report of the findings was made to the Society at the Seventy-Second General Meeting of the Society for New Testament Studies in 2017 in Pretoria, South Africa, by its president, Carl R. Holladay, Charles Howard Candler Professor of New Testament at Emory University. A more substantial report by way of a letter was attached to the newsletter of October–December 2017.[25] This was a year, it should be noted, in which the number of losses surpassed, by 30 percent, the number of admissions—the fifth in a row. At that same meeting, moreover, the creation of a subcommittee, The Future Shape of SNTS, chaired by Holladay, was announced. A first report of this subcommittee was presented by Holladay at the Seventy-Third General Meeting of the Society for New Testament Studies in 2018 in Athens, with an edited version attached to the newsletter of October–November 2018.[26]

Both the report on the survey and the report of the subcommittee begin to signal major developments in all the traditional and distinctive characteristics of the Society. The former report does so by naming "currents and undercurrents relating to the ethos of the Society and its working mission": the need for younger voices, for more women, for more approaches, and for faces from outside the North Atlantic. It finishes with a call to the membership to take an active role in bringing this about. The latter report begins to outline concrete steps to be taken toward addressing such needs. First is a proposal to introduce a new category of membership, associate member. This would preserve the elite standards assumed while opening the door to a broader membership, leading to greater diversity in all areas. Second is a proposal to reconsider the criteria for inviting guests, relaxing present limitations, as well as for evaluating membership, considering other types of publication. In addition, the subcommittee recommends, among other things, expanding the critical range of the seminars offered and strength-

---

25. Studiorum Novi Testamenti Societas, *SNTS Newsletter* (October–November 2017), https://tinyurl.com/SBL4523g.

26. Studiorum Novi Testamenti Societas, *SNTS Newsletter* (October–November 2018), https://tinyurl.com/SBL4523h.

ening the project of the international initiatives. Needless to say, it will be interesting to see what comes to pass; for now, the Society can only be commended for its efforts. If only this had happened long ago, following the trend across the academic world as a whole, including the field of historiography, but the self-perception of elitism is never, alas, without danger.

A Concluding Contrast

I argued in the introduction that the context of the Society for New Testament Studies is indispensable for an appropriate and appreciative understanding of Dr. Kitzberger's work, both as a whole and in terms of this collection of her studies. That was its point of incubation and its point of departure. It was there that she moved from the grand model of historical criticism to the grand model of literary criticism, via the movement of reader-response criticism, as a result of her participation in and work for the seminar group The Role of the Reader in the Interpretation of the New Testament/Hermeneutics and the Biblical Text, beginning in 1990 and lasting through the 1990s. This seminar group represented in itself an anomaly within the Society: a sharp deviation from the long-established theoretical-methodological framework of the Society. After all, what did the problematic of reading and readers in interpretation have to do with the focus on the first and intended historical readers of the text?

In this introduction to her work, I have used this anomaly, and her own academic-intellectual development within it, as a window on the trajectory of the field of studies and its social-cultural context from the turn of the century through the present. This I have done by contrasting the critical project of Dr. Kitzberger and the state of affairs of the Society for New Testament Studies. This contrast can be summarized in terms of critical orientation, social-cultural ethos, and critical ramifications.

What happened is telling. On the one hand, the contrast shows continued adherence on the part of the Society to the model of scientific historical criticism, with little space, if any at all, for other critical approaches. Nothing took the place of the seminar on biblical hermeneutics after its conclusion in 1999, despite all that had happened already and was happening at the time in the field of studies. On the other hand, the contrast also reveals a critical effervescence, if I may so put it, on the part of Kitzberger by exploring different aspects of reader-response criticism, with a focus throughout on the reader as individual figure. Thus, from 1996 through 2002 she moved swiftly from activation of the personal voice, through exploration of transformative experiences, to invocation of autobiographical narrative.

How it happened is no less telling. On the one hand, in addition to its unswerving commitment to a sole critical framework, the Society remained moored to its elitist self-conception and unattentive to the absence and role of faces and voices of the Other in its midst, whether in terms of women or in terms of the non-Western. On the other hand, with her explorations in the realm of reader response, Kitzberger pursued her work in inclusive fashion, calling on faces and voices from all parts of the globe and from all identity formations in society and culture.

What ensued is most revealing. The Society was brought face to face in 2016, ironically through the insight of a woman president, with the specter of ongoing and unremitting decline as a result of its tenets and practices. A call to reflection on its state of affairs across the board was issued, with transformation in mind. The fact that such a realization and summons came forty years after the beginning of the transformation of the discipline in 1975 should not go unsaid. In the meantime, the field of studies continued its path into multiplying variations of ideological criticism, explorations in the reception of the text throughout the world, and the rise of cultural studies with its emphasis on the appeal to the Bible in society and culture at large. In this regard, the Society of Biblical Literature serves as an example of organizational integration and leadership. Where Kitzberger would have gone is, alas, impossible to say, but one thing is clear—she would not have stayed in place.

What lies in the future for the Society for New Testament Studies, the matrix of her work? There is a clear determination to change as well as a clear sense of direction, but the outcome is not yet clear, not to me, anyway. The efforts come so late, and there is so much to overcome. I should think that a thorough critical analysis of its trajectory is very much in order, perhaps by way of a seminar group. As for Kitzberger, what the publication of this volume shows, yet again, is her invaluable contribution to the field by way of reader response. She reminds us all, in and through such work, that the individual critic should not be forgotten—that the personal voice is always present, that transformation is always at work, and that the autobiographical self is always engaged in any and every task of interpretation. In sum, the volume is most welcome, and I reaffirm my gratitude to her for this kind invitation to write a foreword to its publication and thereby recover part of the history of our field of studies.

Introduction

From Historical Criticism to Narrative and Reader-Response Criticism

It was a hot summer's day in July 1990 at the Università Cattolica del Sacro Cuore in Milan when my personal life and professional career were profoundly changed, without yet knowing it. Sitting in this lecture hall without air conditioning was testing for the body, but the intellectual challenge far outweighed the physical. I had been invited to join a seminar group that had worked together for several years within the context of the General Meetings of the Society for New Testament Studies and was regarded as the avant-garde group because of its most unusual focus, The Role of the Reader in the Interpretation of the New Testament. Then, biblical interpretation in this context was still exclusively committed to the historical-critical paradigm with its focus on authors. I, too, was unaware of other approaches or paradigms, except my own excursion into linguistic methods in my doctoral dissertation.[1] Apart from this, I took the traditional way biblical texts were interpreted for granted.

During this first seminar session in July 1990 I understood—nothing! There was a lively debate about a recently published book by one of the seminar members, Edgar V. McKnight's *Post-modern Use of the Bible: The Emergence of Reader-Oriented Criticism*.[2] I was virtually transported into another world, a new paradigm, as it were, comparable—in hindsight—to the transition, for example, from a three-dimensional to a four-dimen-

---

1. Ingrid Rosa Kitzberger, *Bau der Gemeinde: Das paulinische Wortfeld οἰκοδομή/ (ἐπ)οικοδομεῖν* (Würzburg: Echter, 1986).

2. Edgar V. McKnight, *Post-modern Use of the Bible: The Emergence of Reader-Oriented Criticism*, 2nd ed. (Nashville: Abingdon, 1990). Since I had not preregistered for the seminar, I had no information about its agenda and program for this year when I joined in.

sional world. I listened, trying to grasp what the discussion was all about, ready to learn and reorient myself. In the second and third sessions, I experienced glimpses of a new horizon, the rising of a sun that would become the new center of my own work several years later, leading me into ever-new dimensions of biblical scholarship as I journeyed on.

Following this initiation experience at Milan University, I was invited by the chairs of the seminar group, Bernard C. Lategan (University of Stellenbosch, South Africa) and James W. Voelz (Concordia Lutheran Seminary, St. Louis), to join them again the following year and to present a response paper. I gladly accepted, even though I did not really know what I was letting myself in for. But I was ready to move forward, open to the challenge. However, the paper I was supposed to respond to did not arrive in time before the conference. Therefore, I made a rather last-minute suggestion to present a short paper of my own instead. This was graciously accepted, and so I presented my first international conference paper, "A Feminist-Intertextual Reading of Matthew 9:18–26," at the 1991 General Meeting of the Society for New Testament Studies in Bielefeld-Bethel, conveniently not far from my place of residence in Münster. The temperatures were more temperate than in Milan, yet the debates were heated. It was a small seminar group, and I was the only woman, a situation not unfamiliar to me in my professional career. In my paper, I had already made a big step, or so I thought, into new directions. For the first time, I applied a narrative-critical approach and the concept of intertextuality, besides my focus on feminist interpretation. I had become fascinated with narrative criticism,[3] then virtually nonexistent in German biblical scholarship. And intertextuality was still a concept in hiding, waiting to be disclosed by biblical scholars. Humbly but enthusiastically, I presented my reading of the woman's healing and the girl's resurrection story. "This is just old-fashioned stuff!" thus one of the seminar members responded immediately after I had finished. This was another kind of initiation experience. A lively discussion followed, nevertheless, and other seminar members were more appreciative of what I, the newcomer, had to offer. At this meeting I learned that what was a new, and therefore exciting, approach to biblical texts in one context was considered old-fashioned in another. Consequently, I

---

3. Compare the similar experience of Francis J. Moloney: "my own first flush of excitement over the possibilities of narrative criticism." See Moloney, "John 21 and the Johannine Story," in *Johannine Studies 1975–2017*, WUNT 372 (Tübingen: Mohr Siebeck, 2017), 521.

became aware of the wide range of approaches practiced in different parts of the world, at different times, within our discipline, and the challenge of such a complex situation. This, too, was an inspiration and motivation for my future work.

A few days before the Bethel meeting, Daniel Patte's paper had arrived in the mail, too late to write a response paper, yet there was still time to read it, despite its almost book length (and eventually it did become a book).[4] For the first time I was confronted with such strange terms as "meaning-producing dimensions" and the legitimacy of different readings of a text. This was indeed very confusing and unsettling for someone trained to discover *the* meaning of a text, even though in practice it had never been achieved. Thus, when I presented my own reading I was already prepared for alternative readings of the same text and their legitimacy. This implied a complete reversal of perspective and a new ethical accountability and responsibility for the readings we choose. It opened the way to dialogue and the possibility that more than one interpreter can be right.

John and the Synoptics, First Act

The summer of 1990 was momentous also for another reason. Following the General Meeting of the Society for New Testament Studies in Milan in July, I attended, for the first time, the Colloquium Biblicum Lovaniense in Leuven in August, on "John and the Synoptics." I was simply electrified and fascinated by this topic, and the never-ending quest and ever-challenging subject became the focus of my own work. When I was invited to present another paper at the General Meeting of the Society for New Testament Studies in Madrid in July 1992, I chose a topic accordingly, "Love and Footwashing: John 13:1–20 and Luke 7:36–50 Read Intertextually." It was very well received, and I was simply flattered to receive two offers for publication. Eventually, it appeared in a newly founded journal, just perfect as I was venturing out into new territory.[5]

---

4. Daniel Patte, *Discipleship according to the Sermon on the Mount: Four Legitimate Readings, Four Plausible Views of Discipleship, and Their Relative Values* (Valley Forge, PA: Trinity Press International, 1996).

5. Ingrid Rosa Kitzberger, "Love and Footwashing: John 13:1–20 and Luke 7:36–50 Read Intertextually," *BibInt* 2 (1994): 190–206. *Biblical Interpretation: A Journal of Contemporary Approaches* was initiated by David E. Orton, who invited me to publish my paper. Ten years later, I was honored to become a member of the editorial board.

Crossing Geographical and Textual Borders: The Rise of Interfigurality

In 1993, I crossed another border as I journeyed, for the first time, into the New World. The General Meeting of the Society for New Testament Studies was held in Chicago, and I was invited to present another paper in the seminar, then renamed Hermeneutics and the Biblical Text. Basic hermeneutical questions have been on my own agenda since then. I presented a reading of "Mary of Bethany and Mary of Magdala—Two Female Characters in the Johannine Passion Narrative: A Feminist, Narrative-Critical Reader Response."[6] This is my first conference paper included in this volume, for three reasons. First, it shows my earliest reader-response criticism, in which I imagined a female first reader in the Johannine community. This approach engendered a lively discussion about reader constructs and reading strategies.[7] Second, this paper is crucial because of my focus on characterization, a then-neglected aspect of narrative criticism. Therefore, I was very fortunate to have Elizabeth Struthers Malbon respond to my paper, since she had more or less simultaneously coedited a *Semeia* volume on characterization.[8] Her own focus on Markan characters[9] and mine on Johannine (and Synoptic) characters was a perfect match. Third, in this paper I introduced the concept of interfigurality into New Testament studies. I had come across this fascinating concept and the neologism coined by Wolfgang G. Müller in a collected volume published in 1991.[10] When, many years later, Elizabeth Struthers Malbon invited me to write an article on interfigurality for the *Oxford Encyclopedia of Biblical Interpretation* (published in 2013), I was, unfortunately, unable to do so at the time, and eventually no other author was found. Therefore, this volume may also serve as a substitute for the encyclopedia article and,

---

6. Ingrid Rosa Kitzberger, "Mary of Bethany and Mary of Magdala—Two Female Characters in the Johannine Passion Narrative: A Feminist, Narrative-Critical Reader Response," in this volume.

7. Edgar V. McKnight interpreted my approach as a "reading strategy" in the discussion following my paper.

8. Elizabeth Struthers Malbon and Adele Berlin, eds., *Characterization in Biblical Literature*, Semeia 63 (1993).

9. See, in particular, Elizabeth Struthers Malbon, *In the Company of Jesus: Characters in Mark's Gospel* (Louisville: Westminster John Knox, 2000).

10. Wolfgang G. Müller, "Interfigurality: A Study on the Interdependence of Literary Figures," in *Intertextuality*, ed. Heinrich E. Plett, RTT 15 (Berlin: de Gruyter, 1991), 101–21.

even better, as a textbook for this concept, in theory and practice. According to Müller, interfigurality refers to "interrelations that exist between characters of different texts," and it presents "one of the most important dimensions of intertextuality."[11] All essays in this volume are informed, one way or another, by this concept.

John and the Synoptics, Second Act

By applying the concept of interfigurality to reading Johannine characters at the interface with Synoptic characters, I also offer a new paradigm for the relation between John and the Synoptics. From my reader-response perspective, I have become increasingly convinced that John's audience must have been familiar with the Synoptic Gospels, at least one or the other. Therefore, it was a wonderful experience to encounter advocates of historical-critical methods who had arrived at the same conclusion, the dependence of John on the Synoptics, from their author-oriented perspective. I especially remember my pleasant conversation with Maurits Sabbe, during another Colloquium Biblicum Lovaniense, on the anointing stories, acknowledging and appreciating each other's work, across different paradigms. Almost two decades later, I was sitting in a Viennese café with Benedict T. Viviano, OP, when all of a sudden he asked me, "Was John dependent on the Synoptics?" As my answer was a simple yes, he reached out to me, over his lovely Austrian cake, and shook hands with me.[12] We had been together in one place many years before, without, however, meeting each other.[13] This was the Joint Session of the Synoptic Gospels and Johannine Literature sections at the 2001 Annual Meeting of the Society of Biblical Literature in Denver. This joint session was indeed a lively demonstration of the ongoing debate on the relation between John and

---

11. Müller, "Interfigurality," 101.

12. This little anecdote is mentioned for two reasons: first, it shows that biblical scholars by vocation never stop thinking about their work, and second, it is an affirmation of my Austrian identity, even though, or because, I have lived abroad for the greater part of my life.

13. Obviously, I missed his paper as I had to catch my flight back to San Francisco before the final session, in which he presented. Coincidentally, we had been in the same place again many years later—in a seminar at the 2010 General Meeting of the Society for New Testament Studies in Berlin, at which I also met Bernard C. Lategan and Edgar V. McKnight again, thus coming full cycle since the 1990 General Meeting in Milan.

the Synoptics, and of the legitimacy and respect with regard to applying different paradigms and methods in New Testament interpretation within the context of the Society of Biblical Literature.

My first Society of Biblical Literature paper, presented at the International Meeting in Münster in July 1993, was on "The (Intended) Anointing of Jesus by Women: The Interrelationship between the Anointing Stories (Mark 14:3–9 / Matt 13:3–16 / Luke 7:36–50 / John 12:1–8) and the Easter Morning Stories (Mark 16:1–8 parr.)." Comparing the different stories, I applied both a diachronic, historical-critical approach and a synchronic, narrative-critical and reader-response approach. A German professor's comment, in private encounter afterward, was indeed encouraging. "Your paper was the best one in this section!" he enthusiastically proclaimed. Since then, I have not been spoiled by too many equally appreciative reactions from German New Testament scholars, most of whom are committed to and aware of only the historical-critical paradigm. However, I have always regarded myself privileged to have been trained in the historical-critical methods *and then* moved out of the old paradigm to a new paradigm. I am familiar with both and qualified to dialogue with colleagues from different backgrounds, just as the scribe who is like the mistress of a household bringing out of her treasure, what is new and what is old (see Matt 13:52).

From Social Location to Personal Voice and Autobiographical Criticism

The International Meeting of the Society of Biblical Literature in Budapest in July 1995 introduced me to further new dimensions and methods in biblical interpretation. In particular, I was intrigued and fascinated to learn about social location, flesh-and-blood readers, contextualization, diversity, and decolonialization in a paper on "Cultural Studies and Biblical Criticism" by Fernando F. Segovia, whom I had already known as a member of the Society for New Testament Studies seminar group. Consequently, my horizon was tremendously widened and my own approach profoundly changed. There was no way back to hypothetical first readers. From now on, my interest was focused on real readers, social location, the variety and diversity of readings. I realized the liberating power of such an approach. It was the beginning of speaking with my own voice, finally claiming my readings as my own.[14]

---

14. In her response to my Chicago paper, Elizabeth Struthers Malbon had already

Coincidentally, or providentially, at this Society of Biblical Literature International Meeting in Budapest I also met Vicky Peters from Routledge again, whom I had first met a year earlier at the General Meeting of the Society for New Testament Studies in Edinburgh. We had both listened to Segovia's paper and entered into a lively discussion about it. Eventually, Peters informed me about a volume in the making, on the personal voice in classical scholarship, and asked whether I would be tempted to do one on the personal voice in biblical interpretation. I agreed enthusiastically. And it seemed to be just the right time to kindle the same enthusiasm in colleagues from around the globe who joined in the project. It is another lovely coincidence that Richard Stoneman, who strongly supported my book at Routledge, is now based at the same university as the series editor of this present volume, David G. Horrell.

The year 1996 marked the final and essential turning point in my career, when Fernando F. Segovia, then chair of the Johannine Literature section, invited me to present a paper at the Annual Meeting of the Society of Biblical Literature in New Orleans. This was the beginning of a new phase in my life, when the Annual Meetings became an essential part of my schedule and I joined this global community focused on that special time of the year. Papers had to be written, and books published in time to be on the book displays,[15] and most of our activities were planned in view of these days before Thanksgiving. These Annual Meetings became to me the celebration of our intellectual harvest and another kind of family reunion. Most of the essays in this volume were papers presented at the Annual Meetings of the Society of Biblical Literature and inspired by dialogue with colleagues from different parts of the world I encountered in this context. Without these meetings, and projects resulting from them, the greater part of my work would not be. It is essentially dialogic in nature.

---

redirected my perspective when she commented: "Although we can inform ourselves (and others) about the possible or even probable situations and presuppositions of readers other than our own, our readings remain our own. We must claim them as such." In a footnote in my published paper, I had already voiced a prophetic insight when I stated: "I am well aware that the imagined female first reader is a construct and has much of a self-portrait."

15. Two of my edited volumes were first presented, and their births celebrated, at Annual Meetings of the Society of Biblical Literature: Ingrid Rosa Kitzberger, ed., *The Personal Voice in Biblical Interpretation* (London: Routledge, 1999), at the meeting in Orlando in 1998; and Kitzberger, ed., *Transformative Encounters: Jesus and Women Re-viewed*, BibInt 43 (Leiden: Brill, 2000), at the meeting in Boston in 1999.

In November 1996, upon accepting the invitation to New Orleans, I was also invited by Fernando F. Segovia and Daniel Patte to lecture at Vanderbilt University and by Edgar V. McKnight to lecture at Furman University[16] prior to the Annual Meeting. At Vanderbilt I presented my first social-location reading, of the Samaritan woman's story in John 4, followed by an exciting discussion with faculty and students from different social locations, many of them border crossers like myself. I decided to include this paper in the present volume, as it testifies to where and how I started voicing myself. A later rereading of the Samaritan woman was explicitly autobiographical and published in my collected volume *The Personal Voice in Biblical Interpretation*.[17] However, Leticia Guardiola-Sáenz was perfectly right when she remarked, during a personal encounter at the New Orleans meeting, that my chapter is indeed a rewriting. Later someone commented on the Internet that it is "a fabulous postmodern reading." He, too, was right, at least with regard to postmodern. By then, I had come a long way, a very long way indeed, since the supposedly objective historical-critical scholarship I had grown up with and practiced.

When I prepared an invited paper for the Research Consultation on Ideology, Power, and Interpretation at Selly Oak, Birmingham University, in 1997, Segovia commented, "You are rapidly moving out of the German orbit!" He, too, was right. In fact, I had already moved out of my German context, following my vocation of developing further personal voice and autobiographical biblical criticism. The price was high, in terms of my professional career, but it was a liberating and exciting process and has become my passion ever since. Most of the essays assembled here are informed by this autobiographical approach, also including those not attributed to the section explicitly focused on "Characters in John and My Self-Text." Being critical was henceforth no longer possible without being autobiographical,[18] analyzing my own self-text in front of the biblical text

---

16. I was deeply honored to present within the distinguished A. J. Head Lectures in the Humanities, on "The Quest for Living Water: Dimensions of Feminist Biblical Interpretation."

17. Ingrid Rosa Kitzberger, "Border Crossing and Meeting Jesus at the Well: An Autobiographical Re-reading of the Samaritan Woman's Story in John 4:1–44," in Kitzberger, *Personal Voice in Biblical Interpretation*, 111–25.

18. See also Daniel Patte, "Can One Be Critical without Being Autobiographical? The Case of Romans 1:26–27," in *Autobiographical Biblical Criticism: Between Text and Self*, ed. Ingrid Rosa Kitzberger (Leiden: Deo, 2002), 34–59.

and the in between. My "out of the German orbit" paper, inspired by the Mars expedition, is included in this volume, "'The Truth Will Make You Free' (John 8:32): The Power of the Personal Voice and Readings of/from the Gospel of John."

(Post)Feminist Criticism

Among the participants of this small group of twelve (very symbolic indeed) gathered together for the Birmingham Research Consultation was Elisabeth Schüssler Fiorenza. I felt most privileged and honored to participate in this group of highly esteemed professors, and meeting Schüssler Fiorenza again, after our first personal encounter in the summer of 1993 at Harvard, was timely and a source of renewed inspiration. When I became a feminist, decades ago, it was a lonely and painful enterprise, since there was no one else around then with whom I could have shared in the struggle as I embarked on a voyage to new shores. Schüssler Fiorenza's pioneer work, *In Memory of Her*,[19] was a profound source of inspiration and encouragement, as well as a companion, on my own journey. And her quotation of Paula Blanchard, in her conclusion to Margaret Fuller's biography, had become a motto also for my own work: "Her achievement cannot be measured except in terms of the handicap under which she gained it.... But in carving a niche for herself on the enormous wall of resistance that faced her, she left a foothold for others."[20] It is my sincere hope that generations of my students, and perhaps some colleagues too, in different places, have found such a foothold in me from where they could move on in their own journeys.

All essays in this volume are inspired and informed by feminist criticism. However, my understanding of feminist-critical interpretation was transformed several times. This implied also a critical revision of my own work, and it applies in particular to reading the women in John. Eventually, I deconstructed the happy paradise and advocated also a reading against the grain, taking into account the ambivalence of the Johannine story and narratives. Especially informative in this regard are my Chicago paper "Mary of Bethany and Mary of Magdala" and my New Orleans paper

---

19. Elisabeth Schüssler Fiorenza, *In Memory of Her: A Feminist Theological Reconstruction of Christian Origins* (New York: Crossroad, 1983).

20. Schüssler Fiorenza, *In Memory of Her*, xxiv; quote from Paula Blanchard, *Margaret Fuller: From Transcendentalism to Revelation* (New York: Dell, 1979), 342.

"'How Can This Be?'" in this volume. Apart from employing a different reading strategy, my feminist approach, initially focused on women and female characters, later included also men and male characters, and the relation between them became an essential part of my interfigural readings. In the process, gender boundaries were transcended, thus opening up new horizons not only in biblical scholarship but also in our lives in front of the texts. It is a vision still to be realized. My essay "Transcending Gender Boundaries in John" is the most comprehensive in this regard and therefore included in this volume. For a more detailed survey of my own development, you are welcome to read the first part of this essay, "From Madrid to Orlando, and Beyond: My Personal Transformative Encounters with Gospel Women and Men." Amy-Jill Levine's comment in her introduction to the *Feminist Companion to John* was just to the point:

> Ingrid Rosa Kitzberger's "Transcending Gender Boundaries in John," transcends more than simply gender categories; she escapes boundaries set by discrete narratives, methodologies, even prevailing definitions of what constitutes "feminist" interpretations. At present, she finds herself moving to a "post-feminist hermeneutics" motivated substantially by her interest in male as well as female characters.... Kitzberger demonstrates how characters transcend expected gender roles, and how interfigural readings transcend almost all of biblical scholarship. The result of these broken barriers is not chaos; it is freedom for both characters and readers.[21]

I voiced a postfeminist hermeneutics for the first time in my paper "Untying Lazarus—A Sisters' Task? Revisioning Gender and Characterization in John 11" at the 1998 Society of Biblical Literature Annual Meeting in Orlando. The positive reactions from the audience, both male and female, were overwhelming. It seemed that I had barked up the right tree, voicing a vision when the time was right. However, since then there has been a backlash in many contexts, academic and nonacademic. Therefore, many times I found myself returning to feminist interpretation and advocating women's liberation, as I realized that postfeminism is not possible where feminism has never taken deep roots and patriarchy is still prevailing. On the other hand, I have been blessed by encountering and speaking with

---

21. Amy-Jill Levine with Marianne Blickenstaff, eds., *A Feminist Companion to John*, 2 vols. (Sheffield: Sheffield Academic, 2003), 1:14.

women and men who share my vision of transcending gender boundaries and creating a different world, with freedom for both characters and readers. May this collection also contribute to this goal, yet to be achieved, and encourage you, dear readers, to embark on your own journeys as you share in mine.

The Design of This Volume

Since my "interfigural readings transcend almost all of biblical scholarship," as A.-J. so nicely put it, organizing this volume of essays was indeed a challenge. Arranging them chronologically would have had the advantage of clearly showing my own progress and development, thus partly reflecting also developments within our field of New Testament studies in general and Johannine studies in particular. However, for readers' convenience, I have arranged them in parts according to the respective priority of focus.

Part 1, "Reading Strategies," includes the New Orleans paper "'How Can This Be?'" mentioned above, and the paper "How Can You Read John?! The Pains and Pleasures of Reading the Fourth Gospel," presented at the 2004 Society of Biblical Literature International Meeting in Groningen. Both testify to the multidimensionality and ambiguity of reading John and my ongoing passionate struggle whenever I return to this gospel that has become my favorite, the focus of my research and my life inspired by it.[22] In the first essay, I advocate a reading with the grain *and* a reading against the grain, as I was struggling with the challenge of reading the Gospel of John from my feminist perspective but also from my theological perspective, regarding the gospel as Scripture that is relevant for all Christian believers, including myself. By rereading the female characters in John and focusing on their configuration, their interrelatedness within the gospel, I show their "christological Internet" and deconstruct the feminist paradise and the myth of happy endings. In the second essay, I focus on the complex and ambivalent reading experience, thus sharing in the challenge all readers and interpreters, from different backgrounds, are confronted with when they approach this gospel.

---

22. Quite in line, though not completely, with Elizabeth Struthers Malbon's dedication to the Gospel of Mark. See Malbon, "The Poor Widow in Mark and Her Poor Rich Readers," *CBQ* 53 (1991): "the dynamic *process* of reading and of reading readings may be for some of us worth 'a whole life'" (604).

Part 2, "Reading Characters in John, the Synoptics, and the Hebrew Bible," contains four essays, all of them informed by the concept of interfigurality.

My first conference paper presented on American soil, "Mary of Bethany and Mary of Magdala," mentioned above, is a border-crossing piece also for its methodological approach. The focus is on these two female characters, their configuration in the passion narrative, and with other (female and male) characters in the gospel story, and on the reading process as a first-time reading (as different from later rereadings). However, the boundaries of the Fourth Gospel are also transcended in this essay by applying the concept of interfigurality and thus opening it up to the Synoptic Gospels, especially the stories of Jesus's being anointed by a woman. My first comprehensive essay, "Synoptic Women in John: Interfigural Readings," is not included here, as it overlaps with "Transcending Gender Boundaries" and the latter is more comprehensive. Besides, *Transformative Encounters: Jesus and Women Re-viewed*, which originally contained this essay, was reprinted in paperback by SBL Press and is thus easily available.[23]

"Stabat Mater? Rebirth at the Foot of the Cross" addresses the question of how Jesus's mother came to stand at the cross in John's crucifixion account, which differs considerably from the Synoptic accounts. This essay crosses the borders between the gospels, in particular by relating Jesus's mother to Luke's widow of Nain and Simeon, but also the borders between the biblical text and my self-text. This essay is interfigural, interpersonal, and autobiographical. Originally presented at the Jesuit School of Theology in Berkeley and at the 2002 Society of Biblical Literature International Meeting in Berlin, it also crossed the borders between continents, in the context of my own relocation.

"The Three Marys and the Fourfold Gospel" surveys these prominent female characters, Mary, Jesus's mother, Mary of Magdala, and Mary of Bethany, across the gospels, focusing on their different characterization in each gospel and advocating an interfigural reading to address this diversity. It is also informed by Jewish midrash[24] and the notion that all texts are intertextual. Part of this paper was originally presented as a lecture at the University of Limerick, Ireland.

---

23. Kitzberger, *Transformative Encounters*.
24. See Daniel Boyarin, *Intertextuality and the Reading of Midrash* (Bloomington: Indiana University Press, 1994).

"Aging and Birthing: Open-Ended Stories and a Hermeneutics of Promise" transcends the borders between the New Testament and the Hebrew Bible, showing the intratextuality and the hermeneutics of promise in all biblical writings. Intratextuality refers to the semantic axes or axes of meaning that structure the Bible as a whole, and "to search for them implies to read the Bible anew, from a hermeneutical perspective and supported by semiotics."[25] The hermeneutics of promise is based on the notion that all biblical texts are open texts, literally and in particular pragmatically. They are meant to be continued in the readers' lives and become a "generator of hope."[26] Gospel characters (Nicodemus, Simeon, and Anna) meet Torah characters (Abram/Abraham and Sarai/Sara) in a transformative way and open up new possibilities of beginning for present readers. This essay is included here in grateful memory of J. Severino Croatto, who widened my horizon significantly and in whose honor this essay came into being. It was my first to be published in Latin America.[27]

Part 3, "Characterization and Gender," assembles the two essays mentioned above, which focus explicitly on gender, although it is an essential category throughout this volume. From "Untying Lazarus—A Sisters' Task? Revisioning Gender and Characterization in John 11" to "Transcending Gender Boundaries" I had come a long way, and yet these two essays are closely related and connected. From focusing on a male character, Lazarus, who has become the object in the Johannine text and its readings, and advocating a postfeminist hermeneutics, which implied the revisioning of my own feminist readings, to advocating a reading that transcends gender boundaries altogether, it was a logical development, even though it took a couple of years. This second essay focuses on two Johannine characters, Jesus and Nicodemus, and their configuration and interfigurality with female as well as male characters. In their respective

---

25. J. Severino Croatto, *Die Bibel gehört den Armen: Perspektiven einer befreiungstheologischen Hermeneutik*, ÖEH 5 (Munich: Kaiser, 1989), 71. Croatto focuses on the "semantic axis" of the "liberation of the oppressed."

26. See also J. Severino Croatto, "The Function of the Non-fulfilled Promises: Reading the Pentateuch from the Perspective of the Latin-American Oppressed People," in Kitzberger, *Personal Voice in Biblical Interpretation*, 38–52, esp. 50.

27. Another essay appeared in Arequipa, Peru, a few years later, on the initiative of Edmundo Alarcón: Ingrid Rosa Kitzberger, "Caracterization en el Cruce," *RT* 19 (2005): 50–61. It is the Spanish translation of my (unpublished) paper "Characterization at the Crossroads" (paper presented at the Annual Meeting of the Society of Biblical Literature, Denver, November 20, 2001).

encounters with Mary of Bethany, the Synoptic anointing women, Luke's Mary, Jesus's mother, Matthew's magi, and Sophia/Chokmah from the Hebrew Bible and deuterocanonical writings, gender borders are transcended as male characters are enriched with female dimensions.

Part 4, "Characters in John and My Self-Text," contains three essays. First is the Birmingham conference paper mentioned above, "The Truth Will Make You Free," my first explicitly autobiographical reading, in which I offer a new reading of the characters in John 20 and 21: Mary of Magdala, Simon Peter, and the Beloved Disciple. Second is "Reading and Rereading the Samaritan Woman's Story," my first social-location reading, presented a year earlier at Vanderbilt University, in which I was rereading this story from my own border-crossing location and from the woman's perspective. Third is "Flowing Identities,"[28] written from my locations in Münster and Berkeley, thus signifying also my transatlantic border-crossing journeys and the reconstructions of textual and personal identities. The biblical text and my own self-text are perceived as flowing, ever anew in each encounter. John's stories of Nicodemus and Lazarus are chosen as intertexts for interpreting life stories and vice versa. A first version of this essay was presented at the 2000 Annual Meeting of the Society of Biblical Literature in Nashville, within the Semiotics and Exegesis section, which focused on personal voice/autobiographical biblical criticism.

Part 5, "Teaching Strategies," contains an updated lecture originally presented at the University of Sheffield, "Models of Discipleship and Teaching Strategies: Learning from John." It reflects on some aspects that have become essential to my understanding of teaching, which is closely related to my approach in biblical interpretation and thus corresponds to the "Reading Strategies" of part 1 and as applied throughout this volume. My respect for the Otherness of biblical texts, and my respect for the Otherness of my students, is reflected in my encounters with them. Paradigms of biblical interpretation and teaching strategies are closely linked and inform each other.[29]

---

28. See how my mind has changed also with regard to the titles—from my (chronologically) first essay included here, "Mary of Bethany and Mary of Magdala," to this one, from the longest to the shortest title!

29. Unless otherwise indicated, all biblical quotations in this volume are from the NRSV.

Part 1
Reading Strategies

"How Can This Be?" (John 3:9): A Feminist-Theological Rereading of the Gospel of John

How Can This Be? The Quest for the Impossible: Vacillating between Paradigms

"How can this be?" Nicodemus asked and thereby addressed the impossible within the old paradigm and the possible within the new paradigm into which Jesus had invited him. "How can a human being [ἄνθρωπος] be born when he or she is old?"[1] is a futile question within the old paradigm, because it is impossible for one to enter a second time into his or her mother's womb and be born again (John 3:4). However, in terms of the new paradigm, the question of "how" (v. 9) makes sense because to be reborn[2] of the Spirit (vv. 5, 8) is possible. So everything depends on the paradigm and the frame of reference from where the question is asked.

"How can this be?" is also the question of this paper. In effect, how is a feminist and theological reading and interpretation of the Gospel of John possible? In asking about the how, I assume that it *is* possible in the first place and that the quest therefore makes sense. At first sight, however, a feminist interpretation and a theological interpretation seem to exclude each other. On the one hand, feminist interpretation is always and by

---

This chapter first appeared as "'How Can This Be?' (John 3:9): A Feminist-Theological Re-reading of the Gospel of John," in *Literary and Social Readings of the Fourth Gospel*, vol. 2 of *"What Is John?,"* ed. Fernando F. Segovia, SymS 7 (Atlanta: Scholars Press, 1998), 19–41.

1. This is my own translation; all other quotations in this volume, unless otherwise indicated, are from the NRSV.

2. I translate "reborn," although ἄνωθεν can also mean "from above," because of the focus on rereading in this paper. At the same time, however, being born "from above" also implies being reborn—born again after the first, physical birth.

definition a critical interpretation: it starts from a hermeneutics of suspicion and implies analyzing the texts from a distance. The women and the gender ideology reflected in the texts are placed thereby at the center of the inquiry and become the primary focus of attention. On the other hand, theological interpretation starts from a hermeneutics of correlation and trust in the reliability of the texts: it places God, or Jesus, at the center of the inquiry and allows the text's message to influence one's life. Thus, while the first approach implies a reading against the grain, the latter implies a reading with the grain. How can the two ever go together? This seems to be as impossible a task as returning into the mother's womb and being reborn. In other words, the question of how would seem to be as futile as Nicodemus's first question.

The question of this paper, therefore, addresses and struggles with what seems impossible. It has risen out of my social location as a feminist within the academic discipline and my struggle for women's liberation, on the one hand, and my status as a church member and believing Christian who considers the gospel as a document of faith, on the other hand.[3] I have critically analyzed the gospel from the perspective of feminist hermeneutics in one context, but the Gospel of John has also been for me a special source of spiritual nourishment and belief in another context. Feminist-critical and theological-spiritual interpretation of the Gospel of John have so far lived side by side and rather independently of each other. The question I wish to address in this paper is, therefore, an existential question, insofar as it addresses the question of how two equally important and legitimate approaches can be brought into interaction with each other. It is also a question that addresses the practice of biblical scholarship, the ethics of interpretation,[4] and the effects our interpretations have on others.

The more concrete question of this paper is as follows: How can a feminist and thus a critical and suspicious reading of the Gospel of John be

---

3. By *document of faith*, I mean a document of the faith of the people behind the text, which is both a constant challenge to and constant empowerment for my own faith. See in this regard R. Alan Culpepper, "The Gospel of John as a Document of Faith in a Pluralistic Culture," in *Readers and Readings of the Fourth Gospel*, vol. 1 of *"What Is John?,"* ed. Fernando F. Segovia, SymS 3 (Atlanta: Scholars Press, 1996), 107–27. Culpepper uses the term to signify "a text that shapes the character and content of one's religious beliefs" (107).

4. See Daniel Patte, *Ethics of Biblical Interpretation: A Reevaluation* (Louisville: Westminster John Knox, 1995), esp. 37–71.

considered legitimate in the light of the stated aim of the gospel to evoke or strengthen faith in Jesus Christ (20:30–31), which calls for a theological reading as defined above? In other words: Can the Gospel of John be read against its own purpose and self-definition, against how it obviously wants to be read? While a simultaneous feminist and theological reading would seem impossible, a shift of paradigm—as in Nicodemus's case—may open the way to new possibilities. As it is, however, such possibilities are not yet visible and have to be searched for, with open-mindedness.

Nicodemus's experience may serve as a model in this process. Twice he asks, "How can this be?" and neither time does he really get an answer from Jesus; nor, for that matter, does he receive any guidelines regarding how to search on his own for an answer. Actually, the only answer he does get from Jesus, though indirect, is that the first question (about a literal understanding of rebirth) is out of place and has to be replaced by another, that is, by the quest for the rebirth of the Spirit. Nicodemus, therefore, is left puzzled when Jesus starts on his long monologue (vv. 11–21). In the process, the reader of the gospel also gets the message: live with the question! When Nicodemus turns up briefly later on, in the context of the increased controversy over Jesus, he remarks, "Our law does not judge people without first giving them a hearing to find out what they are doing, does it?" (7:51). So also, in order to find an answer to the controversial question raised in this paper, it is appropriate first to hear and learn about the impact and dimensions of a feminist interpretation of the Gospel of John.

Feminist Perspectives on/of John

Since Raymond Brown's evocative and pioneering article on the roles of women in the Gospel of John in 1975, the importance of women in this gospel has been widely accepted; indeed, in the course of the past two decades, such a judgment has been reinforced and reformulated by the work of many others.[5] Whether or not the women in the gospel are seen in the light of the importance and leadership of women in the Johannine

---

5. Raymond E. Brown, "Roles of Women in the Fourth Gospel," *TS* 36 (1975): 688–99. See, e.g., Sandra M. Schneiders, "Women in the Fourth Gospel and the Role of Women in the Contemporary Church," *BTB* 12 (1982): 35–45; Turid Karlsen Seim, "Roles of Women in the Gospel of John," in *Aspects of the Johannine Literature*, ed. Lars Hartman and Birger Olsson, ConBNT 18 (Uppsala: Uppsala University Press, 1987), 56–73; Sjef van Tilborg, *Imaginative Love in John*, BibInt 2 (Leiden: Brill, 1993), esp.

community, they are regarded as disciples—even paradigms of true discipleship—missionaries, and apostles. Besides the role of Jesus's mother, the outstanding roles of the Samaritan woman, of Mary and Martha of Bethany, and of Mary Magdalene have been emphasized and confirmed.[6] Therefore, the Gospel of John has become a happy dwelling place for feminists. "Come and see" (1:39) has been a standing invitation to critics of the sexism of the biblical tradition. In John, it has been argued, it is different: at least in this gospel and in the Johannine community alternatives to patriarchal and sexist traditions can be found.[7]

The paper I presented at the 1993 General Meeting of the Society for New Testament Studies in Chicago, which was later published in a revised version,[8] was very much in line with this very positive evaluation of women in John. In my analysis of the characters of Mary of Bethany and Mary of Magdala in their relation to each other, as well as to other female and male characters in the gospel, I applied a feminist, narrative-critical reader-response approach and arrived at the following "conclusion":

> In spite of its male author and its male narrator the Gospel of John shows an outstanding interest in female characters and remarkable sensitiveness concerning their characterization. Therefore, the imagined actual reader [i.e., a woman in the Johannine community] could follow, more or less, the trace provided for the intended or implied reader and fill it

---

ch. 4, "Loving Women"; van Tilborg, *Reading John in Ephesus*, NovTSup 83 (Leiden: Brill, 1996), 122–25.

6. See Elisabeth Schüssler Fiorenza, *In Memory of Her: A Feminist-Theological Reconstruction of Christian Origins* (London: SCM, 1988), 323–34, who concludes that "these five women disciples are paradigms of women's apostolic discipleship as well as their leadership in the Johannine communities" (333). Van Tilborg discusses the prominence of women in John in the context of the position of women in Ephesus and notes that the women's "very special position in John's text ... runs parallel with what happens in Ephesus with and around women" (*Reading John in Ephesus*, 154).

7. According to Schüssler Fiorenza, not only John but also Mark "highlight the alternative character of the Christian community, and therefore accord women apostolic and ministerial leadership," and she adds, "The 'light shines in the darkness' of patriarchal repression and forgetfulness, and this 'darkness has never overcome it'" (*In Memory of Her*, 334).

8. See "Mary of Bethany and Mary of Magdala—Two Female Characters in the Johannine Passion Narrative: A Feminist, Narrative-Critical Reader Response," in this volume.

up with her own experience and creativity. Resisting reading or "reading against the grain" was not necessitated by these texts.[9]

In the present paper I should like to investigate further this issue of the position and evaluation of women in John and ask on how secure a ground positive results actually stand. I shall do so by applying a reader-response approach, with a focus on reading and rereading and their impact on interpretation.

Reading as *first-time reading* is different from any rereading of a text. It implies a sequential and temporal reading; it refers to plot and plotted time as different from story time.[10] First-time reading, therefore, implies that the reader knows only what she/he has read so far. *Rereading*, on the other hand, opens new perspectives and enables a different appropriation of the text. Wolfgang Iser has described this process as follows:

> When we have finished the text, and read it again, clearly our extra knowledge will result in a different time sequence; we shall tend to establish connections by referring to our awareness of what is to come, and so certain aspects of the text will assume significance we did not attach to them on first reading, while others will recede into the background.... The time sequence that he [the reader] realized on his first reading cannot possibly be repeated on a second reading, and this unrepeatability is bound to result in modification of his reading experience. This is not to say that the second reading is "truer" than the first—they are, quite simply, different: the reader establishes the virtual dimension of the text by realizing a new time sequence. Thus even on repeated viewings a text allows, and indeed induces, innovative reading.[11]

---

9. See "Mary of Bethany and Mary of Magdala," in this volume.

10. See Norman R. Petersen, *Literary Criticism for New Testament Critics*, GBS (Philadelphia: Fortress, 1978), 49–50.

11. Wolfgang Iser, "The Reading Process: A Phenomenological Approach," in *Reader-Response Criticism: From Formalism to Post-Structuralism*, ed. Jane P. Tompkins (Baltimore: Johns Hopkins University Press, 1980), 56. See also Matei Calinescu, *Rereading* (New Haven: Yale University Press, 1993). See further the description of the "first-time reader/multiple-reader axis" as one of the "reading constructs and strategies" by Fernando F. Segovia, "Reading Readers of the Fourth Gospel and Their Readings: An Exercise in Intercultural Criticism," in Segovia, *Readers and Readings of the Fourth Gospel*, 237–77, esp. 241–42. Segovia notes, "A first-time reader construct approaches the text as a fresh reader altogether (largely paralleling, therefore, the experience of the narratee)—without any previous knowledge of the text.... The

Thus, rereading always means starting from a privileged position, due to the increase in knowledge as a result of first-time reading: different parts of the text can be related to each other and viewed in a different light; new dimensions can be realized. In this paper, *rereading* conveys three further meanings as well: (1) *reencountering* the characters in the gospel; therefore, rereading women in John is also a new experience and different from reading/encountering them for the first time; (2) *revisioning* the stories by stepping outside the framework and ideology provided by the author and narrator;[12] and (3) *reevaluating* texts, with reference to a shift of paradigm. Thus, a reading with the grain can turn into a reading against the grain, and vice versa.

Reading and Rereading Women in/into John

The Christological Internet of Women in John

When one considers the functions and features of female characters in John, it is quite puzzling that none of them has an ongoing role within the story. They enter on the stage only once or twice and then are gone forever. For example, Jesus's mother disappears in Capernaum after the wedding at Cana (2:1–12) and returns only briefly under the cross, together with her sister, Mary the wife of Clopas, and Mary Magdalene (19:25). The Samaritan woman, who plays such a prominent role in one of the longest stories of the gospels (4:1–42), vanishes completely after Jesus leaves Sychar two days later. Mary and Martha of Bethany are important in chapter 11, in the context of their brother's resurrection, and again in chapter 12 (12:1–8), where Jesus is their dinner guest and is anointed by Mary, but, in spite of the fact that they are loved by Jesus (11:5), they also have no ongoing role in John's story of Jesus. Finally, Mary Magdalene, who so suddenly and unexpectedly turns up under the cross (as the Samaritan woman did at the well) and becomes the primary witness of Jesus's resurrection in chapter 20, dissolves—after her encounter with Jesus—into the silence and

---

multiple-reader construct approaches the text as a seasoned reader—with previous and extensive knowledge of the text; attentive to the whole of the narration and aware of problems and cycles of the text" (241–42).

12. See J. Cheryl Exum, *Fragmented Women: Feminist (Sub)versions of Biblical Narratives*, JSOTSup 163 (Sheffield: JSOT Press, 1993), preface, esp. 11.

darkness out of which she has come. Neither John 1:1–19:24 nor John 21 mentions her.

Because of this strange fact that female characters have no ongoing role and receive no further development, they have been considered "minor characters."[13] Obviously, such a judgment stands in contrast to the importance attributed to them as disciples, apostles, and missionaries. The importance of these women, however, comes fully into light only by rereading the gospel. Only then, from an overarching point of view, does it become evident that an important aspect of their characterization is their *configuration*—how they are related to one another.[14]

To begin with, the Samaritan woman is developed further in the character of Martha of Bethany. Martha's confession that Jesus is the Messiah is the goal toward which the Samaritan woman might develop. Martha confirms what the Samaritan woman could only put as a question, "He cannot be the Messiah, can he?" (4:29). Martha's answer is, "I believe that you are the Messiah, the Son of God, the one coming into the world" (11:27).

In a similar way, the character of Mary of Bethany, though she leaves the stage after 12:8, is developed further in the character of Mary Magdalene in chapter 20. Mary of Bethany encounters Jesus after the death of her brother, Lazarus, whose raising becomes an important incident leading to Jesus's death. Mary Magdalene encounters Jesus after his own resurrection. Thus, both encounters come about when facing death. Mary of Bethany experiences Jesus's power to raise Lazarus from the dead, while Mary Magdalene experiences Jesus's overcoming of death in his own person. Thus, Mary Magdalene's experience is an intensification of Mary of Bethany's experience, and she is also commissioned to proclaim Jesus's resurrection.

In terms of configuration, it becomes obvious that not only the Samaritan woman and Martha but also Mary of Bethany and Mary Magdalene form complementary pairs, respectively.[15] Mary Magdalene is further related to the Samaritan woman, since both are assigned an apostolic and

---

13. R. Alan Culpepper, *Anatomy of the Fourth Gospel: A Study in Literary Design*, FFNT (Philadelphia: Fortress, 1983), 106.

14. For the concept of configuration—as different from interfigurality—see Wolfgang G. Müller, "Interfigurality: A Study on the Interdependence of Literary Figures," in *Intertextuality*, ed. Heinrich E. Plett, RTT 15 (Berlin: de Gruyter, 1991), 117.

15. For more details on the parallelism between chapter 11 and 20:11–18, see "Mary of Bethany and Mary of Magdala," in this volume.

missionary role. It goes without saying that Mary and Martha, as sisters, are developed as characters in relation to each other.

The narratives establish a further configuration between Jesus's mother and Mary Magdalene, who—within the story world—meet for the first time under the cross (or arrived there together, or whatever). Yet another dimension of configuration between Jesus's mother and Mary Magdalene can be detected. Jesus's mother acts as a mediator at the beginning of the gospel and at the beginning of Jesus's public mission, whereas Mary Magdalene encounters Jesus after the fulfillment of his mission and is appointed as missionary and mediator in the proclamation of the resurrection message. Moreover, as the disciples are reported to have believed in Jesus after his first sign, which was prepared and initiated by his mother (2:3–5), so are the disciples expected to believe in Mary Magdalene's message (20:17–18). There is, of course, also a configuration between all women witnesses under the cross: Jesus's mother and Mary Magdalene are also related to the mother's sister and to Mary the wife of Clopas.[16]

The female characters in John are not only defined and developed by means of configuration. The internet is further determined by its christological dimension. All female characters are cast within a highly christological setting and prove vital to the revelation of Jesus's identity within the unfolding of the gospel's plot. From the time before the coming of Jesus's hour (2:4) to the early morning hours of Easter day (20:1), his encounters with women become prominent locations of revelation. Jesus's identity is progressively revealed to the readers in those stories where women figure prominently.

---

16. The alert reader will have realized that the woman caught in adultery does not show up in this configuration of women in John. Although there is no doubt that, according to manuscript evidence, this story in 7:53–8:11 was inserted later into the gospel, in the synchronic reading presented in this paper this does not matter, because the story is now part of the gospel text as a unity. However, no configuration between this unnamed woman and the other women can be ascertained. In terms of narrative development, she seems to be as isolated and ostracized as she is as adulteress. I suppose, nevertheless, that her presence in the gospel text has influenced the reception of the Samaritan woman in such a way that her relation to six men has been interpreted in moral categories derived from the issue of adultery, although the two cases are totally different from each other. The only similarity is that Jesus talks to both women when they are alone and that both women's stories are rendered within a patriarchal framework.

In the Cana wedding story Jesus's mother initiates his first sign, by means of which he reveals his glory (2:11), and then she witnesses, together with her sister, with Mary the wife of Clopas, and with Mary Magdalene, his final glorification, when he is lifted up on the cross (19:25; see 3:14–15; 17:1).

It is highly significant as well that Jesus utters his first "I am" saying in his encounter with the Samaritan woman and, later on, another such saying in his encounter with Martha. Talking about the coming of the Messiah (4:25), Jesus reveals to the Samaritan woman his true identity, "I am he, the one who is speaking to you" (v. 26). Face-to-face with Martha after Lazarus's death and engaging in a discussion about resurrection (11:23–24), Jesus proclaims, "I am the resurrection and the life" (v. 25).[17]

Jesus's encounter with Mary of Bethany reveals a deeply human trait of the Christ, when he is depicted as weeping with her (11:35). Later on, Jesus is revealed as the anointed one by Mary's prophetic act (12:1–8).

Finally, in his encounter with Mary Magdalene, Jesus reveals his postresurrection identity and his final destiny, the return to his Father (20:11–18).

Therefore, when in 20:30–31 the narrator addresses the readers and reveals the purpose of the Gospel of John—"that you may come to believe that Jesus is the Messiah, the Son of God, and that through believing you may have life in his name"—the readers are reminded of Martha's confession (11:27)[18] as the fulfillment of the Samaritan woman's tentative belief in the Messiah (4:29). The readers also recall Jesus's mother: although she was given only a preparatory role in engendering the faith of the disciples (2:12), she became a witness to Jesus's fulfilling his mission as he died on the cross (19:25–30). Although playing a minor role, yet of great importance, the mother's sister, Jesus's aunt, and Mary the wife of Clopas are also remembered, as is Mary of Bethany's act of faith as she anointed Jesus before his death (12:3–8). Finally, Mary Magdalene's belief in the resurrected Christ and her testimony to him come to the reader's mind when invited to believe that Jesus is the Messiah, the Son of God.[19]

---

17. For the relevance of the "I am" sayings, see D. Mark Ball, *"I Am" in John's Gospel: Literary Function, Background and Theological Implications*, JSNTSup 124 (Sheffield: Sheffield Academic, 1996), 60–67, 101–10.

18. See also van Tilborg, *Reading John in Ephesus*, 124: "Historical memories of the important role of women in the Jesus-movement and the actual writer's intentions meet in the character of Martha, the ideal model of the intended reader."

19. See Robert Kysar, *John's Story of Jesus* (Philadelphia: Fortress, 1984), 85: Mary Magdalene "stands as one of John's models for what it means to believe."

The "you" of 20:30–31 addresses a plurality of readers, a plurality of implied readers in the gospel, and a plurality of first readers as well as present, real flesh-and-blood readers of the gospel.[20] The christological internet of the gospel women is of special importance to female readers, insofar as it provides encouraging role models and thus functions as an invaluable source of faith.

Therefore, a reading against the grain is not necessitated by these texts. On the contrary, the lives of the christologically interrelated gospel women seem to flow out into the female readers' lives. Even feminists can be content with this special result. In addition, we can go one step further and search for more women in the gospel, that is, search for women who might have been lost in androcentric-inclusive language.

Is There a Woman in This Text?[21]

The well-known fact that all biblical texts testify to androcentric-inclusive language raises the question of whether women are included in those passages of the gospel that seem to speak of men only because of the male terms applied. Two examples may serve as test cases.

(1) How does Martha know? "Your brother will rise again," Jesus says to Martha, and she answers, "I know that he will rise again in the resurrection on the last day" (11:23–24). This dialogue is continued by Jesus's self-revelation, "I am the resurrection and the life" (v. 26), and Martha's christological confession, "Yes, Lord, I believe that you are the Messiah, the Son of God, the one coming into the world" (v. 27). In the process, Martha's initial belief in the resurrection on the last day is transformed into belief in the resurrection here and now. How does Martha know about the resurrection on the last day? Before chapter 11 Martha is not even mentioned in John's Gospel, and within this narrative unit Martha does not receive any information about the resurrection. So, how could she have known? This is just one of the many gaps in the story, and it calls forth the reader's activity and decision regarding how to fill this gap.[22]

---

20. See Craig R. Koester, "The Spectrum of Johannine Readers," in Segovia, *Readers and Readings of the Fourth Gospel*, 5–19; see also Culpepper, *Anatomy of the Fourth Gospel*, 221, 225.

21. See Mary Jacobus, "Is There a Woman in This Text?," in *Reading Women: Essays in Feminist Criticism* (New York: Columbia University Press, 1986), 83–109.

22. See Edgar V. McKnight, *Post-modern Use of the Bible: The Emergence of*

Within the reading process the gap functions as a signal to the reader to search for an answer. Very often, answers can only be found by way of the reader's imagination. In this case, however, the answer is provided within the gospel context itself.

In chapter 6, following the multiplication of the loaves and fishes, Jesus teaches the crowd that has come searching for him: "And this is the will of him who sent me that I should lose nothing of all that he has given me, but raise it up on the last day. This is indeed the will of the Father that all who see the Son and believe in him should have eternal life; and I will raise them up on the last day" (6:39–40). Rereading chapter 6 in the light of chapter 11 provides the clue for the puzzling fact of Martha's knowledge: she knows about the resurrection on the last day because she was part of that crowd. This is, at least, the only answer the reader can obtain from internal evidence within the gospel itself. Of course, this answer to one question raises yet another question: How did Martha (and Mary?) come from Bethany near Jerusalem to the Sea of Galilee? At the same time, this narrative gap in chapter 11 addresses the issue of inclusive language, and the answer suggests—though of course it cannot be proved—that Martha, and also Mary, have to be seen as present and included in passages other than chapters 11 and 12. Consequently, the fact that Jesus loves Mary, Martha, and Lazarus (11:5) enables the reader to imagine them also present at the Last Supper, when Jesus shows his love to "his own" by washing their feet (13:1–5).

"Did I not tell you," Jesus asks Martha later in chapter 11, when they arrive outside Lazarus's tomb, "that if you believed you would see the glory of God?" (v. 40). No, he has *not* told her, we may conclude, because nowhere before in this scene or in the larger gospel narrative has Jesus said anything like this to her. Only we, the readers, were informed by the narrator that Lazarus's illness would not lead to death but rather to God's glory, "so that the Son of God may be glorified through it" (11:4). Jesus's question, therefore, points to another gap in the narrative that has to be filled by the reader. In contrast to the first gap concerning Martha's knowledge about the resurrection, this puzzle cannot be solved by searching for Martha in the preceding chapters. However, later on Jesus prays to his Father that those whom he has given him may be with him where he is

---

Reader-Oriented Criticism, 2nd ed. (Nashville: Abingdon, 1990), 222–41; Iser, "Reading Process," 55.

and see the glory God has given him (17:24). Whether Jesus had not told Martha about the glory of God before their arrival at Lazarus's tomb, which is a possibility, or had told her but this fact is (deliberately?) not rendered in the course of the narrative, Martha may be considered as included in Jesus's departing prayer in chapter 17. This assumption makes even more sense if she—together with Mary—was present already at the Last Supper (ch. 13), where the footwashing and the farewell discourses are located. Again, rereading provides a key for the reconsideration of androcentric texts as inclusive of women.

(2) Farewell to Mary Magdalene. Raymond E. Brown was the first to relate Mary Magdalene's recognition of the risen Christ when he calls her by name (20:16) to the shepherd discourse in chapter 10 (v. 17). Since that time, Mary Magdalene has been regarded as one of those who belong to "his own" (10:3–5). This insight has not been taken seriously enough. It implies, so I would argue, that Mary Magdalene must be imagined as present also at the Last Supper in chapter 13 and among "his own" to whom Jesus addresses his farewell words (chs. 14–17).[23] Therefore, everything said to the disciples is said also to Mary Magdalene (and probably—as we have seen—to Martha and Mary as well).

"You will look for me," Jesus prophesies, "and as I said to the Jews so now I say to you, 'Where I am going you cannot come'" (13:33). The only one who really looks for Jesus on Easter morning is Mary Magdalene. "Whom are you looking for?" Jesus himself, the supposed gardener, asks her (20:15). Furthermore, she cannot go where he goes, that is, to the Father, but instead is sent to bring the message to his "brothers" (v. 17).[24]

Likewise, what Jesus has to say in 16:16–22 seems to be said in particular to Mary Magdalene. Like the woman giving birth, who has pain when her hour is come but whose anguish is turned into joy when she is delivered of her child (vv. 20–22), so also Mary Magdalene, after her

---

23. According to Fernando F. Segovia, who stresses the unity of John 13–17, "Jesus and an unidentified number of disciples are present in the room, although several are specifically mentioned." See Segovia, *The Farewell of the Word: The Johannine Call to Abide* (Minneapolis: Fortress, 1991), 3. Although Segovia does not raise the question of gender, "the unidentified number of disciples" is open to a variety of named or unnamed, male or female, disciples.

24. Sandra M. Schneiders understands ἀδελφοί as inclusive of brothers *and* sisters, that is, the disciples are men and women. See Schneiders, "John 20:11–18: The Encounter of the Easter Jesus with Mary Magdalene—A Transformative Feminist Reading," in Segovia, *Readers and Readings of the Fourth Gospel*, 164, 166.

sorrow when facing Jesus's death, is full of joy when she sees Jesus again on Easter morning (20:16–18).[25] Thus, Jesus's promise that the disciples will see him again after not seeing him for "a little while" (16:16) is first fulfilled in his encounter with Mary Magdalene, who thus becomes the first witness to the resurrection and is empowered to proclaim, "I have seen the Lord" (20:18). In fact, the "little while" (μικρόν) is even shorter for her than for all the other disciples, because she is not only the first to see him again but also the one (together with the Beloved Disciple) to have seen him last, at the crucifixion (19:25–27).

Again, describing the state of sorrow of his disciples, Jesus further mentions that they will weep and mourn. In fact, Mary Magdalene is the only one who is portrayed as weeping (20:11, 13, 15). Finally, in chapter 17 Jesus prays to his Father not only for those whom he has sent into the world (v. 18) but also for those who believe in him through their word (v. 20). How can one *not* think of Mary Magdalene when rereading chapter 17 in the light of chapter 20? In chapter 20 the (other) disciples are those who are expected to believe in the resurrected Christ through her word. (Also, thinking of the Samaritan woman is perhaps indicated in 17:20, because the people of Sychar come to believe in Jesus Christ through her testimony in 4:39.)

In all these examples, it becomes obvious that Mary Magdalene has to be included in the group of Jesus's own and has to be considered a disciple.[26] To be sure, more examples of inclusive rereading could be added, both with reference to Mary Magdalene and the other female characters in John. Just as the first mention of the women, Mary Magdalene and the others, as witnesses of Jesus's crucifixion in Mark 15:40–41 constitutes a clear text signal for rereading the whole gospel as inclusive of these women (because they have followed him since Galilee), so there are also text signals in John's Gospel that call forth a similarly inclusive rereading.

---

25. Mary Magdalene's joy is not mentioned explicitly in the text, but it is implicit in her transformation from weeping to the exclamation ραββουνι and in her proclamation of the Easter message to the disciples. The disciples' rejoicing, however, is mentioned explicitly (20:20).

26. See Segovia's notes on the theme of birth in John, which in 16:21, he argues, "differs considerably"; here, he points out, "it is a fundamental shift in the attitude of the disciples that is compared to a process of birth, elsewhere it is the process of becoming a disciple that is formulated in terms of birth" (*Farewell of the Word*, 254). Thus, through the motif of birth also Mary Magdalene's status as disciple is confirmed.

Therefore, the initial question, "Is there a woman in this text?" can and must be answered positively: yes, there are women in the gospel text, even where they are not explicitly mentioned. Rereading provides a key with which to search for them and find them, like the woman in the parable who finds the lost coin after searching carefully (Luke 15:8–9).

To sum up, reading and rereading women in or into John, as presented here, results in an appreciation of their importance and seems very much in accordance with feminist interests. Hence, a reading with the grain and, consequently, a feminist-theological interpretation is possible.

Reading against the Grain?

All readings that stress the importance of women in the Gospel of John and its positive view of them as disciples, apostles, and missionaries, as well as their relevance for the gospel's Christology, concentrate on those meaning dimensions in the text that confirm such a view. There is in fact ample evidence for the validity and legitimacy of this position.[27] However, a close reading and several rereadings of the Samaritan woman's story, shaped by my own life experience and social location, have opened my eyes to other dimensions of the text in chapter 4, which in turn have had

---

27. The reasons and legitimacy for calling one or the other woman a disciple, a missionary, and/or an apostle vary in the relevant literature. Sometimes there are just statements without real argumentation. I should like to mention here briefly on what meaning dimensions in the text, in my opinion, these titles can be based: (1) Martha and Mary may be called disciples insofar as Martha speaks of "the teacher" who is calling for Mary (11:28) and both are loved by Jesus (11:5) as he loves "his own" (13:1). (2) The Samaritan woman can be considered a missionary because, on account of her testimony, the townspeople of Sychar come to believe in Jesus as the Messiah (4:39). I would also argue that she can be called a disciple because of the parallelism between her leaving of the water jar behind (v. 28) and the leaving of the nets behind by the first Synoptic disciples (Mark 1:16–18). (3) All three titles can be attributed to Mary Magdalene: she is a disciple insofar as she addresses the resurrected Christ as ραββουνι (20:16) and belongs to "his own," since she recognizes him when he calls her by name (10:3–5); she is an apostle and missionary insofar as she is commissioned and sent by Jesus to proclaim the resurrection message and carries out this mission (20:17–18). (4) For Jesus's mother, none of these titles is justified, given the lack of appropriate dimensions in the texts. However, she may be defined in other categories. Van Tilborg calls both the Samaritan woman and Mary Magdalene "evangelists"; in fact, he argues, Mary Magdalene "is appointed by Jesus as his only evangelist of the resurrection" (*Reading John in Ephesus*, 123).

profound consequences for my view of the Samaritan woman's characterization.[28] Such reading and rereading raised the question, and ultimately the necessity, of rereading/revisioning the portrayal of the other women in John and hence their positive portrayal in the gospel story. Against my conviction of not so long ago, the necessity of reading against the grain started to dawn on me.

The Truth Will Make You Free: Rhetorical Incarnation

A vital aspect of the gospel is the fact that its message is conveyed by narrative devices and is unfolded in the sequential telling by the narrator and, consequently, the sequential perception by the reader during the reading process. Therefore, it is the actual rhetoric of the narrative that alone can provide the basis of any interpretation. However, this important dimension of the incarnation of the word has been very much neglected within biblical scholarship, with the result that most interpretations are neither based on actual readings of the texts nor constitute a reflection on the reading process.[29] Such neglect has also affected interpretations of women in John, which have often been shaped more by interest in some sort of content rather than the actual flow of the narrative and the reader's response.

Given the limited space of the present study, I am unable to present close readings of all the relevant texts of women's stories in John. I do want to point out, however, some features in each of these stories that I discov-

---

28. See Ingrid Rosa Kitzberger, "Border Crossing and Meeting Jesus at the Well: An Autobiographical Re-reading of the Samaritan Woman's Story in John 4:1–42," in *The Personal Voice in Biblical Interpretation*, ed. Kitzberger (London: Routledge, 1999), 111–27.

29. See in this regard the pioneering monograph by Jeffrey L. Staley, *Reading with a Passion: Rhetoric, Autobiography, and the American West in the Gospel of John* (New York: Continuum, 1995). See also Margaret Davies, *Rhetoric and Reference in the Fourth Gospel*, JSNTSup 69 (Sheffield: Sheffield Academic, 1992); Ingrid Rosa Kitzberger, "Love and Footwashing: John 13:1–20 and Luke 7:36–50 Read Intertextually," *BibInt* 2 (1994): 190–206; Robert Kysar, "The Making of Metaphor: Another Reading of John 3:1–15," in Segovia, *Readers and Readings of the Fourth Gospel*, 21–41; and the reading commentaries by Francis J. Moloney, *Belief in the Word: Reading John 1–4* (Minneapolis: Fortress, 1993); Moloney, *Signs and Shadows: Reading John 5–12* (Minneapolis: Fortress, 1996); Moloney, *Glory Not Dishonor: Reading John 13–21* (Minneapolis: Fortress, 1998).

ered in the course of close readings and that I believe must be considered in order to move toward an answer to the basic question of this paper.

By close rereadings of the Samaritan woman's story in 4:1–42, I came to discern dimensions in the text that I had not seen before, when I had concentrated more on the content and was quite happy to find the female disciple and missionary there. Like the disciples on their way to Emmaus who did not recognize Jesus (Luke 24:16), so also some dimensions in John 4 were there, all along, yet not recognized by me until, in a kind of revelatory process, my eyes were opened. One day, sitting at the well and siding with the woman, I became aware of the sexist and racist bias of the story, which reflects not only the stereotypical Jewish attitude toward the Samaritans but also the patriarchal attitude toward women.

The first bias is put on the lips of the woman herself (v. 9); the other is located in the minds and hearts of the disciples (v. 27). "How is it that you, a Jew, ask a drink of me, a woman of Samaria?" (v. 9), the woman asks Jesus. Later, when the disciples return to the well, "they were astonished that he was speaking with a woman, but no one said, 'What do you want?' or 'Why are you speaking with her?'" (v. 27). The reader is taken along this track, and the message is conveyed to him/her that this view is all right. The woman is defined as "the other" and inferior. Having internalized the patriarchal worldview and self-definition—viewing herself in the ancestral line of fathers and sons (vv. 12, 20), not of mothers and daughters—she is portrayed as a stranger also to herself, not only as an alien to others. In spite of her outstanding theological qualifications, which become obvious in the discussion regarding worship and the expectation of the Messiah (vv. 20–26), she is reduced to her sexuality, with the value judgment about the history of her relationships placed on her lips ("what I ever did," vv. 29, 39). In the end, she is also deprived of her missionary achievement by her townsfolk. When they tell her that they no longer believe because of her words, for they have meanwhile heard Jesus himself (v. 42), they inflict injustice on her, because in fact there were two different groups and two different ways of coming to belief. While the first group believed because of the woman's words (v. 39), the second group believed because of Jesus's words (v. 41).

To sum up, the unfolding of the narrative proceeds in a retrograde direction. Positive and even liberating potentials are diminished by dimensions conveying a very different message. The enthusiasm about the conversion of a whole Samaritan village as well as the woman's role in this process have blinded many readers and interpreters, even feminists, to the oppressive dimensions in the text. To be aware of the text's rhetorical ambivalence, however, is a necessary step toward liberating truth.

Once my feminist eyes were opened to counterreading and revisioning John 4, a rereading of chapters 11, 12 and 20, as well as of chapter 2, became necessary as well, and they brought to light text dimensions that had hitherto been neglected by interpreters, including myself.

Although the characterization of Mary and Martha in chapters 11 and 12:1–8 is a very dynamic process between text and reader, as I have shown in my Chicago paper "Mary of Bethany and Mary of Magdala," the retrograde in the development, especially in the characterization of Martha, becomes obvious nevertheless. Not long after her climactic christological confession, Martha is depicted as demonstrating disbelief, when she reminds Jesus of the odor in Lazarus's tomb (11:39). Jesus's question in the next verse, "Did I not tell you?" conveys the message to the reader that, given Jesus's disclosure to her about God's glory, she should have known better. Thus, the reader's perception of Martha is negatively influenced and the previous positive view corrected.

Because of the discrepancy between the point of view of the narrator and the reader, on the one hand, and that of Mary Magdalene, on the other hand, when she supposes Jesus to be the gardener (20:15), she is portrayed as demonstrating lack of insight and belief. Later on, she is further depicted as reacting inadequately when she tries to hold back Jesus. The narrative takes the reader along this path of perception. Whether or not these dimensions are subsequently overshadowed by her recognition of Jesus as ραββουνι, thereby acknowledging him as teacher, and her fulfillment of his missionary order depends largely on the reader. The narrative does not force a final decision on the reader.

The character of Jesus's mother is by no means developed unambiguously. In spite of Jesus's statement that his hour has not yet come (2:4), she makes preparations for Jesus's action and thereby demonstrates disobedience. At the same time, such behavior also shows her belief in his power. The mother's reaction and attitude become constitutive of his first sign. However, at the end of the narrative, only the disciples are said to have come to believe in him (2:11); his mother is not included.

To sum up, all stories in which women figure prominently prove ambivalent. The women are portrayed not only as disciples, apostles, missionaries, and believers, but also as nonbelievers, as doubting or misunderstanding individuals. In addition, their images are distorted by the stories' patriarchal frame of reference. This is the truth that can only

Deconstructing John's Feminist Paradise: Not Happy but Open Endings

When one takes seriously into account readings and rereadings as well as the effect of the rhetoric of the narratives, the paradise sketched by many feminists has to be deconstructed. The messages of the texts are ambivalent. Therefore, different interpretations of the "women's stories" are legitimated by the texts themselves. Moreover, not one of these stories reveals in fact a happy end.[30]

Jesus's mother goes down from Cana to Capernaum in the company of Jesus, his brothers,[31] and his disciples, and they stay there for a few days (2:12). She does not come to believe in Jesus—at least the text does not say so explicitly.[32] The wedding story at Cana is thus open-ended in this regard. Moreover, no information whatsoever is given regarding his mother between this moment in her life and Jesus's crucifixion.

The Samaritan woman's missionary achievement is diminished in the "end," when the townspeople tell her that it is no longer on account of her words that they believe (4:42). This story does not really have an end either. We never get to know what becomes of the woman, whether she returns to the man who is not her husband and what her position among the townsfolk becomes later on, after Jesus's departure from Sychar.

We are not provided a picture of the postresurrection life of Martha and Mary with their brother Lazarus. We are not even informed how they react to Lazarus's resurrection itself, his coming out of the tomb after four days. The question also remains unanswered whether it is to them to whom

---

30. Van Tilborg considers the stories, except for that of the mother, as "stories with a happy ending," though he goes on to state that the stories are "also somewhat ambiguous" (*Imaginative Love*, 207; in more detail, 177–208).

31. Van Tilborg considers it possible to understand ἀδελφοί as inclusive of "sisters" (*Imaginative Love*, 13–17).

32. Of course, it is legitimate to deduce the mother's belief from her instructions to the servants, "Do whatever he tells you" (2:5), relying on the following interpretation: the narrator does not have to mention her coming to belief because she believes *already*. However, the text in its actual form is open and ambivalent. The mother's belief becomes explicit only much later on, when she is portrayed as a witness to Jesus's crucifixion (19:25–27).

Jesus's command is addressed, "Unbind him and let him go" (11:44).[33] The only further information about the sisters is provided in chapter 12 when they invite Jesus for dinner, which he enjoys in the company of Lazarus and in the course of which Mary anoints him while Martha serves him (12:1–8). Yet while we get to know at least that Lazarus's life is threatened by death, as is Jesus's life (vv. 9–11), the future fate of Martha and Mary is left completely in the dark.[34]

Mary Magdalene's story on Easter morning remains open-ended as well. When she brings Jesus's message to the disciples, the story ends (20:18). But, in fact, this is not an end either. The happy end has been inferred over and over again by wishful thinking. The essential question is: How do the disciples respond to her message? The text does not tell us. The actual sequence of the narrative in 20:19–23 suggests rather that they either did not receive Mary Magdalene's message at all or did not believe her, as in the case of the apostles in Luke's account of the Easter morning (24:10–11). Otherwise, why should they have stayed shut behind doors because of fear of the Jews (v. 19)?

To sum up, shut out of a paradise of feminist bliss, we, the readers, are left with fragmentary and open texts and with the task of either writing the

---

33. See Staley, *Reading with a Passion*, 75: "In view of these multiple responses to Lazarus' sickness and death and the role of Mary and Martha in the story, it seems strange that the narrator concludes the miracle without offering the encoded reader any immediate insight into the sisters' reaction to receiving back their brother (cf. Mark 5:42). Jesus does not publicly restore Lazarus to them (cf. Luke 7:15–16) nor does the narrator make a note of the disciples' reactions (cf. John 2:11)." See also Wilhelm Wuellner, "Putting Life Back into the Lazarus Story and Its Reading: The Narrative Rhetoric of John 11 as the Narration of Faith," *Semeia* 53 (1991): 119–20. See also my chapter "Untying Lazarus—A Sisters' Task?," in this volume.

34. It may be considered whether the sisters can be included in "the crowd … who continued to testify" (12:17) at Jesus's entry into Jerusalem (vv. 12–19) and who are also characterized as those "that had been with him when he called Lazarus out of the tomb and raised him from the dead" (v. 17). Eugen Ruckstuhl believes that Martha and Mary retreated, as possible, from public view so as not to be persecuted themselves, while their brother Lazarus emigrated from Judea or Palestine. See Ruckstuhl, *Jesus, Freund und Anwalt der Frauen: Frauenpräsenz und Frauenabwesenheit in der Geschichte Jesu* (Stuttgart: Katholisches Bibelwerk, 1996), 120. In order to protect the sisters, then, the Jerusalem tradition of the passion narrative also passed over in silence Lazarus's resurrection. Only the Johannine tradition knows about it, due to the information the Beloved Disciple got from Lazarus's sisters.

ends of the stories ourselves by means of our own imagination, or else of living with the tension created by such open ends.

How Can This Be? Blessed Are Those Who Reread

Rereading the Gospel of John from a feminist perspective as outlined in this paper leaves us with a double message[35] and a great deal of ambivalence. Feminist interpretation has turned out to be both a reading with the grain and a reading against the grain. On the one hand, being aware of the importance of women in John, their christological relevance, and their function in achieving the aim and purpose of the gospel (20:30–31) makes possible a reading in which feminist hermeneutics and the theological claim of the gospel can be correlated with each other. On the other hand, being conscious of all those dimensions in the text that call forth a reading against the grain or counterreading raises the question whether and how all that is written in this gospel can engender or strengthen belief. It seems rather that a resisting reading is called for and that the reliability of the gospel's claim of truth is fundamentally questioned.

However, it is not only feminist interpretation that has to struggle with the problem of ambivalence or even of contradiction in John's Gospel.[36] All readers, in fact, have to come to terms somehow with other striking features or puzzles of the text, such as the contradictory statement concerning Jesus's baptizing (3:22, 26; 4:1–2)[37] and the strange pattern of communication throughout involving both questions left unanswered (3:4–11; 11:40)[38]

---

35. It is important to recognize this double message also in John, although it is not as strong as the double message in Luke, which has been more readily acknowledged. See, e.g., Turid Karlsen Seim, *The Double Message: Patterns of Gender in Luke-Acts*, SNTW (Edinburgh: T&T Clark, 1994).

36. See also a number of other serious and difficult problems mentioned by Culpepper, such as the ethical issue of anti-Judaism, of the marginalized and the oppressed, and of theological exclusivism ("Document of Faith," 112–25). For the conflict between the spirituality and the anti-Judaism of the Gospel, see Werner H. Kelber, "Metaphysics and Marginality in John," in Segovia, *Readers and Readings of the Fourth Gospel*, 129–54, esp. 129–36.

37. In 3:22 and 3:26 Jesus's baptizing activities are explicitly mentioned, but this is corrected shortly afterwards in 4:1–2 by saying that it was not Jesus himself who baptized but his disciples.

38. In ch. 3 Nicodemus does not get an answer from Jesus when he asks how a rebirth is possible. In ch. 11 Jesus asks Martha "Did I not tell you?" (v. 40), but no

and answers that have little to do with the questions posed (e.g., 6:25-26; 12:34-35; 20:15).[39] It becomes quite obvious that the implied readers and the real readers of the gospel are readers who are able to live and deal with tensions and puzzles that are not solved in the story, readers who are able to live with questions that remain unanswered, readers who, therefore, cannot remain passive recipients but are encouraged and empowered to take an active and critical part in the production of meaning. It is *such* readers who are expected to (come to) believe in Jesus through all that is written down, in spite of—or because of?—all the ambivalences and even contradictions.

Consequently, both the gospel's theology and theological interpretation have to be redefined. In this paper I started out with the question "How can this be?" and conceived of feminist interpretation and theological interpretation as separate from, or even opposed to, each other by their very nature. However, a shift of paradigm has occurred in this regard. Just as feminist interpretation does not only imply a reading against the grain but can also be a reading with the grain, so can theological interpretation no longer be conceived solely in terms of reading with the grain. Given the impact and importance of the gospel's rhetoric—that is, the ebb and flow of the narrative, with its twists and turns, its complexities, puzzles, contradictions, and openness—the gospel's theology and its theological interpretation have to be redefined.

---

answer of Martha is recorded, quite aside from the fact that in the course of the narrative Jesus has not told her any such thing.

39. In 6:25 the crowd, which after the multiplication of the loaves and fishes searches for Jesus and finally finds him on the other side of the sea, asks him about the time of his arrival, but Jesus "answers" them by revealing their real motivation for looking for him (v. 26). In 12:34 the crowd asks Jesus for the identity of the Son of Man; Jesus responds by talking about walking in light or in darkness (vv. 35-36). In 20:15 Jesus asks Mary Magdalene why she is crying and whom she is looking for. Mary Magdalene does not give an answer but asks him, the supposed gardener, where he has taken "him." See in this regard Kysar, who notes, with reference to John 3:1-15, that the passage "also takes for granted a certain willingness on the part of the reader to recognize and deal with polyvalence" and "makes enormous demands on the reader" ("Making of Metaphor," 30). See also Segovia on "compositional difficulties" (*Farewell of the Word*, 23-25). For unanswered or wrongly answered questions, see also my chapter "How Can You Read John?! The Pains and Pleasures of Reading the Gospel of John," in this volume.

Theology can no longer be considered in terms of content, preexistent and abstracted from the text, but should be more adequately conceived as part of the form, the rhetoric of the gospel. Such a position takes seriously into account the essential message of the gospel that the Word became flesh, was incarnated, and can therefore only be experienced in concrete reality.[40] If theology is actually embedded in the narrative,[41] this implies that all the questions, puzzles, ambivalences, and open endings are also an expression of the gospel's theological message. Encountering the gospel text in the process of reading and rereading is, therefore, a theological experience. Taking this process seriously into account correlates with Jesus's claim that he is "the Way" (14:6).[42] Consequently, theological interpretation has to be based on the awareness that revelation happens in the midst of all the complexities and contradictions of the gospel, and of life, and can no longer be based on a reading in accordance and agreement with the gospel's message. Besides, this message is also multidimensional, not just one grain with which or against which one can read.

Therefore, both theological interpretation and feminist interpretation are faced with the challenge as well as the task and responsibility of deciding how to read. However, from the point of view of a hermeneutics

---

40. Daniel Patte gives as his "fundamental theological conviction that it is in concrete, contingent historical contexts that God reveals Godself." See Patte, *Discipleship according to the Sermon on the Mount: Four Legitimate Readings, Four Plausible Views of Discipleship and Their Relative Values* (Valley Forge, PA: Trinity Press International, 1996), 56. A text is in fact also a concrete historical reality.

41. See Gail O'Day, *Revelation in the Fourth Gospel: Narrative Mode and Theological Claim* (Minneapolis: Fortress, 1986). O'Day argues for "an understanding of the Johannine theology of revelation that takes seriously the Gospel narrative itself," thus taking "the dynamics and interplay of the Fourth Gospel text itself as part of the revelation experience" (44–45). See also Stephen D. Moore, *Literary Criticism and the Gospels: The Theoretical Challenge* (New Haven: Yale University Press, 1989), 55–68 (ch. 5: "The Place of Gospel Theology in a Story-Centered Gospel Criticism"); Sandra M. Schneiders, *The Revelatory Text: Interpreting the New Testament as Sacred Scripture* (San Francisco: Harper, 1991).

42. See O'Day: "Getting to 'the end' is not the goal of Johannine narrative…. Rather, the way and the goal are frequently one. This narrative dynamic corresponds to the Fourth Gospel's understanding of who Jesus is: 'I am the way, and the truth, and the life' (14:6)" (*Revelation in the Fourth Gospel*, 100). See also the motif of the journey as essential for the plot of the Gospel: Fernando F. Segovia, "The Journey(s) of the Word of God: A Reading of the Plot of the Fourth Gospel," in *Fourth Gospel from a Literary Perspective*, 23–54.

of liberation, not just feminist hermeneutics, the liberating potentials of the text will always have to be read against the oppressive ones, because only then is it possible to experience the truth that makes free (8:32).[43] A feminist interpretation that stands up to such a challenge becomes a truly theological interpretation, and it is an interpretation born from struggle.

And blessed are those who face the challenge of rereading the gospel in this way. The proclamation of the twofold purpose of the gospel, to believe and to have life in his name, is closely linked with the blessing in verse 29. Thus argues Fernando F. Segovia: "With 20:30–31 the narrator reinforces the blessing of 20:29 by exhorting and enticing the narratees to believe in Jesus, without seeing and on the basis of the biographical account itself, by claiming that only in Jesus can they ultimately find 'life' in this world and indeed 'life' that surpasses anything described in these pages."[44] "Blessed are those who have not seen and yet have come to believe" (v. 29) actually means, then, in the light of 20:30–31, "Blessed are those who read and reread the gospel and believe." Not seeing Jesus but encountering him in the rhetorical incarnation of the word in the gospel narrative is envisioned by the author as a means of coming to believe in him. This belief is, as we have seen, born from the experience of struggling with a very ambivalent and multidimensional text. The promise to have life in his name (v. 31) implies, therefore, a kind of life that is not a smooth and comfortable resting place but rather for active participation, engagement, and struggle.

As Jesus has to struggle with the dualism of darkness and light (see, e.g., 1:5; 3:19–21), so also feminist interpretation has to struggle when it seeks to come to terms with the light of the positive evaluation of women in this gospel and the shadows of the negative characterization of female characters as well as the darkness of the sexist and patriarchal bias of the stories.

Like the first audience of the gospel, any later reader and any present reader is a postresurrection reader. Therefore, the promises that Jesus gives to those who believe in him for the time after his departure are relevant

---

43. See Fernando F. Segovia, who also finds himself "both nodding and shaking" his head as he reads the gospel; however, he argues that "speak one must, against all odds, for change and transformation, for wellbeing and justice, and for a God who needs to be very much present everywhere." See Segovia, "The Gospel at the Close of the Century: Engagement from the Diaspora," in Segovia, *Readers and Readings of the Fourth Gospel*, 216.

44. Fernando F. Segovia, "The Final Farewell of Jesus: A Reading of John 20:30–21:25," in *Fourth Gospel from a Literary Perspective*, 175.

also to those readers of the gospel who regard it basically as a document of faith. A feminist-theological rereading of the gospel is, therefore, empowered by these promises. Three of them deserve special mention: (1) the disciples will be sent the Paraclete, the Spirit of Truth, who will be with them forever and will guide them into all truth (14:16–17; 16:13); (2) the living water that Jesus gives will become a spring of water in the believer, welling up into eternal life (4:13–14); (3) rebirth of the Spirit implies partaking in its freedom to come and go wherever it wants (3:8).

If we take these promises seriously into account, they might be considered to be at work and effective also in the interpretation of the gospel. The sending of the Paraclete empowers us to trust that it is the Spirit of Truth who guides and shapes the way we interpret. The gift of living water and the effects of rebirth in the Spirit empower us to set out on a new path whose aim and destiny are not yet clearly defined and which thus reveals itself only gradually in the process. We are also empowered thereby to trust our own inner wells, the water welling up from our own lives, to go ahead with the autonomy entrusted to us, and to face the challenge of responsibility for our interpretations. A feminist-theological interpretation of the gospel along these empowering lines emerges as an open-ended task, as open-ended as the gospel itself (21:25).

How Can You Read John?!
The Pains and Pleasures of Reading the Fourth Gospel

How Can a Nice Jewish Girl Read the Gospel of John?

In her chapter "A Nice Jewish Girl Reads the Gospel of John," Adele Reinhartz addresses a challenging question that is closely linked to her career as a New Testament scholar in general and as a Johannine scholar in particular.[1] She recollects an encounter with an eminent Jerusalem rabbi who, after she had told him about her research for her doctoral dissertation in New Testament, exclaimed, "What is a nice Jewish girl like you doing in a field like that?" Reinhartz reflects on her journey with the Gospel of John, and the repeated necessity to respond to explicitly or implicitly asked questions about her motivation to engage in this field. The rabbi's question was not a real question; it was rather a rebuke, or at least an expression of amazement. It actually meant, "How on earth can you engage in a field like that!" Besides the fact that the New Testament writings are Christian Scriptures, the anti-Judaism inherent in at least some of them, and John is particularly problematic in this regard, seemed to justify the rabbi's attitude. In her essay, and later in her book *Befriending the Beloved Disciple: A Jewish Reading of the Gospel of John*, Reinhartz presents four different reading strategies as to how to read this gospel: a compliant reading, a resistant reading, a sympathetic reading, and an engaged reading.[2] Such readings can coexist; they are not exclusive of each other. Reinhartz comments that

---

This chapter was originally a paper presented at the Society of Biblical Literature International Meeting, Johannine Literature section, Groningen, the Netherlands, July 28, 2004. Revised for this publication.

1. Adele Reinhartz, "A Nice Jewish Girl Reads the Gospel of John," *Semeia* 77 (1977): 177–93.

2. Adele Reinhartz, *Befriending the Beloved Disciple: A Jewish Reading of the Gospel of John* (New York: Continuum, 2001).

they are "modes of reading John with which I do battle every time I open this text."³ By offering these reading strategies, she provides an answer to the rabbi's question and thus overcomes his rebuke that she should not—or, how could she?!—engage in Christian Scriptures. Reinhartz demonstrates that she *can*, even with regard to the Gospel of John, and her priority is to show the *how* over against the *why*.

How Can You Read John?!

The Complex Experience of Reading John

The double aspect of the comment—signified by the question mark and the exclamation mark—applies to any reader of this gospel, no matter where one comes from and what one's particular motivations and interests might be.

"How can you read John?" and "How can you read John!" I, too, have asked these questions over and over again since I started to focus on this gospel in my research and writing. I have come a long way in rereading John, journeying through different paradigms and applying different reading strategies. My mind has changed with regard to reading this gospel in particular and reading biblical texts in general.

"How can this be?" I asked, taking up Nicodemus's question, in a paper I presented at the Annual Meeting of the American Academy of Religion/Society of Biblical Literature in New Orleans in 1996.⁴ Then, my main concern was the question, "How is a feminist *and* theological reading of the Gospel of John possible?" This seemed an impossible task, because the first required, or so I thought initially, a reading *against* the grain, whereas the latter required just the opposite, a reading *with* the grain. I struggled with this difficult task, which I had set myself, until the last moment. I wrote the final paragraph in my hotel room in Greenville, South Carolina (where I had lectured and stayed for a week at Furman University), early in the morning before heading to New Orleans, and I added some finishing touches even during the flight. In the process of working on this paper, my own presuppositions changed completely. Consequently, I figured out that a feminist as well as a theological reading could, and in fact had to, be

---

3. Reinhartz, "Nice Jewish Girl Reads the Gospel of John," 180.

4. See " 'How Can This Be?' (John 3:9): A Feminist-Theological Rereading of the Gospel of John," in this volume.

re-viewed both as a reading *with* the grain and a reading *against* the grain. This insight gave way to a much more dynamic reading strategy than I had imagined possible. In this paper, I also demonstrated how much my mind had changed since the paper I had presented at the General Meeting of the Society for New Testament Studies in Chicago in 1993, in which I had strongly advocated an overall positive view of women in John.[5] In the New Orleans paper I deconstructed John's "feminist paradise," since the portrayal of women in John is quite ambivalent. Consequently, different reading strategies, inclusive of reading the silences between the textual markers, produce different results.

The ambivalent experience of reading the gospel with regard to women applies, so I concluded, to any reading, because the gospel text is full of ambivalences and tensions, even contradictions, gaps, twists and turns, in the narrative ebb and flow. In addition, there are questions without answers, or answers that do not match with the questions. Thus, reading the Gospel of John has increasingly become a multidimensional, often very mixed experience, ranging between frustration and liberation, between "How can you read John!" and "How can you read John?" Amid this wide range of experiences, one general experience was essential: as I worked on this gospel text, it worked on me; it became a subject processing its object, transforming my own subjectivity. I have been wrestling with this gospel like Jacob with God's angel at the Jabbok, leaving me wounded *and* blessed.

As I studied and closely read this gospel, I was increasingly puzzled, marveling at what is perhaps the most peculiar biblical text and, for sure, the strangest among the four canonical gospels.

"*What Is John?*" is the title of the two volumes, edited by Fernando F. Segovia, containing the papers of the Johannine Literature sections at the Annual Meetings of the Society of Biblical Literature, which demonstrate the wide range of readings of this gospel. Termed after Pilate's question at Jesus's trial, "What is truth?" (John 18:38), the contributions attest to the very personal nature of each reading, resulting from unique encounters between text and self, each with many meaning dimensions that multiply in the encounter.

---

5. See "Mary of Bethany and Mary of Magdala—Two Female Characters in the Johannine Passion Narrative: A Feminist, Narrative-Critical Reader Response," in this volume.

"What are the gospels?" is another question raised by biblical scholars who are concerned with the genre of the gospels.[6] In my paper "'The Truth Will Make You Free' (John 8:32): The Power of the Personal Voice and Readings of/from the Gospel of John," my answer to the question regarding the specific character of the gospels was quite different and simple:

> They are fragments, puzzles, a sketch rather than a finished picture. They actually withhold more information than they render, and more often than not they leave the readers frustrated. There are gaps and breaks in the stories, ambivalences, and even contradictions, and open ends, often connected with the disappearance of characters we have just got acquainted with.... I have become more and more aware of how strange the character of the Gospels is in general and of John in particular. Taking seriously into account the rhetoric of the texts, instead of abstracting some kind of content from them, the great demand the Gospels put on their readers becomes apparent. Why has the good news come down to us in such a strange and sometimes even bewildering shape? So I have been asking myself. The intentions of the authors are beyond our reach. If I ever happen to meet the evangelists in heaven, for sure I will ask them this question. Meanwhile I am more concerned with the effect such fragmentary and puzzling texts have on us, generations of readers, what they do to us and how we react to them.[7]

In this paper, therefore, I shall explore further the strange nature of John's Gospel and its effect on readers, past and present.

Reading Characters and Communication in John

Taking up Nicodemus's question, "How can this be?," for my New Orleans paper, the question served as a leitmotif for my own investigation. Consequently, however, I became more and more involved with the character of Nicodemus himself, and I was puzzled, even embarrassed, as to how he was treated by Jesus. He asks twice, "How can this be?," with regard to rebirth from above; and both times he is left without an answer (John 3:4,

---

6. Richard A. Burridge, *What Are the Gospels? A Comparison with Graeco-Roman Biography*, SNTSMS 70 (Cambridge: Cambridge University Press, 1992); Detlev Dormeyer, *Evangelium als literarische und theologische Gattung*, EdF 263 (Darmstadt: Wissenschaftliche Buchgesellschaft, 1989).

7. See "'The Truth Will Make You Free' (John 8:32): The Power of the Personal Voice and Readings of/from the Gospel of John," in this volume.

9). Instead, Jesus reproaches him because he, a teacher of Israel, should understand (v. 10). I strongly felt that there is something quite wrong in this dialogue, if it can be called a dialogue in the first place. After all, Nicodemus indeed wants to know. I realized how much this narrative is related to myself, and I wondered what my reaction to not being provided with an adequate answer would be. Most certainly, I would be quite frustrated or even angry. On the other hand, from this scene in John and from my own experience, I learned that sometimes we have to live with a question without an answer, and thus live with an open end and journey on, nevertheless, until we perhaps grow into an answer—just like Nicodemus in the course of John's story, and especially in his final encounter with Jesus, when he lays his bloodstained body in the tomb (19:38–42). It is precisely then, at Jesus's death, that he is reborn from above and thus finds the answer by becoming Jesus's disciple.

The puzzle with regard to Nicodemus applies also to other characters in John, even though we, the readers, are always in a privileged position compared to the characters in the story. We have read the prologue, and thus we know more than any of the characters who encounter Jesus and, due to their ignorance, display their misunderstandings. In addition to the theological impact, these conversations are intriguing for the way communication works, or, for that matter, does *not* work.

When Jesus encounters the Samaritan woman at the well in chapter 4, a communication similar to that between Jesus and Nicodemus takes place. While the latter is left without an answer and reproached for not understanding, without being given any chance to understand in the first place, the Samaritan woman is confronted with another quite strange response on Jesus's part: "If you knew the gift of God, and who it is that is saying to you, 'Give me a drink,' you would have asked him, and he would have given you living water" (4:10). Jesus tells her what she would have gotten had she asked the right question. However, she does not have any chance to ask such a question in the first place. Blaming a person for not doing what she has not even a chance to do—this is indeed a quite neurotic and deeply damaging kind of communication.

The Gospel of John is replete with such very strange patterns of communication, when questions are not answered, or the answers do not match with the questions, or when a person is being reprimanded even when they cannot be accounted responsible.

Further examples of answers not matching with the questions may highlight this. In chapter 6, when Jesus and the disciples have crossed the lake after the multiplication of the loaves and fish, the crowds follow them. When they finally find him they ask, "Rabbi, when did you come here?" He answers, "Very truly, I tell you, you are looking for me, not because you saw signs, but you ate your fill of the loaves" (6:25–26). This is indeed a very strange communication, if we consider it in simply human terms. Jesus does not answer their question; he does not tell them when he came to the other side of the lake. However, he answers on another level, his own level, by responding to the people's hidden motivation. He reads their minds and responds accordingly. In this case, therefore, the mismatch is not as dramatic as in the previous examples of Nicodemus and the Samaritan woman, because the crowd's question is not really essential. After all, it does not matter when Jesus and the disciples came to this place, especially since the people have found them anyway.

When Mary Magdalene encounters the resurrected Jesus in the garden, without, however, recognizing him, he asks her, "Woman, why are you weeping? Whom are you looking for?" She answers, "Sir, if you have carried him away, tell me where you have laid him, and I will take him away" (20:15). This, too, is not an appropriate answer. Jesus, of course, knows that Mary Magdalene is searching for *him*. And we, the readers, also know this, from our privileged position, and we know why she is weeping. However, from Mary's point of view, we would expect her to answer Jesus's questions, supposing him to be the gardener (v. 15), and explain to him her reason for weeping and whom she is searching for. The story could have been developed differently, as in the encounter between the risen Jesus and the two disciples on their way to Emmaus in Luke's Gospel (24:13–35), where they voice the reason for their sorrow. In John's story, however, Mary Magdalene seems to take for granted that the gardener knows who she is speaking about. But what if not? If we imagine identifying with the gardener and suppose he is asking real questions, wanting to know about another person's sorrow, and being confronted with a question, not an answer, in return, a question that implies an action on your part, of which you, however, have no idea: "If you have carried him away …"

In addition to these strange patterns of communication, the gospel text provides not just ambivalent but even contradictory information, paradoxes, as it were. For example, we, the readers, are informed by the narrator that Jesus baptized, and, on the other hand, that he did not baptize (3:22; 4:1–2). What are we supposed to do with this information? How do we react?

When being confronted with strange patterns of communication and contradicting information, a reader's very identity is at stake. Not least due to the research in communication by Paul Watzlawick and his team at the Mental Research Institute in Palo Alto, California, it has been affirmed that confusion and disinformation create tension in the person affected, a tension that has to be resolved one way or another. In any case, a person facing such a situation of failure in communication will search for a point of reference from which certainty can be established.[8]

Apart from these failures in communication, the characters in John's Gospel pose serious problems. More often than not, they turn up suddenly, without being adequately introduced, and also disappear suddenly, leaving the reader with a deep void and a varying degree of confusion.

Nicodemus turns up again, after his strange encounter with Jesus at night in chapter 3, only briefly in chapter 7, when he defends him against his fellow Pharisees. And he only returns to the stage at the end of the gospel, in chapter 19, when he, together with Joseph of Arimathea, buries Jesus's body (19:38-42). Therefore, the text does not provide a clear portrayal of Nicodemus, which has resulted in very different scholarly and ordinary readings. Whether he comes to believe in Jesus or not is a matter of how the text of John's Gospel is read and how the various meaning dimensions are activated.

The same applies to Jesus's mother. After the Cana wedding and her going down to Capernaum (2:1-12), she disappears completely. However, she comes as a surprise when she reappears in chapter 19, standing at the foot of the cross (19:25-27). Whether she comes to believe in Jesus cannot be answered with certainty, but the end of the story indicates that eventually she does so. For a reader encountering Jesus's mother in chapter 2, the ensuing reading of John's story becomes quite a frustrating experience, as he or she would like to get to know what happened to her later on.

The reader encounters a similar experience with regard to the Samaritan woman, who does not even turn up again in John's story of Jesus. After meeting the woman for the first time, he or she might want to have her back, sooner or later. But the reader's expectation is frustrated completely. What happens to her after Jesus and his disciples leave Sychar remains in the dark.

---

8. Paul Watzlawik, *Wie wirklich ist die Wirklichkeit? Wahn—Täuschung—Verstehen* (Munich: Piper, 1976).

The Beloved Disciple, after all the guarantee of the gospel's authenticity (21:24), is not introduced until chapter 13, where he features in the narrative of the footwashing. Later he stands at the foot of the cross, together with the women (19:25-27). On Easter morning, he runs to the tomb, together with Simon Peter, after Mary Magdalene informs them; and he comes to believe at the sight of the empty tomb (20:1-10). Finally, he briefly returns to the stage in chapter 21, mentioned in the course of the narrative of the miraculous catch of fish (v. 7), and again in the gospel's final scene, when he is referred to in the dialogue between Jesus and Peter (vv. 20-23).

Mary Magdalene is first mentioned only very late, at the foot of the cross (19:25), although, because of her prominence in chapter 20, she obviously was one of Jesus's most eminent followers. Nevertheless, she disappears completely after Easter morning. Not even her actual report of the good news to the other disciples, and their respective responses, are narrated in the gospel story. There is only the narrator's comment that Mary Magdalene goes to the disciples and announces to them, "I have seen the Lord," and she tells them what Jesus said to her, without explicitly mentioning what "these things" are (20:18).

Encountering Johannine characters is thus, generally, a very frustrating experience. No ongoing relationship between readers and characters is made possible, and many a reader's questions are left unanswered. Encountering Johannine characters is a most fragmentary experience that confronts readers with their own fragmentary lives, including broken-up relationships, and reminds them of encounters that did not turn into ongoing relationships, however significant the encounter with a certain person may have been. Encountering Johannine characters, therefore, shares in a characteristic of Jesus himself, the "elusive Christ,"[9] whom no one can get hold of, who escapes and hides away repeatedly in the gospel story and thus demonstrates that he only "tented" on earth (1:14); he did not come to settle down.

Gaps, Tensions, Open Ends: Reading (into) Silences

Besides the characters, the sequences of scenes in John are often puzzling.

After the Cana wedding, not only does Jesus's mother disappear, but also Jesus provides no small surprise. Just after the more pleasant event

---

9. See Mark Stibbe, "The Elusive Christ: A New Reading of the Fourth Gospel," *JSNT* 48 (1991): 20-38.

of turning water into wine at a wedding, he is immediately depicted as cleansing the temple in Jerusalem (2:13–23). This very sudden change of location, as well as the contrast in the missions he performs, raises considerable questions on the part of the reader. It is not at all easy to adapt to such sudden changes in location and portrayal of character and to come to terms with the gaps and tensions created thereby.

On a smaller scale, such changes, gaps, ambivalences, and tensions occur also within the individual narratives in John's Gospel.

For example, in the context of Lazarus's resurrection, Mary of Bethany is introduced as the one who has anointed Jesus (11:2), even though the actual anointing takes place later, in chapter 12 (vv. 1–12).

Furthermore, after her encounter with Jesus, Martha tells her sister that "the teacher" is calling for her (11:28), although in fact nothing like that has been mentioned previously. What should a reader make of such a puzzling comment?

Only a little later, at Lazarus's tomb, Jesus reminds Martha, "Did I not tell you that if you believed, you would see the glory of God?" (11:40). However, in the course of the narrative Jesus has not said so. Once again, this sounds like an unjustified reproach on Jesus's part, similar to the reproaches Nicodemus and the Samaritan woman are confronted with.

Finally, in the farewell narrative Jesus admonishes his disciples, "Rise, let us be on our way" (14:31), but then he continues with a lengthy parable on the wine in chapter 15. Thus, Jesus's request to rise addressed to his disciples is made obsolete as he continues his teaching.

To sum up: The Gospel of John is full of gaps, tensions, even contradictions, and the readers have to come to terms with them, one way or another. This is indeed no easy task. However, there is also a lot of potential in the text to be unraveled by the readers. And the problems become a challenge.

The Pains and Pleasures of Reading John

By focusing on the reading process within a reader-response approach, the distinct character especially of the Gospel of John becomes obvious, and also how much form and content belong together and cannot be separated, just like the Word become flesh, incarnated.[10]

---

10. See Gail O'Day, *Revelation in the Fourth Gospel: Narrative Mode and Theologi-*

Reading John is an event, a process, and it is multidimensional. Encountering the gospel implies exposing oneself to this process and accepting to be worked on by a text that becomes the subject. It implies giving up the desire, so often found in biblical scholars and ordinary readers, to control and master the text and to extract "the meaning."

On the other hand, a very active reader is called for by the very nature of this gospel, with all its gaps, tensions, and open endings. Reading John implies making choices as to how one reads, thereby filling in gaps, solving tensions, finishing open-ended stories, last but not least in one's own life. Thus, reading John is, perhaps more than reading other biblical texts, an exercise in taking responsibility for one's own readings and for the worlds created by them, including the effects of our readings on others. Consequently, it is also an exercise in the ethics of biblical interpretation.[11]

Due to its open character, the gospel text is full of potential and thus offers room for the reader's creativity and the pleasures that come along with it.[12] The reader's ability to venture out on his or her own, trusting and partaking in the Spirit that comes and goes wherever it wants (3:8), is indeed a liberating process.

Reading John is an experience of pain *and* pleasure.

Reading with a Passion, the title of Jeffrey L. Staley's pioneer work in autobiographical biblical criticism on the Gospel of John, can also explicate the very nature of reading this gospel. Passion is both pain *and* pleasure.[13]

The Labour of Reading is the title of a collection of essays on biblical interpretation, "illuminating the complex relation between labor, pleasure, desire, alienation and action," and understanding labor as "much more than simply hard work; it can also be seen as a complicated and driving force that moves readers through a range of emotions, responses, and practices."[14] Reading is labor, hard work, always, but it is also a birthing

---

cal Claim (Minneapolis: Fortress, 1986).

11. See Daniel Patte, *Ethics of Biblical Interpretation: A Reevaluation* (Louisville: Westminster John Knox, 1995); Elisabeth Schüssler Fiorenza, *Rhetoric and Ethic: The Politics of Biblical Studies* (Minneapolis: Fortress, 1999).

12. See Robert Alter, *The Pleasures of Reading in an Ideological Age* (New York: Simon & Schuster, 1989).

13. Jeffrey L. Staley, *Reading with a Passion: Rhetoric, Autobiography, and the American West in the Gospel of John* (New York: Continuum, 1995).

14. Fiona C. Black, Roland Boer, and Erin Runions, eds., *The Labour of Reading: Desire, Alienation, and Biblical Interpretation*, SemeiaSt 36 (Atlanta: Society of Biblical Literature, 1999), 2.

process. "When a woman is in labor, she has pain, because her hour has come. But when her child is born, she no longer remembers the anguish because of the joy of having brought a human being into the world" (16:21). Bringing new readings of John's Gospel into the world is also a good reason to rejoice, for those of us who have given birth and those who receive our newborns with open arms and minds.

Part 2
Reading Characters in John, the Synoptics, and the Hebrew Bible

Mary of Bethany and Mary of Magdala—Two Female Characters in the Johannine Passion Narrative: A Feminist, Narrative-Critical Reader Response

1. Introduction

The focus of this investigation is on *two female characters* in John's Gospel, Mary of Bethany and Mary of Magdala.[1] Key are the development and the unfolding of these characters within the passion narrative and their relation to other female and male characters. According to R. Alan Culpepper, "one of the most interesting elements of any story is the cast of

---

This chapter was originally a paper presented at the General Meeting of the Society for New Testament Studies in Chicago, August 1993, in the seminar Hermeneutics and the Biblical Text (chaired by Bernard C. Lategan and James W. Voelz). I am indebted to Elizabeth Struthers Malbon (Blacksburg, Virginia) for her response paper and—besides all the other responses from seminar members—especially to Detlev Dormeyer (Münster), Bas van Iersel (Nijmegen, the Netherlands), Wilhelm Wuellner (Berkeley), and Francis Watson (London) for their critical comments. Without Bas van Iersel's encouragement, however, this paper might never have been presented to readers other than the first readers and audience. It was originally published in *NTS* 41 (1995) and dedicated to Eugen Ruckstuhl (Lucerne, Switzerland), my great benefactor, who encouraged me to work on Mary Magdalene.

1. For the "legitimacy of treating people described in a historical writing as characters" see R. Alan Culpepper, *Anatomy of the Fourth Gospel: A Study in Literary Design*, FFNT (Philadelphia: Fortress, 1983), 105. Detlev Dormeyer points to the double function of proper names as historical persons and characters in *Das Neue Testament im Rahmen der antiken Literaturgeschichte: Eine Einführung*, DA (Darmstadt: Wissenschaftliche Buchgesellschaft, 1993), 59–60. For an analysis of the historical basis of John's narrative, in discussing Culpepper's work, see Eugen Ruckstuhl, "Jesus und der geschichtliche Mutterboden im vierten Evangelium," in *Vom Urchristentum zu Jesus*, ed. Hubert Frankemölle and Karl Kertelge (Freiburg im Breisgau: Herder, 1989), 256–86.

characters"; and "Much of the power of the Fourth Gospel comes from its vivid characterizations and their effects upon the reader."[2] Nevertheless, not much attention has been paid so far to characterization[3] in John (and to characterization in general),[4] and female characters have been even more neglected and treated like stepdaughters.[5] This holds true also

---

2. Culpepper, *Anatomy of the Fourth Gospel*, 7.

3. According to Powell, "it is the process through which the implied author provides the implied reader with what is necessary to reconstruct a character from a narrative." See Mark Allan Powell, *What Is Narrative Criticism?* (Minneapolis: Fortress, 1990), 52.

4. See Culpepper, *Anatomy of the Fourth Gospel*, 115. But see Jan A. du Rand, "The Characterization of Jesus as Depicted in the Narrative of the Fourth Gospel," *Neot* 19 (1985): 18–36; Jeffrey L. Staley, "Stumbling in the Dark, Reaching for the Light: Reading Character in John 5 and 9," *Semeia* 53 (1991): 55–80; see also Jan A. du Rand, "Plot and Point of View in the Gospel of John," in *A South African Perspective on the New Testament*, ed. J. Hartin Petzer and Peter J. Martin (Leiden: Brill, 1986), 149–69, where he deals also, though only briefly, with characters (see 154–56). See now also Elizabeth Struthers Malbon and Adele Berlin, eds., *Characterization in Biblical Literature*, *Semeia* 63 (1993), especially the contribution by David R. Beck, "The Narrative Function of Anonymity in Fourth Gospel Characterization," 143–58; and Marianne Meye Thompson, "'God's Voice You Have Never Heard, God's Form You Have Never Seen': The Characterization of God in the Gospel of John," 177–204.

5. Even Culpepper is far from having done justice to them. He categorizes the Samaritan woman, Mary and Martha, and Mary Magdalene as "minor characters" and spends only one page or two pages on them respectively (see *Anatomy of the Fourth Gospel*, 132–44). Though du Rand's topic ("Plot and Point of View") is not characters, it is nevertheless surprising that, for example, he does not even mention Mary Magdalene when dealing with the resurrection of Jesus "as narrated within the framework of the appearances" (see 167).—*Positive exceptions* are (though their approaches are not narrative critical) Raymond E. Brown, "Roles of Women in the Fourth Gospel," *TS* 36 (1975): 688–99; Sandra M. Schneiders, "Women in the Fourth Gospel and the Role of Women in the Contemporary Church," *BTB* 12 (1982): 35–45. Turid Karlsen Seim's excellent investigation shows some narrative-critical elements, despite her introductory remark that her description of the women is "not … dependent on any specific terminology or methodological frame of reference." See Seim, "Roles of Women in the Gospel of John," in *Aspects of the Johannine Literature*, ed. Lars Hartmann and Birger Olsson, ConBNT 18 (Uppsala: Uppsala University Press, 1987), 56. See also Martinus C. Boer, "John 4:27—Women (and Men) in the Gospel and Community of John," in *Women in the Biblical Tradition*, ed. George J. Brooke, SWR 31 (Lewiston, NY: Mellen, 1992), 208–30. For a narrative-critical evaluation see now also the ingenious commentary by Sjef van Tilborg, *Imaginative Love in John*, BibInt 2 (Leiden: Brill, 1993), esp. ch. 4, "Loving Women."

for female characters in the Gospel of Mark, which has been the focus of interest in narrative-critical studies.[6]

Underlying my character analysis is the *open view of character* as advocated by Seymour Chatman,[7] in which characters are not only evaluated by the functions of their actions in relation to the plot but are treated as autonomous beings and assessed in the way we evaluate real people. David Rhoads describes this approach very well when he states:

> In this approach we analyze not only what characters do but also who they "are." The interpreter reconstructs what kind of "persons" the characters are from the narrator's descriptions and characterizations, the characters' interactions with others, their motives, and so on, then assign them traits, noting how the traits are revealed and whether they change in the story. The interpreter reconstructs characters only from evidence suggested within the boundaries of the narrative world.[8]

The concepts of configuration and interfigurality as defined by Wolfgang Müller[9] are applied and are crucial for this investigation. While

---

6. An exception is Elizabeth Struthers Malbon, "Fallible Followers: Women and Men in the Gospel of Mark," *Semeia* 28 (1983): 29–48; Malbon, "Disciples/Crowds/ Whoever: Markan Characters and Readers," *NovT* (1986): 104–30. Surprisingly, most investigations into the characters of the disciples in the gospels have taken for granted that the term refers to men only. See, e.g., Robert C. Tannehill, "The Disciples in Mark: The Function of a Narrative Role," *JR* 57 (1977): 386–405; Hans-Josef Klauck, "Die erzählerische Rolle der Jünger im Markusevangelium: Eine narrative Analyse," *NovT* 24 (1982): 1–26; Joanna Dewey, "Point of View and the Disciples in Mark," in *1982 Society of Biblical Literature Seminar Papers*, ed. K. H. Richards, SBLSP 21 (Chico, CA: Scholars Press, 1982), 97–106. However, if we take the androcentric-inclusive language fully into account, we need to look afresh at this topic in narrative-critical analysis.

7. Seymour Chatman, *Story and Discourse: Narrative Structure in Fiction and Film* (Ithaca, NY: Cornell University Press, 1978), 107–38.

8. See David Rhoads, "Narrative Criticism and the Gospel of Mark," *JAAR* 50 (1982): 411–34. Culpepper restricts the applicability of this concept with regard to the Gospel of John (*Anatomy of the Fourth Gospel*, 102). I will show, however, that Chatman's program has also value for those characters in the gospel who appear only briefly, as the female characters do.—A plot-centered approach to characters in Mark is advocated by Robert C. Tannehill, "The Gospel of Mark as Narrative Christology," *Semeia* 16 (1979): 57–95, esp. 58. This is in contrast to Rhoads, who decides in favor of an open approach also to Mark ("Narrative Criticism," 417).

9. Wolfgang G. Müller, "Interfigurality: A Study of the Interdependence of Lit-

configuration "is the constellation or grouping of the characters,"[10] the term *interfigurality*, which was coined by Müller as a neologism, refers to "interrelations that exist between characters of different texts."[11] Interfigurality, according to Müller, represents "one of the most important dimensions of intertextuality."[12] Configuration refers here to the relation between Mary of Bethany and Mary of Magdala (and other female and male characters related to them) in the Gospel of John. The concept of interfigurality, on the other hand, is applied in order to define more specifically the relations between the characterization of the two Marys in John and in the Synoptic Gospels. By applying this interfigural view I will show that the author of John must have known the Synoptic Gospels and transformed the material provided by them.[13] I also assume and consider it very likely that not only the author but also his audience, readers or listeners, were familiar with the Synoptic traditions. Otherwise, as I will show, some text signals that indicate intertextuality could not have been noticed as such by the readers, and consequently several dimensions of the texts would have remained concealed to them and some puzzles would have remained unsolved.[14]

---

erary Figures," in *Intertextuality*, ed. Heinrich E. Plett, RTT 15 (Berlin: de Gruyter, 1991), 101–21.

10. Müller, "Interfigurality," 117; see also 114.

11. Müller, "Interfigurality," 101.

12. Müller, "Interfigurality," 101. That such relations, nevertheless, have found little attention so far in intertextual theory and criticism may be due to two main reasons, Müller presumes. One is the suspicion generally felt toward character-oriented studies; the other is the absence of a critical term for this aspect of intertextuality. Therefore, Müller looks "at character as a strictly structural and functional textual element" and coins "the neologism *interfigurality*," "because without it important aspects and problems of intertextuality would not come into view" (101–2).—Due to my open view of character I use Müller's term *interfigurality* but do *not* follow his look at "character as a strictly structural and functional textual element."

13. See also Thyen's investigation into John 11–12. See Hartwig Thyen, "Die Erzählungen von den bethanischen Geschwistern (Joh 11,1–12,19) als 'Palimpsest' über synoptischen Texten," in *The Four Gospels 1992: Festschrift Frans Neyrinck*, ed. Frans Van Segbroeck et al., BETL 100 (Leuven: Leuven University Press; Peeters, 1992), 2021–50. In spite of some similarities, however, my approach and its results are quite different, and unlike Thyen I do *not* draw the conclusion that John used no other sources than the Synoptic Gospels. However, historical judgments are not within the range of my approach.

14. If, however, one believes that only the author of John but not his audience knew the Synoptic Gospels, as some of my colleagues did in response to my Society

Special attention is paid to the position of the *narrator, his point of view*, and the consequences for the *presentation of female characters*.¹⁵ The question is considered how a male point of view shapes the presentation of women as well as the reader's perception of and attitude toward these female characters.¹⁶ The narrator's point of view is distinguished from the characters' points of view, as Rhoads has put it: "The narrative reveals the point of view of the narrator, and the narrator in turn shows us the points of view of the characters, in the course of telling the story."¹⁷ Of special interest in character analysis are those cases where the narrator's point of view, and consequently the reader's point of view, differ from that of the characters, where "the readers are put in a privileged position."¹⁸ Important in this analysis are the spatial and temporal plane and the psychological plane of point of view, that is, "the physical place or the point of view in time from which someone views something" and the "states of the characters' minds, such as thinking, feeling, or experiencing."¹⁹

---

for New Testament Studies seminar paper, the reading process would differ from those readings presented here.

15. If we take for granted that the real author of the Gospel of John was a man, then consequently the implied author's and the narrator's point of view are male points of view. See also van Tilborg, *Imaginative Love*, 170; Alice Bach, "Signs of the Flesh: Observations on Characterization in the Bible," *Semeia* 63 (1993): 64.—For a distinction between the implied author and the narrator in John, see Culpepper, *Anatomy of the Fourth Gospel*, 16 (following Wayne C. Booth). This distinction is necessary in spite of the fact that "In John, the narrator is undramatized and serves as the voice of the implied author."

16. For the influence of the narrator on his or her readers generally (without raising questions of gender issues), see Culpepper, *Anatomy of the Fourth Gospel*, 4. Also Rhoads, "Narrative Criticism," 421; Powell, *What Is Narrative Criticism?*, 53–54.

17. Rhoads, "Narrative Criticism," 421.

18. Edgar V. McKnight, *Post-modern Use of the Bible: The Emergence of Reader-Oriented Criticism* (Nashville: Abingdon, 1990), 256; see also 254–62, "Actualizing the Reader of Biblical Texts." According to Robert M. Fowler, this "incongruity" is "the essence of irony." See Fowler, "Irony and the Messianic Secret in the Gospel of Mark," *Proceedings: Eastern Great Lakes Biblical Society* 1 (1981): 29. For the different relationships between narrator and reader, and narrator and characters, see also Rhoads, "Narrative Criticism," 420, following Norman R. Petersen, "'Point of View' in Mark's Narrative," *Semeia* 12 (1978): 97–121. For point of view in/on a gospel, see further Stephen D. Moore, *Literary Criticism and the Gospels: The Theoretical Challenge* (New Haven: Yale University Press, 1989), 25–40. For the narrator and point of view in John, see Culpepper, *Anatomy of the Fourth Gospel*, 13–40.

19. Rhoads, "Narrative Criticism," 421. Rhoads follows Uspensky's analysis of

The starting point of my character analysis is a *strictly reader-oriented approach* to narrative. This implies that story and discourse, content and form, are inseparable.[20] In my investigation into female characterization in John, I will pay special attention to the introduction of the characters and their progressive unfolding within the narrative.[21] At issue are the questions when and how a reader learns of somebody and something and how she/he is affected by this. Focus, therefore, is on the reading experience as a temporal and responsive, as well as creative and dynamic, process by which meanings of texts are established.[22] This necessitates a close reading

point of view in narrative and his distinction of four planes; besides those already mentioned, there are the ideological and the phraseological plane. See Boris Uspensky, *Poetics of Composition* (Berkeley: University of California Press, 1973). These planes of point of view are also underlying the studies of du Rand, "Plot and Point of View," and Petersen "'Point of View' in Mark's Narrative."

20. See Rhoads, "Narrative Criticism," 414; John Darr, *On Character Building: The Reader and the Rhetoric of Characterization in Luke-Acts* (Louisville: Westminster John Knox, 1992). See also Fred W. Burnett, "Characterization and Reader Construction of Characters in the Gospels," in *Listening to the Word of God: A Tribute to Boyce W. Blackwelder*, ed. Barry L. Callen (Anderson, IN: Anderson University Press, 1990), 69-88.

21. This, unfortunately, has not been done by Culpepper, especially in dealing with the "minor characters," among them the Samaritan woman, Mary and Martha, and Mary Magdalene; see *Anatomy of the Fourth Gospel*, 132-44. See also Moore's critique in *Literary Criticism*, 93-95. Robert M. Fowler points out that focus has been placed on the story level of the narrative, while neglecting the discourse level or the rhetoric. See Fowler, *Let the Reader Understand: Reader-Response Criticism and the Gospel of Mark* (Minneapolis: Fortress, 1991), 2. But to my opinion he draws the wrong conclusion by shifting emphasis from the story to the discourse and by considering "the discourse as opposed to the story of the Gospel narrative" (4). The solution to the problem is not either/or, but narrative criticism and reader-response criticism belong together and form an ideal couple. A combination of both approaches also underlies Staley's analysis of Johannine characters in "Stumbling in the Dark," esp. 54; see also Powell, *What Is Narrative Criticism?*, 16-21, esp. 21. On introduction, see Culpepper, *Anatomy of the Fourth Gospel*, 6: "Characters are fashioned by what the narrator says about them, particularly when introducing them."

22. See Fowler, *Let the Reader Understand*, 3; also McKnight, *Post-modern Use*, 217-72, "The Role of the Reader," esp. reading as "progressive actualization" and "multiple actualizations" (235-41); Detlev Dormeyer, *Der Sinn des Leidens Jesu: Historisch-kritische und textpragmatische Analysen zur Markuspassion*, SBS 96 (Stuttgart: Katholisches Bibelwerk, 1979), 107-9. Wayne C. Booth distinguishes between two techniques of characterization, telling and showing; the latter requires harder work on the part of the reader. See Booth, *The Rhetoric of Fiction*, 2nd ed. (Chicago: University

of the texts, as presented in the second part, which reflects the (possible) communication process between text and reader. Gaps, discontinuity, ambiguity, and so on in the texts deserve special consideration, because they have a unique function within the reading process and are the real turning points in the narrative. The reader is forced to fill in gaps and make decisions and by doing so creates the meaning of the text accordingly and uniquely.[23] Thus, texts are experienced by the reader as texts that are *open* to different possible and legitimate interpretations.[24]

The concrete actualization of a text depends largely on *the reader's social location*, his or her context.[25] Therefore, in my narrative-critical

---

of Chicago Press, 1983), 3–20. See also Powell, *What Is Narrative Criticism?*, 52–53. See also Bar-Efrat's categories of direct and indirect shaping of characters; again, the latter calls for the reader's active participation. See Shimon Bar-Efrat, *Narrative Art in the Bible*, BLS 17 (Sheffield: Sheffield Academic, 1989), 47–92, esp. 64. On process, see Wolfgang Iser, "The Reading Process: A Phenomenological Approach," in *Reader-Response Criticism: From Formalism to Post-structuralism*, ed. Jane P. Tompkins (Baltimore: Johns Hopkins University Press, 1980), 50–69, esp. 54. See also Fowler, *Let the Reader Understand*, 1–5, "The Reading Experience"; and Stanley Fish's "method of analysis which takes the reader, as an actively mediating presence, fully into account." See Fish, "Literature in the Reader: Affective Stylistics," *NLH* 2 (1970): 123. See also Moore, *Literary Criticism*, part 2, "Gospel Criticism as Reading" (71–170).

23. See Iser, "Reading Process," 55: "Literary texts are full of unexpected twists and turns, and frustrations of expectations.... Indeed, it is through inevitable omissions that a story gains its dynamism. Thus, whenever the flow is interrupted and we are led off in unexpected directions, the opportunity is given to us to bring into play our own faculty for establishing connections—for filling in the gaps left by the text itself"; "one text is potentially capable of several different realizations, and no reading can ever exhaust the full potential, for each individual reader will fill in the gaps in his own way, whereby excluding the various other possibilities." See also McKnight, *Post-modern Use*, 223–41 (esp. on ambiguity, poetic omission, paratactic thinking, temporal and logical discontinuity, progressive actualization, and multiple actualizations). See Dormeyer, *Sinn des Leidens Jesu*, 11–12. Also see Robert Alter, *The Pleasures of Reading in an Ideological Age* (New York: Simon & Schuster, 1989), 206–38, "Multiple Readings and the Bog of Indeterminacy."

24. See McKnight, *Post-modern Use*, 241: "The meaning of a text is inexhaustible, because no context can provide all the keys to all of its possibilities." See also Francis Watson, ed., *The Open Text* (London: SCM, 1993).

25. This has been the focus of the seminar The Role of the Reader in the Interpretation of the New Testament (since 1993 Hermeneutics and the Biblical Text) at the General Meetings of the Society for New Testament Studies for the past years. See also Bernard C. Lategan's introduction to *Scriptura* 9 (1991): 1–6.

approach to female characters I have decided to imagine a female first reader, that is, a woman in the Johannine community,[26] who reads the narratives about Mary (and Martha) of Bethany and Mary of Magdala in John 11, 12, and 20 as parts of the whole gospel narrative. Although to some extent the response to the texts might be independent of gender issues, I am convinced that it does make a difference whether a man or a woman encounters these female characters during the reading process, because it takes place not only on an intellectual but also on an emotional level. By learning about female characters a female reader is offered models of identification, and this has an impact on her sense of identity and self-esteem. It is assumed that not only some potentials of the texts are actualized but also the reader herself is actualized and transformed.[27] Underlying my approach is a *feminist hermeneutics* that focuses on the reconstruction of women's history and on the critical analysis of women's stories as rendered by a male author in a patriarchal society.[28]

---

26. The imagination of such a reader remains hypothetical, of course, for it cannot be proved whether a woman in the Johannine community really read the texts as I do here. I am well aware that the imagined female first reader is a construct and has much of a self-portrait. Naturally this is so because of the hermeneutical situation, as Elizabeth Struthers Malbon expressed in her response: "Although we can inform ourselves (and others) about the possible or even probable situations and presuppositions of readers other than our own, our readings remain our own. We must claim them as such." Imagination has to be distinguished from historical reconstruction, which belongs within the historical-critical paradigm and is therefore not an issue here. This imagination of a female first reader might be considered "a reading strategy," as Edgar McKnight interpreted my approach in the discussion following the presentation of my paper.

27. See McKnight, *Post-modern Use*, 254–63, "Actualizing the Reader of Biblical Texts." See also Fish, "Affective Stylistics," 160–61 (talking about his method): "It is a method which processes its own user, who is also its only instrument. It is self-sharpening and what it sharpens is *you*. In short, it does not organize materials, but transforms minds." See also James W. Voelz, "Multiple Signs and Double Texts: Elements of Intertextuality," in *Intertextuality in Biblical Writings: Essays in Honour of Bas van Iersel*, ed. Siepke Draisma (Kampen: Kok Pharos, 1989), 27–34, 33: "It is … the text of the life-experience of the interpreter which is being interpreted in each 'application.'"

28. In my own feminist approach, I have been very much inspired by Elisabeth Schüssler Fiorenza's pioneer works: *In Memory of Her: A Feminist-Theological Reconstruction of Christian Origins* (New York: Crossroad, 1983); *Bread Not Stone: The Challenge of Feminist Biblical Interpretation* (Boston: Beacon, 1984); *But She Said: Feminist Practices of Biblical Interpretation* (Boston: Beacon, 1993).

2. Mary of Bethany and Mary of Magdala—A Female First Reader's First-Time Reading of John 11:1–46, 12:1–8, and 20:1–18

The following readings are based on an imagined female reader who reads the gospel for the first time. This implies that she only knows what has been mentioned so far in the narrative and does not know what will be told later on. First-time reading is taken seriously into account as a *sequential and temporal reading*, and it differs essentially from any second reading or even several rereadings of a text.[29] First-time reading refers to the plot and plotted time, as different from story time, according to Norman Petersen's definition: "The narrative world is comprised of all events described or referred to in the narrative, but in their causal and logical sequence, whereas the plotting of this world is to be seen in the ways its components have been selected and arranged in a sequence of narrated incidents. These ways are plot devices."[30]

The first reader imagined here is an informed reader, not a naive reader.[31] She has knowledge gained from the experience of reading (or hearing) other texts, that is, the Synoptic Gospels, as well as participating in the life experiences of a Christian community and therefore being familiar with the Christian kerygma.

Reading John 11:1–46

> Now a certain man was ill, Lazarus of Bethany, the village of Mary and her sister Martha. It was Mary who anointed the Lord with ointment and wiped his feet with her hair, whose brother was ill. (11:1–2)

---

29. For the difference see Iser, "Reading Process," 55–56.

30. Norman R. Petersen, *Literary Criticism for New Testament Critics*, GBS (Philadelphia: Fortress, 1978), 49–50; see also Rhoads, "Narrative Criticism," 415; Culpepper, *Anatomy of the Fourth Gospel*, 53–75.

31. See Dormeyer's distinction of different types of readers or reader attitudes, which are naive reader, critical reader (in my terminology, informed reader), and critical researcher: Detlev Dormeyer, "The Implicit and Explicit Readers and the Genre of Philippians 3:2–4:3, 8–9: Response to the Commentary of Wolfgang Schenk," *Semeia* 48 (1989): 156; these levels are constructed according to Roman Ingarden, *Gegenstand und Aufgaben der Literaturwissenschaft: Aufsätze und Diskussionsbeiträge (1937–1964)*, ed. Rolf Fieguth (Tübingen: Niemeyer, 1976), 17–22.

At the beginning of the narrative, our reader is confronted with this awkward setting. A man, first unspecified, is then given a name and defined by the place he comes from (or lives in), that is, Bethany. This is identified as the village of Mary and her sister Martha, which implies that the reader knows already who Mary and Martha are. Puzzling, however, is the fact that so far the reader has not heard anything about Mary and Martha in this gospel. Therefore, knowledge of these women must originate from an extratextual source, either from oral tradition or from another written tradition.[32] The story-world is opened up to the reader's world, and both are meant to be related to each other.

Mary is more concretely identified as the one who anointed the Lord, but nowhere previously was our reader informed about such an incident. The narrator invites the reader to remember knowledge gained somewhere else and to integrate it into the reading of a new story. Mary is said to have anointed the Lord and wiped his feet; that is, there are indeed two acts mentioned, the anointing and the wiping, with two different objects: the Lord, that is, the whole person, and a part of him, his feet. This special feature in the text is a clear signal for our reader to open up this text to the anointing stories in the Gospels of Mark and Matthew, on the one hand, and the anointing story in the Gospel of Luke, on the other hand.[33] In Mark (14:3–9) and Matthew (26:6–13) the story of an unnamed woman in Bethany, who anointed Jesus's head with precious ointment, is told. Jesus interprets her act as the anointing of his body beforehand for his burial (Mark 14:8; Matt 26:12). The woman's act is thereby portrayed as a pro-

---

32. See Culpepper on "John's Readers," where he deals with "the gospel's depiction of its authorial audience or intended reader." The starting point is the question, "What does the narratee know, and when does he or she know it?" This question is focused on five areas: persons (or characters), places, languages, Judaism, and events (*Anatomy of the Fourth Gospel*, 212–23). According to Culpepper, Lazarus must be introduced; Mary and Martha are known to the reader. But Culpepper does not answer the question where the knowledge of these persons, and also events, comes from (see 212).

33. See Maurits Sabbe, "The Anointing of Jesus in John 12, 1–8 and Its Synoptic Parallels," in Van Segbroeck et al., *Four Gospels 1992*, 2051–82. Sabbe's approach is historical-critical, and he concentrates on the author's use of sources; he believes in direct dependence of John on the Synoptics. See also Ingrid Rosa Kitzberger, "Love and Footwashing: John 13:1–20 and Luke 7:36–50 Read Intertextually," *BibInt* 2 (1994): 190–206. Despite a widely used explanation, I do not consider 11:2 a prolepsis referring to 12:1–8. The aorist of the verbs is one reason against it; the other is the fact that the two acts described here are not identical with what is narrated in 12:1–8.

phetic sign, because she is foreseeing Jesus's death, and it is a confession of the suffering Messiah, which differs from Peter's confession, who confesses Jesus as the Messiah but rejects his suffering (see Mark 8:27–30). Mary's second act referred to in John 11:2, that is, the wiping of Jesus's feet with her hair, draws the reader's attention to the anointing story in Luke's Gospel (7:36–50). This tells about an unnamed woman, a sinner, who wets Jesus's feet with her tears, then wipes them with her hair, and finally anoints them with precious oil (vv. 37–38). The motivation for her act is her great love (v. 47). The reader is already familiar with the women in Mark's, Matthew's, and Luke's stories. Now she is invited to identify these unnamed women with Mary of Bethany, or at least she is invited to assign some of their character traits to Mary. These traits are: she can foresee Jesus's death and acts accordingly; she confesses him as the suffering Messiah; and she loves him very much.

In the initial setting Mary is considered to be the main character: she is mentioned first, whereas Martha is mentioned second and defined as "her sister" (John 11:1), and also Lazarus is defined as "her brother" (v. 2).[34] This is very unusual, because normally a man is not defined by a woman; it is the other way around, as the reader might have expected.

The sisters send to Jesus, saying, "Lord, he whom you love is ill" (v. 3). Thereby the reader learns that the sisters know Jesus quite well and they also know where he is at the present moment, although he is hiding himself (see 10:39–40). It is also obvious that Jesus knows Lazarus so well that from the information "he whom you love" Jesus knows who is meant. It is a love relationship that exists between Jesus and Lazarus,[35] but Jesus also loves the two women (11:5). Surprisingly, Martha is mentioned first now, and Mary is defined by her, as her sister. The reader will expect that the focus is going to be shifted from Mary to Martha. Jesus's reaction seems not at all to be in accordance with his love for the three of them; he remains where he is for two more days (v. 6).

The narrator shifts the focus very suddenly to Bethany in verse 17. He uses the literary device of anticipation, because Jesus in fact finds Lazarus

---

34. See Brown, "Roles of Women," 694: "Martha and Mary ... seem to have been better known than Lazarus."

35. See Fernando F. Segovia, *Love Relationships in the Johannine Tradition: Agape/Agapan in 1 John and the Fourth Gospel*, SBLDS 59 (Chico, CA: Scholars Press, 1982). There is no real difference between the use of *philein* (see 11:3) and *agapan* (see 11:5) in John's Gospel. See also van Tilborg, *Imaginative Love*, esp. 230–38.

in the tomb only later, in verse 38. The note that Lazarus has been in the tomb four days (v. 17) assists the reader in bridging the gap in the story (neither Lazarus's death nor Jesus's way to Bethany are narrated). She can link the initial scene to the following scene, where Mary and Martha are back on stage again. The mention of four days is also significant, because it informs the reader indirectly that Lazarus is already dead when Jesus is informed about his illness. The reader learns about Jesus's omniscient point of view. He knows already of Lazarus's death when all other characters in the story—and until verse 13 also the reader herself—do not yet know. This implies that Lazarus does *not* die because Jesus stays two days longer where he was. Therefore, the reader can again be sure of Jesus's love for Lazarus, Mary, and Martha, and she expects Jesus to prove his love now.[36]

The narrator's information that many of the Jews have come to Martha and Mary to console them concerning their brother (v. 19) may cause the reader to expect Jesus to do the same. But remembering Jesus's words that "this illness is not unto death but for the glory of God, so that the Son of God may be glorified by means of it" (v. 4), she knows that something more special is going to happen.

When Martha, who is mentioned first again (see v. 5), hears that Jesus is coming, she goes to meet him, while Mary stays at home. Martha is described as active and reacting spontaneously. The reader is not told who informs Martha, and she does not know whether Mary also hears of Jesus's coming but decides not to go—for whatever reason—or whether she does not receive the news. The gap brought about by not telling has to be filled by the reader herself. Whatever answer she will find, it undoubtedly influences her evaluation of Mary. If the reader decides that Mary does not know about Jesus's arrival, Mary is not to be blamed for staying at home. If, on the other hand, the reader believes that Mary does know, she will wonder about Mary's motivation for her reaction. However, the textual ambiguity frustrates the reader's desire for a definite answer, and therefore she will remain uncertain whether her image of Mary is correct. Now she learns of Martha's encounter with Jesus. The narrator does not tell how they actually meet. No greeting and so on is mentioned. This is another gap in the story that must be filled by the reader's imagination. Martha addresses

---

36. Later on, in 13:1, the narrator's comment that Jesus loves "his own" to the end is proved by his footwashing.

Jesus only with a harsh but also ambivalent reproach: "Lord, if you had been here, my brother would not have died" (v. 21). Thus she blames Jesus, but she also demonstrates her belief in Jesus's power over life and death. It is quite telling that Martha reproaches Jesus because of his absence but *not* because of his delay after he was called. Martha's belief and trust in Jesus are further proved by her confession, which follows immediately: "Even now I know that whatever you ask from God, God will give you" (v. 22). This initiates a dialogue between them. This conversation is a theological and intellectual talk about Lazarus's resurrection. Jesus reveals himself as "the resurrection" and "the life." The conversation culminates in Martha's confession that Jesus is the Messiah, the Christ, that is, "the anointed one," and that he is the Son of God who is coming into the world (v. 27). This very remarkable confession on the lips of a woman[37] reminds the reader of another woman mentioned previously in the Gospel, that is, the Samaritan woman (John 4).[38] In her encounter with Jesus at the well she confesses her belief in the coming of the Messiah, the Christ (4:25). But although Jesus tells her that he *is* the Messiah (v. 26), she nevertheless asks, "Can this be the Christ?" (v. 29). This doubtful question is now answered by Martha; thereby configuration between the two women is brought about. The reader interprets one woman in the light of the other and considers them together. Thus also a plot development is achieved. Martha gives the answer that the Samaritan woman might be able to give later on.

By Martha's confession configuration is also established with her sister Mary, whose implicit confession of the suffering Messiah is referred to in 11:2, where she is identified as the one who anointed the Lord. Therefore, our reader learns that *both* sisters have confessed Jesus as the Messiah, though in a different way: by verbal expression and by active demonstration. After her confession Martha informs her sister about Jesus's arrival and tells her that he is calling for her (v. 28). This piece of information causes an ambivalent reaction in the reader. On the one hand, it confirms for her that until now Mary did not know of Jesus's arrival and conse-

---

37. See Brown, "Roles of Women," 693.
38. See Iser, "Reading Process," 54: "Whatever we have read sinks into our memory and is foreshortened. It may later be evoked again and set against a different background with the result that the reader is enabled to develop hitherto unforeseeable connections.... The new background brings to light new aspects of what we have committed to memory; conversely these, in turn, shed their light on the new background."

quently she cannot be blamed that she did not accompany Martha when she went to meet Jesus (v. 29). On the other hand, however, the reader is confused because nowhere previously has the narrator mentioned that Jesus actually sent for Mary; he only has Martha say so. This calls forth the reader's imagination to solve the problem of ambivalence in the text. The reader might conclude that Martha is a liar and speculate about her motivation. But it is equally likely that there is another gap in the story: the narrator does not mention Jesus's calling for Mary, just as he also does not mention when Lazarus died and how Jesus made his way to Bethany. Whether the reader decides for one or the other alternative, it will have an impact on her evaluation of Martha's character. She is either a liar, even if her motivation is positive, or a mediator between Jesus and her sister. Martha refers to Jesus as "the teacher" (v. 28). Thereby the narrator informs the reader implicitly that he considers these women to be Jesus's disciples.[39]

Mary is depicted as even more spontaneous than her sister. She rises immediately and goes to Jesus, who is still in the place, outside the village, where Martha met him (vv. 29–30). It seems to be significant that both women leave their house, the traditional domain of a woman. Mary's movement is described from the point of view of other characters in the story, that is, the Jews who were with her in the house, consoling her (v. 31). When these men and women see her rise quickly,[40] they suppose that she is going to the tomb to weep there (v. 31). The reader, sharing the narrator's omniscient point of view, knows where Mary is really going. In this case, too, the discrepancy between what characters in the story know and what the reader knows adds to the dynamism and effect of the text, which is partly ironical. But the *Jews' supposition* has also an impact on the characterization of Mary. It informs the reader that it would be very likely that she goes to the tomb to weep there. Thus she is characterized as very emotional. When Martha rises, nobody thinks that she is going to weep at the tomb. Therefore, this short note about the Jews' supposition adds to the characterization of both, Mary and Martha, directly and indirectly.

When Mary encounters Jesus, she falls at his feet, saying, "Lord, if you had been here, my brother would not have died" (11:32). This echoes the

---

39. See Culpepper, *Anatomy of the Fourth Gospel*, 140–41. But he gives no reason *why* he considers them to be disciples. According to Brown, Martha, Mary, and Mary Magdalene are "intimate disciples of Jesus" ("Roles of Women," 694).

40. See Wuellner, who believes that "at least half of which [the funeral party] must have been women" ("Lazarus Story," 119).

reproachful comment Martha made when she met Jesus. Mary's remark is as ambivalent as Martha's was, because it implies Mary's belief in Jesus's power over life and death, and falling at Jesus's feet denotes her devotion. In the next sentence the narrator informs the reader, from Jesus's point of view ("he saw"), that Mary is weeping indeed, and so are the Jews who have come with her (v. 30). The scene becomes very emotional now; Jesus is also deeply moved and starts weeping (vv. 33–36).[41]

He asks where they have laid Lazarus. The Jews' (and Mary's?) answer, "Lord, come and see" (v. 34), recalls a scene from the gospel's beginning. When the first (going-to-be) male disciples, Andrew and another disciple of John the Baptist, meet Jesus and ask him where he is staying, Jesus also answers, "Come and see" (1:39). These two disciples and later on another disciple, Nathanael, address Jesus as "Rabbi," that is, "teacher" (1:38, 49). Also Martha refers to Jesus as "the teacher" when she informs Mary of his arrival (v. 28), and so do the disciples in 11:8. By becoming aware of this parallelism between 1:35–51 and 11:28–34, and thus of the implicit configuration between Martha and Mary, on the one hand, and the first male disciples, on the other hand, the reader may draw the conclusion that the present scene is also about discipleship.

Jesus's emotional reaction convinces the Jews of Jesus's love for Lazarus (11:36). The issue of their love relationship is reinforced (see vv. 3, 5) and so is the reader's expectation as to how Jesus will prove his love. The reproachful remark of some of the Jews, "Could not he who opened the eyes of the blind man have kept this man from dying?" (v. 37), affects the reader, reactivating her previously experienced doubt about Jesus's love for Lazarus.

Only now Jesus indeed comes to the tomb. The narrator comments that it is a cave, and a stone lays on it (v. 38). This description is an important piece of information for the reader, and it creates dramatic tension. Jesus gives orders that the stone be taken away (v. 39). Martha's down-to-earth remark that there is already an odor, for Lazarus has been dead for four days, recollects and fulfills the anticipation of verse 17. Jesus reminds Martha that he said to her, "Did I not tell you that if you would believe you

---

41. See Culpepper, who points out that there are "more references to Jesus' emotions in John 11 than in any other chapter, and at this point they become particularly intense" (*Anatomy of the Fourth Gospel*, 110). Otherwise, Jesus is characterized as distant and aloof in John's Gospel and "demonstrably less emotional than in the synoptic gospels" (109–11).

would see the glory of God?" (v. 40). "No, he did not," the reader might answer, or at least the narrator never mentioned it. Only the reader, sharing the narrator's omniscient point of view, knows that "Lazarus' illness is not unto death; it is for the glory of God, so that the glory of the Son of God may be glorified by means of it" (v. 4). But knowing that Martha believes and that she confessed Jesus as the Messiah (v. 27), the reader can infer that she will see the glory of God. While Jesus's order to remove the stone is carried out (by whom, the narrator does not reveal), Jesus is depicted as praying to his Father (v. 41). The climax of the whole story is Jesus's calling Lazarus out of the tomb; and he comes out, his hands and feet bound with bandages and his face wrapped with a cloth (vv. 43-44). Jesus gives orders to unbind him and let him go (v. 44). But who should do so and who actually carries out this order—whether the sisters or some of the Jews—is again not mentioned, nor is anything said about the sisters' reactions. Thus the story has, to some extent, an *open end*.[42]

What *is* told, however, is the Jews' reaction, which is belief in Jesus, on the one hand, and reporting to the Pharisees, on the other hand (11:45, 46). Surprisingly, the Jews are described as those who had come to Mary; unlike in verse 19, Martha is not mentioned here. Thus the reader becomes aware that Mary and Martha played different roles in the story. Mary was portrayed as the main character (besides Jesus) in the very beginning (see vv. 1-2), in her encounter with Jesus, of course (vv. 31-32), and again at the end of the story (v. 45), where the reader gains the impression that the Jews had come mainly to assist Mary, not so much Martha. Mary is characterized as more emotional and vulnerable than Martha, who appears

---

42. Wuellner has pointed to this open end and calls it "a startling 'gap' which the reader is to fill, or rather *not* to fill.... The unfinished task of untying Lazarus becomes the reader's task of untying the text.... This challenge to readers to untie this text is not only unfinished; due to the rhetoric of the narration of faith, it is an unfinishable task" ("Lazarus Story," 119-20). Wuellner refers to Robert Young, ed., *Untying the Text: A Post-structuralist Reader* (London: Routledge & Kegan Paul, 1981). Meanwhile, a narrative-critical reading of the Lazarus story (including characterization) has been presented by Mark Stibbe, who—not knowing of my more or less simultaneous presentation of a conference paper—complained about the neglect of this story in literary analysis. See Stibbe, "A Tomb with a View: John 11.1-44 in Narrative-Critical Perspective," *NTS* 40 (1994): 38-54. But see Wuellner, "Lazarus Story"; Wuellner, "Rhetorical Criticism and Its Theory in Cultural-Critical Perspective: The Narrative Rhetoric of John 11," in *Text and Interpretation: New Approaches in the Criticism of the New Testament*, ed. Peter J. Martin and J. Hartin Petzer, NTTS 15 (Leiden: Brill, 1991), 171-85.

to be more an intellectual and thinking type of person. She was the main character (besides Jesus) in all the other parts of the story (see vv. 5, 20–28, 39).

By shifting the focus from one sister to the other, first making one the main character of the story and then the other, the narrator influences the reader to evaluate them *equally*. Both are important, their different attitudes and ways of reacting are legitimate, and both have a close relationship to Jesus. However different the two sisters are, Jesus is shown as reacting to each of them in accordance with their respective personality. He discusses intellectual-theological issues with Martha, and he weeps empathetically with Mary.

Reading John 12:1–8

Meanwhile, the reader has learned of the council's decision to put Jesus to death (11:53) because of the many signs he has done (v. 47), the last of which is Lazarus's resurrection. And she also learns of the chief priests' and Pharisees' orders that if anyone knows where Jesus is, he should let them know, so that they might arrest him (v. 57).

In the initial setting of the new episode the reader learns that six days before the Passover Jesus comes to Bethany, where Lazarus is, whom Jesus raised from the dead (12:1). By referring to the story of Lazarus's resurrection, the narrator anticipates Jesus's own death. The reader wonders how Mary, Martha, and Lazarus will react, whether they will obey the chief priests' and Pharisees' orders. But knowing of the deep love relationship between Jesus and the sisters and their brother, the reader will not expect them to be obedient. This is proved as correct when she learns that they prepare a meal for Jesus. Martha serves, while Lazarus is one of those at table with Jesus (v. 2). Thereby a very significant negative configuration is established between the chief priests and the Pharisees, on the one hand (see 11:57), and the Bethany family, on the other hand. Hostility and love form a sharp contrast.

This mention of a meal may remind the reader of another story she knows already, Luke's story of Martha and Mary (Luke 10:38–42),[43] and interfigurality is established. In Luke, Martha takes the initiative; she

---

43. Of course, the reader could have recollected this story already in John 11:1–2 (the consecutive reading would have been different then), but I consider it more likely that she does so only now due to the text signal "meal."

receives Jesus into "her house" (v. 38); Mary is defined as her sister (v. 38). While Mary is sitting at Jesus's feet and listening to his teaching (v. 39), Martha is serving (v. 40). Martha complains that she has to do the serving alone and asks Jesus to tell Mary to help her (v. 40), but Jesus answers her that Mary has chosen the good portion, which shall not be taken from her (v. 42). It is a very different portrait of both sisters that is presented to the reader now in John's story. The impression that both sisters are equal, which was gained already by the Lazarus story, is confirmed here. *Both* sisters prepare the meal for Jesus, and while Martha serves, Mary is going to anoint Jesus's feet with precious ointment of pure nard (John 12:3). Thus *both* women serve Jesus as their guest.

Mary is shown as anointing Jesus's feet and then wiping them with her hair (v. 3). This act seems to be illogical, because one does not anoint somebody with such expensive ointment and then wipe it away. This peculiarity, however, may be a signal for the reader to establish intertextuality with Luke's story of the anointing of Jesus's feet by the sinful woman (7:36–50). This text was already evoked previously, when Mary was identified as the one who had wiped Jesus's feet with her hair (11:2). There, the sinful woman's great love becomes also a character trait of Mary. The present narrative denotes that Mary, unlike the woman in Luke, is *not* a sinner. This becomes obvious by the gap in the text. As Mary is no sinner, she has no reason to weep, and there is no need, therefore, to wipe the tears away before anointing Jesus's feet. (This is the sequence of action in Luke.) The interfigurality established between Mary of Bethany and the sinful woman is thus marked by both identification and redefinition.

In contrast to Mary's act of service and reverence, Judas Iscariot, one of Jesus's disciples, is introduced as the one "who was to betray him" (12:4). This characterization, which is achieved by a prolepsis from the narrator's retrospective point of view,[44] portrays Judas in negative configuration with Lazarus, Mary, and Martha, who do *not* betray Jesus. However, only the reader receives this information about Judas's forthcoming betrayal; the other characters in the story do not know. They experience Judas as one of the disciples, not as the betrayer. Judas objects to Mary's "waste": "Why was this ointment not sold for three hundred denarii and given to

---

44. See Culpepper, *Anatomy of the Fourth Gospel*, 27–32 (on the retrospective point of view). According to Culpepper, the mention of Judas's betrayal belongs to the "internal prolepses," which "have an important role in building dramatic intensity" (63).

the poor?" (v. 5). This reproachful remark informs the reader about the value of the ointment and thus how dear Jesus is to Mary. Again only the reader, not the characters in the story, is granted insight into Judas's thinking and motivation: "This he said, not that he cared for the poor but because he was a thief, and as he had the money box to take what was put into it" (v. 6). Mary and Judas are put in sharp contrast, they are portrayed as *type and antitype*. The reader's evaluation of them is thereby influenced. Against the dark foil of Judas, Mary's character shines even more brightly. This impression is confirmed by Jesus's reaction, siding with Mary and defending her against her accuser: "Let her alone, let her keep it for the day of my burial. The poor you always have with you, but you do not always have me" (vv. 7–8). Interfigurality is again established between Mary of Bethany and the woman who anoints Jesus in the stories of Mark and Matthew. Through Jesus's words, his imminent death comes into full view for the first time, though the reader has been prepared for it already. The reference to the day of *Jesus's burial* is another device of anticipation or internal prolepsis.[45]

Reading John 20:1–18

The narrative about Mary Magdalene on Easter morning reminds the reader of her first encounter with this woman in the scene of Jesus's crucifixion. There, Mary Magdalene is mentioned together with Jesus's mother, her sister, and Mary the wife of Clopas, as standing by the cross (John 19:25). Mary Magdalene is only introduced, without any further information. Obviously, the reader knows already then who this woman is.[46] From

---

45. See Culpepper, *Anatomy of the Fourth Gospel*, 63. When later on the reader learns of Jesus's burial (see 19:38–42), she will remember this scene in Bethany. And she will link *Nicodemus*—and also *Joseph of Arimathea*—to Mary. Both spend an unusual amount of ointment or spices on Jesus: Mary spends one pound of nard oil worth three hundred denarii, the men spend about a hundred pounds' weight of myrrh and aloe (v. 39). But, unlike the scene in Bethany, none accuses the men because of their "waste." Joseph of Arimathea is referred to as "a disciple of Jesus, but secretly, for fear of the Jews" (v. 38), whereas Mary, Martha, and Lazarus do not conceal their relationship to Jesus. They really belong to "his own," i.e., his disciples, as our reader will have learned by the time she reaches ch. 19, because Jesus loves "his own" to the end (see 13:1), and he loves Mary and Martha and Lazarus (see 11:5).

46. But see Culpepper, *Anatomy of the Fourth Gospel*, 216: "It would be precarious to infer any prior knowledge of the women at the cross on the basis of the references

her knowledge of the Synoptic Gospels, and most likely also from oral tradition alive in her community, the reader knows that Mary Magdalene was the most eminent of Jesus's female disciples, who followed him from Galilee to Jerusalem (see Mark 15:40–41 parr.). Interfigurality between the character of Mary Magdalene in John and in the Synoptic tradition is also an issue here.

Mary Magdalene comes to the tomb on the first day of the week, early in the morning, while it is still dark (John 20:1). Mary's knowledge concerning the location of the tomb marks a gap in the story, because she was not present at the burial (see 19:38–42). The reader recalls other texts that mention Mary Magdalene and "the other Mary" witnessing the burial scene (see Mark 15:47; Matt 27:61; see also Luke 23:55), and thereby she can fill in the gap. But the reason *why* Mary comes to the tomb is not mentioned either; the reader can only imagine. Mary sees that the stone has been taken away (John 20:1). This information puzzles the reader, because in the burial scene the tomb is not described; it is only referred to as a new tomb in a garden near the place where Jesus was crucified (see 19:41–42). However, the tomb stone features in the Easter morning stories of the Synoptic Gospels (see Mark 16:3; Matt 28:2; Luke 23:2). Thus interfigurality is alive also in this case. But even more important is the configuration between Mary Magdalene and Mary of Bethany, and the parallelism between the Easter morning story and the Lazarus story. Lazarus's tomb is described as a cave, and a stone lays on it (11:38). Jesus gives orders to take the stone away (v. 39), and so they do (v. 41). Now, in this scene, Mary Magdalene sees that the stone of Jesus's tomb has been taken away *already* (20:1). By linking this story to the Lazarus story, the reader may also find out the reason for Mary Magdalene's coming to the tomb. It is most likely that she wants to weep there, just as the Jews supposed Mary of Bethany to do (see 11:31). Mary Magdalene, instead of looking properly, runs to Simon Peter and the other disciple, the one whom Jesus loved, and tells them: "They have taken the Lord out of the tomb, and we do not know where they have laid him" (20:2). It is also surprising that she informs the disciples that "we do not know," because she was the only one, so the narrator says, who went to the tomb. The "we" is, once again, a text signal that evokes interfigurality. It refers to the Easter morning stories in the Synop-

---

to 'Mary the wife of Clopas' and 'Mary Magdalene' (19:25), but the reader may have heard their names before."

tic Gospels, where two or more women are mentioned. The present text thus indicates that Mary Magdalene is the most important among them, and so only *her* story is told.

The narrator's focus then shifts to the race of Simon Peter and the disciple whom Jesus loved (see v. 3). While the other disciple is the first to arrive at the tomb (v. 4), Peter is the first to enter it (v. 6); but the other disciple is the first to believe (v. 8), whereas Peter does not come to believe. The narrator mentions the disciples' return to their home (v. 10), but he does *not* tell how *Mary Magdalene* got back to the tomb (this is another gap in the story); she simply is there again in verse 11, and stands *weeping* outside the tomb. The reader has supposed already from remembering the Lazarus story that Mary has come to weep at the tomb. Now she is assured of it.

Only now Mary looks into the tomb (v. 11) and sees "two angels in white, sitting where the body of Jesus has lain, one at the head and one at the feet" (v. 12). The reader is surprised about Mary's knowledge of Jesus's placement, because she was not present at the burial. The mention of Jesus's body, head and feet, however, denotes another signal of interfigurality. Evoked are the *anointing stories* of the Synoptic Gospels: in Mark's and Matthew's stories (Mark 14:3–9; Matt 26:6–13) the woman anoints Jesus's head as a substitute for his whole body; in Luke's story (7:36–50) the woman anoints Jesus's feet, and so does Mary of Bethany. Therefore, in fact, the reader is *not* informed about Mary Magdalene's knowledge of the position of Jesus's body in the tomb, but she is invited to link Mary Magdalene to the women who anointed Jesus.

The angels' question, "Why are you weeping?" (John 20:13), seems inadequate as it is addressed to a person who has lost a loved one. However, this question prepares the reader for learning of Mary's reason for weeping: now it is the fact that Jesus's body has been taken away, not his death as such. Mary's turning around marks also the turning point in the story: she *meets Jesus* but does not know that it is he (v. 14). Mary's point of view thus differs from that of the reader (and of the narrator). *She* knows what Mary does not know. As previously in John's Gospel, an ironical dimension is thus added to the story. Jesus also asks her about her reason for weeping and adds, "Whom do you seek?" (v. 15). This question seems out of place. But by linking this text to a previous text in the gospel, a new and meaningful dimension emerges. When the (going-to-be) first male disciples followed Jesus, he also turned round and asked them, "What do you seek?" (1:37–38). Now the question refers to Jesus as a person ("whom") and not to what he represents or presents ("what"). Mary Magdalene is linked to the male (going-to-be) disciples, thereby her discipleship is stated implicitly. However, she still does not recognize Jesus, but supposes him to be the gardener (20:15). This remark adds to the ironical dimension, which is further intensified by Mary's request to tell her where he has laid Jesus's body (v. 15). This reminds the reader of Jesus's asking for Lazarus's tomb, "Where have you laid him?" (11:34). The narrator thereby influences the reader's evaluation of Mary's question, which is justified and legitimate, as Jesus's question was.[47] When Jesus addresses Mary by her name, she recognizes him immediately, addressing him as "Rabbouni" (20:16). Thus her discipleship is confirmed. The fact that she recognizes Jesus when he calls her by her name reminds the reader of Jesus's speech in chapter 10. Those who belong to him are those who hear his voice and follow him (see 10:4).[48] Consequently, Mary also belongs among those who are "his own"—she is a disciple.[49] Surprisingly, just after this intimate encounter, Jesus rejects Mary's closeness[50] and her holding on to him, because he has not yet ascended to the Father (20:17).[51] Instead, she is commissioned to bring Jesus's message to the "brethren" (v. 17), and so she does (v. 18). Mary Magdalene is now characterized as a missionary, as an apostle. The reader is reminded of another female missionary, the Samaritan woman.[52] Because of her testimony many inhabitants of Sychar came to believe (see

---

47. In sharp contrast, Culpepper considers Mary's question a further proof of her unenlightenment on this Easter morning (*Anatomy of the Fourth Gospel*, 144).

48. Culpepper has not noticed this significant connection between ch. 10 and ch. 20, when he comments: "Witnessing each of the key moments of the passion story gives her no advantage or insight.... When she recognizes Jesus it is not through seeing the risen Lord, but through hearing his words.... Neither the empty tomb nor the vision of Jesus lifted the veil for Mary Magdalene, only the words of Jesus" (*Anatomy of the Fourth Gospel*, 144). But see Brown, "Roles of Women," 694.

49. Similarly Brown, "Roles of Women," 694–95.

50. Culpepper remarks on this scene: "In fact, although touching and physical contact with Jesus are important in the synoptic gospels, there is none of this in John. The only time the word 'to touch' ... is used in 20.17—'Don't touch me!'" (*Anatomy of the Fourth Gospel*, 11).

51. Culpepper considers this verse as the locus classicus of the difficulty in defining the prolepses; it belongs to the "mixed prolepses," whose "function is to tie the experience of the intended readers ... to the final events in the ministry of Jesus"; they "link Jesus to the church" (*Anatomy of the Fourth Gospel*, 63–64).

52. Brown mentions the Samaritan woman's missionary function and Mary Magdalene's "quasi-apostolic role" (see "Roles of Women," 691–92). See also Culpepper,

4:39). So, the other disciples, too, should come to believe because of Mary's testimony, "I have seen the Lord" (20:18). Configuration between the two women is established.

Reconsidering the whole passage the reader has just read, she becomes fully aware of the many parallels between Mary Magdalene's encounter with Jesus and Mary of Bethany's encounter with him. Both happened when facing death. Mary of Bethany meets Jesus after Lazarus's death, Mary Magdalene meets Jesus after his own death. When Mary of Bethany got up quickly, after learning of Jesus's arrival, the Jews supposed that she was going to the tomb to weep there, and she was weeping when she met Jesus (11:31). And so was Mary Magdalene (20:15; see v. 13). When the funeral party came to the tomb, Jesus gave orders to take away the stone, and so they did (11:38–39, 41). The sequence in Mary Magdalene's story is just the other way around. The setting is after Jesus's death. When Mary Magdalene comes to the tomb, the stone is taken away already, and she meets Jesus afterwards. The encounters of both women with Jesus are very close and emotional. Both seem to be a similar type of person, however individual and different they are otherwise. Both are, so our reader has learned, Jesus's disciples and belong to "his own": Mary of Bethany because Jesus loves her as he loves "his own" (see 11:5; 13:1), and Mary Magdalene because, by recognizing Jesus's voice, she belongs to his flock of sheep who hear his voice (see 10:4). And in both cases Jesus is called "teacher" (see 11:28; 20:16). By realizing this configuration, new light is shed on the characterization of both women; one is portrayed in the light of the other. When recollecting the Easter morning story after finishing the reading process, the reader becomes aware of the configuration not only between Mary of Magdala and Mary of Bethany but also between Mary Magdalene and the male characters in the story, Simon Peter and the Beloved Disciple. Surprisingly, all three of them are first, though in different ways. The Beloved Disciple arrives at the tomb first and sees the linen cloths first (20:4), but Peter is the first to enter the tomb, also seeing the linen cloths and the napkin (vv. 6–7). The Beloved Disciple is the first to believe (v. 8), while Peter does not come to believe. But Mary Magdalene is the first to see the risen Jesus and also the first to be commissioned by him.

Anatomy of the Fourth Gospel, 137: She "becomes a missionary ... is given an apostolic role" and "is a model of the female disciple."

Concluding Reflections

No conclusions can be drawn and no summary presented. Open-ended as the Gospel of John (see 21:25) are its characterizations. Characterization has turned out to be an *unfinished task* on the author's (and narrator's) side, and it is an *unfinishable task* on the reader's side. The texts relevant for our investigation into female characters in John provided the broad outlines, but the actual picture was painted when and how the reader covered the dry bones with flesh and skin and breathed her spirit into them so that they became alive (see Ezek 37:5, 10). Characterization thus was—and will always be—a very *personal and individual issue*.[53] Without the reader's activity, the texts and the characters in them would have remained only dead objects. By the reader's creativity, however, life was put back not only into the Lazarus story,[54] but also into the Mary-and-Martha story and into the Mary Magdalene story.

But the reader herself also gained life and nourishing bread[55] during and through her encounter with these female characters in the story. Her self-esteem and sense of identity were strengthened by learning about the important roles of women in Jesus's life. As a member of the Christian community who keeps Jesus's legacy alive, she could infer from these stories the importance of women in her present community, where men and women are equal.[56]

In spite of its *male author* and its *male narrator* the Gospel of John shows an outstanding interest in female characters[57] and remarkable sensitivity concerning their characterization. Therefore, the imagined actual reader could follow, more or less, the trace provided for the intended or

---

53. See Ilona N. Rashkow, "In Our Image We Create Him, Male and Female We Create Them: The E/Affect of Biblical Characterization," *Semeia* 63 (1993): 105–13, esp. 107–9, 112.

54. See the title of Wuellner's article ("Lazarus Story").

55. See Schüssler Fiorenza, *Bread Not Stone*.

56. Brown notes that John "reports that tradition through the optic of his own times, so that he tells something about the role of women in his own community," in which "women and men are already on an equal level" ("Roles of Women," 698 n. 4, 699).

57. See Seim, "Roles of Women," 57: "The roles of women genuinely coincide[s] with an explicit interest of the Gospel of John itself, very visible on its textual surface."

implied reader[58] and fill it with her own experience and creativity. Resisting reading or reading against the grain is not necessitated by these texts.[59]

Configuration and interfigurality turned out to be essential for the characterization of female characters. Although they had no ongoing role but entered on the stage and left again after featuring within one scene or two, at the most, they became important characters through their development in relation to one another and to other characters. The interfigural view shed light on the transformation and new interpretations of characters already known from the Synoptic tradition, and the reader was vacillating between the hitherto known and the new information.[60] Configuration and interfigurality as vital aspects of literary characterization reflect and do justice to the fact that no woman and no man is an island or secluded entity but is embedded into a network of relationships—to other persons, to their own world, and to worlds and texts other than their own. Mary Magdalene as the most important of Jesus's female disciples is, in John's Gospel, closely and specifically related to Mary of Bethany (which has been the focus of this investigation), but she is also related to Martha, the Samaritan woman, and to Jesus's mother (which was outside the scope of this analysis).

Characterization can, therefore, only be approached adequately if *all* aspects of a text are taken into account and if each individual character is

---

58. See Wolfgang Iser, *Der implizite Leser*, UTB 163 (Munich: Fink, 1972); Hannelore Link, *Rezeptionsforschung: Eine Einführung in Methoden und Probleme*, UTB 215, R 80 (Stuttgart: Kohlhammer, 1980), 41–43. For the problems connected with this concept, see Wilhelm Wuellner, "Is There an Encoded Reader Fallacy?," *Semeia* 48 (1989): 41–54, esp. 43.

59. Bach names the "crucial ambiguity for the feminist reader," which "revolves around the narrator's providing one version of how female characters behave within the situations in which they have been placed, and another *imagined* version that might be provided by the female figure—if one could reconstruct her story" ("Signs of the Flesh," 69). See Rashkow, "In Our Image," 109: "In Bach's reading, there is an adversarial relationship between narrator and narratee unless the reader and the storyteller share either theological, gender, or political codes." According to van Tilborg, the patriarchal *oikos*-mentality is absent from the Johannine stories of women (*Imaginative Love*, 170–71).

60. *Interfigurality* has to be distinguished clearly from *harmonization* of the gospels. While the latter composes a portrait of a character by combining information from different sources and valuing them equally, interfigurality denotes the transformation and redefinition of an earlier tradition, the outcome of this process has priority over other traditions.

considered within the context and the background against which he or she is portrayed. The open view of character corresponds with the open-ended task of characterization, which is an *ongoing process*. The reader, female or male, is invited to respond to *my* response to the characterizations of Mary of Bethany and Mary of Magdala in John in her or his own individual and creative way.

Stabat Mater? Rebirth at the Foot of the Cross

There she stood
at the foot
of the cross

grounded	*surprisingly—*	*for 84 years*
yet pierced	*re-born*	*witnessing*
was her heart	*of the Spirit*	*trusting*
like her son's	*who comes*	*embracing—*
hands and feet	*and goes*	
fulfilled	*and you do not*	
the prophecy	*know how*	
of the old man	*and where*	*There she was*
encountering	*no re-turn*	*lying*
her newborn	*into the womb*	*in her bed*
before he returned	*they returned*	*journeying*
home—	*home—*	*home—*
	mother and son	
		in the night

+++

I wrote the first draft of this paper in spring 2002 and presented it to the Faculty Colloquium of the Jesuit School of Theology at Berkeley on April 24. On July 20, 2002, I presented the paper in the Johannine Literature section (chaired by Fernando F. Segovia) at the Society of Biblical Literature International Meeting in Berlin. I thank colleagues and friends from both sides of the Atlantic and Pacific for their encouraging and stimulating responses. Special thanks to Mayer I. Gruber, Orna Teitelbaum, and Erica Martin for reading and commenting on various drafts of this paper.

Originally published as Ingrid Rosa Kitzberger, "Stabat Mater? Re-birth at the Foot of the Cross," *BibInt* 11 (2003): 468–87.

Εἱστήκεισαν δὲ παρὰ τῷ σταυρῷ τοῦ Ἰησοῦ ἡ μήτηρ αὐτοῦ καὶ ἡ ἀδελφὴ τῆς μητρὸς αὐτοῦ, Μαρία ἡ τοῦ Κλωπᾶ καὶ Μαρία ἡ Μαγδαληνή
Ἰησοῦς οὖν ἰδὼν τὴν μητέρα καὶ τὸν μαθητὴν παρεστῶτα ὃν ἠγάπα, λέγει τῇ μητρί, Γύναι, ἴδε ὁ υἱός σου. εἶτα λέγει τῷ μαθητῇ ᾽Ιδε ἡ μήτηρ σου. καὶ ἀπ᾽ ἐκείνης τῆς ὥρας ἔλαβεν ὁ μαθητὴς αὐτὴν εἰς τὰ ἴδια. (John 19:25–27)

Stabat Mater

At the foot of the cross they stood with her—composers, painters, sculptors, portraying her in tunes, colors, forms, making her eternal, transcending death. The faithful witness to the one dying, her beloved son. Mother and son united in suffering. Mater Dolorosa.

"Your search string resulted in too many hits," I am informed, searching the Internet for the musical representations of the Stabat Mater. My hit is Franz Schubert's version, of course, my fellow Austrian's gifted intonation, soul searching and heart rending, which he composed at the age of only nineteen.

Too many hits. Often with a sword piercing her whole body, Jesus's mother has journeyed through the centuries, stopping over in churches and art galleries, and in private devotional pictures, stuck into prayer books. [I have a few of them floating around, enriching my spiritual life, comforting especially in times of pain and crisis.[2]]

Stabat Mater. Steadfast, grounded, belonging, taken for granted. She has always been there, hasn't she? What would Jesus's crucifixion be without her? Take the mother away, and Jesus's agony on the cross turns into utmost loneliness. "My God, my God, why have you forsaken me?" With his mother at his side, or at his feet, he might make it through, to the other side of life. No motherless child; only the father is missing.

∞

Standing at the foot of the cross she had lived her life. Hers was a difficult life, from early on, with much suffering in it. Yet her faith would never

---

2. My most recent crisis resulted from breaking my right foot on August 29, 2001, soon after I had arrived on Berkeley's Holy Hill. During the agonizing weeks and months that followed, two pictures in my prayer book featuring the crucifixion with Jesus's mother at the foot of the cross (together with Mary Magdalene and the Beloved Disciple) were a source of consolation, hope, and courage to "stand upright," like Jesus's mother, even though I was physically unable to do so.

waver or weaken; steadfast she stood, identifying with Jesus's mother at the foot of the cross, joining in her suffering and compassion. Compassion for others, who were not her own sons and daughters, shaped her life, transforming death into life, birthing new relationships beyond biological bonds. "These are my brothers, and my sisters, and my mother."

Shortly before her eighty-fourth birthday she finally journeyed home, after having fallen into a coma on the feast of Saint Rosa of Lima, her patron saint, and also my mother's and mine. It was during the night of September 14/15, 1998, in the borderlands between the feasts of the Triumph of the Cross and Our Lady of Sorrows,[1] early in the morning, when it was still dark. I was working on a paper about Lazarus in John 11 at that time. When she was laid into the tomb after five days, there was no one to call her out again. I would never have let her go, though, with or without the unbinding. After two months, in November, I went to Disney World in Orlando with Lazarus[2] and my beloved friend Rosa, both happily resurrected at the foot of the dolphins,[3] swimming in living waters. "Out of the believer's heart shall flow rivers of living waters."

Surprise Encounters: Jesus's Mother in John and the Synoptics

The Mother's Journey in John, and My Personal Journey with Her

There she stood. In John's portrait of Jesus's crucifixion, his mother belongs in the picture. Together with her sister, with Mary the wife of Clopas, Mary Magdalene,[4] and the Beloved Disciple, she witnesses the death of her son.

---

1. I thank Carmen de la Vega (JSTB) for providing the English names of the feasts. In German, they are Kreuzeserhöhung (Elevation of the Cross) and Sieben Schmerzen Mariä (Mary's Seven Sorrows).

2. I presented the paper "Untying Lazarus—a Sisters' Task? Revisioning Gender and Characterization in John 11" at the Annual Meeting of the Society of Biblical Literature in Orlando, Johannine Literature section, on November 22, 1998. The revised version is first published in this volume.

3. The Dolphin is one of the major hotels in Disney World and served as the headquarters for the conference. On top of the building two creatures are portrayed swimming. However, their resemblance to actual dolphins may legitimately be questioned.

4. It has been debated whether three or four women are mentioned at the cross, that is, whether the sister of Jesus's mother (and thus Jesus's aunt) is identical with Mary the wife of Clopas. There are two main reasons to not identify them: first, it is rather unlikely (though not impossible) that two sisters of the same family were named Mary,

Her presence appears to be self-evident to the reader of the gospel who has finally arrived at chapter 19, after a long journey[5] with Jesus, through Galilee, Samaria, and up to Jerusalem, back and forth. We have watched Jesus encountering many diverse characters, but he never stopped over for too long. Thus, he demonstrated the very nature of the Logos-become-flesh, his tenting, not housing (1:14), as he remained an "alien non-resident individual"[6] throughout his earthly career.

As he is to return to his Father and is lifted up on the cross, he draws all to him (12:32–33), including his own mother. He has not met her since the Cana wedding, which seems ages ago, when his hour had not yet come (2:4). Now that his hour has come,[7] his mother returns. Both scenes are closely related to each other, and the reader is invited to recall the Cana episode when she or he reads the scene on Golgotha.

Jesus's mother at the foot of the cross comes as a surprise to any reader of the gospel, whether a first reader in the Johannine community or a present reader. "How can this be?" many a reader might have asked, throughout the centuries. So has this real flesh-and-blood reader in front of this text,

---

and second, the four women make for a good contrast to the four soldiers (19:23). For the wide-ranging speculations on the identity of the women (including even a solution of two), see Raymond E. Brown, *The Gospel according to John: XIII–XXI*, AB 29a (New York: Doubleday, 1970), 904–6; Brown, *The Death of the Messiah: From Gethsemane to the Grave*, ABRL (New York: Doubleday, 1994), 2:1013–15.

5. See Fernando F. Segovia, "The Journey(s) of the Word of God: A Reading of the Plot of the Fourth Gospel," *Semeia* 53 (1991), 113–32. For the reader-response approach as applied in this paper, see Edgar V. McKnight, *Post-modern Use of the Bible: The Emergence of Reader-Oriented Criticism*, 2nd ed. (Nashville: Abingdon, 1990); McKnight, *The Bible and the Reader: An Introduction to Literary Criticism* (Philadelphia: Fortress, 1985); Jane P. Tompkins, ed., *Reader-Response Criticism: From Formalism to Post-structuralism* (Baltimore: Johns Hopkins University Press, 1980); Robert M. Fowler, *Let the Reader Understand: Reader-Response Criticism and the Gospel of Mark* (Minneapolis: Fortress, 1991).

6. Leticia A. Guardiola-Sáenz, "Border Crossing and Its Redemptive Power in John 7:53–8:11: A Cultural Reading of Jesus and the *Accused*," in *Transformative Encounters: Jesus and Women Re-viewed*, ed. Ingrid Rosa Kitzberger, BibInt 43 (Leiden: Brill, 2000), 282–83. See also Mark Stibbe, "The Elusive Christ: A New Reading of the Fourth Gospel," *JSNT* 44 (1991): 20–38.

7. According to Brown, "the hour" refers to the "passion, crucifixion, resurrection, and ascension," which marks also his glorification (*John*, 241). With the feast of Passover coming close (11:55; 12:1), Jesus's hour comes, too (12:23; 13:1).

who has been puzzled by the mother's presence in John's account of the crucifixion and has returned to it time and again.

Since my friend Rosa's death during the night between the feasts pertaining to Jesus's cross and his mother's witnessing with sorrows, my self-text has engaged in autobiographical intertextual dialogue with John's text.[8] Consequently, new dimensions have been added to both texts, and it resulted in an increased urgency to address the riddle of Jesus's mother standing at the foot of the cross. September 14/15, 1998, has definitely changed my rereading of John. My surprise about Jesus's mother at the cross is forever linked to my surprise about the way a biblical text can transform a believer's life and death, and thus how the horizons of the world of the text and of the world of the reader in front of the text can merge.

"After this he went down to Capernaum with his mother, his brothers, and his disciples; and they remained there a few days" (2:12). Thus ends the narrative of the wedding at Cana (2:1–12). As John's story of Jesus unfolds, the disciples journey on with him because they have come to believe in him (2:11), while his brothers, before too long, quit because they do not believe in him (7:5). After staying in Capernaum for a few days (2:12), Jesus is, all of a sudden, present in Jerusalem, where he cleanses the temple (2:13–17). What a profound change of career, compared to the pleasure of transforming water into wine, however reluctantly Jesus carried it out, following his mother's will in the end. The narrative gap[9] with regard to Jesus's itinerary is remarkable and places a heavy task on the reader's imagination as to how to fill this gap. But even more pronounced is the narrative gap with regard to his mother, because she disappears completely after the brief interlude in Capernaum. Where did she go to

---

8. For the encounter between the biblical text and the self as text, see Ingrid Rosa Kitzberger, ed., *The Personal Voice in Biblical Interpretation* (London: Routledge, 1999); Kitzberger, *Autobiographical Biblical Criticism: Between Text and Self* (Leiden: Deo, 2002); Jeffrey L. Staley, *Reading with a Passion: Rhetoric, Autobiography and the American West in the Gospel of John* (New York: Continuum, 1995); Janice Capel Anderson and Jeffrey L. Staley, eds., *Taking It Personally: Autobiographical Biblical Criticism, Semeia* 72 (1995).

9. On the impact of narrative gaps on the reading process, see Wolfgang Iser, "The Reading Process: A Phenomenological Approach," in Tompkins, *Reader-Response Criticism*, 55; McKnight, *Post-modern Use*, 223–41; Robert Alter, *The Pleasures of Reading in an Ideological Age* (New York: Simon & Schuster, 1989); Meir Sternberg, *The Poetics of Biblical Narrative* (Bloomington: Indiana University Press, 1985).

after the "few days"? Did she return home? Obviously, she did not journey on with Jesus, since she is never mentioned during the years of his ministry. And the question whether she believed in her son, before or after his first sign, is still hotly debated among biblical scholars in the twenty-first century.[10]

The narrative gap caused by the silence about the mother's whereabouts and her attitude toward Jesus leaves the reader puzzled, and yet she or he must journey on with the open questions and the ambivalence. Likewise, only a little later the reader needs to journey on with Nicodemus and his unanswered question, "How can this be?," referring to rebirth (3:9).[11]

When the reader finally encounters Jesus's mother again toward the end of the gospel, after perhaps having given up all hope to ever meet her again,[12] the open question is finally transformed into an answer. At least now, at the foot of the cross, so the reader can conclude, Jesus's mother has come to believe in her son, and she testifies to it by her very presence.[13]

---

10. Belief is stated explicitly only with regard to the disciples (2:11). There are basically two readings of the mother's belief. First, it is expressed in her informing Jesus about the lack of wine, and thus in her implicit quest for a "sign" that she believes he can perform. Second, the very same action is regarded as lack of belief because Jesus rebukes her since his hour has not yet come. Due to the open text and the ambivalence engendered by it, both readings are possible and legitimate. For the multidimensionality of biblical texts and different readings, see Daniel Patte, *Ethics of Biblical Interpretation: A Reevaluation* (Louisville: Westminster John Knox, 1995), Patte, *Discipleship according to the Sermon on the Mount: Four Legitimate Readings, Four Plausible Views of Discipleship, and Their Relative Values* (Valley Forge, PA: Trinity Press International, 1996).

11. For the heavy demands on readers of John, who have to come to terms with puzzles, ambivalences, even contradictions, and open questions, see "'How Can This Be?' (John 3:9): A Feminist-Theological Rereading of the Gospel of John," in this volume.

12. In 6:42 the mother is indirectly mentioned by the Jewish leaders within the bread-of-life discourse: "Is not this Jesus, the son of Joseph, whose father and mother we know? How can he now say, 'I have come down from heaven'?" Some textual witnesses, however, omit the mother; but this is obviously secondary, since it is the easier variant.

13. Wayne C. Booth distinguishes between two techniques of characterization: telling and showing. See Booth, *The Rhetoric of Fiction*, 2nd ed. (Chicago: University of Chicago Press, 1983), 3–20. Shimon Bar-Efrat speaks of direct and indirect shaping of characters. See Bar-Efrat, *Narrative Art in the Bible*, BLS 17 (Sheffield: Sheffield Academic, 1989), 47–92, esp. 64. In both cases, the latter categories demand more activity on the part of the reader.

Steadfast and grounded she stands there, a silent witness.[14] And it is Jesus now, as opposed to the Cana episode, who takes the initiative when he entrusts his mother and the Beloved Disciple to one another (19:27) and thereby establishes a new relationship between them that transcends physical, flesh-and-blood family ties and becomes the core of a new family of brothers and sisters (20:17).[15] "From that hour the disciple took her into his own home" (19:27). While the narrator does not tell when the two actually leave the crucifixion scene, it is obviously not right away, as the sequence of the narrative indicates.[16] Nevertheless, finally they must have departed into the disciple's house,[17] and it is there that Jesus's mother dis-

---

14. See Robert G. Maccini, *Her Testimony Is True: Women as Witnesses according to John*, JSNTSup 125 (Sheffield: Sheffield Academic, 1996), ch. 8. His evaluation of the mother, however, differs greatly from mine, especially with regard to the mother's faith and her function in the scene.

15. The identity of the Beloved Disciple has troubled the minds of scholarly readers throughout the centuries and has produced vast literature. See, e.g., James H. Charlesworth, *The Beloved Disciple: Whose Witness Validates the Gospel of John?* (Valley Forge, PA: Trinity Press International, 1995), who filled 437 pages! Basically, all attempts to identify him with a named person (e.g., Lazarus) need to be rejected, since the author obviously intended to leave him anonymous. Whether or not he was an actual historical person, and the prominent witness to and guarantee of the Jesus tradition within the Johannine community, has been debated and answered differently. However, the fact that he is portrayed as the ideal disciple does not exclude historicity. In my view he was both: ideal *and* historical.

Ἀδελφοί can, and indeed needs to, be understood as inclusive of sisters, if the androcentric language is seriously taken into account. Consequently, the disciples are male and female. For the new family, note also Jesus addressing his mother as "woman" (2:4; 19:26). Her biological motherhood is no longer essential. This is in line with the family-critical ethos of the Synoptic tradition (see Mark 3:31–35 parr.). See also Q 11:27–28, where Jesus rejects the woman's praise of the womb and the breasts of his mother. Against Maccini's claim that the mother at the cross serves "as a guarantor of Jesus' humanity" (*Her Testimony is True*, 196, 199).

16. This seems to be another case of prolepsis, one of John's narrative devices; see, e.g., 11:17 and 11:38; 11:2 and 12:3. The difference here is that the actual realization, i.e., their arrival in the house, is not narrated.

17. The Greek is εἰς τὰ ἴδια, which is reminiscent of the prologue (1:11), now reversed and a new family created. See Francis J. Moloney, *Glory Not Dishonor: Reading John 13–21* (Minneapolis: Fortress, 1998), 145. See also 16:32: Jesus's prediction of the disciples' flight (ἕκαστος τὰ ἴδια); another link is the hour. The deeper, symbolical meaning of the expression does not exclude the existence of an actual home in Jerusalem. Against Brown, *John*, 907, and Brown, *Death of the Messiah*, 1023–25 ("his own realm of discipleship," 1025). See Frans Neirynck, "ΕΙΣ ΤΑ ΙΔΙΑ: Jn 19, 26 (et

appears again, this time forever, into the darkness of the unknown out of which she has initially come in chapter 2. The Beloved Disciple, on the other hand, returns in chapter 20, when he—together with Simon Peter—runs to the tomb on Easter morning (20:3-4) after having been informed about the empty tomb by Mary Magdalene (vv. 1-2). Jesus's mother may, by implication, be regarded present also, if we take seriously the note that the Beloved Disciple took her home. Because the narrator does not tell us when Mary Magdalene gets back to the tomb (20:11),[18] we can imagine that she encounters Jesus's mother in the disciple's home, while the two men are running to the tomb, and she joins them there later. The narrative gap allows for such a reconstruction and reimagination.

Birth and Rebirth: Jesus's Mother at the Interface between John and the Synoptics

In John, Jesus's mother does not actually give birth to him. Thus, the Fourth Gospel differs considerably from the infancy narratives in Matthew (chs. 1-2) and in Luke (chs. 1-2) but meets with Mark's silence about Jesus's physical birth.[19] While her role as mother is not questioned in Mark, no

---

16, 32)," *ETL* 55 (1979): 357-65; Neirynck, "La traduction d'un verset johannique, Jn 19, 27b," *ETL* 57 (1981): 83-106. For a literal reading, see also Eugen Ruckstuhl, who considers the Beloved Disciple a Jerusalem disciple of Jesus. See Ruckstuhl, "Der Jünger, den Jesus liebte," in *Jesus im Horizont der Evangelien*, SBABNT 3 (Stuttgart: Katholisches Bibelwerk, 1988), 371-73.

18. In 20:11 Mary Magdalene is back at the tomb, but how and when she got there is not narrated. Within the historical-critical paradigm, this gap has been interpreted in terms of redaction criticism: the episode of the disciples' race to the tomb was inserted into the original Mary Magdalene story (20:1, 11-18). This has had far-reaching consequences for the evaluation of the three characters and their relation to one another. Within a narrative-critical reader-response approach the question is essential: What does the text do to the reader, and how does one make meaning of it? Depending on how the reader fills the gap, different readings are possible and legitimate.

19. It is remarkable that Mark starts with the proclamation of John the Baptist and Jesus's baptism, temptation, and the beginning of his Galilean ministry (1:1-15), without revealing any information about Jesus's beginnings to his readers. When they first encounter Jesus, he is already a grown-up man and ready to start his public career. See Morna D. Hooker, *Beginnings: Keys That Open the Gospels* (Harrisburg, PA: Trinity Press International, 1997). On the different portrayal of Jesus's mother in the New Testament, see Ingrid Rosa Kitzberger, "Mary, Mother of Jesus," in *Religion Past and*

matter how ambivalent she is portrayed during Jesus's ministry (see 3:21–35), in John the mother's role seems to have been co-opted by the heavenly Father, out of whose womb[20] the Logos became flesh (1:14–18) and into which he finally returns, after rejecting Mary Magdalene's attempt to hold him back (20:17).

While Jesus's mother is deprived of her birthing privilege, rebirth is offered as an option to anyone, whether female or male, who is ready for the challenge and the adventure.[21] In fact, rebirth turns out to be *the* choice, no matter how long the process takes.

"How can anyone be born after having grown old? Can one enter a second time into the mother's womb and be born?" (3:4). Nicodemus,[22] the old and established rabbi, is, strangely enough, confronted with Jesus's call to start all over again. So are we, the readers. Birth in terms of rebirth

---

Present: Encyclopedia of Theology and Religion, ed. Hans Dieter Betz et al. (Leiden: Brill, 2010), 8:113–14.

20. The Greek κόλπος (1:18) can mean "bosom" and "womb." Most translations, however, render it as "bosom" (RSV) or alternatively, "heart" (NRSV). Obviously, it is difficult to imagine a father with a womb. See Judith M. Lieu, who draws attention to the tradition of the maternal God of prophecy and psalmody in the Hebrew Bible (Hos 11:1–4; Isa 42:14; Ps 139:13) and considers Deut 32:18 as closest (though with regard to John 18:37): God is the one who has given birth to his people. See Lieu, "The Mother of the Son in the Fourth Gospel," *JBL* 117 (1998): 76. See also Mayer I. Gruber, *The Motherhood of God and Other Studies*, SFSHJ 57 (Atlanta: Scholars Press, 1992), who refers, inter alia, to Second Isaiah (3–15). See also Sandra M. Schneiders, who speaks of the "femininity of God" and favors the reading "born" from God in 1:13. Ἐγεννήθησαν can mean both: "born" or "begotten." See Schneiders, *Written That You May Believe: Encountering Jesus in the Fourth Gospel* (New York: Crossroad, 1999), 122–23.

21. See Francis J. Moloney, "An Adventure with Nicodemus," in Kitzberger, *Personal Voice in Biblical Interpretation*, 97–110. See Lieu's evocative insight that "Jesus himself is the paradigm" since he not only came "from above" but was also born "from above"; see John 18:37 ("Mother of the Son," 75–76).

For a fresh look at the mother in John, see Liliana M. Nutu, "Opening Mouths and Legs, or Women's Talk: Can One Hear the Mother of Christ in John's Gospel and Leeloo in Luc Besson's *The Fifth Element*?" This chapter was meant to be included in a volume, edited by myself, *Voicing/Silencing Wo/men*. However, due to the delay of submission of other papers, the volume has not (yet) materialized.

22. For a more detailed study of Nicodemus, see Ingrid Rosa Kitzberger, "Synoptic Women in John: Interfigural Readings," in Kitzberger, *Transformative Encounters*, 88–102; "Aging and Birthing: Open-Ended Stories and a Hermeneutics of Promise," in this volume; "Transcending Gender Boundaries in John," in this volume.

from above,[23] of water and Spirit (3:3–8), is one of the main agenda in John's Gospel. Physical birth is superseded and substituted by spiritual (re) birth. In this sense, it denotes becoming disciples of Jesus and members of his heavenly family: God's children and Jesus's brothers and sisters (see 1:12–13; 20:17).[24] Only 16:21 refers to a physical birth and a woman in labor, but also in this case it is used as a metaphor and applied to the disciples' process from sorrow over Jesus's departure to the lasting joy when seeing him again (16:16–24).[25]

Standing at the foot of the cross, together with the other witnesses, Jesus's mother is reborn when she receives the Spirit (19:30),[26] which Jesus had promised to give at the time of his glorification. "Let anyone who is thirsty come to me, and let the one who believes in me drink," Jesus cries out on the last day of Sukkot. "Now he said this about the Spirit, which believers in him were to receive; for as yet there was no Spirit, because Jesus was not yet glorified" (7:37–39). So the narrator comments. Now that Jesus is hanging on the cross, the time of his glorification has come; and his mother is among the first to receive the Spirit and consequently be reborn. Before blood and water flow out from Jesus's pierced side (19:34),[27] rivers of living water flow out from her, the believer (see 7:38), so the reader can conclude.

---

23. The Greek ἄνωθεν can mean "again" and "from above." I translate it as "rebirth from above" because, in fact, both meanings are inherent at the same time in John's use of the term.

24. See the intriguing title by Wes Howard-Brook, *Becoming Children of God: John's Gospel and Radical Discipleship*, B&L (Maryknoll, NY: Orbis Books, 2001).

25. See Fernando F. Segovia, *The Farewell of the Word: The Johannine Call to Abide* (Minneapolis: Fortress, 1991), 254. The theme of birth "differs considerably from that found in the remainder of the Gospel." It refers to those who have become disciples already and who undergo a birthing process related to Jesus's death and resurrection.

26. The Greek text is παρέδωκεν τὸ πνεῦμα. The translation "gave up his spirit" (e.g., NRSV) is, therefore, inaccurate. However, the surface meaning of Jesus breathing his last is by no means excluded. See Jean Zumstein, who offers an excellent approach that considers both the literal and the symbolical meaning in this passage: "Der erste Sinn schließt den zweiten Sinn nicht aus, wie umgekehrt der zweite Sinn den ersten nicht aufhebt." See Zumstein, "Johannes 19, 25–27," *ZTK* 94 (1997): 146 n. 54.

27. Despite the myriads of interpretations of "blood and water," for sure the water refers also to the Spirit and is thus the fulfillment of Jesus's prophecy in 7:38–39, and consequently a parallel to 19:30 (the giving of the Spirit); see Brown, *John*, 949–50. All characters in 19:25–27, including the mother, may be considered as still present in 19:34.

Therefore, the scene of Jesus's death is also a birthing scene.[28] Apart from the mother's (and the other witnesses') rebirth, a new son is born to her when Jesus entrusts her and the Beloved Disciple to each other and thereby redefines them as mother and son (19:26–27).[29] Thus, the mother experiences at the same time the death of one son and the birth of another.[30]

To sum up, Jesus's mother is reborn at the foot of the cross in a double sense: first, as she reenters the stage after her long absence since chapter 2, and second, as she testifies to her belief, receives the Spirit, and becomes a disciple of Jesus. Both kinds of rebirth come as a surprise,[31] since the reader might have expected neither the one nor the other.

Equally surprising is the mother's presence in the Johannine account of the crucifixion when we read it in the context of the Synoptic Gospels. Thus, she shares in the riddle of the relationship between John and the Synoptics that has attracted the attention of readers ever since the Fourfold Gospel came into being.[32] In the Synoptic Gospels Mary turns up

---

28. Lieu, who relates the crucifixion scene, and in particular Jesus's mother, to the woman of the parable in 16:21, comments: "So is this a birthing or a dying? …; we meet birth here only when we encounter death. Indeed, the birth, which is not narrated in this Gospel, becomes through 16:21 a death, or is the death a birth?" ("Mother of the Son," 73). For the closeness, if not identification, of death and birth in John, see also my chapter "Flowing Identities," in this volume.

29. The flow of blood and water from Jesus's pierced side (19:34) could also be regarded as an actual birth, with the water referring to the amniotic fluid. See Maccini, who considers it the last and greatest sign, "for it signifies the new birth and life that the death of the Messiah brings" (*Her Testimony Is True*, 205). Within the Johannine context, blood and water may also have eucharistic and baptismal connotations (see John 3; 6). See Zumstein, "Johannes 19, 25–29," 147–48.

30. While the Father in heaven is reunited with his son Jesus, his mother on earth is united with her "new" son. I thank Orna Teitelbaum for this intriguing comment in her email of February 28, 2003.

31. John is indeed a gospel of surprises on several levels. With regard to characters, and in particular those mentioned at the foot of the cross, i.e., the mother's cowitnesses, it is striking that all three other women, including Mary Magdalene, turn up the first time within the gospel story, and the Beloved Disciple was mentioned only once and introduced late, in John 13.

32. See D. Moody Smith, *John among the Gospels: The Relationship in Twentieth-Century Research* (Minneapolis: Fortress, 1992); Adelbert Denaux, ed., *John and the Synoptics*, BETL 101 (Leuven: Leuven University Press; Peeters, 1992); Graham N. Stanton, "The Fourfold Gospel," *NTS* 43 (1997): 317–46; Martin Hengel, *The Four Gos-*

during Jesus's ministry, but she is not present among the women who witness Jesus's crucifixion from afar (Mark 15:40–41 parr.). These, on the other hand, are not mentioned in John, except the most prominent female witness, Mary Magdalene.[33]

Rereading Jesus's Mother in John: Intertextual/Interfigural Characterization

In addressing the question of Jesus's mother standing at the foot of the cross in John's Gospel, an author-oriented approach within the historical-critical paradigm could be applied, focusing on source and redaction criticism. However, such an attempt can never move beyond mere hypothesis, with more or less credibility.[34] In the remainder of this paper, therefore, I shall continue with the reader-response approach applied so far, presenting my own readings, with particular focus on intertextuality and in particular interfigurality[35] as hermeneutical keys. By viewing the Johannine focus text in the light of Synoptic intertexts, new dimensions are added to the

---

pels and the One Gospel of Jesus Christ: An Investigation of the Collection and Origin of the Canonical Gospels, trans. John Bowden (London: SCM, 2000).

33. The lists vary also among the Synoptics. Mark mentions Mary Magdalene; Mary, the mother of James the younger and Joses; and Salome, out of an anonymous larger group (Mark 15:40–41). Matthew lists Mary Magdalene; Mary, the mother of James and Joseph; and the mother of the sons of Zebedee, out of the larger, unnamed group (Matt 27:55–56). Luke mentions the women generally at the crucifixion (Luke 23:49) and provides names only in the Easter morning narrative: Mary Magdalene, Joanna, Mary the mother of James, and the other women (24:10; diff. 8:3, Susanna). There is also a difference in timing. In the Synoptics, the witnesses are mentioned *after* Jesus's death, in John *before* his death. This, of course, is a logical narrative sequence if Jesus is to speak with his mother and the Beloved Disciple.

34. Different answers have been presented in historical-critical scholarship on John 19:25–27, ranging widely with regard to possible sources accessible to John and the historical evaluation of the scene.

35. Naturally, my own readings are subjective, and I claim them as such! On real readers versus reader constructs in reader-response criticism, see Fernando F. Segovia, ed., *Readers and Readings of the Fourth Gospel*, vol. 1 of *"What Is John?,"* SymS 3 (Atlanta: Scholars Press, 1996); Segovia, *Literary and Social Readings of the Fourth Gospel*, vol. 2 of *"What Is John?,"* SymS 7 (Atlanta: Scholars Press, 1998). On intertextuality, see, e.g., Owen Miller, "Intertextual Identity," in *Identity of the Literary Text*, ed. Mario J. Valdes and Miller (Toronto: University of Toronto Press, 1985), 19–40; Siepke Draisma, ed., *Intertextuality in Biblical Writings: Essays in Honour of Bas van Iersel* (Kampen: Kok Pharos, 1989), 15–26. The term *interfigurality* was coined by Wolfgang G. Müller and refers to the relationship between characters in different texts.

characterization of Jesus's mother in John,[36] and new light is shed on the reader's surprise encounter with her at the foot of the cross.

Rereading Jesus's Mother in John and Mark

A reader who is familiar with the Synoptic Gospels will recall their accounts of Jesus's crucifixion when reading the Johannine account. The reader will think of the women who witnessed, prominent among them Mary Magdalene (Mark 15:40–41 parr.). Consequently, the mother missing out in the Synoptics becomes evident. However, when one reads Mark's account very carefully, Jesus's mother can become visible nevertheless, because she is hidden under the surface of the text.[37] Before Jesus breathes his last, he cries out with a loud voice, in Aramaic: "Eloi, eloi, lema sabachthani?" which is translated "My God, my God, why have you forsaken me?" (15:34). Thus, Jesus is portrayed reciting the first line of Ps 22 (Ps 21 LXX) and thus joining in the lament of the suffering righteous of the Hebrew Bible. In fact, the entire crucifixion scene in Mark is replete with allusions to Ps 22, in particular as pertaining to the mockery of Jesus (see 15:29–32). However, the recontextualization of Ps 22 in Mark 15 happens in a reverse order.[38] Consequently, Jesus's cry, rephrasing the first line of Ps 22, forms the end and the climax. This may indicate that his cry is a cry of complete despair, devoid of the trust in God and without God's response, which follows only in the second half of Ps 22. However, such an interpretation that takes God's silence at face value need not be the only way to read the text. Just as the reader knows that the silence of

---

See Müller, "Interfigurality: A Study on the Interdependence of Literary Figures," in *Intertextuality*, ed. Heinrich E. Plett, RTT 15 (Berlin: de Gruyter, 1991), 101–21.

36. On characterization, see, e.g., John Darr, *On Character Building: The Reader and the Rhetoric of Characterization in Luke-Acts* (Louisville: Westminster John Knox, 1992); Elizabeth Struthers Malbon and Adele Berlin, eds., *Characterization in Biblical Literature*, Semeia 63 (1993).

37. I first referred to this intertextual reading and the mother's (indirect) presence in Mark's crucifixion scene in "Synoptic Women in John," 107 n. 80. This footnote was the germ for this paper. Thanks to Amy-Jill Levine for her encouraging response.

38. See Vernon K. Robbins, "The Reversed Contextualization of Psalm 22 in the Markan Crucifixion: A Socio-rhetorical Analysis," in *The Four Gospels 1992: Festschrift Frans Neyrinck*, ed. Frans Van Segbroeck et al., BETL 100 (Leuven: University Press; Peeters, 1992), 2:1161–83; Robbins, *Exploring the Texture of Texts: A Guide to Socio-rhetorical Interpretation* (Valley Forge, PA: Trinity Press International, 1996), 48–50.

the women at the very end of the gospel (16:8)[39] has been overcome and turned into voice (because the gospel, and the Christian community to which she or he belongs, exist!), so Ps 22 in Mark 15 can, and perhaps needs to, be read in such a voicing-the-silence manner. In fact, the entire Ps 22 is evoked by an intertextual reading.[40] This implies that the second half of the psalm, which voices the trust in God, is evoked, too. Consequently, Jesus's mother becomes visible.

"Yet it was you who took me from the womb; you kept me safe on my mother's breast. On you I was cast from my birth, and since my mother bore me you have been my God" (Ps 22:9–10). In, paradoxically, addressing his now-absent Father (Mark 15:34), Jesus invokes both his mother's presence, her womb and her breasts, and his Father's presence at his birth. Thus, through an intertextual reading, death and birth are joined together in Mark's account of the crucifixion.

Reading John 19:25–27, Mark 15:34—and through it Ps 22—comes alive as an intertext and transforms the focus text. Such rereading is confirmed by the allusion to and quotation of Ps 22 in the very context of John's crucifixion scene, when the soldiers cast the lot over Jesus's garment (19:23–24 = Ps 22:18).

Reading Jesus's mother into Mark's account of the crucifixion is underscored by the designation of Jesus as "son of Mary" in Mark 6:3.[41] It is only here in the New Testament that Jesus is defined in relation to his mother and not his father,[42] which would have been the more common use. Thus, mother and son are related to each other in a more pronounced manner.

When reading Jesus's mother at the foot of the cross in John, both Markan intertexts, the crucifixion scene and the scene at Nazareth, come

---

39. It is generally acknowledged (based on textual witnesses) that the gospel originally ended with v. 8.

40. Intertextual reading activates the entire intertext and thus differs essentially from mere quotation. Besides that, the latter is author oriented and belongs into the historical-critical paradigm.

41. See Detlev Dormeyer, "Die Familie Jesu und der Sohn der Maria im Markusevangelium (3:20f, 31–35; 6:3)," in *Vom Urchristentum zu Jesus: Für Joachim Gnilka*, ed. Hubert Frankemölle and Karl Kertelge (Freiburg im Breisgau: Herder, 1989), 109–35. The Nazareth scene in Mark 6:1–6 reflects the unbelief of the townspeople who claim to know who Jesus is because they know his family. There is not sufficient evidence to interpret "son of Mary" as referring to his supposed illegitimacy.

42. See diff. John 1:45; 6:42: "son of Joseph."

into play. As a consequence, the mother's presence is no longer so puzzling as it was at first sight.

Rereading Jesus's Mother in John and Luke

Encountering Jesus's mother at the foot of the cross, a reader who is familiar with the Synoptic Gospels will open up this text to another intertext, this time a passage from the Lukan infancy narrative. When Jesus's parents bring the newborn into the temple (Luke 2:22-24),[43] the old Simeon is there already and recognizes the baby as the one he has been waiting for all his life, as the fulfillment of God's promises. Finally, having seen salvation, he is ready to go home (2:25-32). But he does not do so before having uttered a prophecy addressed to the mother: "This child is destined for the falling and the rising of many in Israel, and to be a sign that will be opposed so that the inner thoughts of many will be revealed—and a sword will pierce your own soul too" (2:34-35).[44] In the context of Luke's

---

43. The temple (ἱερόν) refers to the temple court, not the temple sanctuary (ναός). See Raymond E. Brown, *The Birth of the Messiah: A Commentary on the Infancy Narratives in the Gospels of Matthew and Luke*, ABRL (New York: Doubleday, 1993), 438-39. On the reason for the visit to the temple, see Brown, *Birth of the Messiah*, 448-51, and Joseph A. Fitzmyer, *The Gospel according to Luke I-IX*, AB 28 (Garden City, NY: Doubleday, 1981), 421, 425. The plural "their" purification (2:22) is better attested than the singular and has puzzled many interpreters. Brown refers it to both parents, "even though there is no Jewish tradition for the purification of the father," and he rejects Origen's interpretation, who referred it to Mary and Jesus, as "implausible, since the child was to be presented or consecrated to the Lord, but not purified" (*Birth of the Messiah*, 436). However, Mayer I. Gruber drew my attention to "some as yet otherwise known Second Temple sect, which held that the child as well as the mother had to be purified" (email communication dated May 8, 2000). See Joseph Baumgarten, "Purification after Childbirth and the Sacred Garden in 4Q265 and Jubilees," in *New Qumran Texts and Studies: Proceedings of the First Meeting of the International Organization for Qumran Studies, Paris 1992*, ed. George J. Brooke with Florentino Garcia Martinez (Leiden: Brill, 1994), 3-10; Frank Zimmerman, "Origin and Significance of the Jewish Rite of Circumcision," *PR* 38 (1951): 103-12; Mayer I. Gruber, "Purity and Impurity in Halakic Sources and Qumran Law," in *Wholly Woman, Holy Blood: A Feminist Critique of Purity and Impurity*, ed. Kristin de Troyer et al. (Harrisburg, PA: Trinity Press International, 2003), 65-76.

44. The Greek ψυχή, translated as "soul," denotes "the locus of emotion and affections, the heart" (Brown, *Birth of the Messiah*, 441). For the numerous mariological and pastristic interpretations of the phrase, see 462. Brown refers to the closest Hebrew Bible vocabulary in Ezek 14:17: "Let a sword pass through the land so that I may cut

Gospel, the prophecy refers to Mary's share in the division over Jesus and the suffering that will result from it. Only in the long run the division that Jesus himself brings (see 12:51–53) will lead to his crucifixion. In Luke 2, however, it does not yet come into the picture.

Reading John 19:25–27 in the light of Luke 2:22–38, the Johannine text turns out to be a reinterpretation of Simeon's prophecy: the piercing of the mother's soul now refers to her pain as she witnesses her son's crucifixion.[45]

Besides Simeon, the prophetess Anna, a widow of eighty-four years,[46] encounters the newborn Jesus in Luke's temple scene. She also recognizes him, praises God, and speaks to all about this child's significance (vv. 36–38). Although it is not mentioned explicitly, it can be assumed that Anna also embarked on her last journey soon after. Therefore, she may be remembered as well when reading John 19:25–27, in particular with regard to the women witnesses.

John 19:25–27 can be opened up to yet another intertext in Luke. Out of the company at the foot of the cross, only two become characters in this short scene, when Jesus entrusts his mother and the Beloved Disciple to each other: "Woman, behold your son," he addresses his mother, and "Behold, your mother," he addresses his disciple. Consequently, the disciple takes her to his home (19:25). A new relationship between them is established and a new family is born.[47] However, the very fact that

---

off man and beast." It is "a selective sword of judgment ... a sword for discrimination" (Brown, *Birth of the Messiah*, 463–64).

45. This reinterpretation is most vividly reflected in the arts, where Jesus's mother has been portrayed as standing at the foot of the cross with a sword piercing her body. This artistic representation has strongly influenced the reading of Luke 2:34–35, so that Simeon's prophecy has been interpreted as referring to the crucifixion. This, however, does not do justice to the original story context of Luke.

46. Anna's age has been debated, depending on the choice of textual variants (ὡς or ἕως in v. 37). Accordingly, eighty-four refers either to her total age or to the time of her widowhood. Brown chose the latter version; consequently, Anna's age would be about 103 (*Birth of the Messiah*, 442). I prefer eighty-four, for reasons of credibility. Besides that, it matches perfectly with my friend Rosa's age at her death (she died shortly before her eighty-fourth birthday).

47. Brown regards it as a "revelatory formula," in which "the one who speaks is revealing the mystery of the special salvific mission that the one referred to will undertake; thus, the sonship and motherhood proclaimed from the cross are of value for God's plan and are related to what is being accomplished in the elevation of Jesus on the cross" (*John*, 923). The idea of adoption or succession, as other scholars have suggested, need not be excluded, since different layers of meaning are possible. Besides

the mother and the disciple are entrusted to each other is striking, not only because it presupposes that the disciple was a motherless child, but especially because it presupposes that Jesus's mother had no other male relatives to care for her after Jesus's departure. Although Jesus is referred to as the "son of Joseph" in John (1:45; 6:42), Joseph never turns up as a character in John's story, not even in the early days at the Cana wedding. On the other hand, Jesus's brothers are mentioned (7:3–10), but the narrator informs us that they did not believe in Jesus (7:35). Therefore, when Jesus's mother stands at the foot of the cross, she is portrayed as a woman without a husband, probably a widow, and without any other sons who could care for her. While Jesus's brothers are most likely still alive, because of their unbelief they are no longer considered to be real brothers, and they are replaced by his disciples (see 20:17). Seeing Jesus's mother as a widow and Jesus as her only son, an alert and informed reader who is familiar with the Synoptic Gospels will recall one particular story: the widow of Nain and the raising of her only son in Luke 7:11–17. Thus, the possibility of an intertextual, and in particular an interfigural, reading is opened up.

In Luke 7, the woman is a widow, and the deceased son is her only son (7:12).[48] Filled with compassion, Jesus tells the woman, "Do not weep" (v. 13), and then addresses the son, "Young man, I say to you, arise" (v. 14). Immediately, "the dead man sat up, and began to speak" (v. 15). "And he gave him to his mother," the narrator concludes the quick resurrection (v. 15). A comment on the enthusiastic reaction of the crowd and the spreading of the news follows (vv. 16–17).

The parallels to the crucifixion scene in John are obvious,[49] but so are the inversions. In Luke, Jesus restores life to the only son of a mother who is a widow and reestablishes their relationship. In John, it is the dying only son of a mother, who also appears to be a widow, who establishes a new

---

that, the filial care for his mother, the most literal meaning, is certainly present, beyond all symbolic meanings.

48. Μονογενὴς υἱὸς τῇ μετρὶ αὐτοῦ. It is significant to note that the son is related to the mother, not the other way around. See John 1:14: μονογενοῦς παρὰ πατρός.

49. Note, however, that Jesus's mother does *not* weep. The weeping is left to Mary Magdalene on Easter morning (20:11, 13, 15). However, in the famous hymn of the Middle Ages, dated 1306, the mother is depicted as weeping: "Stabat mater dolorosa / iuxta crucem lacrimosa." Accordingly, the tears feature also in the musical representations, such as that of Franz Schubert.

relationship between his mother and another young man, who becomes her son. In John, the moment of Jesus's death is at the same time a moment of birth, since a new son is born to his mother. This parallels the resurrection, a kind of rebirth, of the widow's son in Luke.

Rereading John 19:25–27 in the light of Luke 7:11–17, therefore, adds new dimensions also to the characterization in John, in particular with regard to Jesus's mother.

Jesus's Mother, John, and Myself

Arriving at the end of my intertextual and interfigural reading journey, I still cannot help wondering about John, the author of the gospel,[50] and how he (or she?) came to place Jesus's mother at the foot of the cross. Historically, the presence of family or friends as witnesses right at the cross is very unlikely, if not impossible.[51] The Synoptic accounts, with the women standing afar, are more reliable for that matter. The consequence that Jesus's mother never stood at the foot of the cross may be shocking and upsetting to many believers for whom the mother, remaining faithfully with her son in his agony, has become a role model and a source of comfort and strength. I wonder what my friend Rosa would say if she were able to read this chapter. In a spiritual sense, of course, the mother could very well have been with her son in his last hour, supporting him even if she was unable to stand near. Consequently, there is truth in the Johannine crucifixion scene, an inner truth that has been projected onto the outer reality, something that is not uncommon in John's Gospel.

Nevertheless, the question remains how John came to do what he did, and, on the literary level, place Jesus's mother at the foot of the cross. Based on my previous work on John and the Synoptics from a reader-response perspective, it seems, nevertheless, very likely that John used the Synop-

---

50. Please note that I am not changing paradigms. However, asking historical questions has not ceased in the reader-response critic that I am. This is legitimate as much as it is natural. For possible female authorship, see Schneiders, *Written That You May Believe*, part 3, "Because of the Woman's Testimony ...," 211–32.

51. See Willibald Bösen, who refers to Tacitus, *Ann.* 6.10, 19; Suetonius, *Tib.* 61. See Bösen, *Der letzte Tag des Jesus von Nazareth: Was wirklich geschah* (Freiburg im Breisgau: Herder, 1994), 322–23. That the crucified was surrounded by relatives and friends refers to later rabbinic evidence; see Brown, *Death of the Messiah*, 1029. Gustaf Dalman refers in particular to marital legislation. See Dalman, *Jesus—Jeshua: Studies in the Gospels* (New York: Ktav, 1971), 201.

tic Gospels as sources, also in creating the crucifixion scene, and he used the sources in a very creative way. Consequently, his rewriting the Synoptics might not have been so very different from my rereading them. This would entail the following: He used the implicit mention of Jesus's mother in Mark 15:34 (= Ps 22:1) as a starting point and had it confirmed by Mark 6:3 ("son of Mary"). In addition, he reinterpreted the temple scene in Luke 2:21–38, in particular Simeon's prophecy, so that the piercing of the soul now refers to the suffering of Jesus's mother when she stands at the foot of the cross. Furthermore, the brief scene in which Jesus entrusts the mother and the Beloved Disciple to each other is modeled, in reverse order, after the raising of the widow of Nain's son in Luke 7:11–17.[52]

I would not mind if John's brain worked similarly to mine; in fact, I would be delighted. However, nothing can be said for sure about him (or her) who died into his (her) gospel and is no longer accessible apart from his (her) textual incarnation.

Journeying Home, or, "The End Is Where We Start From"[53]

Returning "home," Jesus's mother and the Beloved Disciple do not return to where they came from, but to a new home, the foundation of the post-Easter community. In Acts 1:14 the mother is indeed mentioned as a member of the Jerusalem church.

The story of Jesus's mother in John is open-ended, just like the gospel itself, despite its double ending (20:30–31; 21:24–25). Like all biblical texts, it is open-ended on a literary level, but especially it is pragmatically open and as such it wants to be continued in our own lives.[54] Revisiting Jesus's

---

52. Maurits Sabbe, a strong advocate of John's direct dependence on the Synoptics, considers Luke 23:49 and the parallels in Mark 15:40 and Matt. 26:56 as the inspiration for John; and in addition, "Synoptic sayings about a symbolic family relationship to Jesus, and the Matthean terminology for the Christians as brothers among themselves (Mt 5,23.24.49; 7,4.5; 18,12.21.35; 23, 8) or in relation to Jesus (Mt 12,48.50; 25,40; 28,10)." See Sabbe, "The Johannine Account of the Death of Jesus and Its Synoptic Parallels (Jn 19,16b–42)," *ETL* 70 (1994): 40.

53. T. S. Eliot, "Four Quartets, Little Gidding," V, ii.1–3, in *The Complete Poems and Plays of T. S. Eliot* (London: Guild, 1986), 197.

54. J. Severino Croatto, "The Function of the Non-fulfilled Promises: Reading the Pentateuch from the Perspective of the Latin-American Oppressed People," in Kitzberger, *Personal Voice in Biblical Interpretation*, 38–52; Croatto, *Biblical Hermeneutics: Toward a Theory of Reading as the Production of Meaning*, trans. Robert R. Barr

mother at the foot of the cross opens up the possibility for readers, past and present, to return "home" where home was not but now is, thereby embarking on a new journey, full of promise.[55] Jesus's mother becomes a generator of hope[56] as she moves on beyond death to a community born from death.

Stabat Mater? If she ever did, she is no longer there. She has journeyed on, thus sharing in the flowing identity of the rivers of living waters that signify believers. *Panta rhei*, and the end is where we start from, Jesus's mother and John and I. Homeward bound –>

(Maryknoll, NY: Orbis Books, 1987): "What is genuinely relevant is not the 'behind' of a text, but its 'ahead,' its 'forward'—what it suggests as a pertinent message for the life of the one who receives or seeks it out.... The Bible is an open text. Precisely as a *text*, it is open."

55. See Croatto, "Function of the Non-fulfilled Promises," 50: "The unfinished journey, however, indicates the 'not yet' of the promises. They must be fulfilled *now*."

56. Croatto refers to the "journeys of the patriarchs and the sons and daughters of Israel through the desert, with their crises, their risks, and their suffering" ("Function of the Non-fulfilled Promises," 50). See also my chapter "Aging and Birthing: Open-Ended Stories and a Hermeneutics of Promise," in this volume.

The Three Marys and the Fourfold Gospel

Transformative Encounters on the Seashore

"Mary," he called out, with his soft yet determined voice. Turning around, they looked at him, expectantly. Feeling a gentle breeze enfolding them, they did not know where he had come from. All of a sudden he was there, standing right in front of them on the seashore, where they had gathered early in the morning while it was still dark.

"Here I am, Lord!" Mary, the one who was—just for a change—on home ground, answered, her voice trembling with awe and wonder, recognizing Jesus immediately when he called her name. "Is it I, Lord?" she hesitantly asked, becoming aware of all the other Marys with her. "I have heard you calling in the night," she added more firmly now. "I will go, Lord. If you lead me, I will hold your people in my heart."

"Come and have breakfast," Jesus invited the women, leading them to a charcoal fire on the beach, with fish and bread on it. None of them dared to ask him, "Who are you?" because by now they all knew it was the Lord. Jesus came and took the bread and gave it to them, and did the same with the fish.

This was now the second time Jesus appeared to Mary Magdalene after he was raised from the dead, but the first time he appeared to the other Marys.

When they had finished breakfast, Jesus asked them, "Do you love me?" "You know that we love you more than anyone else," the seven Marys answered spontaneously, as with one voice. After this, Jesus singled out the single women, took them aside, and said to them, "All authority in heaven and on earth has been given to me. Go therefore and make disciples of

---

This chapter was originally a lecture at Mary Immaculate College, University of Limerick, Ireland, June 3, 2004. I was able to present only part of my lecture—a fragmented woman presenting a fragmented paper.

all nations, baptizing them in the name of the Father and the Son and the Holy Spirit, and teaching them to obey everything that I have commanded you. And remember, I am with you always, to the end of the age."

And so, without returning home, they went: Mary of Nazareth, Jesus's own mother, who had never left her hamlet, apart from a few family visits in the Galilean neighborhood; Mary of Bethany, a village woman too, who loved stability and housing guests; and Mary of Magdala, the only city woman among them, who had already traveled far and wide on business.

According to tradition, Mary, Jesus's mother, journeyed as far as Ephesus in Asia Minor and stayed there, while Mary of Magdala and Mary of Bethany sailed on to the coast of southern France, proclaiming the gospel and baptizing many. Apostolic, their mission was called by those who recognized them with their hearts.

"Who Do They Say I Am?":
Reading the Three Marys in the Four Gospels

When Jesus addresses this question to his disciples, they come up with three answers, before providing their own, the correct one, voiced through Peter (Mark 8:27–28). When I asked my students, in a class at the Graduate Theological Union in Berkeley in fall semester 2001, who they thought Jesus was, they presented many more answers, which was not surprising since the students came from very different churches, faith traditions, ethnicities, and cultural backgrounds. "A radical Jew," was the answer that impressed me most, because it came from my Jewish student Orna, who was reading the New Testament for the first time. "Jesus and Women: Transformative Encounters" was the topic that had brought the most diverse group of students together, sharing their desire to learn more about women in the New Testament tradition and their relevance for present-day churches.

"Who do they say I am?" This question could also be asked by New Testament women in general and by the Marys in particular. First of all, the question of identity with regard to the Marys is necessary because eight women mentioned in the New Testament bear this name, and except two they are found in relation to Jesus, or even in his immediate company.[1] This is not unusual since Mary (Miriam) was by far the most popular

---

1. See my articles on "Mary, Mother of Jesus," "Mary and Martha," and "Mary

name in Palestine in Second Temple Judaism, borne by over 25 percent of the female population.² Consequently, "Which Mary?" is the question to start with, before investigating further into their identity markers, or those attributed to them. By the way, without having statistics, the situation as pertaining to the Marys in present-day Ireland seems to be similar to that of first-century Palestine. Most Irish women I have met, at home or abroad, were called Mary or Marie.³

The three most prominent Marys of the gospel tradition are Mary of Nazareth, Jesus's mother, Mary of Magdala, and Mary of Bethany, and on these "three Marys of great renown" I shall focus.

If they asked the question "Who do they say I am?" with regard to their specific identity, their characterization and significance, they would most likely encounter more answers than a book can hold. Re-viewing two thousand years of reading and interpreting the gospels, a thousand images appear, often very different from each other, sometimes so different that one and the same woman can no longer be recognized. This is further complicated by the wide range of traditions, often in the form of legends, that developed over the centuries, reflecting the respective times as well as male attitudes toward women. In addition, different women were conflated into one, which was Mary Magdalene's fate in particular.

However, not only the history of interpretation and the history of reception have produced such puzzling results. Just a look into the gospel texts themselves confronts readers, past and present, with diversity, ambivalence, even contradictions, besides some common features, of course, thus raising new questions, rather than answering those a reader might bring to the text, in search of the authentic Marys.

To start with, investigating the three Marys, we can notice that their most striking characteristic is their brokenness, their fragmentation. As "fragmented women"⁴ they share the fate of all women in patriarchal societ-

---

Magdalene," in *Religion Past and Present*, ed. Hans Dieter Betz et al. (Leiden: Brill, 2010), 8:113–14, 121, 122.

2. Tal Ilan, "Notes on the Distribution of Jewish Women's Names in Palestine in the Second Temple and Mishnaic Periods," *JJS* 40 (1989): 186–200.

3. I thank Sr. Mary T. Brien, PhD, my former student in Berkeley, who—back on her Irish home ground—drew my attention to the opening at Limerick University, encouraged me to apply, and accompanied me during the interview days.

4. J. Cheryl Exum, *Fragmented Women: Feminist (Sub)versions of Biblical Narratives*, JSOTSup 163 (Sheffield: JSOT Press, 1993).

ies and writings. What we have is in fact only the tip of the iceberg, using the image Elisabeth Schüssler Fiorenza coined in her pioneer work, *In Memory of Her: A Feminist Theological Reconstruction of Christian Origins*.[5] However, in terms of potential, a volcano might perhaps provide a more vital image.

The traces of all three Marys in the gospels are very scarce indeed. This applies even to Jesus's mother. They are mentioned only a few times, without much further information and hardly a voice and subject identity granted to them. And yet their significance and impact both in Jesus's life and ministry and that of later generations, including the churches for whom the gospels were originally written and those who handed them on, is evident. After all, they *are* mentioned, even with their names, while other women became anonymous or disappeared completely.

A brief survey of the portrayal of the three Marys in the four gospels will be illuminating. I start with the Fourth Gospel, the youngest and latest in a vibrant and challenging process of oral traditions, first written collections, and gospel writing. For many reasons it is the most puzzling and challenging of our canonical gospels, also with regard to women and especially the three Marys.

The Gospel of John

In John 19:25-27, at the foot of the cross, four women[6] and a man are presented as witnesses and faithful to the last. Two of the women are named Mary: Mary (the wife) of Clopas, and Mary Magdalene, besides Jesus's mother, who, however, is never named Mary in the Fourth Gospel. She first turned up at the Cana wedding, in chapter 2, but then disappeared after she had gone down to Capernaum, together with Jesus's brothers and the disciples (2:12). Whether her initiating Jesus's first sign of turning the water into wine testified to her belief in him, or whether she came to believe in him because of it, or whether her behavior was inappropriate, since she did not respect Jesus's hour (which had not yet come), is heavily debated among scholars. No clear answer can be given, the text is open. At the foot

---

5. Elisabeth Schüssler Fiorenza, *In Memory of Her: A Feminist Theological Reconstruction of Christian Origins* (New York: Crossroad, 1983).

6. The debate on the number of women has to be decided in favor of four (not three), because it is unlikely that Mary (the wife) of Clopas is identical with the sister of Jesus's mother. Even though the name Mary was so popular in Second Temple Judaism, it is unlikely that parents would have given the same name to two of their daughters.

of the cross Jesus's mother comes indeed as a surprise, because she has never been on the stage of his public ministry, which, after all, lasted three years, according to John's timing. Before Jesus dies, he entrusts his mother and the Beloved Disciple to each other, as a new pair of mother and son, and the disciple finally takes her into his house (19:26–27). This is all we get to know about Jesus's mother in John. She does not even give birth to him, which is reserved to the heavenly Father, out of whose womb the Word-become-flesh was born (1:13, 18). The biological bond between Jesus and his mother, whom he addresses as "woman" (2:4; 19:26), is superseded by the spiritual bond. Rebirth from above, through the Spirit (see 3:3, 6), is the option and challenge offered to everyone, including his own mother.

Mary Magdalene is mentioned the very first time at the foot of the cross, without any further information about her (19:25). Her presence and identity seem to be taken for granted. And yet, in contrast to the silence about her throughout the gospel, she becomes the main protagonist in the Easter morning story in chapter 20, when the resurrected Christ first appears to her and commissions her to proclaim the good news (20:11–18).

Finally, Mary of Bethany, together with her sister Martha, features only in chapters 11 and 12, and is also never mentioned during Jesus's early ministry, though Jesus is said to have loved them and their brother Lazarus (11:5) and obviously was a frequent guest in their house in Bethany near Jerusalem. When Mary of Bethany is introduced, she is defined as the one who anointed Jesus (11:2), although the act itself occurs only later, in chapter 12. In the context of her brother's death, she is portrayed as the more emotional one of the two sisters, who weeps and laments (11:33), whereas Martha is the more logical and argumentative woman (11:21–27). However, both are equal, and both are presented as hostesses when Jesus returns to their house for Lazarus's resurrection dinner (12:1–8). While Martha serves at the table, Mary serves their guest by anointing him with precious oil, thus preparing him prophetically for his own burial.

Just as Jesus's mother and Mary of Magdala are related to each other, through their standing together at the cross as well as by framing Jesus's life story (chs. 2 and 20), Mary of Bethany and Mary of Magdala are also related to each other, by narrative devices that parallel the scenes at Lazarus's tomb and at Jesus's tomb.[7]

---

7. See "Mary of Bethany and Mary of Magdala—Two Female Characters in the Johannine Passion Narrative: A Feminist, Narrative-Critical Reader Response," in this volume.

The Gospel of Mark

In Mark, the first and oldest gospel, Jesus's mother is portrayed quite differently, though Mark shares with John the absence of a birth or infancy narrative featuring her. Jesus turns up as an adult, without any information, at least in the beginning, about where he has come from. Only in chapter 6 is Jesus's origin from Nazareth mentioned, in the context of his townspeople rejecting him. It is only here in the entire New Testament that Jesus is defined as "the son of Mary" (6:3) by those who claim to know who he is. In chapter 3 Jesus's mother enters the stage the first time, when she, together with his brothers, comes to see him (3:31–32) after she was most likely already among his "own," his family who had tried to restrain him because they thought he had gone out of his mind (3:21). Facing his mother and brothers, Jesus redefines his family as those who are with him and listen to his teaching and who do the will of God (3:33–35). Thus, in principle his mother is not excluded, since members of the old, biological family can become members of the new, spiritual family. However, nowhere in the gospel is she portrayed as coming to believe in her son and following him. There is a huge gap with regard to Jesus's mother in this gospel, and the portrait is not very much in favor of her.

Mary Magdalene is mentioned the first time as one of the women witnesses to Jesus's crucifixion, together with another Mary, the mother of James the younger and Joses, Salome, and many others. They are defined as those who have followed him, served him, and come up with him to Jerusalem (15:40–41). Thus, they are portrayed as real disciples, in terms of Mark's terminology and concept. At Jesus's burial, both Marys watch where the body is laid (15:47). Consequently, they are able to return, together with Salome, when the Sabbath is over, in order to anoint Jesus's body. However, this has become obsolete, and they become the first addressees of the Easter message, commissioned to pass it on to the male disciples. But they seem to fail, when the narrator states that "they said nothing to anyone, for they were afraid" (16:8). Nevertheless, the very existence of the Gospel of Mark testifies to the contrary, which is part of this gospel's irony. If the women had remained silent, there would be no gospel.

The Gospel of Luke

With regard to Jesus's mother, the Third Gospel is the most enthusiastic of them all. She features prominently within the birth and infancy narratives in chapters 1 and 2. Right at the beginning, she is introduced both by her town Nazareth and her name Mary, besides being defined as a "virgin" (Luke 1:26–27). Jesus's origin is portrayed as the work of the Holy Spirit, and Mary as the Lord's faithful maiden. She accepts her vocation communicated by the angel Gabriel (1:26–38), who announces Jesus's birth to her, just as later, according to the legend, another angel had the same task of announcing the birth of a son to Saint Kevin's mother (though without supernatural conception) and that he would become "a father of many monks."[8] In no other gospel is Mary given so much voice, culminating in her song of praise that has come to be known as the Magnificat (1:46–55).

Within the birth narrative in chapter 2, as different from chapter 1, the virginal conception is no issue. Mary and Joseph (who was not mentioned in chapter 1) are indeed simply called "the parents" (2:27, 43, 48) and "the child's father and mother" (2:33). The same applies to the narrative about the twelve-year-old Jesus in the temple (see 2:43, 48) and the narrative of Jesus's rejection in his hometown, Nazareth, where the townspeople ask, "Is not this Joseph's son?" (4:22).

Obviously, two different traditions are behind chapter 1, on the one hand, and chapters 2 and 4, on the other. Apparently, the evangelist had no problem integrating both traditions into his gospel without harmonizing them.[9]

Mary Magdalene is mentioned first among the women who followed Jesus, after having been healed from bad spirits and illnesses, and who provided for him materially (8:2–3). It is only here that Mary Magdalene is characterized as the one who was liberated from seven demons, which has especially kindled (male) interpreters' imagination and fantasy in the course of history. Mary Magdalene, and the others, are not viewed as disciples in the proper sense but as material providers for the Jesus movement, thus indicating that they were wealthy. Without explicit mention of her name, Mary Magdalene is assumed among the women who has come

---

8. Michael Rodgers and Mark Losack, *Glendalough: A Celtic Pilgrimage* (Blackrock: Columba, 1996), 17–18.

9. The lecture was part of my interview for the chair in New Testament at Limerick. I was not offered the position and wonder whether speaking about the nonvirginal conception at Mary Immaculate College might not have been so ideal (even though *immaculate* refers to Mary's own conception; but it is often linked to Jesus's conception). However, Luke—and also Matthew—had no problem with the nonvirginal conception and/or temporal virginity.

with Jesus from Galilee to Jerusalem, who witness his crucifixion, and who see where Jesus's body was laid (23:55). Together with Mary the mother of James and other women she prepares the spices and goes to the tomb in order to anoint Jesus's body. Instead, they receive the Easter message through the two men and pass it on to the apostles, who, however, disregard it as idle tale and do not believe them (24:1-12).

Mary and Martha, who, apart from the Gospel of John, are mentioned only in Luke, feature just within the short narrative 10:38-42. They live in a village somewhere in Galilee and welcome Jesus and the disciples into their home. Strictly speaking, it is only Martha who hosts and serves Jesus, while Mary sits at Jesus's feet and listens to his words, like a true disciple of her teacher. Over against Martha's complaint that Mary leaves all the work to her, Jesus clearly favors Mary over Martha, since the former has chosen the better part.

The Gospel of Matthew

Starting with his lengthy genealogy, Matthew situates Mary within a line of "irregular women" through whom God, nevertheless, works his salvation (Matt 1:1-16). In chapter 1, Mary's virginal conception is assumed. The reference to Isaiah 7:14 in Matthew 1:23 confirms it, but does not prove it. However, Jesus's designation as the "son of the carpenter" in Matthew 13:55-56, as well as the mentioning of his brothers and sisters, suggests that Mary's virginity was understood as temporary, indicated also in 1:25. In Matthew, as completely different from Luke, Joseph is the main protagonist in the birth and infancy narratives. He is the agent, who receives dreams to guide him; Mary is the object of his care and concern, or more specifically, "the child and his mother" (1:18-25; 2:13-23). During Jesus's ministry, Mary is also depicted as coming to Jesus, together with his brothers, and being confronted with Jesus's definition of his true, new family (13:46-50).

Mary Magdalene, together with Mary the mother of James and Joseph, and the mother of the sons of Zebedee, and many other women, is introduced as one of those who remain faithful to the end and witness Jesus's crucifixion (27:55-56). Mary Magdalene and the other Mary sit opposite the tomb when Jesus is buried (27:61) and return after the Sabbath "to see the tomb" (28:1). Encountering the angel, they are commissioned to pass on the resurrection news to the disciples, and they encounter Jesus himself after their departure from the tomb (28:8-10).

The Fourfold Gospel and the Challenge of Reading Intertextually

Since the Fourfold Gospel came into being in the second century, it has challenged readers, if they allowed for the differences and even contradictions, not overlooking them or trying to harmonize them. Reading the three Marys in the Fourfold Gospel is thus like a test case, or a prism, for the more comprehensive problem reflected in it.

The shift from having and using just one gospel to accepting four gospels as authoritative and legitimate representations of the one gospel was perhaps the most momentous event in early Christianity and marked a paradigm shift.[10] Since then, one gospel was always read, consciously or not, in the light of the others. One text was opened up to other texts, in whatever way and direction, independent of their original chronology and sequence. Intertextuality became an essential part of reading the gospels. Consequently, the focus text as well as the intertexts were radically transformed; neither remained the same.

This affected also the characters woven into the texture of the texts. Thus, the Mary of one gospel was transformed by her encounter with her alter ego in one or more of the other gospels. The results are manifold and differ considerably, due to different readers who activate the intertextual potential ever anew in each reading.

This process becomes more complex and multidimensional when we take seriously into account that intertextuality did not commence with the creation of the Fourfold Gospel but was there long before. In fact, in the beginning there was intertextuality.

Intertextuality is at the core of all biblical tradition, both the Hebrew Bible and the New Testament, with regard to writing and reading. All biblical Scriptures were produced in dialogue with, and in rereading and rewriting, other texts, whether written or oral. And all readers, in turn, were reading intertextually from the very beginning, reading the text in front of them in the context of other texts they knew, past and present, and in the context also of their own lives, their self-texts.

To be sure, "intertextuality ... is not a characteristic of some texts as opposed to others but part of the structure of the literary text as such," as Daniel Boyarin states in *Intertextuality and the Reading of Midrash*, in which he attempts a new approach to midrash, viewing it "as a kind of

---

10. Graham N. Stanton, "The Fourfold Gospel," *NTS* 43 (1997): 317–46.

interpretation that continues compositional and interpretive practices found in the biblical canon itself."[11] "The intertextuality of Midrash is thus an outgrowth of intertextuality within the Bible itself."[12]

What Boyarin says with regard to midrash and the Torah may be applied also to New Testament texts, especially the narrative gospel texts, and their interpretations. However, this requires a new approach and a new paradigm.

"Intertextuality is just a playing around," so the (then) professor of New Testament at the University of Münster commented, most self-consciously, on my chapter "Synoptic Women in John: Interfigural Readings" in my book *Transformative Encounters: Jesus and Women Re-viewed*, in a recent brief and nontransformative encounter.[13] Obviously, he also did not appreciate any of my other publications I had sent him earlier, all of them applying the concept of intertextuality in general and interfigurality in particular. I understood that he, a serious scholar and professor with many obligations, had no time, of course, to "play around." A clash of paradigms, as it were.

For more than a decade I have been fascinated with this new approach. Colleagues and students from very different backgrounds, both Jewish and Christian, have responded favorably, or even enthusiastically, and inspired me to keep going.

Reading intertextually has drastically changed my understanding of the nature of biblical texts and of myself in front of the texts, especially since I had come from an exclusively historical-critical paradigm, attempting to discover *the* meaning of the text. This unquestioned belief had been greatly disturbed and finally deconstructed when I had joined, not aware of the consequences, the seminar The Role of the Reader in the Interpretation of the New Testament at the General Meeting of the Society for New Testament Studies in Milan in 1990. Learning of many "meaning-producing dimensions" in a biblical text, and several possible and legitimate interpretations,[14] was like an earthquake, or perhaps the

---

11. Daniel Boyarin, *Intertextuality and the Reading of Midrash* (Bloomington: Indiana University Press, 1994), 14.

12. Boyarin, *Intertextuality and the Reading of Midrash*, 15.

13. Ingrid Rosa Kitzberger, "Synoptic Women in John: Interfigural Readings," in *Transformative Encounters: Jesus and Women Re-viewed*, ed. Kitzberger, BibInt 43 (Leiden: Brill, 2000), 77–111.

14. Daniel Patte, *Ethics of Biblical Interpretation: A Reevaluation* (Louisville: Westminster John Knox, 1995); Patte, *Discipleship according to the Sermon on the*

eruption of a volcano, turning things upside down. Since then I have seriously paid attention to the incarnation of the biblical text, the concrete texture of the text, the ebb and flow of a narrative, with turning points, gaps, and ambivalences. I have been attentive to my own reading process and that of others, curious to understand why different people, both ordinary and scholarly readers, read a text differently.

Intertextuality has become the key to understand this process and to use it as a hermeneutical concept and tool to interpret Scripture.

When on June 3, 1998, exactly six years ago today, I flew over to London to submit the script for my book *The Personal Voice in Biblical Interpretation* to my publisher, a new chapter was opened in my intertextual approach.[15] Since then, I have seriously taken into account also the intertexture of a reader's self-text, including my own. "Can one be critical without being autobiographical?" Patte asks this challenging question in his chapter to my edited volume *Autobiographical Biblical Criticism: Between Text and Self.*[16]

Reading intertextually is disturbing because it challenges the concept of the text as a closed, self-contained unity that can be dealt with and controlled by the reader or interpreter.

Reading intertextually requires a true openness and willingness to be changed and even transformed in the process, to encounter the biblical text as Other, as a subject that processes me as much as I process the text.

Intertextuality is, by its very nature, dialogical, dynamic, creative, border crossing. It acknowledges the rich potential and the surplus of meaning of every text, and especially the biblical texts, and of the readers in front of the texts. Intertextuality takes into account the flowing identities of both text and reader[17] who encounter each other ever anew, opening up new intertexts.

Reading the gospels intertextually acknowledges the very nature of the gospel as the living Word of God.

Mount: Four Legitimate Readings, Four Plausible Views of Discipleship, and Their Relative Values (Valley Forge, PA: Trinity Press International, 1996).

15. Ingrid Rosa Kitzberger, ed., *The Personal Voice in Biblical Interpretation* (London: Routledge, 1999).

16. Daniel Patte, "Can One Be Critical without Being Autobiographical? The Case of Romans 1:26–27," in *Autobiographical Biblical Criticism: Between Text and Self*, ed. Ingrid Rosa Kitzberger (Leiden: Deo, 2002), 34–59.

17. See my chapter "Flowing Identities," in this volume.

With reference to several patristic writers and one recent author, Graham Stanton concludes his article "The Fourfold Gospel" by comparing it "to the rivers of Paradise which flow from the Garden of Eden into the whole known earth at that time (Gen 2.10–14)," and he comments: "The Biblical image of rivers and living, flowing waters was often linked to the gift of the Spirit, as it was by the Fourth Evangelist."[18] And the Spirit blows where it wills (John 3:8); it cannot be caged in.

In his chapter "The Role and Function of the Gospels as Literature," McKnight asks the crucial question, "Is there a function of Gospel texts comparable to the function of literary texts—a function that is faithful to the nature of the Gospels and that remains in a dialectical relationship to dogmatic and historical references?" His answer:

> The Gospels may be viewed in terms of the discovery and creation of a world that is a divine gift and not simply the consequence of human quest and achievement. When the reference of the text is seen as a world of grace and truth, narrow dogmatic and historical references are relativized, no longer seen as the primary goal of study. This world-creating or world-revealing function of the Gospels is comparable to the way art and poetry function in enabling readers to create worlds, to come to know who they are and where they come from and are going, and to better understand their place in life and relation to nature and their fellows.[19]

"The text of the Torah is gapped and dialogical, and into the gaps the reader slips, interpreting and completing the text in accordance with the codes of his or her culture." Thus Boyarin explains the process in which the rabbis were rereading the Bible and creating midrashim.[20] Coincidentally, I used a very similar image for the first time in my paper " 'The Truth Will Make You Free' (John 8:32): The Power of the Personal Voice and Readings of/from the Gospel of John," presented at the International Research Consultation on Ideology, Power, and Interpretation at the University of Birmingham in August 1997.[21] There I compared the structure and surface of the gospel narratives with the rocky and uneven surface of Mars, having been inspired by the spectacular Mars expedition and the

---

18. Stanton, "Fourfold Gospel," 345–46.
19. Edgar V. McKnight, *Jesus Christ in History and Scripture: A Poetic and Sectarian Perspective* (Macon, GA: Mercer University Press, 1999), 80.
20. Boyarin, *Intertextuality and the Reading of Midrash*, 15.
21. First published in this volume.

stunning pictures. From Croatto I have learned that all biblical texts are open. They are literally open, but especially pragmatically open and need to be continued in our lives.[22]

Epilogue

Standing at the Sea of Galilee, I feel the gentle breeze coming from behind, enfolding me. It is June 1990, and I have been invited to give a sermon to this very mixed small community that has gathered here at Tabgha on this holiday morning to celebrate the Eucharist. With Magdala to my left, I imagine Jesus and Mary Magdalene meeting for the first time over there, when he—embarking on his mission—had come down the Wadi Hammam from Nazareth to the Sea of Galilee. I imagine Mary was the first person he met and called, just as she was the first to whom he appeared after his resurrection.

∞

It is June 2002, and I am attending the Sunday service in Saint Mary Magdalen, the Dominican parish church in Berkeley. A song culminating in the refrain "Here I am, Lord!" which I hear for the first time, touches me deeply, containing a calling, without yet knowing exactly what it is.

Since then, I have cross-referenced this song with Mary Magdalene and imagined her first encounter with Jesus as a calling in the night, similar to Nicodemus's encounter with Jesus (see John 3), demanding nothing less than being reborn and embarking on a new journey.

---

22. J. Severino Croatto, "The Function of the Non-fulfilled Promises: Reading the Pentateuch from the Perspective of the Latin-American Oppressed People," in Kitzberger, *Personal Voice in Biblical Interpretation*, 38–52.

Aging and Birthing: Open-Ended Stories and a Hermeneutics of Promise

In my beginning is my end ...
In my end is my beginning.
— T. S. Eliot, *Four Quartets, East Coker*

How can anyone be born after having grown old?
Can one enter a second time into the mother's womb and be born?
— John 3:4

Can a child be born to a man who is a hundred years old? ...
Shall I indeed bear a child, now that I am old?
— Genesis 17:17; 18:13

Personal Voices, or How Age Matters

"How old was she?" he asked me after I had finished reading the text to him. "I don't know," I said, "the text does not tell us. Perhaps she was your age, perhaps mine."

The question was an immediate response to John 20:11–18 and referred to Mary Magdalene. I was puzzled, even more so as a mentally handicapped young man, almost twenty-six at the time, asked me this question. Being illiterate, Rainer enjoyed my reading biblical texts to him last year when I worked as chaplain in the psychiatric clinic where he lives. In fact, I myself had not questioned Mary Magdalene's age all these years of being a New Testament scholar and had just taken for granted

---

This chapter was first published as "Aging and Birthing: Open-Ended Stories and a Hermeneutics of Promise," in *Los caminos inexhauribles de la Palabra: Las relecturas creativas* en *la Biblia y* de *la Biblia; Homenaje a J. Severino Croatto*, ed. Guillermo Hansen (Buenos Aires: Lumen-ISEDET, 2000), 387–411.

that she was about Jesus's age, until I encountered a picture portraying Mary Magdalene, together with the Madonna and Child, and about the same age as Jesus's mother, in the Barber Institute of Fine Arts at the University of Birmingham (UK) in the summer of 1997, when attending the General Meeting of the Society for New Testament Studies there.[2] Besides the evocative effect of Mary Magdalene's encounter with Mary and Jesus already soon after his birth, my reimagining her as an older woman strongly affected my rereadings of all the New Testament passages in which she is explicitly or implicitly mentioned.

A similar experience and effect happened in the wake of encountering another picture, this time on a simple card and not in such a renowned art gallery, of Thomas encountering the resurrected Jesus, according to John 20:24–29.[3] Thomas is portrayed as an old man, with gray hair and a gray beard. As with Mary Magdalene, I had, until then, taken for granted that he was about Jesus's age and thus a young, not an old, man. What a difference it made to see the old man kneeling before Jesus and touching his pierced side!

For sure, age is an important aspect of characterization, and the way we as readers perceive a biblical character depends also on the age of the man or woman in question. And yet it is striking, how, more often than not, the age of a biblical character, in particular in the New Testament, is not mentioned in the text. Thus, unless we have other, perhaps more indirect, indications, this gap in the text, and thus its openness, calls for and challenges the reader's activity and constructive imagination. Consequently, also, his or her chance of identifying with a biblical character depends partly on the reconstruction of the age of this character. Hence, as we are focusing on age, we might shift from identifying with one character to another as we move through the different ages in our own lives, from young to old, no matter how we define these stages.

Since reimagining Mary Magdalene as maybe being a middle-aged woman like myself,[4] I have come to reread John 20:11–18 in particular,

---

2. Gaudenzio Ferrari (?), *The Madonna and Child with St Mary Magdalene and a Bishop*.

3. "Der auferstandene Herr und Thomas" ("The Risen Lord and Thomas"), prayer-book illustration, from the workshop of the "Meister der Maria von Geldern," dated around 1420, in private ownership.

4. If she was indeed about the same age as Jesus's mother, then, by the time Jesus started his mission and Mary Magdalene joined him as one of his disciples, she was

one of my favorite biblical texts, with very different eyes, and transformation has happened within both worlds, the gospel story-world and my own story-world, influencing each other in a mutual and intertextual fashion.[5]

As I am increasingly confronted with my own aging process, having turned forty-five last year, while not knowing whether I shall live long enough to experience the "second" half of life, I am happy to write this chapter in honor of someone who has just turned seventy, yet in fact feels middle-aged, and for sure has remained young at heart.

For the past couple of years, and in particular since preparing a paper for the Johannine Literature section at the Annual Meeting of the American Academy of Religion/Society of Biblical Literature in New Orleans in 1996, I have become especially attracted to Nicodemus.[6] He was soon to be followed by other biblical characters who are old and yet seem to experience a turning point in their lives as they are confronted with the chance of a new beginning. This is expressed in terms of birth or rebirth. Consequently, aging and birthing come together and eventually become one and the same process. Or, alternatively, they are stories of old people encountering a newborn child. Therefore, this paper is about my fascination for some of the biblical stories that feature old men and women who experience a new beginning as they are approaching the end of their lives. These are stories of hope and promise, for all of us, regardless of our age.

---

probably in her mid-forties. There is, in fact, also a historical indication that Mary Magdalene may indeed have belonged to the same generation as Jesus's mother, due to their Hasmonean name Mary (Mariam), which became popular only after Herod's murder of his wife Mariamne. "The name Mary was given to girls in the generation ahead of Jesus as a nationalistic gesture of protest against Herod. Thus, Mary of Magdala may well have been old enough to be Jesus' mother." See Marianne Sawicki, "Magdalenes and Tiberiennes: City Women in the Entourage of Jesus," in *Transformative Encounters: Jesus and Women Re-viewed*, ed. Ingrid Rosa Kitzberger, BibInt 43 (Leiden: Brill, 2000), 192.

5. On the intertextual relation between the biblical text and the reader as text, between the biblical story-world and the reader's story-world, see Ingrid Rosa Kitzberger, ed., *The Personal Voice in Biblical Interpretation* (London: Routledge, 1999). See also Janice Capel Anderson and Jeffrey L. Staley, eds., *Taking It Personally: Autobiographical Biblical Criticism*, Semeia 72 (1995); Jeffrey L. Staley, *Reading with a Passion: Rhetoric, Autobiography and the American West in the Gospel of John* (New York: Continuum, 1995).

6. See "'How Can This Be?' (John 3:9): A Feminist-Theological Rereading of the Gospel of John," in this volume.

In exploring these stories, I draw on the concepts of intertextuality and interfigurality, and thus on the relation between texts and the relation between characters in different texts.[7] In particular, I explore the relation between the Gospel of John and the Hebrew Bible, on the one hand, and between the Gospel of John and the Synoptic Gospels, on the other hand.

Thus, this paper also contributes to the *intratextuality* of the Bible and reveals what I consider one of its significant semantic axes.[8]

My approach is a reader-response approach, which takes seriously into account the reader's active role in reconstructing the text within the reading process.[9] Consequently, characterization, too, is understood as achieved by a reader reading biblical characters.[10]

---

7. For the concept of intertextuality, see, e.g., Owen Miller, "Intertextual Identity," in *Identity of the Literary Text*, ed. Mario J. Valdés and Miller (Toronto: University of Toronto Press, 1985), 19–40; Siepke Draisma, ed., *Intertextuality in Biblical Writings: Essays in Honour of Bas van Iersel* (Kampen: Kok Pharos, 1989), 15–26. The term *interfigurality* was coined by Wolfgang G. Müller and refers to "interrelations that exist between characters of different texts" and presents "one of the most important dimensions of intertextuality." See Müller, "Interfigurality: A Study on the Interdependence of Literary Figures," in *Intertextuality*, ed. Heinrich F. Plett, RTT 15 (Berlin: de Gruyter, 1991), 101. See "Mary of Bethany and Mary of Magdala—Two Female Characters in the Johannine Passion Narrative: A Feminist, Narrative-Critical Reader Response," in this volume; Kitzberger, "Synoptic Women in John: Interfigural Readings," in Kitzberger, *Transformative Encounters*, 77–111.

8. On intratextuality, see J. Severino Croatto, *Die Bibel gehört den Armen: Perspektiven einer befreiungstheologischen Hermeneutik*, ÖEH 5 (Munich: Kaiser, 1989), 66–72. On the relation between *intratextuality* and *intertextuality*, see 72. On semantic axes see Croatto, *Die Bibel gehört den Armen*, 70–71, 85. These "semantic axes" or "axes of meaning" structure the Bible as a whole, and to search for them implies to read the Bible anew, from a hermeneutical perspective and supported by semiotics (71). In his volume, Croatto focuses on the "semantic axis" of the liberation of the oppressed.

9. On reader-response criticism, see Edgar V. McKnight, *Post-modern Use of the Bible: The Emergence of Reader-Oriented Criticism* (Nashville: Abingdon, 1990); McKnight, *The Bible and the Reader: An Introduction to Literary Criticism* (Philadelphia: Fortress, 1985); Jane P. Tompkins, ed., *Reader-Response Criticism: From Formalism to Post-structuralism* (Baltimore: Johns Hopkins University Press, 1980).

10. See John Darr, *On Character Building: The Reader and the Rhetoric of Characterization in Luke-Acts* (Louisville: Westminster John Knox, 1992); Elizabeth Struthers Malbon and Adele Berlin, eds., *Characterization in Biblical Literature*, Semeia 63 (1993); Fred W. Burnett, "Characterization and Reader Construction of Characters in the Gospels," in *Listening to the Word of God: A Tribute to Boyce W. Blackwelder*, ed. Barry L. Callen (Anderson, IN: Anderson University Press, 1990), 69–88.

Rebirth of an Old Man: The Story of Nicodemus

He was a Pharisee and a leader of the Jews. One night he decided to go to Jesus. He did not really know why he did so, yet there was this strong urge to get to know this strange, self-appointed rabbi personally and talk with him. "Rabbi," he addressed his colleague, "we know that you are a teacher who has come from God; for no one can do these signs that you do apart from the presence of God." And he waited with curiosity for Jesus's response. Yet, when it came, after a long silence, Nicodemus was completely taken by surprise. "Very truly, I tell you, no one can see the kingdom of God without being born from above." The old man looked up into the night sky and pondered these strange words. He was not sure he had understood them correctly. "Perhaps Jesus meant to say 'being born again'?" he started musing to himself. Finally, he decided to ask Jesus, "How can anyone be born after having grown old? Can one enter a second time into the mother's womb and be born?" It was both his curiosity and his humor that made him confront Jesus with this question. He knew, of course, that what he heard himself saying was impossible. And yet, there was something in Jesus's words that sparked a deep longing, buried in Nicodemus's heart. As he was growing older, he had started yearning for some kind of new beginning, but he did not know where and how to search for it. And now here it was, this strange challenge offered to him by this strange rabbi, who, by the way, could have been his grandson.

∞

Nicodemus is one of the characters unique to the Gospel of John, and—as with so many other characters—we are presented with only a fragmentary picture of the old Pharisee. He enters the stage only three times within the gospel story.

The first time we learn about him is in the narrative of his coming to Jesus by night, as rendered in John 3. It is indeed a strange encounter of one of the Pharisees deciding to visit Jesus in private. But even more surprising is the topic of their conversation. Just imagine Jesus confronting the old man with the subject of a possible rebirth from above![11] For sure, Jesus—

---

11. The Greek word ἄνωθεν can mean both, "again" and "from above." I translate it as "rebirth from above" because, in fact, both meanings are inherent at the same time

or the author of the gospel for that matter—could have chosen a woman, possibly in child-bearing age, in order to develop this typical Johannine topic of "birth of water and the Spirit" (vv. 5, 8) or "rebirth from above" (v. 7). Yet, it is the old man Nicodemus who is faced with the possibility of becoming a "child of God" (1:12–13). Thus, we are also confronted with the invitation that the gospel extends to its readers, whether past or present, to become "children of God" and be "born from God" (1:12–13; see 20:30–31) through encountering Nicodemus. Thereby, the invitation becomes even more challenging and fascinating, because it implies that this promise of a new beginning, inherent in the invitation, is extended to all ages, even to an old and well established man such as Nicodemus. It implies the promise that age does not matter with regard to the new birth or, alternatively, that even in old age there is the chance of a fundamental change in life. In the gospel context, the talk about rebirth is also the invitation to, and birth into, a new community,[12] with members of all ages, as it were.

However, Nicodemus does not yet know all that and, in fact, at this early stage in the gospel story we as readers do not know this either. Though we do know that the talk about rebirth has to do with becoming a "child of God," as we have—different from Nicodemus—read the prologue (1:1–18), we learn only later about the community dimension of this experience of initiation, at the very latest when Jesus, before his death, gathers together "his own" in chapter 13 in order to entrust his commandment of love to them.

Having listened to Jesus's strange talk about (re)birth of water and the Spirit, Nicodemus is left puzzled, and so are we. "How can these things be?" he asks (3:9). "Are you a teacher of Israel, and yet you do not understand these things?" (v. 10). Jesus's answer comes as a hard blow indeed, blaming Nicodemus for his lack of understanding, though he seems to try hard to find out by asking a second question, "How?" (see v. 4). And when

---

in the Johannine use of the expression. That Nicodemus was old can be deduced from his question "How can anyone be born after having grown old?" (John 3:4).

12. The expression "kingdom of God" (3:3), which is used only here in John's Gospel and recalls Synoptic terminology, is, according to Moloney, transformed here and refers to the Johannine community, and "rebirth of water and the Spirit" refers to baptism and to entering into this community. See Francis J. Moloney, *Belief in the Word: Reading John 1–4* (Minneapolis: Fortress, 1993), 112–13. See also Craig R. Koester, *Symbolism in the Fourth Gospel: Meaning, Mystery, Community* (Minneapolis: Fortress, 1995), 163–67.

Jesus starts on his long monologue,[13] he also does not provide an answer, and neither does he so much as give Nicodemus a hint on how to answer the question for himself. Thus, Nicodemus is left with the unanswered question. And so are we, the readers. Hence, Nicodemus in the story, and we reading the story, have to journey on with this question and find the answer for ourselves,[14] in the course of the narrative and in the course of our lives.

The second time Nicodemus enters the stage of the gospel story is in chapter 7, where he advocates for Jesus when he is put on trial by the chief priests and fellow Pharisees, who want to arrest him (vv. 32, 45–49). "Our law does not judge people without first giving them a hearing to find out what they are doing, does it?" Nicodemus comes to Jesus's help (v. 51). This seems to be the second, though rather indirect, encounter between Jesus and Nicodemus, but no conversation takes place on this occasion, and there is not the slightest hint from Jesus as to the still-open question. However, this question becomes even more important now that Jesus is confronted with increased hostility, and, in fact, he foretells his own death only a little later (8:21–30). "I am from above," he defines himself in this context (v. 23). While Nicodemus may no longer be present to listen to Jesus's words, any alert reader of the gospel will think of Jesus's previous talk about "rebirth from above." Hence, birth and death come close together. Yet, how this can be, we do not (yet) know.

The third and last time Nicodemus comes to the fore is after Jesus's death, when he joins Joseph of Arimathea in burying Jesus's body in a garden tomb near the place where he was crucified (19:38–42). Nicodemus is identified as the one who had at first come to Jesus by night (v. 39). This is a clear text signal for us readers to link the scene of their last encounter to the scene of their first encounter. And watching (by reading the text) and imagining (by filling in the gaps in the story) Nicodemus anointing Jesus's bloodstained body with the huge amount of a hundred

---

13. The monologue begins in 3:11 and continues through to v. 21. However, Jesus's words to Nicodemus merge with the voice of the narrator, and thus not the whole passage is addressed to Nicodemus. See Derek Tovey, "From Teller-Character to Reflection-Character: The Narrative Dynamic in John 3," in *Narrative Art and Act in the Fourth Gospel*, JSNTSup 151 (Sheffield: Sheffield Academic, 1997), 148–67.

14. The motif of the journey is essential for the plot of the gospel. See Fernando F. Segovia, "The Journey(s) of the Word of God: A Reading of the Plot of the Fourth Gospel," *Semeia* 53 (1991), 113–32.

pounds in weight of myrrh and aloes (v. 39), we may wonder whether he was pondering Jesus's strange words of rebirth when being faced so very concretely with his death.

Each of the three encounters between Jesus and Nicodemus is an open-ended narrative. At their first encounter, not only do we not hear a response of Jesus to Nicodemus's question, but we are also left ignorant as to what happened after that. We also do not get to know how and when Nicodemus and Jesus parted company that night. The scene in chapter 7 is also very fragmentary, especially because the text does not tell us anything about the encounter between the two, who obviously have not met since their first encounter. We are left curious as to what happened on a more personal level, how they looked at each other, if at all, what they might have said to each other, and so on. The storyteller, or narrator, obviously was not interested in the development of the relation between the old rabbi and the young rabbi. Or, alternatively, he or she might have chosen to leave the texts open-ended and full of gaps, just the way these texts are. During their final encounter, when Nicodemus is faced with the now-silenced Jesus, he can no longer ask him, "How can these things be?" (see 3:9). Thus, the question becomes more urgent for us as readers. After Nicodemus—together with Joseph or Arimathea—has laid Jesus's body in the tomb (19:41–42), he disappears from the scene, just as he had appeared that first night. However, we as readers journey on,[15] even after Nicodemus's long journey seems to have ended at the garden tomb. We do so with the fragments, questions, and puzzles that we have gathered all along the way of reading John's Gospel. And, in spite of its double ending, the whole gospel remains an open-ended story (20:30–31; 21:25). However, it is precisely because of its open end that the gospel continues in our own lives, in fact in the lives of all readers, whether past or present, young or old. By not answering the question "How?" of rebirth within the story-world, it remains a question to be answered by *us*. Therefore, rebirth is one of the challenges and promises that remain open when we close John's story.

---

15. See Francis J. Moloney, "An Adventure with Nicodemus," in *The Personal Voice in Biblical Interpretation*, ed. Ingrid Rosa Kitzberger (London: Routledge, 1999), 97–110; see 105–6: "My journey with Nicodemus is open-ended.... Nicodemus and I have come a long way, but more adventures lie ahead of us.... At this moment, hopefully only beginning the latter half of my autobiography, I recognize Jesus at the tomb and wonder where my adventure with Nicodemus will lead me." Moloney was fifty-eight years when he wrote these sentences.

As for Nicodemus, we are encouraged to reconstruct his open story by our own reading. I have argued elsewhere that—by taking the context of the gospel seriously into account—we can assume that Nicodemus was in fact reborn when he placed Jesus's body to rest.[16] By openly—and no longer secretly—encountering and honoring Jesus, he shows that he has followed Jesus's call to rebirth and has become one of his disciples.[17]

There is still much more to his story, which we can find out when rereading it carefully. Much has been said about the timing of Nicodemus's first visit at night. And many interpreters who portrayed a very negative picture of Nicodemus, claiming that he never overcame his initial ignorance and did not progress on his journey,[18] take the night as a starting point for their negative evaluation. By reading the night in chapter 3 within the context of the Johannine dualism between darkness and light, night and day, which permeates the whole gospel (see 1:1–4), Nicodemus is considered as belonging to the night. However, there is no necessity or even sufficient evidence for such a reading, as I have demonstrated elsewhere.[19] On the other hand, it is exactly the timing at night that suggests a positive interpretation and opens up this text to other texts, in particular from the Hebrew Bible.

I had been reading and rereading the narrative in John 3 for a long time and became increasingly fascinated by Nicodemus's visiting Jesus by night and their strange conversation about rebirth. I had kept pondering over it even when I was not reading the story. I had started to journey with Nicodemus.[20] One day, or rather night, it happened that I looked up into the sky, and it was a wonderful night with myriads of stars shining brightly. Suddenly the text John 3 opened up for me in two ways.

First, I reimagined the scene of this first encounter as being out in the open, under the night sky, and that changed the scene tremendously. Until

---

16. Kitzberger, "Synoptic Women in John," 94–95, 98.

17. For a positive evaluation of Nicodemus, see Francis J. Moloney, *Glory Not Dishonor: Reading John 13–21* (Minneapolis: Fortress, 1998), 149. Fernando F. Segovia draws attention to the fact that in John the process of becoming a disciple is expressed in terms of birth. See Segovia, *The Farewell of the Word: The Johannine Call to Abide* (Minneapolis: Fortress, 1991), 254.

18. See, for example, D. D. Sylva, "Nicodemus and His Spices," *NTS* 34 (1988): 148–51.

19. Kitzberger, "Synoptic Women in John," 88–95.

20. Like Moloney, though he had started this journey much earlier and of course in a way different from mine. See Moloney, "Adventure with Nicodemus."

then, I had taken for granted, as most readers and interpreters do, that Jesus was located in a house somewhere in Jerusalem when Nicodemus came to visit him that night. That seems only logical, as we are accustomed to visiting someone in a house. However, there are good reasons to assume that Jesus stayed in the open when Nicodemus came to see him. While we know that Jesus stayed in Bethany near Jerusalem in the house of Mary, Martha, and Lazarus (11:1–44; 12:1–8), with whom he had a close relationship, we never hear that anybody housed him when he was in Jerusalem. He rather seems to have been an "alien non-resident individual," choosing public spaces as the location for himself and his disciples.[21]

Second, and as a consequence of the first point, John 3 opened up to Hebrew Bible texts: those in Genesis featuring Abram/Abraham and Sarai/Sarah. And myriads of new meanings were born from these intertextual and interfigural encounters.

An Old Man and Woman Facing Birth: Nicodemus Encounters Abraham and Sarah

"He brought him outside and said, 'Look toward heaven and count the stars, if you are able to count them.'"

Looking up into the starry night, and pondering Nicodemus and his strange confrontation with rebirth at his old age, the story suddenly opened up for me to Abram/Abraham's story, and to Sarai/Sarah's story as a consequence, beginning in Gen 15. Genesis 17 and 18 were to follow in due course.

---

21. Leticia A. Guardiola-Sáenz's fascinating and challenging interpretation supports my assumption of viewing the scene in ch. 3 as taking place out in the open, under the night sky. See Guardiola-Sáenz, "Border Crossing and Its Redemptive Power in John 7:53–8:11: A Cultural Reading of Jesus and *the Accused*," in Kitzberger, *Transformative Encounters*, 267–91. Referring to the scene in chs. 7 and 8 she comments: "So, while the multitude ... seems to conclude the day in the private spaces of their homes, Jesus spends the night in an open public space, on a hill at the margins of Jerusalem. Jesus, as an alien, non-resident individual of the city, wanders outside the walls of Jerusalem. Excluded from the private spaces of the people's homes, voluntarily or involuntarily, Jesus takes over some of the public spaces, like the Mount of Olives, and transforms them into his private space/home" (282–83). See also Sharon H. Ringe, "Encounters in Public Spaces," in *Wisdom's Friends: Community and Christology in the Fourth Gospel* (Louisville: Westminster John Knox, 1999), 57–58, though Ringe thinks that "Nicodemus' furtive visit ... is engineered to take place under cover" (57).

Genesis 15:1–21 tells the story of God's promise of an offspring and of multitudes of descendants to Abram when he complains about being childless (vv. 1–6). "Count the stars, if you are able to count them," God, who comes to Abram in a vision (v. 1), invites him. And then he adds, "So shall your descendants be" (v. 5). Thus, the promise of an offspring implies also the countless descendants that will come after him, and thus it implies the guarantee of the continuity of Abram's life and lineage. This scene must have happened at night, though the text does not mention it explicitly (as in John 3:1), because stars can only be seen at night! The sequence of the narrative in Gen 15, which contains also the promise of the land (vv. 7–8, v. 18), makes clear that verses 7–21 were originally a narrative independent from verses 1–6, though they form a new unity now. One indicator of the genesis of this Genesis text is the fact that, while it must be night already in verse 5, when Abram is invited to count the stars, the sun is going down in verse 12, and the sun has gone down and it is dark in verse 17. The inconsistency is obvious. And yet, in the present new text of verses 1–21, Abram's age comes into focus more clearly only in verse 15: "As for yourself, you shall go to your ancestors in peace; you shall be buried in a good old age." Though this promise implies that Abram will be "in a good old age" some time later on, when he dies, it nevertheless also suggests that he is already old at the time when God promises him an offspring (and the land). Abram's complaint about being childless, and a slave born in his house becoming his heir (vv. 2–3), implies that he had already reached an age when his hope for any offspring of his own was gone. This is made explicit in the two other narratives featuring the promise, Gen 17:1–27 and 18:1–15, though these texts belong to a different tradition respectively, traditions probably different also from Gen 15:1–6.[22]

In Gen 17 Abram/Abraham's age is explicitly mentioned at the beginning and at the end of the narrative. "When Abram was ninety-nine years

---

22. According to the traditional model of Julius Wellhausen, Gen 17:1–27 is attributed to the P tradition, while Gen 18:1–15 belongs to the J tradition, and so does Gen 16:7–21 (apart from the interpolation vv. 13–16). The provenance of Gen 15:1–6, however, is still being debated; it was formerly attributed to an E tradition. See Gerhard von Rad, *Das erste Buch Mose: Genesis*, ATD 2/4 (Göttingen: Vandenhoeck & Ruprecht, 1981), 140–42, 154, 160. For an overview of the genesis of the Pentateuch and recent new models, see Erich Zenger, "Die Entstehung des Pentateuch," in *Einleitung in das Alte Testament*, ed. Zenger et al., KST 1.1 (Stuttgart: Kohlhammer, 1995), 46–75. As the focus of this paper is on the synchronic level and the final, present form of the Genesis text, further discussion of the diachronic level is not necessary.

old, the LORD appeared to Abram" is how the story begins. Abram's age is mentioned first. Thus, the importance of his old age is made clear right at the very beginning (v. 1), and it is repeated at the end of the scene (v. 24). The focus of Gen 17 is on God's covenant with Abram (vv. 2–7), which will be extended to Abram's offspring and those coming after him (vv. 7–10, 19). The sign for this covenant is the circumcision of every male (vv. 10–14), and it is carried out right away, when Abraham, his son Ishmael (by Hagar), and all the men in his house are circumcised at the end of the story (vv. 23–27). Thus, the promise of an offspring, and of generations after him, is embedded into the story of the covenant that God establishes between himself and Abram. Focusing on the age of Abram, the validity of the covenant makes sense only when it does not come to a close when Abram goes to his ancestors. The guarantee of the continuity of his lineage is expressed also in the new name Abram is given. "No longer shall your name be Abram, but your name shall be Abraham; for I have made you the ancestor of a multitude of nations. I will make you exceedingly fruitful; and I will make nations of you, and kings shall come from you. I will establish my covenant between me and you, and your offspring after you throughout their generations, for an everlasting covenant, to be God to you and to your offspring after you" (vv. 5–7). The promise of the land is only subordinated in this context; it is the land that will be given to Abraham's offspring (v. 8).

While Gen 17:1–14 concentrates on God's covenant with Abram/Abraham and the promise of an offspring and generations to come, the focus shifts to his wife Sarai/Sarah in verse 15. However, she does not enter the stage as a real character, and God does not appear to her as he did to Abram/Abraham. She turns up only indirectly, and God refers to her in his talk to Abraham: "As for Sarah your wife, you shall not call her Sarai, but Sarah shall be her name. And I will bless her, and moreover I will give you a son by her. I will bless her, and she shall give rise to nations; kings of peoples shall come from her" (vv. 15–16). Like Abram, Sarai is given a new name in the process, as the ancestress of nations; yet, God does not give her this new name directly but entrusts the name giving to Abraham. Thereby, as the whole story demonstrates, she is viewed as dependent on and subordinated to her husband. God's blessing her is exclusively directed toward the son she is to give birth to for Abraham (v. 16; see v. 21). Likewise, it will be Abraham's task to name his son Isaac (v. 19). God's promise of a son to him by his wife Sarah catches Abraham completely by surprise, and he bursts out in laughing. "Can a child be born to a man who is a hundred years old? Can Sarah, who is ninety years old, bear a child?" he asks God in a mixture of amusement and bewilderment (v. 17).

Having started to read Nicodemus's story in the light of the Genesis texts, because of the text signal "night," it is here, at the latest, that this intertextual reading seems to be suggested also by the author of the gospel. Abraham's words of pure disbelief and puzzlement, "Can a child be born to a man who is a hundred years old? Can Sarah, who is ninety years old bear a child?" (Gen 17:17), recall and connect with Nicodemus's words, "How can anyone be born after having grown old? Can one enter a second time into the mother's womb and be born?" (John 3:4). While Nicodemus is faced with the possibility of a spiritual (re)birth ("of water and the Spirit," vv. 5, 8) and thus with the chance of himself becoming a "child," a "child of God" as it were (John 1:12–13), Abraham is faced with the physical birth of a son. And Sarah is to bear (and give birth to) this son, and thus her womb is mentioned implicitly, Nicodemus's—and any human being's—mother and her womb turn up in Nicodemus's second question. The parallelism between John 3 and Gen 17 is striking. The intertextuality that is established between these texts implies the interfigurality between Nicodemus and Abraham, as it occus also in Gen 15.

Genesis 18 is a narrative very different from the previous narratives in Gen 15 and 17. The most striking difference is the fact that not only Abraham but also Sarah feature as real characters. Both act and speak, and they are partners in the encounter with the divine. "The LORD appeared to Abraham by the oaks of Mamre, as he sat at the entrance of his tent in the heat of the day" is the way this story begins (v. 1). While it was night in Gen 15, it is just the opposite here: the heat of the day. When the "three men" arrive (v. 2), Abraham does not yet know—unlike us reading the story—who these visitors are. By telling the story from Abraham's point of view, dramatic tension is added. Taking the three men for ordinary visitors, Abraham nevertheless extends his great hospitality to them. He invites them in, provides water for the washing of their feet (vv. 2–5), then hastens into the tent to tell Sarah to make cakes (v. 6), and even runs to his herd and chooses a good calf, which he has the servant prepare (v. 7). When he finally serves his guests, he stands by them under the tree while they eat (v. 8). While doing so, they ask for Abraham's wife, Sarah, who has stayed in the tent (v. 9). One of the guests announces his return in due season and Sarah's having a son by then (v. 10). The change from the "three men" acting to the one speaking and making the promise already indicates what is made explicit only a little later: it was the Lord who appeared to

Abraham and Sarah (v. 13). Sarah listens to the promise at the entrance of the tent (v. 10). "Now Abraham and Sarah were old, advanced in age; it had ceased to be with Sarah after the manner of women,"[23] the narrator comments at this turning point in the story (v. 11). While in Gen 17 Abraham's old age was mentioned right at the very beginning (v. 1), and both his and Sarah's age were mentioned after the promise of a son (v. 17), the age comes in here only toward the end of the story, but also after the promise is made. While in Gen 17 Abraham reacted immediately, here it is Sarah who starts laughing at such news and utters her amusement and disbelief: "After I have grown old, and my husband is old, shall I have pleasure?" she muses to herself. And yet the Lord, either by hearing her words or by being just omniscient, as one might expect, knows about Sarah's reaction, and he questions Abraham (not the woman herself!): "Why did Sarah laugh, and say, 'Shall I indeed bear a child, now that I am old?'" (v. 13). The next question, "Is anything too wonderful for the LORD?" seems to be the question of the Lord himself, not an indirect quotation of Sarah's words. The shift between Sarah's direct words and their quotation by the Lord is significant. For one thing, the latter mentions only her old age,[24] not that of her husband; on the other hand, Sarah's reference to her pleasure is domesticated by referring to her bearing a child, thus referring to the result of and not the act of having pleasure. Voicing sexual pleasure by God himself seemed to be indecent to the author of this story, yet naming it at all, though by Sarah herself, shows his down-to-earth attitude. The traditions in Gen 15 and 17 did not even hint at the act of baby making. Sarah's words, and their variation in the quotation, are reminiscent of Abraham's words in Gen 17:17, in particular the second part: "Can Sarah, who is ninety years old, bear a child?" Here, however, it is Sarah herself who voices her doubts. And in particular the quote "Shall I indeed bear a child, now that I am old?" sounds very much like Abraham's voice, but with the significant shift from Sarah as object to her as subject. However, her words also recall

---

23. In the genealogy Gen 11:27–32 Sarai was introduced as Abram's wife (v. 29), and the childlessness was attributed to her barrenness, not the old age of both husband and wife: "Now Sarai was barren; she had no child" (11:30). It is assumed that both texts, Gen 11 and Gen 18, belong to the same tradition (J).

24. There is also a difference in mentioning the age of Sarah, which in the NRSV does not show up. Sarah's drastic version *balah*, whose literary meaning denotes the rotting of old clothing, is not repeated by the Lord. See von Rad, *Das erste Buch Mose: Genesis*, 162.

Nicodemus's response, "How can anyone be born after having grown old? Can one enter a second time into the mother's womb and be born?" (John 3:4). Again, it seems that the author of John indeed intends that John 3 be read in the light of Genesis, this time Gen 18. By opening the focus text John 3 to the intertext Gen 18, interfigurality is also established here. But this time the interfigurality refers to Nicodemus and Sarah. This is most striking, and it shows the transcendence of gender boundaries,[25] which is such an important feature in the Gospel of John. While Sarah questions the possibility of the actual birth of a child to her, Nicodemus questions his own rebirth and thus his becoming a child. Yet, while Sarah—like Abraham—laughed at the news, Nicodemus seems to be left speechless after his second question, "How?" However, we might imagine him laughing, or at least smiling, when he asked Jesus the first time, about rebirth in old age. By adding the funny remark about returning to the mother's womb, some humor is also added to this story, and a new aspect is added to the characterization of Nicodemus.

Like Nicodemus's story in John, and in fact the Gospel of John as a whole, the narratives in Genesis, and the Pentateuch as a whole, remain open-ended. Though the actual birth of the son to Abraham and Sarah is narrated within the story (Gen 21:1–7), while Nicodemus's rebirth is not narrated and can only be deduced from the unfolding of the story, the Genesis stories nevertheless remain open-ended. The Pentateuch ends without the gift of the land, which thus remains a nonfulfilled promise.[26] Thereby, the text has a function similar to the Gospel of John: its open end opens it pragmatically to its readers, past and present.[27] Thus, the promise,

---

25. See Kitzberger, "Synoptic Women in John"; "Transcending Gender Boundaries in John," in this volume.

26. See J. Severino Croatto, "The Function of the Non-fulfilled Promises: Reading the Pentateuch from the Perspective of the Latin-American Oppressed People," in Kitzberger, *Personal Voice in Biblical Interpretation*, 38–52.

27. As Croatto expresses this so very well: "The work, composed to be read as it is (neither as an Hexateuch nor as an Enneateuch), seeks to generate hope in the addressees and to move them toward a new liberation process.... The Pentateuch, as a new 'unfinished' literary symphony bears a vital message, precisely because it is *unfinished*" ("Function of the Non-fulfilled Promises," 43). "But what, in a literary sense, is closed—and must be read as such—is open *pragmatically*. What I mean by this distinction is that every text proposes something that the reader must 'fulfil' in some way. The text continues in the life of its addressees.... The manner in which the Pentateuch

whether of rebirth or of the land, becomes a promise not only to the characters in the story but also to readers of all ages and locations.

Both my pondering over the old man Nicodemus being faced with rebirth and the timing of his first visit with Jesus at night have opened up his story to the stories of Abraham and Sarah in Genesis, with all the intertextual and interfigural meanings engendered by this encounter. By reading Nicodemus's story in the light of the stories of Abraham and Sarah, new dimensions were added to his characterization. Also, the positive evaluation that I had suggested already as a consequence of reading his story within the context of John's Gospel has been confirmed and even expanded. However, as a result of these intertextual/interfigural readings, new dimensions have been added also to the characterization of Abraham and Sarah. Though, of course, the authors of the Abraham/Sarah traditions had no idea yet of John and a story about Nicodemus, and consequently an intertextual/interfigural reading the other way around does not work if approached author oriented, we as present readers with the whole Bible in our hands can do so. In fact, since Nicodemus's encounter with Abraham and Sarah, I cannot but read their stories in the light of his story, too. Thus the *intratextuality* of the Bible is once again made explicit. *All* texts interpret one another in mutual fashion, and "semantic axes" come to the fore.

Returning to Nicodemus in John, there is still another intertextual/interfigural reading to which the Johannine texts, in particular John 3—and John 19, in due course—open up. Wondering about the strange association of Nicodemus with the issue of (re)birth in John 3, I have come to think of the only other old man in New Testament tradition who is faced with birth: Simeon. And, as a consequence, a woman also comes to the fore: Anna.

An Old Man and Woman Face a Newborn Child: Nicodemus Encounters Simeon and Anna

> Guided by the Spirit, Simeon came into the temple; and when the parents brought in the child Jesus, to do for him what was customary under the law, Simeon took him in his arms and praised God, saying, "Master, now you are dismissing your servant in peace, according to your word; for my eyes have seen your salvation, which you have prepared in the

---

closes is precisely its opening to the praxis of its addressees, whether those in the past or of ourselves as present readers" (39).

presence of all peoples, a light for revelation to the Gentiles and for glory to your people Israel."

For a long time I have been moved by Luke's description of the story of Simeon and his encounter with baby Jesus, as rendered in Luke 2:21–40 and culminating in the above-quoted scene in verses 27–32. There is the story of an old man who has been waiting for this very moment all his long life, and obviously he did not give up hope when year after year passed by. His trust was based on God's words ("according to your words," v. 29), who had addressed the promise and the fulfilment to him: to see salvation with his own eyes before his death (v. 30). Or, in the narrator's voice: "It had been revealed to him by the Holy Spirit that he would not see death[28] before he had seen the Lord's Messiah" (v. 26). When he takes the newborn Jesus into his arms, his life comes to a close and he can go in peace.[29] The arrival of the child and the departure of the old man overlap at this very moment in history, foremost in the history of the old man himself. However, his actual departure is not narrated in the story, which thus remains open-ended. It is again left to the readers to imagine Simeon's death after his encounter with Jesus. But by leaving the story open-ended, another important dimension seems to be communicated by the author or narrator: Simeon's end is in fact a new beginning, a new future lies ahead of him beyond death,[30] and he embarks on the journey toward the new horizon.

There are some striking parallels, though in a reversed manner, between Nicodemus and Simeon. To start with, both are old men, and

---

28. See Joseph A. Fitzmyer, *The Gospel according to Luke 1–IX*, AB 28 (Garden City, NY: Doubleday, 1981), 427: "From this expression Simeon's old age is usually deduced." See the element of peace also in God's promise to Abram in Gen 15:15: "You shall go to your ancestors in peace; you shall be buried in good old age."

29. See Raymond E. Brown, *The Birth of the Messiah: A Commentary on the Infancy Narratives in the Gospels of Matthew and Luke*, ABRL (New York: Doubleday, 1993), 438: "The reference in the Nunc Dimittis to Simeon's willingness to die has led to the plausible supposition that Luke thinks of him as an old man." According to Pseudo-Matthew 15:2, Simeon was 112 years old.

30. It is a most striking and meaningful coincidence that Rembrandt died while working on his last piece, *Simeon with the Christ Child*, with the almost-finished painting left on the easel. Then, on October 4, 1669, he was sixty-three years old and tired from the misery of his last years. Obviously, Rembrandt imagined himself as Simeon when painting the picture. See Jörg Zink, *Was die Nacht hell macht: Rembrandt malt die Weihnachtsgeschichte* (Eschbach: Verlag am Eschbach, 1997), 17–18.

both are faced with rebirth or birth respectively. However, for Nicodemus the challenge of rebirth comes as a complete surprise, while Simeon has been waiting all his life to see the newborn Messiah. While Nicodemus starts on a new journey only now, in his old age, Simeon seems to have come to the end of a very long journey, lasting all his life. But, in fact, also he is about to embark on a new journey in old age. Both stories remain open-ended. While Nicodemus comes to Jesus the first time while he is staying in Jerusalem, and after Jesus's cleansing of the temple and his announcement of the destruction of the temple, thereby meaning his own body (John 2:13–25), Simeon encounters the newborn Jesus when he is brought into the temple in Jerusalem by his parents, when they come to fulfill the requirements of purification (Luke 2:22–24).[31] There is still another important text dimension that links the stories of these two old men together: the (Holy) Spirit. The (re)birth promised to Nicodemus happens in water and the Spirit (John 3:5, 8). The Holy Spirit rested on Simeon all the time he was waiting (Luke 2:25), it was revealed to him by the Holy Spirit that he would not see death before he had seen the Lord's Messiah (v. 26), and it was finally the Holy Spirit who again guided him into the temple that very day (v. 27). By opening up John 3 to Luke 2, the interfigurality between Nicodemus and Simeon becomes obvious, and the story of the first can be read in the light of the latter.[32]

But there are still further dimensions of an intertextual reading. In John 3, Nicodemus is left amazed (v. 7) at Jesus's strange words about rebirth and asks, "How can these things be?" (v. 9). In Luke 2, "the child's father and mother were amazed at what was being said about him" (v. 33) after listening to Simeon's strange words about the newborn child in his

---

31. The temple (ἱερόν) refers to the temple court, as different from the temple sanctuary (ναός). "Since Simeon encounters Mary, he is either in the court of the Gentiles or the court of the women" (Brown, *Birth of the Messiah*, 439). The purification refers to Mary, the mother, as required forty days after birth (for a male child), according to Lev 12. However, the presentation of a firstborn in the Jerusalem temple is mentioned neither in the Hebrew Bible nor in the Mishnah; further, there is nothing about the need of a purification of the firstborn son. See Fitzmyer, *Luke*, 421, 425. See also Brown (*Birth of the Messiah*, 448–51) on the problem of the occasion for the family's coming to the temple: "Luke seems to have confused" the consecration or presentation of the child, on the one hand, and the purification of the mother, on the other hand (447).

32. See also further verbal links between John 3 and Luke 2: human being (ἄνθρωπος; John 3:1, 3; Luke 2:25); "his name" (ὄνομα αὐτῷ; John 3:1; Luke 2:21; see v. 25).

arms (vv. 28–32). However, the parents do not ask any questions. Nor does Mary, when she is confronted with Simeon's prophecy following right away: "This child is destined for the falling and rising of many in Israel, and to be a sign that will be opposed so that the inner thoughts of many will be revealed—and a sword will pierce your own soul" (vv. 33–35). While Mary asked, "How can this be?" after the angel Gabriel had announced Jesus's birth to her (1:26–38, v. 34) and was then put into the picture, she and Joseph seem to react here in the first temple scene just like Mary did later on, after having found the twelve-year-old boy in the temple, who confronted them with the upsetting question, "Why were you searching for me? Did you not know that I must be in my father's house?" (2:49)— "His mother treasured all these things in her heart" (v. 51). Focusing on the amazement, interfigurality is also established between Nicodemus and Mary (and Jesus's father). Though this is only a minor aspect here, I have shown elsewhere how much an interfigural reading between Nicodemus and Jesus's mother is suggested by the Gospel of John.[33]

However, the story of Jesus's presentation in the temple is not yet over after Simeon's encounter with the newborn child and his parents, because he is not alone. Anna, a prophetess and a daughter of Phanuel, of the tribe of Asher, is also there (v. 36). While Simeon comes to the temple, guided by the Spirit, she is already there, as she never leaves the temple and worships there with fasting and praying night and day (v. 37). When the family arrives, she comes to them and "began to praise God and to speak about the child to all who were looking for the redemption of Jerusalem" (v. 38). This scene is much shorter than the previous one featuring Simeon's encounter. And it seems that Anna does not take the newborn Jesus in her arms, as one would have expected (at least when thinking in stereotypical gender roles). At least the story does not tell us that. But once again, it is open to the imagination of the reader to see Simeon hand baby Jesus over to Anna after his blessing Jesus's mother. In spite of the brevity of this second part of the story in the temple, the description of Anna is more

---

33. See Kitzberger, "Synoptic Women in John," 96–99, 109. The interfigurality between Nicodemus and the Lukan Mary (unnamed in John) testifies also to the transcendence of gender boundaries in John (see 109). There are further verbal links between John 3 and Luke 2: the womb (κοιλία) in Nicodemus's words John 3:4 corresponds with the womb (implicit: of Mary) in Luke 2:21 and the womb (in general) in Luke 2:22 (literally: "every male that opens the womb" = the firstborn); the mother (μητήρ) in general in John 3:4 corresponds with mother Mary in Luke 2:34.

detailed than that of Simeon, and we thus get to know more about her biography.[34] The emphasis is on her great age, given as eighty-four,[35] and she is defined as a widow who lived seven years with her husband after her marriage (vv. 36–37). Obviously, she has remained childless.[36] Now, in old age, she encounters the child Jesus, and—being a prophetess—she immediately knows who he is and thus can speak about him right away (v. 38). Different from Simeon, no imminent death is reported, and it is again left to the reader's imagination whether she lived longer or joined Simeon on departing on his last journey. Like Simeon's story, also hers remains open-ended. By Anna's facing the newborn child, intertextuality is also suggested between Nicodemus and her, though it is not as explicit as with Simeon. Anna's prayer by night (and day) might provide another, though minor, link to Nicodemus's visit with Jesus at night (though the scene in Luke 2 obviously happened during the day).

There is still another intertextual link that deserves notice. In Luke 2:35, Simeon addresses Mary with his prophetic foresight that a sword will pierce her soul.[37] Thus, so very soon after Jesus's birth, Mary is already confronted with future suffering that her son's mission will bring about, because it will be a mission including sharp divisions even among the closest family members.[38] As a last consequence, the division[39] that

---

34. The passage Luke 2:22–40 is modeled on 1 Sam 1–2. There, the emphasis is on Samuel's mother, Hanna (Anna). See Brown, *Birth of the Messiah*, 446, 450–51.

35. Anna's age has been debated, depending on the choice of textual variants (ὡς or ἕως in v. 37). Accordingly, eighty-four refers either to her total age or the time of her widowhood. Brown (*Birth of the Messiah*, 442) chose the latter version; consequently, Anna's total age is about 103.

36. Most likely, Simeon was also childless, and perhaps also unmarried; otherwise, we might expect mention of it in the text. However, according to the (apocryphal) Acts of Pilate (17:1), Simeon had two sons, whom Jesus raised from the dead.

37. The Greek ψυχή translated as "soul," denotes "the locus of emotion and affections, the heart" (Brown, *Birth of the Messiah*, 441).

38. Simeon's words about the sword piercing Mary's soul have engendered extensive reflections and interpretations in the past and present, as listed by Brown, *Birth of the Messiah*, 462–63. The most popular one, referring to the *mater dolorosa*, is rejected by both Brown (441, 462) and Fitzmyer (*Luke*, 429). Interpreting the words within the context of Luke's Gospel, Brown understands the sword as one of discrimination (see Ezek 5:1–2; 6:8–9; 12:14–16), which he considers in perfect harmony with Luke 2:34c and 12:51–53, the latter referring to the division among families that Jesus will bring about. Mary, like the others, has to pass the test and recognize the sign (see 2:34c; Brown, *Birth of the Messiah*, 464–65). "And indeed her special anguish, as the

Jesus will bring (Luke 12:51–53) will lead to and be revealed in extreme at his crucifixion.

In John's crucifixion scene, Jesus's mother is portrayed as standing at the foot of the cross, together with three other women: her sister, Mary the wife of Clopas, and Mary Magdalene (19:25–27).[40] Most readers of John who are familiar with the Synoptic Gospels will think of Simeon's prophetic words in Luke 2:35, and intertextuality is established between the Johannine crucifixion scene and the Lukan temple scene,[41] thereby linking together closely death and birth. Viewing the scene at the cross, we are invited to recall Mary's encounter with Simeon and to read the first in the light of the latter and thus have new meaning dimensions added. In fact, by placing Jesus's mother at the foot of the cross, a scene unique to John's Gospel, John himself seems to have reinterpreted Simeon's words as referring to Jesus's death.[42]

Recalling Jesus's physical birth and the newborn child being brought to the temple is further suggested by another important dimension of

---

sword of discrimination passes through her soul, will consist in recognizing that the claims of Jesus's heavenly Father outrank any human attachments between him and his mother, a lesson that she will begin to learn already in the next scene (2:48–50)" (465). Fitzmyer also refers to the transcendence of family ties; see Luke 8:21; 11:27–28 (*Luke*, 430).

39. Note "sword" in the Matthean version of this tradition from Q in Matt 10:34–36. See Brown, *Birth of the Messiah*, 464: "Luke's form of the saying omits the reference to the sword, but in 2:35a he refers to the sword of discrimination with the same meaning that it has in Matthew's form of the Q saying."

40. It has been debated whether three or four women are mentioned at the cross, that is, whether the sister of Jesus's mother is identical with Mary wife of Clopas. There are two main reasons to identify them as two different women: first, it is rather unlikely that two sisters of the same family should have been called Mary, and second, the four women would contrast with the four soldiers in 19:23. However, it remains strange that only the mother's sister (besides the mother herself, of course) is not mentioned by name.

41. This intertextuality has been established also by generations of artists, both painters and sculptors, who portrayed Jesus's mother at the foot of the cross with a sword piercing her, thus symbolizing her pain, which is beyond words.

42. Note the shift in meaning between Luke and John. While the interpretation of the sword as referring to division and contradiction is the most plausible one within the Lukan context (see n. 38), already John, and many subsequent readers of the gospels, reinterpreted Simeon's words and applied them to the anguish of Jesus's mother at the foot of the cross. This, for sure, is a legitimate interpretation.

the Johannine crucifixion scene. Read in the context of the gospel, it is in fact a birthing scene.[43] When hanging on the cross, Jesus gives[44] his Spirit (19:30; see 7:39). Thus, those of his followers witnessing the scene—the four women and the Beloved Disciple (vv. 25–27)—are reborn of the Spirit (see 3:5) and thus become "children of God" (1:12–13). Different from Luke 2, the birth is understood in a spiritual sense. In John 19, therefore, the rebirth (of the Spirit) of Jesus's mother and her actual giving birth to him are brought together by this intertextual reading. Furthermore, Jesus's words about the destruction of the temple (and his raising it up in three days)—thereby referring to the temple of his body (2:19–21)—which are fulfilled now that he is lifted up on the cross, recall the Lukan temple scene.

But the crucifixion scene recalls also the scene of Nicodemus's visit in John 3. After speaking about rebirth, Jesus mentions his death, which is described as the lifting up of the Son of Man (3:14). Thus, birth and death are again closely linked. Besides that, the subject of salvation links John 3 to Luke 2: God sent his Son into the world in order that it might be saved through him (John 3:17); Simeon's eyes have seen God's salvation, which he has prepared in the presence of all peoples (Luke 2:30–31).

By realizing the various intertextual links between the crucifixion scene in John 19 and the temple scene in Luke 2, the intertextual readings of John 3 and Luke 2, and hence the interfigurality between Nicodemus and Simeon, are confirmed. As readers, we are invited to vacillate between the two gospels, and also to vascillate between the chapters in John, and consequently reconstruct new meanings of the texts in the process of reading.

The End Is Where We Start From

We have come a long way. After journeying with Nicodemus through John's Gospel, we left the confines of the gospel and ventured out into the

---

43. See also Judith M. Lieu, who relates the crucifixion scene, and in particular Jesus's mother, to the parable in 16:21. She asks, "So is this a birthing or a dying? ...; we meet birth here only when we encounter death. Indeed, the birth, which is not narrated in the Gospel, becomes through 16:21 a death, or is the death a birth?" See Lieu, "The Mother of the Son in the Fourth Gospel," *JBL* 117 (1998): 73.

44. The NRSV is not correct here. The Greek reads παρέδωκεν τὸ πνεῦμα.

story-worlds of the Hebrew Bible and of the Synoptic Gospels. We witnessed Nicodemus's encounter with Abram/Abraham and Sarai/Sarah, but also with Simeon and Anna. By realizing the interfigurality between Nicodemus and the other characters, all of them have undergone transformation. Nicodemus's characterization has been enriched, and new dimensions have been added. But the same is true the other way around. As a consequence of the intertextual and interfigural readings presented in this paper, we are encouraged and empowered to read also the stories of Abram/Abraham and Sarai/Sarah, Simeon and Anna, in the light of Nicodemus's story and thus have new meaning dimensions added to their characterization, too. Thereby, gender boundaries are transcended. By connecting Nicodemus not only to Abram/Abraham and Simeon but also to Sarai/Sarah and Anna (and to Mary, Jesus's mother), this becomes obvious. For John, gender roles and gender stereotypes seem to have been no limiting boundaries. On the contrary, these boundaries are meant to be overcome. Consequently, reading the Gospel of John calls for a truly liberating praxis of gender antiapartheid also in the lives of its readers, past and present. Such a praxis is modeled on the Johannine community, which is distinguished by equality between men and women.

Encountering these male and female characters, Nicodemus, Abram/Abraham, Sarai/Sarah, Simeon and Anna, and journeying with them for a while, we have come a long way indeed. However, like them we have not come to an end. Reaching the end of our journey through the biblical stories, we are encouraged to embark on our own journeys. Their open-ended stories are also pragmatically open and thus are meant to continue in our lives as readers, past and present. No matter what age we are, these stories of old women and men who are met with the challenge and promise of birth, whether in a physical or spiritual sense, hold a rich potential of promise and hope also for us. The message is: aging, and even death, can be transformed into the experience of birthing and (re)birth. Further, these stories testify to an important semantic axis, and thus to the *intratextuality* of the Bible, which reveals the biblical God—of the Hebrew Bible and the New Testament—as a God of promises for all ages. No matter whether these promises are fulfilled within the story-world or remain unfulfilled by the time we come to the end of the story, they are promises to be fulfilled in the lives of us, the readers. Consequently, these texts in John, Genesis, and Luke call for a hermeneutics of promise, as applied in this paper. Such a hermeneutics makes explicit those meaning dimensions in the texts that testify to God's promises, and it aims at the reconstruction of our own lives[45]—as individuals and communities—according to these promises. This implies that we trust in God's never-ending creative power, in particular when old age and death come on us, and that we be open to a new beginning at any time in our lives. Thereby, T. S. Eliot's words may come true:

> What we call the beginning is often the end.
> And to make an end is to make a beginning.
> The end is where we start from.[46]

---

45. See Anthony C. Thiselton, "Communicative Action and Promise in Interdisciplinary, Biblical, and Theological Hermeneutics," in *The Promise of Hermeneutics*, ed. Roger Lundin, Clarence Walhout, and Thiselton (Grand Rapids, MI: Eerdmans, 1999), 133–39. He deals with promises in the context of speech-act theory and mentions as one of the four senses of his *hermeneutics of promise*: "According to the central traditions of the Old and New Testaments, *communicative acts of declaration, proclamation, call, appointment, command, worship, and most especially promise are constitutive of what it is for the word of God to become operative and effective*" (133). Further, "*Promising* constitutes a *very strong illocutionary act*" (236), and "*promise* provides a paradigm case of *how language can transform the world of reality*" (238). On reconstruction, see John D. Vogelsang, "A Hermeneutics of Reconstruction," *Religious Education* 88 (1993): 167–77: "A hermeneutics of reconstruction is a dialogue between the interpreter and the text where alternatives are released and both are altered, leading to the emergence of new truths and a new social order" (169–70).

46. T. S. Eliot, Four Quartets, Little Gidding, V, ll. 1–3, in *The Complete Poems and Plays of T. S. Eliot* (London: Guild, 1986), 197.

Part 3
Characterization and Gender

Untying Lazarus—A Sisters' Task?
Revisioning Gender and Characterization in John 11

Personal Voices

"Lazarus," he cried with a loud voice, "come out!" There was a hush among the crowd gathered at the tomb, and the silence echoed his words and their beating hearts. Tension was in the air, filled with the odor from the corpse. Moments of eternity, dissolving four days into nothingness. There he was, slowly stumbling out of the tomb, his hands and feet bound with strips of cloth, and his face wrapped in a cloth, a lame and blind man, yet back to life. Staring aghast, they watched him, unbelievingly. "Unbind him and let him go," Jesus said, looking at those around him, encouragingly. But nobody dared to move. "Shall we do it?" the sisters whispered to each other, finally breaking the eternal silence. And the question hung in the air like a great promise.

∞

"Maybe something was wrong with the sisters and their brother," she wondered. "Why was Lazarus ill, and what illness was it that caused his death?" she continued her musings. "Maybe it was psychosomatic," she tried to answer her own questions, "maybe he became ill because his sisters were so overpowering?"

∞

This chapter was originally a paper presented at the Annual Meeting of the Society of Biblical Literature, Johannine Literature section, Orlando, November 22, 1998. Revised for this publication.

"To be alive in this text as a male," he concludes, "is to live the death of Lazarus ... to have one's death celebrated prematurely."

∽

Untying the Text: A Readers' Task?

"Unbind him and let him go," Jesus says, but there is no hint as to who should carry out this task. And there is no record either of who does it in the end. Like so many other gospel stories, especially in John,[2] this one also remains open-ended and thus calls for the reader's activity as to how to finish the story or, alternatively, as to how to live with such an open end. "The unfinished task of untying Lazarus becomes the readers' task of untying the text," according to Wilhelm Wuellner.[3]

Reading the text thus implies reconstructing it. Besides its open end, this story, which is one of the longest in all four gospels, is full of twists and turns, gaps and ambivalences[4] that demand an active reader who makes decisions as to how to read. Consequently, each reader creates his or her unique text. Reading, whether ordinary or critical reading, always involves choices between different meaning dimensions in a multidimensional text,[5] including those meaning dimensions that are embedded in the silences of the text, in what is not said at all, or what is articulated in an

---

2. See "'How Can This Be?' (John 3:9): A Feminist-Theological Rereading of the Gospel of John," in this volume.

3. Wilhelm Wuellner, "Putting Life Back into the Lazarus Story and Its Readings: The Narrative Rhetoric of John 11 as the Narration of Faith," *Semeia* 53 (1991): 120. "There opens up a startling 'gap' which the reader is to fill, or rather, *not* to fill.... The unfinished task of untying Lazarus becomes the readers' task of untying the text (Young). This challenge to readers to untie this text is not only unfinished; due to the rhetoric of the narrative of faith, it is an unfinishable task" (120–21).

4. See also Wuellner, "Putting Life Back," 124: "full of jolts, ruptures, and inconsistences"; Jeffrey L. Staley, *Reading with a Passion: Rhetoric, Autobiography and the American West in the Gospel of John* (New York: Continuum 1995), 55–84, esp. 60–66.

5. On "meaning-producing dimensions" and the multidimensionality of biblical texts, see Patte, *Ethics of Biblical Interpretation*; *Discipleship according to the Sermon on the Mount*. On the terminology of ordinary versus critical reading and the interdependence of both readings, see Patte, *Ethics of Biblical Interpretation: A Reevaluation* (Louisville: Westminster John Knox, 1995); Patte, *Discipleship according to the Sermon on the Mount: Four Legitimate Readings, Four Plausible Views, and Their Relative Values* (Valley Forge, PA: Trinity Press International, 1996); Gerald West and Musa

ambivalent way so that a solution is required that has not been supplied by the author or narrator.

Adopting a strictly reader-oriented approach, my focus is on the reading process and thus on the discourse and the rhetorical analysis of the text. Characterization, therefore, is regarded as not simply being provided by the text but as happening in the reading process, in the creative interaction of the reader with the text.[6] Consequently, characterization is also individual and never static, and it implies choices as to how to read. Therefore, the ethical dimension of any reading, and of biblical interpretation in particular,[7] comes to the fore, that is, the question of how our interpretations affect others, and the responsibility we have for our interpretations and for the worlds created by them.

Feminist-Critical Interpretation: Voicing Women, Silencing Men?

Feminist interpretation is, by its very nature, a critical interpretation and a reading against the grain. Analyzing patriarchal texts involves the naming and overcoming of their sexist and oppressive bias. Voicing women and rereading the texts from their hitherto neglected point of view becomes the preeminent task. Equality, justice and liberation are the goals of this struggle.

For many years I have concentrated my research on feminist interpretation and on women in the New Testament, especially in the Gospel of John. In a paper presented at the General Meeting of the Society for New

---

W. Dube, eds., *"Reading With": An Exploration of the Interface between Critical and Ordinary Readings of the Bible; African Overtures*, Semeia 73 (1996).

6. See Elizabeth Struthers Malbon and Adele Berlin, eds., *Characterization in Biblical Literature*, Semeia 63 (1993); Fred W. Burnett, "Characterization and Reader Construction of Characters in the Gospels," in *Listening to the Word of God: A Tribute to Boyce W. Blackwelder*, ed. Barry L. Callen (Anderson, IN: Anderson University Press, 1990), 69–88; Staley, *Reading with a Passion*, esp. 26–54 (on John 5 and 9) and 55–84 (on John 11); Kitzberger, "Mary of Bethany and Mary of Magdala—Two Female Characters in the Johannine Passion Narrative: A Feminist, Narrative-Critical Reader Response," in this volume; and "How Can This Be?," in this volume.

7. See Patte, *Ethics of Biblical Interpretation*; Elisabeth Schüssler Fiorenza, "The Ethics of Biblical Interpretation: Decentering Biblical Scholarship," *JBL* 107 (1988): 3–17; Fiorenza, *Rhetoric and Ethic: The Politics of Biblical Studies* (Minneapolis: Fortress, 1999); Danna Nolan Fewell and Gary A. Phillips, eds., *Ethics, Bible, Reading as If*, Semeia 77 (1998).

Testament Studies in Chicago in 1993, I focused on the pivotal roles of the sisters Mary and Martha of Bethany in John 11 and 12 and on their importance—together with that of the other women, especially Mary Magdalene—in the Gospel of John, who are related to each other by a "christological internet," as I showed in my paper at the Annual Meeting of the Society of Biblical Literature in New Orleans in 1996.[8]

"Why was he ill, and what kind of illness was it that caused his death?" So one of my senior students asked one day in the seminar Death—Mourning—Life: Perspectives from the New Testament, at the University of Münster in 1996. Once again we were reading John 11, but this time in a different context. This woman in her sixties, another Mary, had become an eager participant in my feminist courses and was fascinated by this new approach to women in the New Testament. Learning about their importance was also an empowering experience for herself. "Maybe his sisters were overpowering"—this remark came quite unexpectedly and puzzled me. However, it initiated a process of gradually revisioning my own feminist interpretations. Honestly, until that very day I had not even thought about Lazarus. He was dead and gone, and even his resurrection, or so it seemed to me, did not have much impact, apart from the fact that it increased the threat of Jesus's own imminent death in the course of the narrative (see 11:53). I had been quite pleased with my evaluation of the sisters and their importance in the story, so that the brother had dissolved into a vague background, resurrected only by my student's curious remarks. These have become a challenge for me ever since.

"To be alive in this text as a male is to live the death of Lazarus … to have one's death celebrated prematurely." "To be alive in this text as a male is to be a participant in the destructive power of patriarchy and androcentrism." Listening to Staley's voice in *Reading with a Passion* affected me deeply.[9] How could this be? I wondered. How could John 11 and feminist interpretations of this text have such a devastating effect on a male reader?[10] Furthermore, I asked: Did the feminist readings themselves, or

---

8. Kitzberger, "Mary of Bethany and Mary of Magdala"; Kitzberger, "How Can This Be?"

9. Staley, *Reading with a Passion*, 83–84.

10. See Staley: "Feminist reader-response criticism has given me a strategy that stirs my blood, but paradoxically the stir is the premonition of my own death, the silencing of my own androcentric voice" (*Reading with a Passion*, 83). "As a male I want to be an assenting reader of this story. I want to identify with the feminist read-

rather the reception of these readings within a certain ideological framework, cause the death of the male reader and his entombment together with Lazarus? Jeff's voice stirred my blood.[11] This was the second motivation for this paper.[12]

Characterization and Gender: Textual and Personal Constructs

In an "open view of character," according to Seymour Chatman, characters are not only evaluated for their functions in relation to the plot of the story but are treated as autonomous beings, like real people.[13] Consequently, everything that provides clues to the character of a literary figure is important in a text: what the narrator tells us about a character, what a character says or does, how a character is related to and interacts with other characters in the story-world. Of special relevance is the introduction of a character, how he or she is first presented to the readers, and how he or she is developed in the course of the narrative.[14]

Within a strictly reader-oriented approach, as applied here, characterization is not only the author's or narrator's way of portraying a character, but even more so it is the activity of the reader who reconstructs a character in the reading process. This, in turn, is strongly shaped and influenced

---

ings, of Martha's bold confession and Mary's brazen anointing.... Yet I find myself resisting any identification with the stinking corpse of Lazarus, the one bound up in linen cloths" (82).

11. Thank you for your voice, Jeff! And though you are afraid that your "reading cannot and should not be taken seriously by contemporary feminist interpreters of the New Testament," here is the proof to the contrary, and to be sure, you are "read, noted and toasted" but not "then resisted and roasted" (Staley, *Reading with a Passion*, 84).

12. For the importance and relevance of personal experience for interpreting biblical texts, see Ingrid Rosa Kitzberger, ed., *The Personal Voice in Biblical Interpretation* (London: Routledge, 1999); Janice Capel Anderson and Jeffrey L. Staley, eds., *Taking It Personally: Autobiographical Biblical Criticism, Semeia* 72 (1995). Besides the voices of Mary and Jeff, this paper was engendered and motivated by the deaths of three very close friends within the past three years: Richard, Eugen, and Rosa, whose funeral services were also related to John 11.

13. Seymour Chatman, *Story and Discourse: Narrative Structure in Fiction and Film* (Ithaca, NY: Cornell University Press, 1978), 107–38. See also David Rhoads, "Narrative Criticism and the Gospel of Mark," *JAAR* 50 (1982): 411–34.

14. See R. Alan Culpepper, *Anatomy of the Fourth Gospel: A Study in Literary Design*, FFNT (Philadelphia: Fortress, 1983), 6: "Characters are fashioned by what the narrator says about them, particularly when introducing them."

by the reader's context, his or her social location and personal voice. Therefore, characterization is the re-creation of characters in the reader's own image and likeness.[15]

Gender, as one important aspect of characterization, is also constructed in the text and reconstructed by the reader. Gender as a social construct thus also becomes a very personal issue for female and male readers respectively. Feminist interpretation implies the deconstruction of women's characterization by male authors or narrators and reconstructing them by overcoming the androcentric and patriarchal bias, starting from a hermeneutics of suspicion. Gender is never neutral. Its construction in the text and its reconstruction by the reader are, therefore, always heavily loaded with values and agendas, different for men and women, whether within a feminist or nonfeminist context and framework. Consequently, reading female and male characters are different processes, depending on whether one is a man or a woman, and so are readings of these readings, as Staley's reception of feminist interpretations of John 11 demonstrates so very well. Just as texts affect us, so our readings and interpretations affect others, whether consciously or unconsciously, whether intentionally or unintentionally. We should always bear this in mind.

Untying Lazarus: A Feminist's Task?

In my feminist interpretation of John 11 and 12 I stressed the importance of the sisters Mary and Martha[16] and their portrayal as equals, thus in contrast to their portrayal according to Luke's Gospel (10:38–42). Focusing on Lazarus, therefore, implies a fundamental shift of perspective and consequently a reading against the grain, a process usually associated, or even synonymous, with feminist-critical readings. Here it is applied both to the reading of the text and to reading feminist readings of the text, including my own.

---

15. See Ilona N. Rashkow, "'In Our Image We Create Him, Male and Female We Create Them': The E/Affect of Biblical Characterization," *Semeia* 63 (1993): 105–13.

16. Kitzberger, "Mary of Bethany and Mary of Magdala" and "How Can This Be?" So did other feminist interpretations of these texts, which had the ambivalent effect on Jeff Staley, who wants to be "an assenting reader of this story" and yet has to be "a resistant reader" (Staley, *Reading with a Passion*, 82–83).

The Characterization of Lazarus

"Now a certain man was ill, Lazarus of Bethany, the village of Mary and her sister Martha" (11:1). At the beginning of chapter 11, all three characters are mentioned for the first time in John's Gospel, and thus this verse—together with verse 2—provides their introduction. However, there is something very unusual. It seems that the readers are already familiar with the sisters, but not with Lazarus, who is introduced by way of Mary and Martha and identified as their brother in verse 2. I have reasoned elsewhere that the sisters are already known both to the author of the gospel and to its audience[17] due to their knowledge of the Synoptic Gospels, here the Gospel of Luke (10:38–42), and through oral tradition. Lazarus, however, has to be introduced. Thus, from the very beginning of the story his relevance and importance ranks second to those of his sisters. Nevertheless, the way he is introduced suggests that he will be the main character in the ensuing narrative. He is mentioned first, at the very beginning of the sentence, and he is its subject. However, any expectations the reader might have to hear a story about Lazarus are very short lived.[18] Being ill, Lazarus immediately disappears from the stage and turns into some mere background foil for the narrative. His sisters, on the other hand, take the initiative by sending for Jesus (v. 3), and Jesus and his disciples come to the fore, speaking *about* Lazarus and about theological issues, including Lazarus as the object and location of God's and his Son's glory to be revealed (vv. 4, 7–15). From being the subject, Lazarus turns very quickly into the object in the course of the narrative. His silence and inactivity are in stark contrast to the activities of the others and their speaking *about* him and *for* him, not *with* him.[19]

---

17. "Mary of Bethany and Mary of Magdala," in this volume. See Culpepper, *Anatomy of the Fourth Gospel*, 211–23, esp. 212.

18. See Wuellner's opinion that "the Lazarus narrative does not seek to narrate the raising of Lazarus as one of the 'many other signs which Jesus performed in the presence of his disciples' (John 20:30), both explicit and implicit in John. Rather, … [it] is written for the purpose of enhancing, confirming the readers' belief in Jesus as the Christ, as the Son of God, and thereby enhancing, confirming the readers' 'having life in His name'" ("Putting Life Back," 113).

19. On speaking with, see Patte, *Ethics of Biblical Interpretation*, 23–25; Patte, *Discipleship according to the Sermon on the Mount*, 389–96. On speaking for, see Linda Alcoff, "The Problem of Speaking for Others," *CC* (1991–1992): 5–32.

Lazarus returns, though indirectly, only in verse 17, when the narrator informs us that "Lazarus had already been in the tomb four days." He died silently, while others were speaking about him. In their individual encounters with Jesus, both Martha and Mary voice their reproach of Jesus because he was not there to save their brother,[20] but they also express their strong belief in him: he could have worked a miracle, and he still can (vv. 21–22, 32). Once again, Lazarus is the object of their conversation, while his subjectivity has been entombed four days earlier, or even longer. Only at the end of the narrative does Lazarus return to the stage, when he responds to Jesus's voicing his name and issuing the order, "Lazarus, come out!" And Lazarus, obedient as he is, stumbles out of the dark, a dead man walking (vv. 43–44).

"Unbind him, and let him go," Jesus finally demands (v. 44). But it remains unclear whom he is addressing, whether the sisters or any of the Jews who have come to console the sisters. While it is quite obvious that Lazarus could not have freed himself and thus the order "Unbind him" makes sense, the order "let him go" is surprising. Why did Jesus not say, after the successful unbinding, anything like, "Take your cloths and go" (see 5:8)? "Let him go" implies the fact that he was bound and therefore in need of liberation, apart from the bandages. But liberation from whom? From his sisters, as my student Mary suggested? We readers are left with this textual ambivalence, the unanswered question and open end. However, Lazarus does not go away, regardless of who finally undertook the task of unbinding him after his resurrection. In chapter 12 he seems to be comfortable at the table with Jesus and a host of other guests, enjoying the dinner prepared by his sisters and served by Martha (12:1–2). But the privilege of being nourished and served, as well as the homely peace, do not last long. He soon becomes a tourist attraction, and the crowds want to see him (v. 9). This, in turn, calls forth the chief priests' and Pharisees' plan to kill him, just as they want to kill Jesus for fear of the people's apostasy (vv. 10–11). So, what has Lazarus gained in the course of events? Nothing, in fact! He was not asked whether he wanted to be resurrected

---

20. Staley notes that while the sisters speak in unison *before* Lazarus's death, when sending for Jesus (11:3), they can only speak for themselves *after* his death. "Thus, it appears that the death of their brother brings with it the sisters' discovery of their own personal voices" (*Reading with a Passion*, 78). Staley wants to "show how the deaths of the story's male characters empower these women, freeing them to ever bolder speech and action" (77).

after successfully accomplishing the most difficult task in life—dying. Being resurrected implies having to go through all this once more. And for Lazarus it even implies the threat of a violent death.

To sum up, apart from his introduction in verse 1, Lazarus is reduced to an object throughout the narrative in John 11. While others speak *about* him and *for* him, he has no voice of his own.[21] Not even on the occasion of his resurrection is he granted that fundamental human right to speak for himself. Unlike the young man of Nain in Luke's Gospel, who—after being raised from the dead—"sat up and began to speak" (7:15), Lazarus remains mute. And unlike the other resurrected gospel characters, Lazarus remains unrelated, in spite of the dinner party in John 12. While the young man of Nain is given back to his mother (Luke 7:15), and the young girl, Jairus's daughter, is touched by Jesus and the witnesses are asked to give her something to eat right away (Mark 5:43 parr.), Lazarus is left in isolation,[22] wrapped and bound in cloths, at the end of the narrative. And Jesus's order to let him go indicates the breakup of existing relationships, not their reestablishment. In fact, Lazarus is forced to go away later on, though this is not narrated, because of the threat of his violent second death.

Throughout John 11, Lazarus is defined by his relation to his better-known sisters. He is described as Mary's brother (vv. 2, 32), as the brother of both Martha and Mary (v. 19), and as Martha's brother (vv. 21, 23, 39). Neither Mary nor Martha is called Lazarus's sister, which is even more surprising in a context where women were usually defined in relation to men, not the other way around. Not much is revealed about the relationship among the strange Bethany family, least of all how they came to live together and without partners, which was again most unusual in their cultural and religious context.[23] Obviously, the sisters were concerned about

---

21. See Staley, *Reading with a Passion*, 83: "What I find doubly disturbing is this: that as a male reader I read through this sign, with its multiple disruptions and designing strategies, as if I were the one to become dead, the one without a voice, pretending to experience precisely that which I find impossible to experience—the silence of the zombie-like Lazarus."

22. See Staley, *Reading with a Passion*, 75: "It seems strange that the narrator concludes the miracle without offering the encoded reader any immediate insight into the sisters' reaction to receiving back their brother (Mark 5:42). Jesus does not publicly restore Lazarus to them (cf. Luke 7:15–16)."

23. Staley, like many other interpreters, speculates about that and supposes that while Lazarus was unmarried, the sisters were married but their husbands had died (*Reading with a Passion*, 68).

their brother and cared for him before, during, and after his illness and resurrection. This seems to be taken for granted. Neither approaches Jesus at the dinner party complaining, "Lord, do you not care that our brother has left us to do all the work by ourselves? Tell him to help us!" (see Luke 10:40). Patriarchal role models are not questioned in this regard. However, the relation between the sisters and the brother need not necessarily be interpreted in traditional patriarchal terms. It could also be viewed in terms of a mother-child relationship, with overprotective and overpowering mother-sisters, thus in line with what my student suggested. The text is ambivalent and open to different interpretations, depending on the reader's ideological presuppositions.

The relationship between Jesus and Lazarus is also ambivalent. Although we are informed by the narrator (11:5) and by the sisters (v. 3) that Jesus loved Lazarus and that he was the friend of Jesus and his disciples (v. 11, "our friend Lazarus"), Jesus's reaction and behavior in the course of the narrative cause doubts. First, he remains where he is for two more days when the sisters send for him (v. 6). Then, in spite of Jesus's tears at the tomb (v. 35), considered to be the proof of his love for Lazarus by the funeral party (v. 36), Lazarus rather remains an object of Jesus's demonstration and revelation of God's glory, and his own sharing in God's power (vv. 4, 15, 40–42).

Lazarus—the ill, dead, and resurrected man—remains a voiceless object, acted on and spoken for and about. His true resurrection and liberation are still to be accomplished.

Untying Lazarus

Untying Lazarus implies reading against the grain of the narrative and stepping out of its ideological framework. A feminist-critical reading for equality, justice, and liberation, therefore, implies the resurrection of Mary and Martha as important characters in John's story-world and as preeminent in Jesus's life.[24] But it implies also the reconstruction and revisioning of the relationship between the sisters and their brother, and the reconstruction of his role in the narrative. On the other hand, a feminist

---

24. See Adele Reinhartz, "From Narrative to History: The Resurrection of Mary and Martha," in *"Women Like This": New Perspectives on Jewish Women in the Greco-Roman World*, ed. Amy-Jill Levine, EJL 1 (Atlanta: Scholars Press, 1991), 161–84.

interpretation that voices the women but silences the man (or the men) remains a reading with the grain, and it reinforces the patriarchal and hierarchical bias inherent even in the Gospel of John, which otherwise transcends many traditional borders and boundaries and also opens new vistas for the relationship between women and men. Staley's experience of being alive in the story only as a dead man is in fact due to the narrative framework and ideology of the text itself, which silences Lazarus, the man who is the most likely of all characters that a male reader would identify with. But it is also the reaction to feminist interpretations that have underscored the role of the sisters, while further silencing the brother. The effect of such a procedure might have gone unnoticed had not an entombed male reader dared to raise his resisting personal voice, and had not a feminist reader bothered to listen carefully. The ethics of biblical interpretation thus involves the continuous critical reflection of our own endeavors and speaking with those who are affected by our readings. This, in turn, may lead to revisioning our task and presuppositions. Feminist interpretation needs to critically analyze not only patriarchal texts and interpretations, but also feminist interpretations, including one's own. Then it is truly ideological criticism[25] and indicates the shift towards a postfeminist interpretation and hermeneutics. Untying Lazarus is thus indeed also a sisters' task. However, it presupposes liberated women who—through struggle and solidarity—have regained and reclaimed their own subjectivity and have learned to speak for themselves with their unique personal voices.

---

25. See Fernando F. Segovia, "Cultural Studies and Contemporary Biblical Criticism: Ideological Criticism as a Mode of Discourse," in *Reading from This Place*, vol. 2, *Social Location and Biblical Interpretation in Global Perspective*, ed. Segovia and Mary Ann Tolbert (Minneapolis: Fortress, 1995), 1–17; Fred Inglis, *Ideology and the Imagination* (London: Cambridge University Press, 1975).

Transcending Gender Boundaries in John

"Do you remember this woman?," he asked those sitting around him whom he loved. And he loved them to the end. So he got up from the table, took off his outer robe, and tied a towel around himself. Then he poured water into a basin and began to wash their feet and to wipe them with the towel that was tied around him.

When he came to Simon Peter, the latter said, "Yes, Lord, I remember. But, you know, she was a sinner, well-known in town, wasn't she? You cannot take her as an example, can you?" Jesus looked deep into his eyes and said, "Unless I wash your feet, you have no share with me." And, after a moment of silence, he asked, "Do you love me more than these?" Simon Peter said to him, "Lord, you know that I love you. Wash me, not only my feet, but also my hands and my head."

And Mary, the one from Bethany, who was sitting next to Simon Peter, smiled knowingly.

∞

"How can this be?" the old rabbi wondered. And he journeyed on with the unanswered question, pondering over it many a starry night.

After all things were fulfilled he bought a mixture of myrrh and aloes, about a hundred pounds' weight, and came to the tomb late in the afternoon, before the sun set. Together with another secret disciple, they wrapped Jesus's bloodstained body into linen cloths, just like a newborn. And they laid him in the tomb. After Joseph had left, Nicodemus remained standing at the tomb, weeping. Then he knelt down and paid homage to his dead king. Opening his treasure chest, he offered him

---

Originally published as Ingrid Rosa Kitzberger, "Transcending Gender Boundaries in John," in *A Feminist Companion to John*, ed. Amy-Jill Levine with Marianne Blickenstaff (Sheffield: Sheffield Academic, 2003), 2:173–207.

myrrh and aloes, more than the body could hold. Suddenly there was a star, shining brightly over the tomb. Looking up into the night sky, Nicodemus instantly knew the answer to his question. From that very moment he was reborn from above.

∽

When he saw the linen wrappings lying there and the cloth that had been on Jesus's head not lying with the linen wrappings but rolled up in a place by itself, he believed. Together with Simon Peter, the Beloved Disciple returned home, and they told them all that had happened.

"How can this be?" Jesus's mother, who had become the disciple's own mother, asked him. "Nothing is impossible with God," Nicodemus said, and he looked into the rising sun.

∽

From Madrid to Orlando, and Beyond: My Personal Transformative Encounters with Gospel Women and Men

"I'm a feminist too," he proudly confessed, responding to the paper I had just presented. It was on footwashing, precisely in John 13 and Luke 7. This was an extremely hot summer's day in July 1992, and a wash all over would, in fact, have been just perfect for us sitting in one of the lecture rooms at the University of Madrid during the General Meeting of the Society for New Testament Studies. The water being poured out in the stories on which we focused increased our desires by way of contrast. "Lord, not only my feet but also my hands and my head," Simon Peter exclaims enthusiastically after his initial rejection of Jesus's washing his feet. "If I do not wash you, you have no part in me," Jesus says, encouraging his disciple to think twice. "He who has bathed does not need to wash, except for his feet, but he is clean all over." Jesus's words echoed in biblical scholars who were wet all over, except at least one. It was one of these very rare occasions when being a women was, just for a change, an advantage for me within an academic setting: I was among the few and privileged women at the conference who were blessed with a private bath, so I was able to have a shower before presenting my paper.

That year, the number of women in this particular seminar setting had increased drastically: there were two of us. Yet the male audience was open and receptive, and my presentation of feminist intertextual readings of John 13:1–20 and Luke 7:36–50 was followed by a lively discussion.[2] This was the first time that I presented a feminist reader-response paper (the first of several others to follow in the ensuing years) at an international conference, and it was exciting. Equally exciting was my experience of meeting a member of a hitherto unknown species: a male feminist. This well-established American professor took me completely by surprise with his confession. I remember vaguely that I tried to convince him that he did not exist, that is, as a feminist. However, in the years to come I occasionally met other male feminists who were equally self-conscious. I learned to let them be, considering the multidimensionality not only of the biblical texts but also of their interpreters and the polyvalence of terms such as *feminist*. At the same time, I developed further my own feminist approach in lecturing and writing. But the anonymous woman of Luke 7 has always held a special place in my scholarly biography, because of the Madrid experience, which was a kind of initiation experience. Besides that, the woman's relation to the Johannine Jesus has been on my mind since that summer in 1992. I shall revisit both texts, John 13:1–20 and Luke 7:36–50, and the characters in them, in this present paper.

As a consequence of my Madrid paper, I was invited for another paper at the following year's General Meeting of the Society for New Testament Studies. Thus in 1993 I went to Chicago together with Mary of Bethany and Mary of Magdala, and I was delighted by Elizabeth of Blacksburg's response to Ingrid of Münster's paper.[3] My feminist, narrative-critical reader response to the characters of the two Marys in the context of John's passion narrative, their relation to other female and male characters in the same gospel, and their relation to female characters in the Synoptic Gospels, marked a turning point in my research. Since then, I have concentrated on women in John, and I have encountered them in ever new ways over the years. Besides the two Marys, the Samaritan woman later on became my special companion and dialogue partner, with whom I

---

2. Ingrid Rosa Kitzberger, "Love and Footwashing: John 13:1–20 and Luke 7:36–50 Read Intertextually," *BibInt* 2 (1994): 190–206.

3. "Mary of Bethany and Mary of Magdala—Two Female Characters in the Johannine Passion Narrative: A Feminist, Narrative-Critical Reader Response," in this volume. At the meeting, Elizabeth Struthers Malbon (Blacksburg, Virginia) presented the response paper.

have journeyed for quite a while now.[4] Reading the Johannine women in Chicago, I advocated a *reading with the grain* and stressed the positive portrayal and importance of women in John.[5] Of course, I was very pleased with my findings, and they were in line with the feminist consensus.

"How can this be?" As I was preparing a paper for the Annual Meeting of the Society of Biblical Literature in New Orleans in 1996, this question—taken over from the Johannine Nicodemus (John 3:9)—was on my mind day and night. Applied to my paper, the question was: How is a feminist *and* theological interpretation of the Gospel of John possible? My pondering over this increasingly difficult question resulted in another fundamental turning point in my research. My New Orleans audience and later the readers of "What Is John?" witnessed how my mind had changed.[6] Now, I advocated both a *reading with the grain* and a *reading against the grain*. The portrayal of women in John, so I concluded, can be regarded in a positive but also in a negative way, depending on which meaning dimen-

---

4. Ingrid Rosa Kitzberger, "Border Crossing and Meeting Jesus at the Well: An Autobiographical Re-reading of the Samaritan Woman's Story in John 4:1–44," in *The Personal Voice in Biblical Interpretation*, ed. Ingrid Rosa Kitzberger (London: Routledge, 1999), 97–110. On November 14, 1996, I presented a lecture on "Reading and Rereading the Samaritan Woman's Story: Characterization and Social Location" at Vanderbilt University, Nashville. A revised version is first published in this volume.

5. Since Raymond E. Brown's pioneering article "Roles of Women in the Fourth Gospel," there has been an increased interest in women in John, and their importance has been stressed. See Brown, "Roles of Women in the Fourth Gospel," *TS* 36 (1975): 688–99. See, e.g., Sandra M. Schneiders, "Women in the Fourth Gospel and the Role of Women in the Contemporary Church," *BTB* 12 (1982): 35–45; Elisabeth Schüssler Fiorenza, *In Memory of Her: A Feminist Theological Reconstruction of Christian Origins* (New York: Crossroad, 1983), who regards the "women as paradigms of true discipleship" (323–33); Turid Karlsen Seim, "Roles of Women in the Gospel of John," in *Aspects of the Johannine Literature*, ed. Lars Hartmann and Birger Olsson, ConBNT 18 (Uppsala: Uppsala University Press, 1987), 56–73; Martinus C. de Boer, "John 4:27— Women (and Men) in the Gospel and Community of John," in *Women in the Biblical Tradition*, ed. George J. Brooke, SWR 31 (Lewiston, NY: Mellen, 1992), 208–30; Sjef van Tilborg, *Imaginative Love in John*, BibInt 2 (Leiden: Brill, 1993), esp. ch. 4, "Loving Women"; Robert G. Maccini, *Her Testimony Is True: Women as Witnesses according to John*, JSNTSup 125 (Sheffield: Sheffield Academic, 1996); Adele Fehribach, *The Women in the Life of the Bridegroom: A Feminist Historical-Literary Analysis of the Female Characters in the Fourth Gospel* (Collegeville, MN: Liturgical Press, 1998).

6. "'How Can This Be?' (John 3:9): A Feminist-Theological Rereading of the Gospel of John," in this volume.

sions in the texts are chosen and activated in the reading process.[7] Thus, the constructive character of interpretation and the ethical dimension of interpretation[8] were emphasized. Encountering these and other gospel women, as well as gospel men, turned out to be a very dynamic process, depending on the individual reader or interpreter. Consequently, also my own encounters with those gospel women and men, with whom I had already journeyed for a while, changed drastically due to my new findings. Transformation happened in the reading process, and in my actual life, as pertaining to my feminist praxis in relation to real women and men in the context of my social location as a Catholic woman, a biblical scholar, and a teacher. While in New Orleans the Gospel of John as a happy paradise for feminists was lost forever,[9] a new freedom was engendered that called for the ethical accountability of and the responsibility for our own readings.

Since taking up Nicodemus's question in 1996, he has become increasingly important to me. This, besides my new approach to the gospel women, marked yet another turning point: this was the first time, since I had become a feminist, that a gospel man (and not a woman) had caught my special attention and later gained my sympathy. Getting involved with this man after I had focused my research on women in the New Testament for a decade and a half, my mind changed once again. Since then, my feminist interpretations have included also men, and I have developed my approach further toward (though not yet arrived at) a postfeminist hermeneutics and toward the creation of a gender *antiapartheid* community of believers and biblical scholars alike. This struggle has been greatly inspired and nourished by reading and rereading the Gospel of John and its portrayal of female as well as male characters, and by the gender-related ethics of equality conveyed in this gospel.

---

7. On "meaning-producing dimensions" and the multidimensionality of biblical texts, see Daniel Patte, *Ethics of Biblical Interpretation: A Reevaluation* (Louisville: Westminster John Knox, 1995); Patte, *Discipleship according to the Sermon on the Mount: Four Legitimate Readings, Four Plausible Views of Discipleship, and Their Relative Values* (Valley Forge, PA: Trinity Press International, 1996).

8. On the ethics of biblical interpretation, see Patte, *Ethics of Biblical Interpretation*; Danna Nolan Fewell and Gary A. Phillips, eds., *Ethics, Bible, Reading as If, Semeia* 77 (1997); Elisabeth Schüssler Fiorenza, "The Ethics of Interpretation: Decentering Biblical Scholarship," *JBL* 107 (1988): 3–17; Schüssler Fiorenza, *Rhetoric and Ethic: The Politics of Biblical Studies* (Minneapolis: Fortress, 1999).

9. On deconstructing John's feminist paradise, see "How Can This Be?," in this volume.

Encountering another Johannine man confirmed the direction I was heading. When, in 1998, I went to Orlando Disney World with Lazarus, I advocated his untying and the empowering of the silenced and marginalized one to speak up for himself.[10] The responses from both the male and female audience showed that I was barking up the right tree.

As a consequence of my transformative encounters with gospel men, in particular with Nicodemus and Lazarus, I henceforth also encountered the women in John, and also in the Synoptics, with different lenses. When I encountered Nicodemus and Jesus's mother in their respective relations to Synoptic women in my chapter "Synoptic Women in John: Interfigural Readings" for the volume *Transformative Encounters. Jesus and Women Re-viewed*,[11] the pathway toward the realization of the transcendence of gender boundaries in John was opened.

In this paper, I, therefore, shall revisit the footwashing Johannine Jesus and the footwashing Lukan woman, on the one hand, and Nicodemus on the other hand. This time, I shall encounter the latter in relation not only to Synoptic women but also to Synoptic men. Thereby, I suggest that in John's Gospel gender boundaries are in fact overcome in the characterization of both male and female characters.

Interfigural Characterization: New Glasses for Old Characters

As I concentrate on characterization as an essential (though often neglected) aspect of narrative criticism, I employ a reader-response approach,[12] in

---

10. "Untying Lazarus—A Sisters' Task? Revisioning Gender and Characterization in John 11," in this volume.

11. Ingrid Rosa Kitzberger, "Synoptic Women in John: Interfigural Readings," in *Transformative Encounters: Jesus and Women Re-viewed*, ed. Ingrid Rosa Kitzberger, BibInt 43 (Leiden: Brill, 2000), 77–111.

12. On reader-response criticism, see Jane P. Tompkins, ed., *Reader-Response Criticism: From Formalism to Post-structuralism* (Baltimore: Johns Hopkins University Press, 1980); Edgar V. McKnight, *Post-modern Use of the Bible: The Emergence of Reader-Oriented Criticism* (Nashville: Abingdon, 1990); McKnight, *The Bible and the Reader: An Introduction to Literary Criticism* (Philadelphia: Fortress, 1985); Robert M. Fowler, *Let the Reader Understand: Reader-Response Criticism and the Gospel of Mark* (Minneapolis: Fortress, 1991); Fernando F. Segovia, ed., *Readers and Readings of the Fourth Gospel*, vol. 1 of *"What Is John?,"* SymS 3 (Atlanta: Scholars Press, 1996); Segovia, *Literary and Social Readings of the Fourth Gospel*, vol. 2 of *"What Is John?,"* SymS 7 (Atlanta: Scholars Press, 1998).

which characterization is regarded as being achieved by a very dynamic process of the reader's creative engagement with the text. Consequently, characterization implies both the construction by the author and the reconstruction by the reader.[13] The latter is a very individual process, as it depends on the choices a reader makes within the reading process. In fact, one and the same text signal can be interpreted in very different ways, due to the actualization and contextualization of certain meaning dimensions within the immediate narrative context or the story at large. By concentrating on the rhetoric and the discourse of the text, the gradual unfolding of a narrative,[14] and thus also the gradual unfolding of a character within the narrative, is taken seriously into account. Just like the plot of the story, also characters cannot be abstracted from the narrative ebb and flow. Thus, no summary or content[15] of a character can be deduced. The readings as presented in this paper are my own readings, and thus the readings of a real reader.[16] Certainly they are not the only possible ones. Due to the

---

13. See John Darr, *On Character Building: The Reader and the Rhetoric of Characterization in Luke-Acts* (Louisville: Westminster John Knox, 1992); Elizabeth Struthers Malbon and Adele Berlin, eds., *Characterization in Biblical Literature*, Semeia 63 (1993); Fred W. Burnett, "Characterization and Reader Construction of Characters in the Gospels," in *Listening to the Word of God: A Tribute to Boyce W. Blackwelder*, ed. Barry L. Callen (Anderson, IN: Anderson University Press, 1990), 69–88.

14. Consequently, also the act of reading is a gradual process. See Stanley Fish, "Literature in the Reader: Affective Stylistics," *NLH* 2 (1970): 123–62. He speaks of the "temporal flow of the reading experience," and in his method "it is assumed that the reader responds in terms of that flow and not the whole utterance … and the report of what happens to the reader is always a report of what has happened to that point" (127). For the difference between story and discourse, see Seymour Chatman, *Story and Discourse: Narrative Structure in Fiction and Film* (Ithaca, NY: Cornell University Press, 1978). See also Gérard Genette, *Narrative Discourse: An Essay in Method* (Ithaca, NY: Cornell University Press, 1980); Wolfgang Iser, "The Reading Process: A Phenomenological Approach," in Tompkins, *Reader Response Criticism*, 50–69.

15. For the "content" as embedded in the form, see Gail O'Day, *Revelation in the Fourth Gospel: Narrative Mode and Theological Claim* (Minneapolis: Fortress, 1986).

16. A real reader is different from any reader constructs, whether first, intended, or implied readers. See also Segovia, *Readers and Readings of the Fourth Gospel*, especially the contribution by Segovia, "Reading Readers of the Fourth Gospel and Their Readings: An Exercise in Intercultural Criticism," 237–77. On the importance of real readers, see also Fernando F. Segovia and Mary A. Tolbert, eds., *Reading from This Place*, vol. 1, *Social Location and Biblical Interpretation in the United States*; vol. 2, *Social Location and Biblical Interpretation in Global Perspective* (Minneapolis: Fortress, 1995).

open nature and the surplus of meaning of any text, different readings are plausible and legitimate.

My character analysis is based on an open view of character as advocated by Seymour Chatman, according to whom characters are not only evaluated by the functions of their actions in relation to the plot but are treated as autonomous beings and are assessed the way we evaluate real people.[17] Therefore, every detail in the text that provides a clue for characterization is taken into account: what a character says or does, what the narrator says about him or her, how she or he is related to other characters, and so on.

In this paper, as in previous papers mentioned above, my focus is on dimensions of characterization that are added by an intertextual approach, and more specifically by an interfigural view of character. The term *interfigurality*, coined by Wolfgang G. Müller, refers to "interrelations that exist between characters of different texts," and it represents "one of the most important dimensions of intertextuality." Thus, interfigurality differs from configuration, which refers to the relation of characters within the same text.[18]

Here, interfigurality refers to the relation between Johannine characters and Synoptic characters. Thus, I suggest also a new approach to the never-ending riddle and scholarly discourse on the relation between John and the Synoptics, which has attracted my attention for the past decade, in fact since attending the Colloquium Biblicum Lovaniense on John and the Synoptics in 1990.[19]

---

17. Chatman, *Story and Discourse*, 107–38. On the other hand, see R. Alan Culpepper, who refers to "the legitimacy of treating the people described in a historical writing as characters." See Culpepper, *Anatomy of the Fourth Gospel: A Study in Literary Design*, FFNT (Philadelphia: Fortress, 1983). Detlev Dormeyer points to the double function of proper names as historical persons and as characters. See Dormeyer, *Das Neue Testament im Rahmen der antiken Literaturgeschichte*, DA (Darmstadt: Wissenschaftliche Buchgesellschaft, 1993), 59–60.

18. Wolfgang G. Müller, "Interfigurality: A Study on the Interdependence of Literary Figures," in *Intertextuality*, ed. Heinrich E. Plett, RTT 15 (Berlin: de Gruyter, 1991), 101, 107.

19. Adelbert Denaux, ed., *John and the Synoptics*, BETL 101 (Leuven: Leuven University Press; Peeters, 1992). See also Frans Neirynck, "John and the Synoptics," *ETL* 45 (1977): 73–106. On John and the Synoptics, see D. Moody Smith, *John among the Gospels: The Relationship in Twentieth-Century Research* (Minneapolis: Fortress, 1992).

By relating Johannine male characters to Synoptic female and male characters, new dimensions are also added to gender as one important aspect of characterization. Gender, as a social construct and as here related to a literary character, is established by the roles attributed to a character within the narrative and by the context in which a character is drawn. Besides that, gender is constructed by the relation of a character to other characters, male and female, of the same text and of other texts, hence by configuration and interfigurality. As with any other aspect of characterization, gender is established both by the construction of the text by its author and by its reconstruction on the part of the reader. Therefore, gendered characterization is also a very individual issue, depending on the readers, whether male or female. Thus, the gendered readings of Jesus and Nicodemus, in their relation to other men and to women, as presented in this paper, are my own readings. I invite you, my readers, to "read with" me[20] and, as a consequence, be empowered to venture out on your own readings of gospel women and men and experience your own transformative encounters.

Love and Footwashing: Jesus and the "Sinner Woman" Revisited

Reading Jesus in John 13:1–20

"Now before the festival of the Passover, Jesus knew that his hour had come to depart from this world and go to the Father. Having loved his own who were in the world, he loved them to the end." This introduction (v. 1) to the ensuing scene in chapter 13, and to the wider context of Jesus's farewell discourse in chapters 13–17, recalls events we encountered previously during the process of reading John's Gospel. At the same time, it raises our expectation for what is to come, because the mention of the forthcoming Passover feast and Jesus's love "to the end" (εἰς τέλος) point toward future events. The reference to Jesus's omniscient point of view with regard to his fate reminds us of what happened up to this point. "His hour" (ἡ ὥρα) had not yet come when Jesus's mother drew his attention to the lack of wine at the Cana wedding, thus implicitly requesting him to act (2:1–12, v. 4). But,

---

20. See Patte, *Ethics of Biblical Interpretation*, 23–25; Patte, *Discipleship according to the Sermon on the Mount*, 389–96; Gerald West and Musa W. Dube, eds., *"Reading With": An Exploration of the Interface between Critical and Ordinary Readings of the Bible; African Overtures*, Semeia 73 (1996).

so we learn, with the feast of Passover coming close (11:55; 12:1), Jesus is aware that "The hour has come for the Son of Man to be glorified" (12:23). Immediately, we are put into the picture with regard to the nature of the "glorification" (δοξάζειν) that defines "the hour": it contradicts human (our) expectations and presents a paradox. Jesus compares it to the dying of the grain, in order that it bears much fruit (12:24). Further, it is about "hating" (μισῶν) one's life in order to keep it for eternal life (12:25). And it has consequences for his disciples: "Whoever serves me must follow me, and where I am, there will my servant be also. Whoever serves me, the Father will honor" (12:26). Following Jesus (ἀκολουθεῖν) and serving him (διάκονειν) are to be understood as synonyms, as Jesus's words suggest. A master-servant relationship and thus a hierarchy is clearly indicated. Yet, because of the context, this seems to be of a different nature from human master-servant relationships. On the other hand, the reader's expectation is raised as to *where to* follow Jesus. Since Jesus raised Lazarus from the dead, the threat of Jesus's own death has drastically increased (11:50–53). When Mary of Bethany anointed him (12:1–8), he himself pointed to his impending death, respectively to his burial, for which the ointments should be kept (12:7). Thus, "his hour," and the path ahead of him, are linked to his death. Following Jesus, therefore, implies the readiness to follow him even unto death.

Despite his omniscience regarding his destiny, Jesus, nevertheless, is depicted in most human terms: "Now my soul is troubled. And what should I say—'Father, save me from this hour?' No, it is for this reason that I have come to this hour. Father, glorify your name" (12:27–28). Only a little later, Jesus's knowledge about the kind of death he is going to die comes to the fore: "And I, when I am lifted up from the earth, will draw all people to myself" (12:32). Jesus's words are commented on by the narrator: "He said this to indicate the kind of death he was to die" (12:33). Glorifying (δοξάζειν) and honoring (τίμαν) as connected to Jesus (and his Father), and consequently to those who follow him, are completely different from human glory and honor. When many of the people, even the authorities, came to believe in Jesus, so the narrator informs us, they nevertheless did not confess it, for fear that they would be put out of the synagogue (12:42); this is further explained by "for they loved human glory more than the glory that comes from God" (12:43).

When we arrive at chapter 13 and learn about Jesus's hour and having loved his own (ἀγαπήσας τοὺς ἰδίους) "to the end," we bring to this text all that has been said so far, and thus also the ambivalent, or, rather, paradoxical information regarding glory and honor, servant and master, Jesus's impending death, and the disciples' following him. Jesus's love, which previously referred to Lazarus, Mary, and Martha of Bethany (11:3 φιλεῖν; v. 5 ἀγαπᾶν),[21] is now related to all of "his own," that is, to those who have followed him so far.[22] It is intensified through its designation as a loving "to the end" (εἰς τέλος).[23] At the same time, the reader's expectation is raised as to what Jesus's love entails, or how he would demonstrate it. Verse 2 specifies the present scene as a meal scene: καὶ δείπνου γινομένου.[24] The side remark referring to Judas's betrayal, and once again to Jesus's knowledge of his return to his Father (vv. 2–3), delays the plot development by way of retardation. At the same time it is a prolepsis: it forecasts the betrayal. Thereby, a sharp contrast is created between Jesus's love for his disciples, which includes even Judas, and the latter's action. Thereby, also a division among "his own" becomes obvious, even before those who are present are even introduced. At least one of his own will *not* follow him to the end (see 12:26).

Then, totally unexpectedly, for us readers just as well as for the characters in the narrative, Jesus gets up from the table, takes off his outer robe, and ties a towel around himself (v. 4). Then he pours water into a basin and begins to wash the disciples' feet and to wipe them with the towel (v. 5). Every detail of Jesus's action is described, and thus the reader becomes engaged into the scene. He or she no longer remains a spectator but becomes a potential addressee of Jesus's action: "Any moment Jesus will come to wash *my* feet," so she or he might envision. But Jesus comes to Simon Peter, who thus becomes a character with whom we can identify. His immediate rejection to Jesus's washing his feet corresponds with our own hesitations and feelings: "Lord, are you going to wash my feet?" (v. 6) and "You will never wash my feet" (v. 8). Though Jesus makes it clear that the meaning of his action cannot yet be fully understood (v. 7), he

---

21. See Fernando F. Segovia, *Love Relationships in the Johannine Tradition: Agape/Agapan in 1 John and the Fourth Gospel*, SBLDS 58 (Chico, CA: Scholars Press, 1982).

22. Regarding ἀγαπήσας, see Raymond E. Brown, *The Gospel according to John XIII–XXI*, AB 29A (New York: Doubleday, 1970), 550: "The participle is a complexive aorist covering the public ministry."

23. See Brown, *Gospel according to John XIII–XXI*, 550: "The phrase *eis telos* has a twofold meaning: 'utterly, completely' and 'to the end of life,' i.e. to the death."

24. Thus begins v. 2 in the Greek text. The NRSV has freely changed the sequence of information in this verse.

defines it as establishing a lasting relationship between himself and his disciples: "Unless I wash you, you have no share with me" (οὐκ ἔχεις μετ' ἐμοῦ, v. 8). Now, Simon Peter enthusiastically wants it all: "Lord, not my feet only but also my hands and my head!" (v. 9). However, Jesus cools him down: "One who has bathed[25] does not need to wash, except for the feet, but is entirely clean. And you are clean, though not all of you" (v. 10). Then, the narrator comments: "For he knew who was to betray him; for this reason he said, 'Not all of you are clean'" (v. 11). It is obvious that the footwashing is a symbolic act: it denotes communion between the giver and receiver ("having a share with"),[26] and it points, in good Johannine fashion, to a double meaning: "clean" (καθαρός) as referring to an outer reality as brought about by water and to an inner state.

Only Simon Peter is explicitly mentioned as an object of Jesus's footwashing. By way of summary, verse 12 concludes: "After he had washed their feet." Having finished his task, Jesus puts on his robe, returns to the table, and asks his disciples the essential question: "Do you know what I have done to you?" (v. 12). Without waiting for their answer, he continues his teaching: "You call me Teacher and Lord—and you are right, for that is what I am. So if I, your Lord and Teacher, have washed your feet, you also ought to wash one another's feet" (vv. 13, 14). Jesus defines his action as an example (ὑπόδειγμα), demanding of his disciples to do as he has done to them (v. 15). He adds further explanation by claiming that servants are not greater than their master, nor are messengers greater than the one who sent them (v. 16). This recalls Jesus's previous statement that "Whoever serves me must follow me, and where I am there will my servant be also" (12:26). Serving Jesus and following him thus means joining his mission of serving, exemplified by his washing the disciples' feet. Any hierarchies are turned upside down and consequently are overcome. "Servants are not greater than their masters" implies that the division becomes obsolete, since the master Jesus acted as a servant. Washing one another's feet,

---

25. Δελουμένος is a perfect participle passive and denotes one who has had a bath. Since my Madrid experience, I envision also Simon Peter (like myself) as having had a bath (or shower) before entering the stage.

26. See Francis J. Moloney, *Glory Not Dishonor: Reading John 13–21* (Minneapolis: Fortress, 1998), 14–15: "The Christian reader of the Johannine story recognizes a veiled reference to the practice of baptism in the early church.... To 'have part with Jesus' through washing also means to be part of the self-giving love that will bring Jesus' life to an end (see v. 1) and is symbolically anticipated in the footwashing (v. 8)."

therefore, establishes equality between the disciples and implies the negation of patriarchal structures.

The characterization of Jesus in chapter 13 is constructed by what he does and by what he says, and by what the narrator says about him. The emphasis is clearly on the former, the act of footwashing, while what is said, by Jesus or by the narrator, adds the explanation and defines the footwashing as a demonstration of love (vv. 1, 34). Certainly, Jesus's action alone would have had dramatic effect on his disciples, as well as on us, the readers. However, misunderstanding might have resulted without any explanation, and the imperative nature of the whole enterprise might have gone unnoticed. Thus, both elements, what is done and what is said, are necessary for the characterization of Jesus. There is no doubt: washing another's feet is an essential part of Jesus's mission and self-understanding, and it is extended to those who follow him: the disciples in the narrative, and any readers of the narrative, past and present. The Johannine Jesus is thus characterized as an antipatriarchal man who advocates the overcoming of hierarchies and, consequently, equality among those following him. This, naturally, implies also equality between men and women.

"Is there a woman in this text?"[27] So we might ask. Reading John 13:1–20, we have encountered only male characters: Jesus, Judas, and Simon Peter. All the others of "his own," who are present at the meal and the footwashing, are mentioned just by way of summary (13:1, 5, 12). Only later is "the disciple whom Jesus loved" introduced (v. 23). Thus, neither the concrete number of disciples present is mentioned, nor is any hint given with regard to their gender. It is consequently left to the reader to fill this narrative gap and to reconstruct the characters.[28] Some clues for this task are provided in the context of the gospel story. Of course the male disciples whom Jesus called at the beginning of his ministry have to be included: besides Simon Peter, there are Andrew, Simon Peter's brother; Philip; and Nathanael (1:35–51). Only when reading chapter 14 do we come to know about Thomas (v. 5), who, so we can conclude, was also present at the meal.

---

27. See Mary Jacobus, "Is There a Woman in This Text?," in *Reading Women: Essays in Feminist Criticism* (New York: Columbia University Press, 1986), 83–109.

28. Narrative gaps call for the reader's activity as how to fill them. See Iser, "Reading Process," esp. 55; McKnight, *Post-modern Use of the Bible*, 223–41; Meir Sternberg, *The Poetics of Biblical Narrative* (Bloomington: Indiana University Press, 1985); Robert Alter, *The Pleasures of Reading in an Ideological Age* (New York: Simon & Schuster, 1989).

But what about women? Though no woman is mentioned explicitly within the narrative (just as Thomas and the other male disciples are not mentioned explicitly), women have to be considered present nevertheless. The textual reference to Jesus's having loved "his own" (13:1) and the designation of this scene as a meal scene open up this narrative to the narratives in chapters 11 and 12. Before chapter 13, only three people were mentioned as being loved by Jesus: Lazarus, Martha, and Mary (11:3, 5). In 12:1–8, they gave a dinner for Jesus (v. 2), because he had raised Lazarus from the dead (v. 1).[29] While Lazarus was one of those at the table with Jesus, Martha served (v. 2), and Mary anointed Jesus's feet (v. 3). This implies that the Bethany family has to be included among Jesus's "own" whom he loved to the end (13:1). Besides that, the "unidentified number of disciples" makes room for more than the disciples who are explicitly mentioned.[30] When we reach the end of the gospel and encounter the resurrected Jesus and Mary Magdalene in the garden (20:11–18), it becomes clear that also Mary Magdalene must have been present at the Last Supper and the footwashing. When she recognizes Jesus by his calling her by name (20:16), she is defined as one of "his own" (see 10:3). Because she is implicitly introduced as one of a group of women who went to the tomb on Easter morning (see "we," 20:2), other women might also be included already in chapters 13–17. Besides these clear text signals that link chapter 13 to other texts in the gospel, thereby making room also for women, the androcentric-inclusive language enables the reader to think of women even when they are not explicitly mentioned. Therefore, "his own" and "the disciples" can be regarded as comprising male and female disciples.[31] This becomes fully obvious only by reading the whole gospel, from beginning to end, and, when arriving at the end, by rereading the gospel and thereby actualizing new meaning dimensions due to increased knowledge.[32]

---

29. It seems to have been a kind of resurrection party. In fact, eating is important after resurrections (see Mark 5:43; John 21:12–13).

30. Fernando F. Segovia, *The Farewell of the Word: The Johannine Call to Abide* (Minneapolis: Fortress, 1991), 3. He also stresses the unity of chs. 13–17. Thus, the presence of Thomas at the footwashing is confirmed.

31. The same refers to the ἀδελφοί (brothers), as family members and as disciples. See Sandra M. Schneiders, "John 20:11–18: The Encounter of the Easter Jesus with Mary Magdalene—A Transformative Feminist Reading," in Segovia, *Readers and Readings of the Fourth Gospel*, 164, 166. For an inclusive reading of the Gospel of John, see also "How Can This Be?," in this volume.

32. Reading as first-time-reading is different from any rereading of a text. See

When reading Jesus in chapter 13, we do not yet know of Mary Magdalene and other (implicitly mentioned) female disciples. However, Martha and Mary have already entered the stage. As mentioned above, the definition of the scene as a meal and the reference to Jesus's love for "his own" open up chapter 13 to the preceding chapters 11 and 12. To imagine these women (and their brother) as present at the footwashing is one consequence of this link between the chapters. But there is more to this. A special relationship is indicated between Jesus and Mary of Bethany.

Jesus Encounters Mary of Bethany

The parallels between 13:1–20 and 12:1–8 are striking.[33] In both scenes, a meal is taking place, with Jesus and some of his disciples present. Both times, something totally unexpected happens. In Bethany, Mary starts to anoint Jesus's feet with precious perfume of pure nard and then dries his feet with her hair (12:3). This, certainly, is not the usual act of hospitality extended toward one's guest. Whatever Mary's original intention may have been (we are not informed about it), Jesus interprets her action in terms of his impending death: "She bought it so that she might keep it for the day of my burial" (v. 7). Thus he responds to Judas Iscariot's objection to Mary wasting the perfume (vv. 4–6). In chapter 13, it is another disciple, Simon Peter, who objects to Jesus's action, and again Judas is introduced in a negative way, this time as the betrayer (in 12:6 he is called a "thief"). In both meal scenes, the unusual action is a symbolic act full of meaning, and both times it involves the feet of the recipients.

Rereading 12:1–8 in the light of 13:1–20 sheds new light on Mary of Bethany. She can be viewed as one who has already carried out what Jesus demands of his disciples, and thus she proved to be a true disciple (see 13:14–15). However, such rereading can also enrich the characterization of Jesus. By establishing configuration between Jesus and Mary of Bethany, a new dimension is added to the former. We can conclude that Jesus acted in a way similar to Mary. In fact, according to the temporal

---

Kitzberger, "How Can This Be?," in this volume; Matei Calinescu, *Rereading* (New Haven: Yale University Press, 1993); Iser, "Reading Process," 56; Segovia, "Reading Readers of the Fourth Gospel and Their Readings," esp. 241–42, on "first time-reader/multiple-reader axis."

33. See also Maurits Sabbe, "The Footwashing in Jn 13 and Its Relation to the Synoptic Gospels," *ETL* 58 (1982): 298–300.

sequence of the narrative, Jesus appears as the one who seems to have been inspired by Mary's action. After all, she was the first who had the idea about the feet. Thus, Mary becomes a role model for Jesus's action. He learned from this woman.

Yet there is a difference between Jesus's action and Mary's action: she *anointed* his feet, while he *washed* his disciples' feet. The similarity of their action is due to both wiping the feet afterwards: Jesus with a towel, Mary with her hair. Thereby, the latter's action is implicitly described as a washing, however strange the sequence of action, that is, the wiping away of the *perfume*, may sound. But it is precisely this sequence that opens up this text to an intertext in the Synoptic Gospels: Luke 7:36–50. There, the sequence is more logical: the woman wets Jesus's feet with her tears, dries them with her hair, and *then* anoints them (v. 38). As I have argued elsewhere, the gap in the Johannine anointing narrative (the missing tears, and hence no washing) opens it up to the Lukan anointing narrative, and thus interfigurality is established between Mary of Bethany and the anonymous Lukan woman.[34]

Due to the configuration between Jesus and Mary of Bethany and due to her interfigurality with the Lukan woman, interfigurality is also established between Jesus and the Lukan woman. In fact, there are more parallels between the latter two, because both are actually *washing* the feet.

Jesus Encounters the "Sinner Woman"

Any reader of John who is familiar with the Synoptic Gospels—we present readers but also most likely part of the first readers in the Johannine community—will think of the Lukan woman when reading John 13. While the Johannine footwashing replaces the Last Supper of the Synoptics and is thus unique to John, there is only one footwashing narrative in the entire gospel tradition apart from John's. Thus, naturally, the one opens up intertextuality to the other, and consequently interfigurality between Jesus and the woman is established.[35]

---

34. See Kitzberger, "Love and Footwashing," 195–96.
35. According to Sabbe, who employs a redaction-critical approach, John 13 is based on the following Synoptic models: the Last Supper, especially the Lukan version; the anointing of Jesus, in particular the Lukan version in 7:36–50, but also the Markan/Matthean version (Mark 14:3–9; Matt 26:6–13); and other Synoptic material ("Footwashing in Jn 13"). For the numerous verbal links between John 13 and Luke 7,

The passage in Luke 7:36–50 is also portrayed as a meal scene. One of the Pharisees (vv. 36, 39), who is later identified by Jesus as "Simon" (v. 40), invites Jesus to eat with him, and so Jesus takes his place at his table (v. 36, literally: he reclined). The expression "and behold" (καὶ ἰδού, v. 37) expresses the unexpected: "And a woman in the city, who was a sinner, having learned that he was eating in the Pharisee's house, brought an alabaster jar of ointment." The narrator introduces her as a "sinner woman" (γυνὴ ἁμαρτωλός), which probably denotes a prostitute. Thereby, the reader's evaluation of the woman is already influenced. On the other hand, his or her expectation is raised as to how the host, Jesus, and the other guests will react. But before anyone has a chance to react, the woman starts to act: "She stood behind him at his feet, weeping, and began to bathe his feet with her tears and to dry them with her hair. Then she continued kissing his feet and anointing them with the ointment" (v. 38). The host's reaction follows right away: "Now when the Pharisee who had invited him saw it, he said to himself, 'If this man were a prophet, he would have known who this woman is who is touching him—that she is a sinner'" (v. 39). This time, it is the Pharisee who defines the woman as a sinner, though he does so only in his thoughts. At the same time, while the Pharisee is sure about the woman, he doubts Jesus's identity, because his expectations with regard to his guest are completely disappointed by Jesus's nonreaction to the woman's scandalous behavior. Jesus, knowing his host's silent considerations, addresses him. We thereby get to know his name as Simon (v. 40).

Jesus then confronts Simon with a parable in which love refers to the canceling of the debts (vv. 41–42). Thus the subject of love is introduced into the narrative, though in a rather strange manner, because the reference is rather to "gratefulness" than what we would normally call "love." After Simon's correct answer to Jesus's question (vv. 42–43), Jesus, for the first time, turns to the woman (v. 44), but only to address Simon and ask him: "Do you see this woman?" (v. 44). The question sounds strange: How could the host *not* have seen the woman? But it also draws Simon's and our attention to her.

It seems odd that Simon, and not the woman, is addressed. In the course of the narrative, she becomes an object of a male discourse: they

---

see "Footwashing in Jn 13," 302–5. I came across Sabbe's article in 1992, after I had already established the link between John 13 and Luke 7. Despite our different methodological approaches to John and the Synoptics, we share the belief that the Fourth Gospel was directly dependent on the other gospels.

speak *about* her, not *with* her, and she is not permitted to raise her own voice. Thus a feminist reading, my reading, is a resisting reading. Nevertheless, a surprising turn follows right away: Jesus blames the Pharisee by contrasting his nonaction with the woman's action: "I entered your house; you gave me no water for my feet, but she has bathed my feet with her tears and dried them with her hair. You gave me no kiss, but from the time she came in she has not stopped kissing my feet. You did not anoint my head with oil, but she has anointed my feet with ointment" (vv. 44–46). By putting the blame on the host, Jesus characterizes the woman as his true host: she did what Simon should have done. However exaggerated and not fully justified Jesus's rebuke is, the woman is thereby fully rehabilitated. Not only is her action regarded as correct rather than as scandalous, as it seemed to this point, but she is also defined as a role model for Simon. Things are completely reversed: the "sinner woman" is a role model for the (righteous) Pharisee! We can assume that not only Simon (and the other guests) in the narrative were completely taken by surprise, but also any readers, from first readers to present readers.

The sequel to the narrative diminishes this climax. The woman is, once again, defined as a sinner, though her sins have been forgiven, as Jesus lets Simon know (v. 47), before he lets the woman herself know! (v. 48). "Your sins are forgiven" and "Your faith has saved you; go in peace" are the only words addressed directly to her (vv. 48, 49).[36] She is no real dialogue partner; rather, she is being patronized. Consequently, the characterization of Jesus, as constructed in the text and as reconstructed by the reading presented here (my reading), is very ambivalent. It is positive as far as the woman is seen as a role model. Yet, it is also negative, because Simon is too harshly blamed and, most of all, because the woman is made an object and is silenced.

The similarities, but also the dissimilarities, between John 13:1–20 and Luke 7:36–50 are evident. In both narratives, the footwashing comes as a surprise, for the characters in the narrative and for the readers. Both

---

36. Luke 7:36–50 is a very complex narrative, with ambivalent and even contradicting messages, e.g., while in v. 47 the woman's sins have been forgiven already, Jesus forgives them in v. 48; and in v. 50 a completely new idea comes into play: the woman's *faith* has *saved* her. Also, whether her love was the reason for the forgiveness of her sins, or followed as a consequence (see v. 47), cannot be answered: the text is contradictory and thus creates many puzzles and raises many problems for a reader. See Kitzberger, "Love and Footwashing," 198–202.

times, someone called Simon objects to the action: Simon the Pharisee and Simon Peter; the first a spectator, the second an addressee. In both narratives, Jesus talks with the one who is scandalized and explains the meaning of the action, the woman's and his own. While Simon the Pharisee is blamed for not acting like the woman, Simon Peter is finally persuaded to let Jesus wash his feet. The most striking fact, however, is the relation between footwashing and love in both narratives. In Luke 7, Jesus defines the woman's action of weeping and bathing his feet with her tears (v. 38) as "footwashing" (v. 44, "you gave me no water for my feet"). According to one semantic axis of the text, love was the woman's motivation for her footwashing and anointing: she showed her great love by acting the way she did. Likewise, the Johannine Jesus demonstrated his love for "his own" by washing their feet, and they are called to follow his example (13:14–15; see 13:34–35).

Opening up John 13:1–20 to Luke 7:36–50, interfigurality is established between Jesus and the woman, and out of the many meaning dimensions of both texts, love and footwashing become the dominant semantic axes. Such intertextual and interfigural reading has far-reaching consequences for the characterization of the Johannine Jesus: he is modeled after a woman, and even more so after a "sinner woman," a prostitute. As she washed his feet, so Jesus, in turn, later washed his disciples' feet. Again, as with Mary of Bethany, Jesus learned from a woman. Although the interfigurality between Jesus and a woman who was considered a prostitute sounds scandalous, it is very much in line with Jesus's scandalous action of footwashing, whereby he made himself a servant and in fact renounced his mastership (13:13–16).

In terms of the relation between John and the Synoptics, the message of such an intertextual reading must have been equally startling for those of the Johannine first readers who were familiar with the Synoptic Gospels, just as it is for us. Traditional norms and ways of thinking are turned upside down and consequently overcome. Though we cannot know what the author of John intended, it seems that he consciously modeled his Jesus on the Lukan "sinner woman." After all, the Johannine Jesus is portrayed as being confronted with the accusation of being himself a sinner (ἁμαρτωλός). His healing the man born blind on a Sabbath in chapter 9 gives rise to a dispute among the Pharisees: "Some of the Pharisees said, 'This man is not from God, for he does not observe the Sabbath.' But others said, 'How can a man who is a sinner perform such signs?' And they were divided" (9:16). Thus, Jesus was considered a sinner by some of the Pharisees. This is confirmed later in the narrative. When the Pharisees call the man born blind for the second time, they tell him: "Give glory to God! We know that this man is a sinner" (v. 24). The healed man answers the Pharisees' accusation: "I do not know whether he is a sinner. One thing I do know, that though I was blind, now I see" (v. 25). And in the course of his dispute with Jesus's opponents the man explicitly denies that Jesus is a sinner: "We know that God does not listen to sinners, but he does listen to one who worships him and obeys his will" (v. 31). On the other hand, the man himself is considered a sinner because of his blindness. "You were born entirely in sins, and you are trying to teach us?" the Pharisees respond. At the beginning of the narrative, Jesus rejected his disciples' questioning of whether the man himself or his parents had sinned, because he was blind from birth (vv. 1–2). Instead, Jesus considers the man's blindness as the site of God's revelation (v. 3).

Viewing John 13:1–20 in the light of chapter 9 confirms the intertextuality between chapter 13 and Luke 7. Besides the semantic axes engendered by love and footwashing, the issue of being considered a sinner links the Johannine and Lukan texts. The interfigurality between Jesus and the woman implies also solidarity: both were defined by *others* as sinners. While we are not informed about the woman's own construction of her identity, we know that Jesus's self-understanding clashed vehemently with the identity imposed on him by others, especially by his opponents.

It is also noteworthy that Simon Peter, the only character featuring besides Jesus in John 13:1–20, is the only one who, in the Synoptic tradition, called himself a sinner. When Jesus calls him as his first disciple, after the miraculous catch of fish, Simon Peter falls down at Jesus's knees, saying, "Go away from me, Lord, for I am a sinful man" (ἀνὴρ ἁμαρτωλός εἰμι, Luke 5:8). Thus, the links between the Johannine texts, John 13 (and John 9), and the Lukan texts, Luke 7 (and Luke 5), are obvious, and the interfigural reading as presented above is confirmed.

The Johannine Jesus: Transcending Gender Boundaries

The configuration between Jesus and Mary of Bethany is significant. Not only is Jesus related to her, but she becomes a role model for him: he learns from her and bases his own footwashing on her anointing his feet beforehand. Such reading, as presented above, adds an important dimension to the characterization of the Johannine Jesus in terms of gender relations.

Even more significant is Jesus's interfigurality with the Lukan "sinner woman." By portraying the male character, Jesus, in the light of a female character, the anonymous woman, gender boundaries are transcended.

Such intertextual reading is strongly encouraged and confirmed by the interfigurality between the Johannine Jesus and another woman: Sophia/Chokmah in the Hebrew Bible and in deuterocanonical writings, in particular in Prov 8 and Sir 24.[37] There, she speaks in the first person, very similar to Jesus's "I am [ἐγώ εἰμι]" sayings in John. Like the Johannine Jesus, she is preexistent and was present already at the beginning of creation, as the first created, and she participated in creation (Prov 8:12–31; Sir 24:3–6, 9). She has built her tent and dwells among humans (Sir 24:8, 10). She offers life and love (Prov 8:17, 35), and she invites humans to eat and drink of her (Sir 24:19–21).[38] She grows among the humans like a tree: like a terebinth she spreads out her branches, and like the vine she buds forth delights, and her blossoms become glorious and abundant fruit (Sir 24:16–17).

Wisdom traditions are present throughout John's Gospel, yet in particular in the prologue and in chapters 6, 7, and 15. Like Sophia/Chokmah, the Johannine Jesus is preexistent and mediated in all creation: "He was in the beginning with God. All things came into being through him, and without him no one thing came into being" (1:2–3, 10). He, the Logos, became flesh and lived among us, literally: "built his tent" (ἐσκήνωσεν, 1:14). He brought life, which was the light of all people, and shone into the dark (1:4–5); and the love between Jesus and his Father, as well as between Jesus and his disciples, permeates the whole gospel. The Johannine Jesus invites people to come to him and eat and drink of him: "I am the bread of life. Whoever comes to me will never be hungry, and whoever believes in me will never be thirsty" (6:35). "I am the living bread that came down from heaven. Whoever eats of this bread will live forever" (6:51).

The entire dialogue between Jesus and the people, which follows the multiplication of the loaves and fishes (6:1–59), refers to the food that

---

37. See, though with a different approach, Martin Scott, *Sophia and the Johannine Jesus*, JSNTSup 71 (Sheffield: JSOT Press, 1992); Ben Witherington III, *John's Wisdom: A Commentary on the Fourth Gospel* (Louisville: Westminster John Knox, 1995); Sharon H. Ringe, *Wisdom's Friends: Community and Christology in the Fourth Gospel* (Louisville: Westminster John Knox, 1999).

38. See Judith E. McKinlay, *Gendering Wisdom the Host: Biblical Invitations to Eat and Drink*, JSNTSup 216, GCT 4 (Sheffield: Sheffield Academic, 1996).

Jesus himself is. Chapter 7, on the other hand, focuses on Jesus as the drink. In the context of the Feast of Booths, he invites the people to drink of him: "Let anyone who is thirsty come to me, and let the one who believes in me drink. As the scripture has said, 'Out of the believer's heart shall flow rivers of living water'" (7:37-38). This drink, so the narrator comments, refers to "the Spirit, which believers in him were to receive" (v. 39). Jesus gives this drink at his crucifixion when he gives the Spirit (19:30, παρέδωκεν τὸ πνεῦμα), and when blood and water flow forth from his body (19:34). Like Sophia/Chokmah, Jesus compares himself to the vine, and his disciples to the branches: "I am the true wine, and my Father is the vinegrower," and "I am the vine and you are the branches. Those who abide in me and I in them bear much fruit, because apart from me you can do nothing" (15:1, 5).

These few hints may suffice to indicate that the Johannine Jesus is modeled after Sophia/Chokmah. Accordingly, Johannine readers who are familiar with the Wisdom traditions are encouraged to establish these interfigural links. Whereas it has been argued that the Johannine Jesus, the Logos, co-opted and actually replaced Sophia/Chokmah,[39] I advocate a different reading. Because Jesus is linked to this female character, he is characterized as both male and female. He is definitely portrayed as a man, as the Son of his Father, but at the same time he is enriched with female traits that originate from Sophia/Chokmah. Thus, if interfigurality is realized, as argued above, the characterization of Jesus changes drastically compared to a reading that remains within the confines of John's Gospel.[40] Again, gender boundaries are overcome in his person, and because Jesus is one with his Father, as he repeats throughout the gospel, and because whoever sees Jesus sees also the Father (e.g., 14:7-11), the Father's charac-

---

39. So, for example, Norman R. Petersen, *The Gospel of John and the Sociology of Light: Language and Characterization in the Fourth Gospel* (Valley Forge, PA: Trinity Press International, 1993), 110-32. See also Alison Jasper, *The Shining Garment of the Text: Gendered Readings of John's Prologue*, JSNTSup 165, GCT 6 (Sheffield: Sheffield Academic, 1998).

40. The interfigurality that is established between the Johannine Jesus and Sophia/Chokmah confirms also the interfigurality between Jesus in John and the "sinner woman" in Luke, because, as Raymond E. Brown notes, "Luke comes closer than does any other Synoptic Gospel to identifying Jesus as the wisdom of God (11:49), a wisdom that can be shared with his followers (21:15)." See Brown, *The Birth of the Messiah: A Commentary on the Infancy Narratives in the Gospels of Matthew and Luke*, ABRL (New York: Doubleday, 1993), 469, where he refers to Luke 2:39-40.

terization is also affected. Consequently, the Johannine God-Father must also be viewed in female terms.[41]

"How Can This Be?": Nicodemus Revisited

Reading Nicodemus in John 19:38–42

At the beginning of the passion narrative, in chapter 13, Jesus demonstrated his love for his disciples by his act of footwashing. At the end of the passion narrative, in chapter 19, two of his disciples, in turn, render a service of love to their dead rabbi. "After these things" (μετὰ δὲ ταῦτα, 19:38), that is, after Jesus's death on the cross, his giving the Spirit to his followers (19:30), and the piercing of his side (vv. 34–37), the two disciples carry out what is left to be done. "Joseph of Arimathea, who was a disciple, though a secret one because of his fear of the Jews, asked Pilate to let him take away the body of Jesus. Pilate gave him permission; so he came and removed his body" (v. 38). Joseph is described as a "secret disciple" (μαθητὴς τοῦ Ἰησοῦ κεκρυμμένος) in retrospect, because here, at the end of the gospel, he turns up for the first time. This implies that, while so far he has been a secret disciple, he now becomes public. He openly goes to Pilate to ask permission for Jesus's body, and he demonstrates his discipleship by providing a proper burial. Nicodemus comes to assist him in this task. Unlike Joseph, Nicodemus featured previously in the gospel, as the narrator indicates in reintroducing him: "Nicodemus, who had at first come to Jesus by night, also came, bringing a mixture of myrrh and aloes, weighing about a hundred pounds" (v. 39). The reference to Nicodemus's first encounter with Jesus links the present scene in chapter 19 to chapter 3. Thereby, the reader is encouraged to recall what happened then, at the beginning of the gospel and at the beginning of Jesus's ministry. The nightly encounter between Jesus and the Pharisee Nicodemus was shaped by the talk about rebirth

---

41. See also Jesus as "born of God" (ἐκ θεοῦ ἐγεννήθησαν) in 1:13; besides that, κόλπος in 1:18 can be translated as "womb." See also Judith M. Lieu, who draws attention to the tradition of the maternal God of prophecy and psalmody in the Hebrew Bible, e.g., Hos 11:1–4; Isa 42:14; Ps 139:13; Deut 32:18—God is the one who has carried from the womb and has given birth. See Lieu, "The Mother of the Son in the Fourth Gospel," *JBL* 117 (1998): 76. See also Lieu, "Scripture and the Feminine in John," in *A Feminist Companion to the Hebrew Bible in the New Testament*, ed. Athalya Brenner, FCB 10 (Sheffield: Sheffield Academic, 1996), 225–40.

from above.⁴² "Very truly, I tell you, no one can see the kingdom of God without being born from above," so Jesus challenged Nicodemus. The old rabbi met this new option offered to him with mere puzzlement, "How can anyone be born after having grown old? Can one enter a second time into the mother's womb and be born?" (v. 4). In his response, Jesus further explained his invitation, "Very truly, I tell you, no one can enter the kingdom of God without being born of water and Spirit" (v. 5). "How can these things be?" Nicodemus asked Jesus after his exploration of the nature of the Spirit, as opposed to the flesh (vv. 6–9). Instead of an answer, however, Jesus rebuked him for his lack of understanding: "Are you a teacher of Israel, and yet you do not understand these things?" (v. 10). When Jesus started on his long monologue (v. 11), thereby merging with the voice of the narrator,⁴³ Nicodemus was left puzzled. Yet, like Jesus, he journeyed on, and we briefly met them together again when Jesus was put on trial by the Pharisees. On this occasion, Nicodemus spoke up for Jesus and defended him against the accusations (7:50–51). Again, Nicodemus was rebuked, that time by his fellow Pharisees (v. 52). Just as after his first encounter with Jesus, so also here Nicodemus disappears from the scene, though, if regarded as belonging among the Pharisees, he turns up implicitly in the ensuing narrative. When we reach the end of the passion narrative, our reencounter with Nicodemus comes as a surprise. It seems, that he—like Joseph—has emerged from the secret and dares to become public,⁴⁴ now that all things are fulfilled. Whereas he came to Jesus by night the first time, he now comes by day to join Joseph in burying Jesus's body.⁴⁵

---

42. The Greek ἄνωθεν can mean both, "again" and "from above." I translate it as "rebirth from above" because, in fact, both meanings are inherent at the same time in the Johannine use of the expression.

43. See Derek Tovey, "From Teller-Character to Reflection-Character: The Narrative Dynamics in John 3," in *Narrative Art and Act in the Fourth Gospel*, JSNTSup 151 (Sheffield: Sheffield Academic, 1997), 148–67.

44. See Moloney, *Glory Not Dishonor*, 149: "Both of these *secret* disciples of Jesus now become *public*." So also Maurits Sabbe, "The Johannine Account of the Death of Jesus and Its Synoptic Parallels (Jn 19, 16b–42)," *ETL* 70 (1994): 53. See Raymond E. Brown, *The Death of the Messiah: From Gethsemane to the Grave; A Commentary on the Passion Narratives in the Four Gospels*, ABRL (New York: Doubleday, 1994), 2:1267: "We are left with the expectation that the public action of Joseph and Nicodemus will lead them to bear witness to Jesus after the resurrection."

45. In John, Jesus is buried while it is still day; in the Synoptics, the burial takes place in the evening, after sunset; see Mark 14:42 (par. Matt 27:57); Luke 23:54. See

Whereas in the early chapters Nicodemus was characterized primarily by what he said, in his dialogue with Jesus in chapter 3 and in his defense of Jesus against the Pharisees in chapter 7, he is now characterized by what he does. Together with Joseph, he does what needs to be done; words seem to have become superfluous when facing Jesus's body. "They took the body of Jesus and wrapped it with the spices in linen cloths, according to the burial custom of the Jews" (v. 40). Silently they fulfill their self-assigned task. By describing the procedure in detail, the narrator emphasizes the act. "Now there was a garden in the place where he was crucified, and in the garden there was a new tomb in which no one had ever been laid. And so, because it was the Jewish Day of Preparation, and the tomb was nearby, they laid Jesus there" (vv. 41–42).

While Joseph features also in the Synoptic Gospels and is thus already known to those readers (Johannine first readers and present readers) familiar with the other gospels,[46] Nicodemus is a character unique to John's Gospel. Equally unique is Jesus's burial. Due to the introduction of Nicodemus in John, Jesus receives a proper burial, according to Jewish custom. While Joseph's part is his requesting Jesus's body from Pilate, Nicodemus's main contribution is the huge amount of spices he brings: a mixture of myrrh and aloes, weighing about a hundred pounds (φέρων μίγμα σμύρνης καὶ ἀλόης ὡς λίτρας ἑκατόν, v. 39). Therefore, while in the Synoptics Jesus is hurriedly placed into the nearby tomb, without any further attendance, in John the two men provide a decent burial. Thereby, they also confirm their discipleship. Nicodemus is characterized as "the one who first came by night," but also by his spices (ἀρώματα, v. 40). These spices, myrrh and aloes, as well as the huge amount of them, are important text signals, because they open up this text to other texts and relate Nicodemus to other characters, in John and outside.

---

also Craig R. Koester, *Symbolism in the Fourth Gospel: Meaning, Mystery, Community* (Minneapolis: Fortress, 1995), 205: "On Good Friday Nicodemus acted before nightfall, while it was still the Day of Preparation (19.42)."

46. See Mark 15:42–47; Matt 27:57–61; Luke 23:50–55. The characterization of Joseph varies: according to Mark, he was "a respected member of the council, who was also himself waiting expectantly for the kingdom of God"; according to Matthew, he was "a rich man" and "was also a disciple of Jesus"; according to Luke, he was "a good and righteous man … who, though a member of the council, had not agreed to their plan and action," and "he was waiting expectantly for the kingdom of God." According to Matthew, the tomb was Joseph's own tomb (27:60).

First, any reader reading John 19:38–42 will recall Mary of Bethany, who, in 12:1–8, anointed Jesus equally graciously, with a pound of costly perfume of pure nard (λίτραν μύρου νάρδου πιστικῆς πολυτίμου, 12:3). Configuration is established between Nicodemus and Mary.[47] She anointed Jesus beforehand for his burial. In fact, Jesus told her adversary, Judas, to leave her alone, "so that she might keep it for the day of my burial" (12:7). Now, the actual day of his burial has arrived, but it is Nicodemus who carries out the anointing. Thus, while both characters, Nicodemus and Mary, are related to each other, there remains also a riddle for the reader, depending on the interpretation of Mary's keeping (τηρήσῃ) the anointment. In any case, there is no doubt that she actually anointed Jesus during the dinner with her family. Thus, John presents in fact a double anointing: one beforehand and one at Jesus's death. This is unparalleled by any other gospel.

Second, Nicodemus's spices open up this text in John to the Synoptic anointing stories, and interfigurality is established between Jesus and the Synoptic women who anointed or intended to anoint Jesus.

Nicodemus Encounters the Synoptic Anointing Women

In the Synoptics, ointments and the act of anointing are related to women only. There, no man comes up with such an idea. It seems that this change of roles was left to the old rabbi.

Nicodemus is related, on the one hand, to the anonymous woman who anointed Jesus in Simon's house in Bethany and, on the other hand, to the women who intended to anoint Jesus's body on Easter morning.[48]

The huge amount of Nicodemus's spices parallels the precious ointments applied by the unnamed woman who entered Simon the leper's house during a meal and anointed Jesus's head (Mark 14:3–9, par. Matt 26:6–13). She used "very costly ointment (of pure nard)" (μύρου νάρδου

---

47. See Sabbe, "Johannine Account of the Death of Jesus," 53: the burial "surely corresponds to the anointing of Jesus by Mary in Jn 12, 7 whose action somehow anticipated the later anointing at the burial."

48. Though he does not expand on this, Sabbe refers to the Synoptic women at Easter: "The anointing of Jesus' body ... also betrays some Synoptic inspiration.... The spices called ἀρώματα (v. 40) correspond to the ἀρώματα in Mk 16, 1; Lk 23, 56; 24, 1 with which the women are occupied at a later stage, when the sabbat was past" ("Johannine Account of the Death of Jesus," 52–53).

πιστικῆς πολυτελοῦς, Mark 14:3; μύρου βαρυτίμου, Matt 26:7). Due to the accusation of waste uttered by some of the guests (Mark 14:4), or the disciples (Matt 26:8), the worth of the ointments is emphasized: more than three hundred denarii,[49] according to Mark; a large sum, according to Matthew. The worth of Nicodemus's spices is not specifically mentioned, but the unparalleled and exceptionally huge amount denotes a similar "waste" of money, if regarded in human, logical terms. Thereby, it is also indicated that Nicodemus was a rich man; at least he could afford what he offered spontaneously.[50] In both Synoptic narratives, the woman's act of anointing Jesus's *head* is interpreted by Jesus as an anointing of his *body* beforehand for his burial (Mark 14:8; Matt 26:12). Thus, the anointing refers to a *pars pro toto*; the head indicates Jesus's whole body. The fact that Jesus's head is anointed most likely indicates also the woman's confession of Jesus as the Messiah, the suffering Messiah, as it were.[51]

The other anointing narratives in the Synoptics are also, and even more so, linked to Jesus's death. According to Mark and Luke, the women disciples come to the tomb on Easter morning in order to anoint Jesus's body and thereby do what was missed at his actual hurried burial by Joseph. According to Mark, there are three women disciples: Mary Magdalene, Mary the (mother) of James, and Salome (16:1). According to Luke, the company, referred to as those who had followed him from Galilee (23:55), comprised more than three women: Mary Magdalene, Joanna, Mary (the mother) of James, "and the other women with them" (Luke 24:10). According to Mark, they "bought spices [ἀρώματα], so that they might go and anoint him" (16:1). According to Luke, the women "prepared spices and ointments" (ἀρώματα καὶ μύρα, 23:56) and came to the tomb "taking the spices [ἀρώματα] that they had prepared" (24:1). However, the intended anointing does not occur, because Jesus's body is no longer there. Matthew is the only evangelist who takes seriously the fact that Jesus was already

---

49. This is the equivalent of a year's income of an average day laborer; see Matt 20:1–16.

50. That he *brought* the spices indicates that he had them already and thus did not have to go and buy them. See Brown, *Death of the Messiah*, 1259: "There is a spontaneity and unexpectedness in 'But there came also Nicodemus.' ... Implicitly he was rich like the Matthean Joseph."

51. To my knowledge, Elisabeth Schüssler Fiorenza was the first to recognize this meaning (*In Memory of Her*, xiv, with reference to the Hebrew Bible prophets anointing the head of the Jewish king; the anointing of Jesus by the woman was a "prophetic sign-action").

anointed beforehand for his burial by the unknown woman; hence there is no need to anoint him a second time. In Matthew, therefore, the women disciples, Mary Magdalene and the "other" Mary (the mother of James and Joseph, 27:56), come to the tomb on Easter morning in order to "see" the tomb (27:1), with no intention of an anointing.

Luke, on the other hand, who in 7:36–50 replaced the anointing of Jesus's head by the anointing of his *feet*, presents the most detailed account of the intended anointing on Easter morning. Whereas in Mark the women buy the spices after the Sabbath (16:1), in Luke they prepare the spices and anointments (ἡτοίμασαν ἀρώματα καὶ μύρα) right after Jesus's death and rest during the Sabbath (23:56), and they bring the prepared spices (φέρουσαι ἃ ἡτοίμασαν ἀρώματα) to the tomb on Easter morning (24:1). The emphasis is clearly on the preparation of the spices and thus on the intended act of anointing. This detailed report in Luke corresponds with the detailed report of Jesus's burial, and in particular the application of Nicodemus's spices, in John.[52] This is corroborated by another astonishing parallel: just as Nicodemus comes along with his spices on the Friday, right after Jesus's death, so the Lukan women prepare their spices also on the Friday, right after Jesus's death. Consequently, the *interfigurality* between Nicodemus and the Synoptic anointing women refers foremost to the Lukan women, Mary Magdalene, Joanna, Mary (the mother) of James, and the others with them. Moreover, their characterization as those who have followed Jesus from Galilee (Luke 23:55) corresponds with Nicodemus's characterization as the one who had at first come to Jesus by night (John 19:39). In both cases, those who attend (or intend to attend) to Jesus's

---

52. It can be debated whether Nicodemus actually *anointed* Jesus's body. The text is not specific on that, but only tells that Nicodemus, together with Joseph, wrapped Jesus's body with the spices in linen cloths (19:40). The answer to the question depends on the nature of Nicodemus's mixture, whether it was oil or powder. According to Brown, σμύρνα rather implies powder, while μύρον, as in John 11:2; 12:3–5; Mark 14:3–8, par. Matt 26:6–12; Luke 7:37–38, and (μύρον καὶ) ἀρώματα, as in Mark 16:1 and Luke 23:56; 24:1, implies oil (*Death of the Messiah*, 1260–64). In any case, however, the anointing of the Synoptic women is activated in the narrative of Jesus's burial in John. Consequently, the reader is encouraged to establish an interfigural link between Nicodemus and the women, even if he used "fragrant, pulverized 'myrrh' and 'aloes' that would be sprinkled in with and/or over the burial wrapping around Jesus," as Brown holds (*Death of the Messiah*, 1264). But see also Brown's note that "Anointing would not necessarily consist of rubbing the oil on the corpse, for it could be dripped from a vessel over the body from head to foot" (*Death of the Messiah*, 1261 n. 50).

burial are those whom he encountered already early during his mission. This parallel implies that, like the women in Luke, Nicodemus has come a long way. However, unlike the Lukan women, he did not travel with Jesus on the road (Luke 8:1–3) but followed him (in a figurative sense) at some distance, until he was, through Jesus's death, finally attracted to the young rabbi (see John 12:32).

The interfigural relation to the Synoptic anointing women adds important dimensions to the characterization of Nicodemus and implies mainly two things. First, Nicodemus's function at Jesus's burial, and thus his character as such, is evaluated in a clearly positive manner. Second, by drawing the portrait of Nicodemus in the light of the Synoptic anointing women, and by attributing the female role of anointing to the man, gender boundaries are, once again, transcended. Nicodemus, the Pharisee and leader of the Jews (3:1), is thus characterized in female terms. This, in turn, corresponds with the context in which he was portrayed at the beginning of the gospel. The talk about rebirth confronts the old man with a subject that would traditionally be expected rather in the context of women's talk than men's. It is striking, therefore, that Nicodemus, and not one of the female characters in John's Gospel, became the dialogue partner for Jesus's elaboration of the necessity of rebirth.

But there is still more to Nicodemus's spices. The myrrh, as part of the mixture that he brings along, opens up the Johannine text to yet another Synoptic intertext and consequently relates Nicodemus to other characters: the magi of Matthew's infancy narrative.

Nicodemus Encounters the Magi

Readers familiar with the Synoptic Gospels, and thus also part of John's audience, may be reminded of the magi from Matt 2:1–12 and relate Nicodemus's gift of myrrh and aloes to their gift of gold, frankincense, and myrrh (2:11). In fact, the narrative of the magi is the only other occasion in all New Testament writings, besides the Johannine account of Jesus's burial, where myrrh (σμύρναν) occurs. Yet, the link between the Johannine burial scene and the passage within the Matthean infancy narrative is much more profound, as a closer look reveals.

The narrative of the magi (μάγοι), or "wise men," who come to pay homage to the newborn "king of the Jews," is unique to Matthew. While in 2:1 the narrator introduces them as the magi from the East (ἀπὸ ἀνατολῶν), who come to Jerusalem, verse 2 provides the reason and intention for their long journey by having them ask, "Where is the child who has been born king of the Jews? For we observed his star at its rising, and have come to pay him homage." Whom they ask is not explicitly mentioned. But whoever the original addressee, King Herod hears this and is frightened, and all Jerusalem with him (v. 3). Calling together all the chief priests and scribes, he inquires of them where the Messiah is to be born (v. 4). Thus, it is King Herod who identifies the "king of the Jews" as the expected Messiah. When he learns that Bethlehem of Judah is to be the Messiah's birthplace, he secretly calls the magi and learns from them the exact time when the star appeared to them (v. 7). As Herod calls the magi now, it is suggested that he was not the addressee of their initial interrogation, though we are not told how the news about the magi came to reach him. These gaps in the narrative are left to be filled by the readers and consequently to revision the scene and sequence of events. Herod instructs the magi to search diligently for the child and let him know when they find him, so that he may also pay homage (v. 8).

Leaving the king, the magi set out again, "and there, ahead of them, went the star that they had seen at its rising, until it stopped over the place where the child was. When they saw that the star had stopped, they were overwhelmed with joy" (vv. 9–10). The star, which they saw at its rising (ἐν τῇ ἀνατολῇ) and obviously have not seen since then, guides them from Jerusalem to their destination in Bethlehem. "On entering the house, they saw the child with Mary his mother," so the narrator continues, "and they knelt down and paid him homage. Then, opening their treasure chests, they offered him gold, frankincense, and myrrh" (ἀνοίξαντες τοὺς θεσαυροὺς αὐτῶν προσήνεγκαν αὐτῷ δῶρα, χρυσὸν καὶ λίβανον καὶ σμύρναν, v. 11). No further details of their visit are rendered, nor is any interpretation provided as far as their gifts are concerned. It seems that, having delivered their gifts, they immediately start on their long journey back home, though on another route because of having been warned in a dream not to return to Herod (v. 12). Having reached their destiny and fulfilled their task, they disappear from the stage, never to return.[53] But we, the readers, remain in the house with the child and Mary his mother, and wonder about the significance of this brief encounter that contrasts with the long journey.

---

53. However, their relics traveled even a longer way, finding their final resting place in the Cathedral of Cologne, two hours by train from my place, Münster. On the magi's adventurous story after their death, see Brown, *Birth of the Messiah*, 197–200.

There are three important semantic signals in this narrative: the star, the king, and the gifts. The link between the star and the magi indicates that these men can be regarded as astrologers, because they were able to interpret the sign in heaven.[54] They also had some knowledge about a forthcoming king of the Jews (βασιλεὺς τῶν Ἰουδαίων) so that they could identify the rising star as "his star" (αὐτοῦ τὸν ἀστέρα ἐν τῇ ἀνατολῇ, v. 2). Thereby, they are clearly defined as gentiles, because the king of the Jews is obviously not their own king but that of another nation. Their encounter and confrontation with "King" Herod makes explicit the conflict between two different kings: the newborn king, on the one hand, and the established king who is frightened of his supposed rival, on the other hand. Finally, the gifts of gold, frankincense, and myrrh are significant because they characterize the receiver as king[55] and so underscore the magi's belief that the newborn baby is indeed the king of the Jews. Thus the gentile magi are the first within Matthew's Gospel story to acknowledge and pay homage to the newborn king.[56]

---

54. So also Brown, *Birth of the Messiah*, 169. For the many interpretations regarding the magi from the East, see *Birth of the Messiah*, 167–70; for attempts to identify the star, see *Birth of the Messiah*, 170–74 (explanations have ranged from a supernova or "new star" to a comet and to a planetary conjunction of Jupiter, Saturn, and Mars).

55. See Joachim Kügler, "Gold, Weihrauch und Myrrhe: Eine Notiz zu Mt 2,11," *BN* 87 (1997): 24–33. See Brown's note that "gold" (Hebrew *zahab*) can refer "both to gold and to a type of incense"; since it is yoked with frankincense in Matthew, the latter is plausible (*Birth of the Messiah*, 176). The reference of gold to Jesus's kingship, of incense to his divinity, and of the myrrh to his death is the product of a later interpretation in a treatise called "Excerpta et Collectanea" that is "associated, probably incorrectly, with the saintly Anglo-Saxon historian, 'the Venerable Bede,' of Jarrow (ca. 700)," but it dates back as early as the second century, because it is found in Irenaeus's *Haer.* 3.9.2 (Brown, *Birth of the Messiah*, 199 n. 59).

56. This parallels the end of the gospel, when in Matt 28:16–20 the disciples are commissioned by the risen Christ to go out into the world and "make disciples of all nations" (v. 19). The same significance of the newborn Jesus not only for the Jewish people, but for all nations, is also inherent in the Lukan infancy narrative in ch. 2, within Simeon's song. See Brown, *Birth of the Messiah*, 459: "In their second chapters both evangelists anticipate the future of the Gospel by already bringing into the birth story the themes of Gentiles who are attracted by the light of God's son." The implicit citations of Isa 60:6 and Ps 72:10–11 in Matt 2 underscore that Jesus is king not only for the Jews but for all nations; see Brown, *Birth of the Messiah*, 187–88. Besides these Scripture references, Matt 2 is based on the Balaam narrative in Num 22–24, in particular on 24:17, where Balaam foretells that a star symbolizing the Messiah will arise. See Brown, *Birth of the Messiah*, 190–96.

Reading John 19:38-42 in the light of Matthew 2:1-12, and linking Nicodemus interfigurally to the magi from the East, makes explicit text dimensions inherent in the Johannine text and adds new dimensions to the characterization of Nicodemus. Like the magi, he has come a long way, though his journey has taken place more on an inner than on an outer level. His first encounter with Jesus by night, and Jesus's challenging talk about rebirth from above (John 3), were, in fact, like a rising star that initiated Nicodemus's start on a new journey, which led him into conflict with his fellow Pharisees and finally to becoming a disciple of Jesus.[57] Like the magi, Nicodemus traveled in the dark,[58] symbolically speaking, until he finally encountered Jesus, the Light, when he entombed him while it was still day. Like the magi who offer their gifts of gold, frankincense, and myrrh and thus pay homage to the newborn king, so also Nicodemus, at the end of his journey, offers myrrh and aloes, thus acknowledging and paying homage to his dead king.[59]

---

57. Thus, his journey parallels the three stages of the magi: they set out in the East; travel to Jerusalem, where they encounter the adversary Herod; and finally arrive in Bethlehem. Nicodemus sets out after his first encounter with Jesus in ch. 3; journeys on to his encounter with the adversaries, his fellow Pharisees, in ch. 7; and finally arrives at Jesus's tomb in ch. 19. Nicodemus's first encounter with Jesus at night, linked to the promise of rebirth, opens up John 3 to God's promise of a child to Abram in Gen 15, where the uncountable stars refer to his offspring. See "Aging and Birthing: Open-Ended Stories and a Hermeneutics of Promise," in this volume.

58. Though not explicitly mentioned in Matt 2, it is implicit that the magi traveled in the dark because naturally stars can be seen only at night, unless the "star" refers to a supernova, which is also visible by day. As the text indicates, they were guided by the star only from Jerusalem to Bethlehem, and not on their entire journey. T. S. Eliot, in his poem "Journey of the Magi," significantly envisions the magi as having journeyed at night: "A hard time we had of it. / At the end we preferred to travel all night" (l. 17). "Then at dawn we came down to a temperate valley.... But there was no information, so we continued / And arrived at evening, not a moment too soon / Finding the place" (ll. 21, 29-31). See *The Complete Poems and Plays of T. S. Eliot* (London: Guild, 1986), 103.

59. The huge amount of spices and the location of the tomb in a garden indicate a royal burial provided for Jesus. See Robert J. Karris, who recalls the funeral of "king" Herod the Great, as rendered in Josephus, *Ant.* 17.198-199, where five hundred servants are carrying spices. See Karris, *Jesus and the Marginalized in John's Gospel*, ZSNT (Collegeville, MN: Liturgical Press, 1990), 59. For this and other references (later rabbinic sources and Jer 34:5) denoting the royal burial for Jesus, see Brown, *Death of the Messiah*, 1260-61. For the kings of Judah being buried in garden tombs (2 Kgs 21:18, 26; and King David's sepulcher being in a garden according to LXX of Neh 3:16), see Brown, *Death of the Messiah*, 1270. Finally, Jesus's royal burial is corroborated by

Like the magi, Nicodemus disappears from the stage after having accomplished his task, and it is left to the reader to imagine what becomes of them thereafter.

Linking Nicodemus to the magi thus further confirms his positive characterization, as indicated above in the discussion of his spices. Thereby, it is also confirmed that he is reborn from above and becomes a "child of God" (see John 1:12–13) when he places Jesus's bloodstained body in the tomb. Thus, death and birth are closely linked together in a very striking way. By viewing Nicodemus in the light of the magi, this link, inherent already in John's story, is further corroborated. While the magi offer Jesus their gifts, in particular the myrrh, at his birth, Nicodemus offers Jesus his gifts, in particular the myrrh, at his death[60] and is himself newly born.

The relation between Jesus's death and his birth, as established above through the intertextual links between the Johannine burial account and the Matthean story of the magi, prepares the way to yet another intertextual link. Besides Nicodemus's spices, the linen cloths into which Jesus's body is wrapped are of special significance. They are relevant when the Beloved Disciple and Simon Peter see them on Easter morning (John 20:5–9), and the former comes to believe because of them. However, these linen cloths are an important text signal for the readers already when they are reading the burial account. Thinking of Jesus's birth by recalling the magi story, a reader familiar with the Synoptic Gospels may recall another passage from the infancy narratives, this time the Lukan version, and Mary, Jesus's mother, comes to the fore.

---

his portrayal as king throughout the passion narrative (see 18:33–40; 19:1–5, 14–16, 19–22). The inscription on the cross identified him as "king of the Jews" (19:19), which is reminiscent of the magi's identification of the newborn.

60. The view of the magi's gift of myrrh as foreshadowing Jesus's suffering and death, as documented from the second century onwards, is probably due to reading Matthew's infancy narrative in the light of the later Johannine burial narrative. There is no indication that myrrh (σμύρνα) was used in burial rites. On the contrary, it is used in much more pleasant settings, e.g., Cant 4:14 (together with aloe, as in John 19:39, and also with frankincense, as in Matt 2:11), and Cant 4:6 (again, together with frankincense). The only instance where myrrh is associated with death, apart from the Johannine burial account, is Mark 15:23, where, within the crucifixion scene, Jesus is offered wine mixed with myrrh (ἐσμυρισμένον οἶνον), obviously as a means to dull the pain; but Jesus rejects it.

Nicodemus Encounters Mary the Mother of Jesus

The Lukan birth narrative in 2:1–20 tells of Joseph's and Mary's journey from Nazareth to Bethlehem to be registered, according to Augustus's decree (vv. 1–5). The mention of Mary's pregnancy (v. 5) prepares the reader for the event that follows after their arrival in Bethlehem. "While they were there, the time came for her to deliver her child. And she gave birth to her firstborn son" (vv. 6–7). In just one sentence the essential event of Jesus's birth is rendered. However, one little detail is fully described: "(She) wrapped him in bands of cloths, and laid him in a manger, because there was no place for them in the inn" (ἐσπαργάνωσεν αὐτὸν καὶ ἀνέκλινεν αὐτὸν φάντῃ, v. 7).[61] The cloths and the manger are obviously significant, because they are mentioned again as a "sign" (σημεῖον) in the angel's annunciation to the shepherds in the second part of the birth story: "This will be a sign for you: you will find a child wrapped in bands of cloth and lying in a manger" (v. 12). Finally, the shepherds find "Mary and Joseph, and the child lying in the manger" (v. 16). The cloths are not mentioned again explicitly, but certainly they are included by implication. The fact that Mary herself wrapped Jesus in bands of cloth, right after she had given birth to him, seems to denote an essential detail. The swaddling is nothing extraordinary but the natural care of parents for a newborn. Thus, Mary is depicted as caring for and nurturing her child from the first moment of his entry into the world. On the other hand, Jesus's humanity is emphasized: he is just like any other human newborn.[62] Yet this very fact of being swaddled becomes a sign for the shepherds so that they can find the "Savior, who is the Messiah, the Lord" (v. 11). Together with the mention of the manger, the cloths signify what kind of savior Jesus is: the opposite of a triumphalist ruler.[63]

---

61. See Brown, *Birth of the Messiah*, 418: with regard to Jesus's actual birth, Luke is "very laconic … in describing the event.… Curiously, Luke seems more interested in telling his audience where Mary laid the newborn baby!"

62. See Brown, *Birth of the Messiah*, 399: "To swaddle a baby is a sign of parental care." Against a "'crib-scene' hermeneutics of Luke 2:1–20," Brown asserts: "The swaddling, far from being a sign of poverty, may be a sign that Israel's Messiah is not an outcast among his people but is properly received and cared for" (419 n. 34). Brown refers to Wisdom 7:4–5 (419–20).

63. According to Brown, "Luke has placed his narrative against the background of the imperial claims of Augustus" (*Birth of the Messiah*, 420). For different interpretations of the manger, see Brown, *Birth of the Messiah*, 399, 419. Brown holds that

"They took the body of Jesus and wrapped it with the spices in linen cloths, according to the burial custom of the Jews" (John 19:40). Reading the concerted action of Joseph and Nicodemus in the Johannine burial account in the light of Luke 2:1–20, the parallels are striking, and the interfigural links become obvious. Just as Mary cared for Jesus immediately after his birth by wrapping him in cloths and laying him in a manger, so Nicodemus (together with Joseph) cares for Jesus right after his death by wrapping him in cloths and laying him in a tomb. Once again death and birth become closely linked. As Nicodemus is portrayed in the light of Mary, he is attributed a caring and nurturing role traditionally considered female. This, in turn, is very much in line with the narrative of Nicodemus's first encounter with Jesus by night[64] and their talk about rebirth, which, significantly enough, is recalled in the burial scene (v. 39). It is also very much in line with the interfigurality established between Nicodemus and Mary in John 3. As I have demonstrated in detail elsewhere,[65] Nicodemus's question "How can these things be?" (3:9) opens up this text to the Lukan infancy narrative in Luke 1:26–38. There, Mary asked the same question, "How can this be?" (v. 34), after the angel Gabriel's annunciation that a child will be born to her. Yet, while Mary is given a detailed answer, referring to the Spirit's coming upon her (v. 34), and is told that "nothing will be impossible with God" (v. 37), Nicodemus is rebuked by Jesus for his lack of understanding. But in the context of their nightly talk the Spirit is of the essence, too: the rebirth implies being born "of water and the Spirit" (John 3:5).

Furthermore, Nicodemus and Jesus's mother (never named Mary in John) are linked together in various ways within John's Gospel,[66] so that the intertextual relations to the Lukan infancy narrative are corroborated. Interestingly, while in John Jesus's mother is not portrayed as giving birth

---

"the manger does not signify poverty but a peculiarity of location caused by circumstances," and, with respect to the character of a sign, refers to LXX Isa 1:3: "God's people have begun to know the manger of their Lord" (419).

64. Note also the relation of the shepherds to the night in the Lukan infancy narrative (2:8).

65. See Kitzberger, "Synoptic Women in John," 96–99.

66. Besides the links through birth and death, their stories in John show some parallels: both are first mentioned at the very beginning of the gospel, in ch. 2 and ch. 3 respectively, featuring in an open-ended story; and they return at the end of the gospel, in ch. 19, where both demonstrate their faith. For the characterization of Jesus's mother in John, see Kitzberger, "Synoptic Women in John," 102–8.

to Jesus, it is the man Nicodemus who is portrayed in the context of (re)birth. The intertextual links between John 19:38–42 and Luke 2:1–20, on the one hand, and between John 3:1–21 and Luke 1:26–38, on the other, establish a firm relation between the Johannine passion narrative and the Lukan infancy narrative. Thereby, death and birth are connected in a striking and evocative manner. This, in turn, is in line with John's depiction of Jesus's death that is at the same time a birth:[67] when, dying on the cross, Jesus gives the Spirit (19:30), those who witness are reborn of the Spirit (see 3:5) and become "children of God" (see 1:12–13). Thus, Jesus's mother, together with the other women and the Beloved Disciple (19:25–27), is viewed here within the (implicit) image of birth in a spiritual sense. Further, as she loses her son Jesus, another son is "born" to her when Jesus entrusts her and the Beloved Disciple to each other, so that Jesus's mother becomes the Beloved Disciple's mother and he becomes her son (vv. 26–27). Then, Jesus returns into the womb of his Father, from whom he was born (see 1:13, 18).

Nicodemus: Transcending Gender Boundaries

Like Jesus in John, also Nicodemus is characterized in such a way that gender boundaries are transcended. In addition to the configuration between him and Mary of Bethany with respect to the anointing of Jesus's body, the interfigurality with the Synoptic anointing women and with Mary the mother of Jesus adds significant new dimensions to his characterization. By attributing to him the roles of anointing, and of caring and nurturing, that were carried out by the (un)named Synoptic women and by the Lukan Mary, respectively, Nicodemus is enriched with female character traits. Besides that, his being linked to the topic of (re)birth, within John's Gospel story and by opening up chapters 19 and 3 to the Lukan infancy narratives, the female dimension of his characterization is

---

67. The blood and water flowing out of Jesus's body (19:34) may also be reminiscent of an actual birth, where the water would refer to the amniotic fluid. Judith M. Lieu, who relates the crucifixion scene, and in particular the mother of Jesus, to the parable in 16:21, notes: "So is this a birthing or a dying? …; we meet birth here only when we encounter death. Indeed, the birth, which is not narrated in this Gospel, becomes through 16.21 a death, or is the death a birth?" ("Mother of the Son in the Fourth Gospel," 73).

further corroborated.[68] On the other hand, he is also linked to Synoptic male characters, the magi in the Matthean infancy narrative. This implies two things. First, the interfigural link between Nicodemus and Mary in the Lukan infancy narrative is underscored; and the relation between the Johannine burial account and the Synoptic infancy narratives, and thus the relation between Jesus's death and birth, is strongly emphasized. Second, the portrayal of Nicodemus in the light of female as well as male Synoptic characters confirms that the author of John freely and consciously crossed gender boundaries and clearly invites his readers to do the same.

Final Reflections: Gender Transcendence and Transformation

The readings presented in this paper concentrated on gender as constructed in the text and as reconstructed by the reader. Thus they emphasized gender as a category of analysis. On the other hand, gender boundaries began to shift and were finally transcended in the course of opening up the Johannine texts to Synoptic (and Hebrew Bible) intertexts. By portraying Jesus and Nicodemus in the light of female (and male) characters and thereby attributing to them roles and character traits previously regarded as female, gender boundaries were in fact overcome in these characters themselves. This seems to imply consequences similar to those of Jesus's footwashing action. While the latter demonstrates the overcoming of hierarchies and patriarchal structures, the transcendence of gender boundaries implies the overcoming of divisions according to gender, of gender *apartheid*, and consequently the establishment of true equality between men and women. Thus, a countermodel of community vis-à-vis patriarchy becomes visible behind the Johannine texts, but even more so in the world in front of the texts, in readers reading in such a way.

As with all readings, a new world is created in the act of reading and as a consequence of it, and in turn readers are invited to enter into this world and read the new text. Of course, we simply do not know how John's first readers read his gospel and which of the suggested intertextual links they were able to establish. It is very likely, though, that part of his audience was also familiar with the Synoptic Gospels (and the Hebrew Bible) and could

---

68. Besides his interfigural relation to Synoptic female characters, Nicodemus is also interfigurally related to Sarai/Sara (besides Abram/Abraham) in the Genesis narratives, as I have shown in "Aging and Birthing: Open-Ended Stories and a Hermeneutics of Promise," in this volume.

read Johannine characters in the light of Synoptic characters (and characters of the Hebrew Bible). The old alternative with regard to the relation between John and the Synoptics—that John, in case he knew the Synoptics, either supplemented or replaced them—needs to be transcended too, because, as the readings in this paper have shown, in portraying Jesus and Nicodemus, the Synoptic (and Hebrew Bible) texts and characters were *transformed*. Consequently, when reading the Johannine texts and characters, readers are invited to recall the texts and characters on which they are based and to vacillate between focus text and intertext. This is a very dynamic endeavor and calls for an active reader who is entrusted and empowered to read in his or her own unique way.

As readers, whether past or present, we encounter texts that are literally and pragmatically open, and so are meant to be continued in us. Thus, we have the choice, ever anew, of how we read, which meaning dimensions and textual links we activate in the process, and which kind of worlds we thereby create. The readings in this paper are my own readings, as stated in the beginning, and I claim and acknowledge them as such. They are readings *of* transformation, in the encounter with literary characters, and they are readings *for* transformation, in the encounter between readers reading characters *with*.

Part 4
Characters in John and My Self-Text

"The Truth Will Make You Free" (John 8:32): The Power of the Personal Voice and Readings of/from the Gospel of John

Personal Fragments

"What is truth?" Pilate asked and returned again to the crowd outside, leaving Jesus and the question behind inside. No answer. Not even Jesus tried to explain, enfolding himself in silence while the noise outside got louder. Death was close upon him, and truth was at stake.

∞

"The truth will make you free," I read, looking out the library window. My eyes catch the golden letters on top of the faculty building. It feels good, inspiring, invigorating. I have just started working on my dissertation, spending a year at the University of Freiburg, and the message is golden as I wish my future to be. Returning three years later, in 1981, I worked inside the building, and I felt the protection and the promise and the inspiration of these words when teaching and researching. No questions. Truth was what it was, the goal of all our endeavors; it was knowledge and wisdom, holding a liberating reward for us.

∞

From the surface of Mars—where the sky is salmon and Earth is a blue morning star—you probably would have noticed the spaceship coming. It

---

This chapter was originally a paper presented at the International Research Consultation on Ideology, Power, and Interpretation at Selly Oak Colleges/Westhill College, University of Birmingham (UK), August 3, 1997. Revised and first published in this volume.

may have been the noise the thing made that caught your attention; although the Martian atmosphere is spent and shredded, it's not too tenuous to carry sound. And it's certainly not too tenuous to make anything that tries to punch through it pay the price, causing the interloper to glow like a meteor as it plunged toward the touchdown somewhere on the ancient world. That you could not have missed.

There was, of course, no one in Mars' Aries Vallis floodplain to mark the moment when NASA'S 3-ft.-tall Pathfinder spacecraft dropped into the soil of the long-dry valley. But there was a planet more than 100 million miles away filled with people who were paying heed when it landed, appropriately enough on July 4.[2]

∞

On the night of the Fourth, when we landed on Mars, I walk the beach and watch the fireworks compete with the stars in the enormous black sky. This is Independence Day, and I am alone. So are we all. This is what we discover at times like these—the first flight around the moon, the moon walk, the probe of Jupiter, the Viking missions, and now this amazing, take-your-breath-away event. Errands into space lift us out of ourselves and return us to ourselves. They tell us that we are alone in the universe, and how terrible and how wonderful an idea that is....

What one man calls cosmic loneliness, another might see as being part of a system in which everything is at once lonely and companionable—rocks, beaches, people. Out there is Mars with its wasted territory. Around here are oceans and a gaseous atmosphere that turns the sky blue. The only justification for our loneliness is that we feel it. Did the Neanderthals experience cosmic loneliness? Is that why they kept quiet?[3]

∞

On the same Fourth of July, on the planet Earth, a contract was signed in London, 11 New Fetter Lane, for a book titled *The Personal Voice in Biblical Interpretation.*

---

2. Thus begins Jeffrey Kluger's article "Uncovering the Secrets of Mars," *Time*, July 14, 1997: 40–41.

3. Roger Rosenblatt, "Visit to a Smaller Planet," *Time*, July 14, 1997: 47.

The Truth in John: A Personal Answer

Pilate's question is still echoing today and fills thousands of pages of scholarly books discussing its meaning and function, and questioning its being a question in the first place. "What is truth?" has become one of the main questions of humankind, like the questions of the whence and where of our existence.

Pilate's question remains unanswered, like so many other questions in John's Gospel.[4] Therefore, the readers, or the audience, have to live with these questions and are invited to find answers themselves. The question "What is truth?" is not answered in the context of the trial scene (see John 18:18–38). However, the answer is provided within the larger context of the gospel. "I am the truth," Jesus reveals himself to his disciples during the farewell discourse when Thomas asks Jesus about his own destiny and the way to it (see 14:5). "I am the way, and the truth, and the life," Jesus answers (14:6).

"I am" is the transformation of the objective into the personal, the move from detachment into engagement. "*What* is truth?" turns out to be the wrong question in the first place. "*Who* is truth?" would have been the appropriate one. The alert and understanding reader knows what Pilate did not, and actually could not, know. He did not belong to Jesus and, therefore, did not listen to his voice (see 18:37).

"*What* are you looking for?" Jesus—turning around—asked the first going-to-be-disciples who were following him (1:37–38). "Come and see," is his invitation to their quest for his abode, and, "They came and saw where he was staying, and they remained with him that day" (1:39). The personal encounter of that day empowered them to become Jesus's disciples and to attract others to him with their personal voices (see 1:40–46). They had not found some*thing* but some*body*.

"*Whom* are you looking for?" Jesus asks Mary Magdalene on Easter morning when she has turned around to him (20:15). Her quest is a most personal one, and it is answered by Jesus with the most personal voice—"Mary." And her personal answer is "Rabbouni" (20:16).

A fundamental shift from what to who marks the way of becoming a disciple in John. And it is only to his disciples that Jesus reveals himself

---

4. See 3:4–11; 11:40; also 6:25–26; 12:34–35; 20:15, etc. See "'How Can This Be?' (John 3:9): A Feminist-Theological Rereading of the Gospel of John," in this volume.

as the truth. The truth in John is personal;[5] it has a face, a body, a voice. And it is experienced in committed community. Discipleship leads to the knowledge of truth, which makes free (see 8:32). The liberating power of the truth is promised to those on the way with him who is "the Way."

Truth is, therefore, dynamic, never static, and it is encountered in the process. As such it is life giving and closely linked to the lives of the readers and interpreters of John's Gospel.

"Rock Festival on Mars," or: The Quest for the Personal

"Barnacle Bill. Yogi. Casper. Scooby Doo. Flat Top. Boo-Boo. The Couch. Scoufflé. After a billion of years of anonymity, a motley collection of rocks on the Martian flood plain called Aries Vallis at last had names of their own. And back on Earth last week, the Pathfinder scientists who had playfully nicknamed the rocks were enjoying, as one of them phrased it, a 'rock festival,' reveling in the torrent of data being yielded by the rock stars and their surroundings."

Thus reports and comments Leon Jaroff in *Time* magazine of July 21, 1997, in his article "Rock Festival on Mars."[6] Even more than just naming the rocks, the scientists perceived them and the Sojourner vehicle in most human terms. Sojourner's encounter especially with Barnacle Bill and later on with Yogi are described as very human encounters, with some erotic connotations not lacking. When Sojourner climbed Barnacle Bill, one of the scientists, Matthew Golombek, joked: "Here we have proof that Sojourner sort of nestled up and kissed Barnacle Bill." And when later Sojourner, by mistake, bumped into Yogi and began climbing it, scientist Justin Maki commented that "it got a little too enthusiastic." The chief engineer dubbed Sojourner "The Little Rover That Could." And he proved it. But when the scientists forgot to wake him (her?), one day he could not, and a team member commented: "On the seventh day, it decided to rest."

Naming and viewing rocks and vehicles on Mars in human terms, as well as the irruption of the human point of view on Mars, demonstrates the human quest for the personal. Peopling Mars with the personal amid the highest degree of objective data and scientific perfection projects the

---

5. On the personal character of truth in John, see also Bernard C. Lategan, "The Truth That Sets Man Free (John 8:31–36)," *Neot* 2 (1968): 70–80; Josef Blank, "Der johanneische Wahrheitsbegriff," *BZ* 7 (1963): 164–73.

6. Leon Jaroff, "Rock Festival on Mars," *Time*, July 21, 1997: 72–74.

human need for personal encounters onto a planet one hundred million miles away from us. Experiencing cosmic loneliness, or just earthly loneliness, calls for a voice that is personal.

Biblical Interpretation and the Personal Voice

When I launched the project *The Personal Voice in Biblical Interpretation*, reactions were overwhelming.[7] Colleagues from all around the globe accepted my invitation; others gave a warm support. Many colleagues, so it seemed to me, had just been waiting for an opportunity to utter their personal voices and reflect on them within biblical criticism. Dried-up valleys on the planet Earth, in scholars' souls, that desired to be filled again with living water.

Paradigms Old and New and the Irruption of the "I"

While the planet Mars one hundred million miles away from us is peopled with human-like creatures, down here on Earth we biblical scholars have been trained to get into distance to our objects, the biblical texts, and mute our personal voices.

Paradigms have risen and declined, though the process differed, depending on the countries we live in and also on the years we have spent within the discipline. While some countries have not yet even got a glimpse of the rise of new paradigms, others have already long forgotten the old ones. However, common to most paradigms is the exclusion of the "I," of the interpreter's personality. Within the historical-critical paradigm we have learned to fragment texts and suppress our personal voices. Within literary approaches the unity of the texts has come into focus, but our own voices were still muted. Even reader-response criticism has, by and large, focused on implied readers and implied audiences, as well as imaginative, constructed intended first readers or audiences.[8] Only with

---

7. Ingrid Rosa Kitzberger, ed., *The Personal Voice in Biblical Interpretation* (London: Routledge, 1999).

8. See Fernando F. Segovia's preface to *Readers and Readings of the Fourth Gospel*, vol. 1 of *"What Is John?,"* SymS 3 (Atlanta: Scholars Press, 1996), vii–viii; Segovia, "Reading Readers of the Fourth Gospel and Their Readings: An Exercise in Intercultural Criticism," in *Readers and Readings of the Fourth Gospel*, 273–77, esp. 240–42. See also my first reader constructions, for example, in "Mary of Bethany and Mary of

the rise of cultural studies, with its focus on real flesh-and-blood readers and their social locations,[9] has the personal started peeping into biblical criticism.

The irruption of the "I" into biblical criticism is a process that takes shape in different methodological approaches. Cultural studies stresses more the communal aspect of an individual "I." The focus on real readers in reader-response criticism shows more interest in the individual, though this is not practiced very often and is still rather disguised in reader constructions. The most personal voice, however, can be heard in explicit autobiographical criticism. So far, there is only one monograph in autobiographical biblical criticism, Staley's *Reading with a Passion*, and the Semeia volume *Taking It Personally: Autobiographical Biblical Criticism*, whose preparation overlapped with that of my own project, without knowing of each other, a very timely coincidence, though.[10]

The irruption of the personal "I" has only started to make itself felt in our discipline, but for sure it is an irreversible process, and a very powerful one, too.

Magdala—Two Female Characters in the Johannine Passion Narrative: A Feminist, Narrative-Critical Reader Response," in this volume.

9. See Fernando F. Segovia and Mary Ann Tolbert, eds., *Reading from This Place*, vol. 1, *Social Location and Biblical Interpretation in the United States*; vol. 2, *Social Location and Biblical Interpretation in Global Perspective* (Minneapolis: Fortress, 1995); see esp. Segovia, "Cultural Studies and Contemporary Biblical Criticism: Ideological Criticism as Mode of Discourse," in Segovia and Tolbert, *Social Location and Biblical Interpretation in the United States*, 1–17. "Meaning emerges, therefore, as the result of an encounter between a socially and historically conditioned text and a socially and historically conditioned reader" (8). See also Anthony Easthope, *Literary into Cultural Studies* (London: Routledge, 1996); R. S. Sugirtharajah, ed., *Voices from the Margin: Interpreting the Bible in the Third World* (London: SPCK, 1991); Daniel Smith-Christopher, ed., *Text and Experience: Toward a Cultural Exegesis of the Bible* (Sheffield: JSOT Press, 1995).

10. Jeffrey L. Staley, *Reading with a Passion: Rhetoric, Autobiography and the American West in the Gospel of John* (New York: Continuum, 1995); Janice Capel Anderson and Jeffrey L. Staley, eds., *Taking It Personally: Autobiographical Biblical Criticism*, Semeia 72 (1995). For a survey and discussion of autobiographical approaches in biblical and literary criticism, see Stephen D. Moore, "True Confessions and Weird Obsessions: Autobiographical Interventions in Literary and Biblical Studies," in Anderson and Staley, *Taking It Personally*, 19–50.

The Power of the Personal Voice

To be sure, the personal voice has always been there in criticism in general and biblical criticism in particular, and has made itself felt in the interpretive process. The muted personal voices have always managed to slip into the "objective" and "neutral" investigations,[11] disguising themselves as, for example, the author's intention, the theology of the gospel, or even as God himself. Powerful they have been, these disguised personal voices, *overpowering*, in fact. In historical-critical commentaries they have found their special dwelling places, and due to the authority of this type of supposedly most objective and neutral literature, they have had the strongest impact and influence on generations.

On the other hand, whenever the personal voice of an interpreter is made explicit it becomes powerful, too, but *em-powering* this time. Daring to speak with one's own personal voice and speaking with others who dare to raise their personal voices, too, becomes an empowering and liberating experience, for oneself and for others. "I am" is the truth for everybody, and it is a liberating truth.

The subjects and biblical texts we choose to interpret are as much influenced by our personal voices as are the readings and interpretations of biblical passages. The choices of certain meaning dimensions, and the neglect of others, echo our personal voices. Personal voice criticism makes this impact explicit.[12] Becoming conscious of our own life stories in the encounter with biblical stories, both are transformed and re-created in each other's image. Consequently, the overpowering muted personal voices in objective criticism can be unmasked, too. Personal voice criticism and ideological criticism go hand in hand.

---

11. See Daniel Patte, "The Guarded Personal Voice of a Male European-American Biblical Scholar," in Kitzberger, *Personal Voice in Biblical Interpretation*, 12–23.

12. According to Nancy K. Miller, personal criticism "entails an explicitly autobiographical performance within the act of criticism." See Miller, *Getting Personal: Feminist Occasions and Other Autobiographical Acts* (London: Routledge, 1991), 1. Susan Fort Wiltshire speaks of the "authority of experience" and claims that "all writing is personal" in her essay "The Authority of Experience," in *Compromising Traditions: The Personal Voice in Classical Scholarship*, ed. Judith P. Hallett and Thomas Van Nortwick (London: Routledge, 1997), 168–81.

Readings from/of the Gospel of John

Readings from John

"Readings *from* John" refers to the personal voice in the gospel itself and to the effect on the readers. To be sure, the author of John had a very personal voice, too, and it shaped the way he narrated his story, how he developed his plot, how he portrayed the characters, inserted value judgments, and so on. The ideological dimension of the point of view is most powerful. Especially problematic are readings from John when the issues of anti-Judaism, exclusivism, dualism, or the patriarchal framework turn up.[13] By simply reading these passages, they have enacted their overpowering and harmful effect. Reading *from* John is never objective and neutral. Therefore, any reading *from* calls forth an ethical stance and decision and has to turn into a reading *of*.[14] But, for sure, there are also texts in John, and they are many, that are liberating and can, therefore, be accepted and transformed into the reader's life; for example, the overcoming of hierarchies within the community of disciples by Jesus's call to serve each other (see ch. 13), and the importance of women in John's Gospel. It is also due to John's personal voice that the role of the Twelve, which is so prominent in the Synoptic Gospels, is hardly evident. Equality marks the group of Jesus's followers. It might be coincidence or synchronicity that we are twelve speakers at this conference, including men and women.

---

13. R. Alan Culpepper draws attention to the problematic ethical issues of anti-Judaism, the marginalized and oppressed, and theological exclusivism in John's Gospel in his essay "The Gospel of John as a Document of Faith in a Pluralistic Culture," in Segovia, *Readers and Readings of the Fourth Gospel*, 112–25. For the conflict between the gospel's spirituality and anti-Judaism, see Werner Kelber, "Metaphysics and Marginality in John," in Segovia, *Readers and Readings of the Fourth Gospel*, 129–54, esp. 129–36.

14. See Fernando F. Segovia, who finds himself "both nodding and shaking" his head as he reads the gospel; however, he argues that "speak one must, against all odds, for change and transformation, for wellbeing and justice, and for a God who need to be very much present everywhere." See Segovia, "The Gospel of John at the Close of the Century: Engagement from the Diaspora," in Segovia, *Readers and Readings of the Fourth Gospel*, 216.

Readings of John

"Readings *of* John" refers to the readings and interpretations of John, to ordinary and critical readings alike.[15] Both are highly informed by the personal voice of the interpreter encountering the texts, even if—as with critical readings—the validity of decisions is proven through textual evidence.

Over the past years I have been especially concerned with two stories in John and with their different interpretations, including my own: the Samaritan woman's story in chapter 4 and Mary Magdalene's story in chapter 20. While the first story was the subject of a lecture I presented at Vanderbilt University in November 1996 and which I interpreted autobiographically in the volume *The Personal Voice in Biblical Interpretation*, I want to return now to Mary Magdalene's story, which has been my subject also in two previous papers.[16]

First, I want to sketch briefly several interpretations of John 20–21 and show how they are based on the personal voices of the interpreters. Second, I want to show how my own reading of chapters 20 and 21 has changed due to personal experience.

Personal Voices in the Readings of John 20–21

From the many dimensions of the interpretation of these chapters, I choose five examples that can be traced through all interpretations, no matter how they are informed, respectively. All of them refer to the characterization of Mary Magdalene.

---

15. See Daniel Patte, *Ethics of Biblical Interpretation: A Reevaluation* (Louisville: Westminster John Knox, 1995), esp. 76–112. He draws attention to the fact that our "critical" readings, too, are based on "ordinary" readings and are bringing them to critical understanding. Segovia notes that "cultural studies calls for critical analogies of all readers and readings, whether located in the academy or not, highly informed or not" ("Cultural Studies and Contemporary Biblical Criticism," 13).

16. On the Samaritan woman's story, see "Reading and Rereading the Samaritan Woman's Story: Characterization and Social Location," in this volume; Ingrid Rosa Kitzberger, "Border Crossing and Meeting Jesus at the Well: An Autobiographical Rereading of the Samaritan Woman's Story in John 4:1–44," in Kitzberger, *Personal Voice in Biblical Interpretation*, 111–27. On Mary Magdalene, see "Mary of Bethany and Mary of Magdala" and "How Can This Be?," in this volume.

1. The Conflict and Competition between Mary Magdalene and the Two Disciples

It has become a quite common interpretation to view the relationship between Mary Magdalene on the one hand and Simon Peter and the Beloved Disciple on the other hand as one of conflict and competition, centering on the question of who was first on Easter morning. This question occurs mainly within the historical-critical paradigm, in particular in literary approaches (of the old kind) and in redaction criticism. The insertion of the two disciples' race to the tomb (20:3–10) into the story of Mary Magdalene (20:1, 11–18), so it has been argued, was motivated by and has engendered this hierarchy, and consequently Mary Magdalene was placed second, especially in relation to the Beloved Disciple, who comes to believe (v. 8) before Mary Magdalene encounters the risen Jesus. This argument is often supported by reference to Jesus's words to Thomas, "Blessed are those who have not seen and yet have come to believe" (20:29). Furthermore, the later addition of chapter 21 to the gospel is quite often, especially in feminist interpretations, considered as devaluing Mary Magdalene's first seeing the risen Lord and her role in general. Thereby, the patriarchal bias and the suppression of women in general and Mary Magdalene in particular is seen at work here. However, such interpretations are not forced on us by the text. It can, in fact, be read in a different way, as I will show in my own reading. I suppose that this conflict theory is based on the dominant experience in our own patriarchal world of hierarchies, which is imposed on the text. Thus, it is interpreted in a reader's own image.

2. The Abandoned Mary at the Tomb

"Instead of standing by the side of Mary Magdalene and comforting her, they [the disciples] return home, without a word to her. The woman remains alone at the tomb, alone in her mourning."

Thus one of my students interpreted the passage in chapter 20, especially verse 11, in her thesis, which I supervised at the University of Münster. Reading this sentence for the first time, I added a question mark; but reading it again, I suddenly understood.

One of the gaps in this story is the fact that it is not narrated how Mary Magdalene got back to the tomb after calling the two disciples (v. 2). For historical-critical interpreters, this is a clear sign of redaction. However, for a reader of the present text who regards it as a unity, the task remains to imagine, in one way or another, how Mary Magdalene returned to the tomb. Did she run after the disciples and arrive at the tomb while they were still there, or after they had already left? How this question is answered, and thereby the gap filled, depends on the interpreter. For my student it was obvious that all three characters were at the tomb together for some time, but that the men left the woman behind, alone, not caring for her; they abandoned her. Knowing the student's biography I understood why she had chosen this reading and how the abandoned child, which is deep inside all of us, I believe, made herself felt. Her father had recently died, her mother had died when she was sixteen, and her stepmother had just thrown her out of her home after the father's death. She was abandoned like Mary Magdalene and was longing for comfort in her loneliness and grief. Her own life experience had informed the reading of the story; her personal voice had merged with the voice of the text. For sure, this is a legitimate reading, though not the only possible one.

3. The Stupid Mary and the Gardener

"Supposing him to be the gardener," Mary Magdalene speaks to Jesus without recognizing him (20:15). This short note has engendered legions of interpretations that revel in stressing Mary's stupidity and blindness, who, so they argue, is slow in realizing and should know better. Even when Jesus is standing right in front of her, she does not know it is him!

This kind of reaction on the reader's part is enabled by the discrepancy between the narrator's and the reader's point of view, on the one hand, and the character's point of view, on the other hand. The reader, therefore, feels superior, having the insight that Mary Magdalene is lacking. While the discrepancy between the different points of view is a literary device in the first place, it finds good soil in the reader's desire to be superior, to be better than somebody else, at the cost of this other. By stressing Mary Magdalene's stupidity, the interpreter actually says, "I am better. I know what you don't!" It is, therefore, an interpretation engendered by only too human a desire, based on everyday experience.

However, the note about the supposed gardener is not so much an information about Mary Magdalene's position as a literary device intended for the reader, with a special function in the reading process. It enables the reader to link this scene to the burial scene (19:38–42) and thereby reminds him or her that the tomb was in a garden.

4. Mary, the Touching Woman

For a long time Jesus's instruction to Mary Magdalene has been translated "Don't touch me" and not "Don't hold on to me" (20:17), which is commonly acknowledged nowadays. The former reading has often been elaborated more precisely in erotic and sexual terms, as the woman touching the man who rejects her. Whenever Mary Magdalene was identified with the "sinner woman" of Luke 7:36–50, the erotic dimension of her action and the rejection by Jesus was stressed even more. However, all those readings, very often by celibate men, were rather the utterances of the interpreter's personal voices than the voice of the text. But even the reading "Don't hold on to me" has been directed against Mary Magdalene, describing her in terms of a woman who cannot let go, who does not realize that Jesus has not just returned into the ordinary world. Misogynist and sexist voices have shaped the interpretation of this wonderful text.

5. Mary, the Successful Apostle and the Happy End

The view of Mary Magdalene as an apostle who was commissioned by the risen Lord is no longer a novelty nowadays. It is based on the concluding verses of the scene in 20:11–18, with the narrative sequence of Mary's commission by Jesus and her announcement to the disciples (vv. 17–18). However, we are not told whether her mission was successful, that is, whether the disciples believed her. The following scene (vv. 19–23) rather suggests that they did not. In any case, the story has an open end. The happy end has been inferred over and over again by the interpreters' wishful thinking. To be sure, we all long for happy ends, and very likely we project this desire onto reality. And the less we have experienced happy ends in our lives, the more we long for them in stories we read. This is human, and it is personal.

John 20–21 and My Personal Voice, or: How My Mind Has Changed

Until quite recently the conflict-competition theory and the happy-end theory have been influential in my own interpretations, too. The latter was shattered last fall when I was preparing my paper "How Can This Be?" for the Annual Meeting of the Society of Biblical Literature in New Orleans and suddenly realized my own wishful thinking. To be sure, I have not been spoiled by too many happy ends in my life, either. The conflict-competition theory took a little longer until it was deconstructed. This happened this spring, though it was prepared by experiences last year, which, however, needed some time to sink into my consciousness. Two experiences changed my mind as to how to read John 20–21.

1. Meeting Brother Peter, the Motherly Monk

He was waiting for me outside the monastery and had stayed up late because a stranger had announced herself. I was met with one of the warmest welcomes I have ever experienced in my life. Early in the mornings he would wake me and all the other guests with a big bell, and he gave me a special treat, sensing that I like to sleep long. He cared for us guests like a mother, always busy and cheerful. From the first day I named him the "motherly monk," and when I told him later he seemed to like it. But there were also other motherly fathers and brothers at Mount Melleray Abbey, the Irish Cistercian monastery. They did all kinds of jobs that are traditionally conceived of as female duties, such as cooking, cleaning, washing, even baking the daily bread, besides following their more male duties, thus overcoming the division between male and female gender roles.

Besides the motherly monks, I experienced, though only temporarily during my stay, a community of men and women in which Paul's vision that in Christ there is neither male nor female (Gal 3:28) had become reality.

Consequently, the conflict-competition theory with regard to John 20–21 was no longer convincing to me, and I started to revision the text. Rereading these chapters was now informed by my experience—I viewed Simon Peter in the image of Brother Peter, the motherly monk, and vice versa. And I started to question the relationship between Simon Peter and Mary Magdalene in John's story-world. The fact that Mary Magdalene immediately ran to the disciples after seeing that the stone was rolled away could be viewed very differently, that is, in terms of a very close and intimate relationship. In such a situation of distress one would definitely not call somebody with whom one is in conflict. There is no explicit mentioning in John as to how and when the two disciples and Mary Magdalene met the first time and how they got along with each other. But the narrative presupposes and takes for granted that the readers know that they had been following Jesus for a while and belonged to his own. Mary Magdalene and the Beloved Disciple are portrayed as standing together at the foot of the cross (19:25–27), which suggests a close relationship not only to Jesus but also to each other. No hierarchies are indicated in the development of the story, and no value judgment as to who is better, more faithful, or whatever, either between Mary Magdalene and Simon Peter or between her and the Beloved Disciple. My personal experience of a different relationship between men and women, a glimpse, as it were, of a different reality, was necessary for me to reread the texts in John in a different key.

2. On Becoming a Sheep

During a period of illness last spring, and deeply affected by two recent deaths, staying in bed and feeling very miserable, I was reading and rereading chapters 20 and 21 of John's Gospel. I was especially struck by one passage to which I had never paid too much attention and which, somewhere in my heart, I had met with a kind of resisting reading. "Feed my lambs," Jesus says to Peter, on this special morning on the seashore of the Sea of Tiberias, and a little later, after Peter's second confession of his love for Jesus, "Tend my sheep" (21:15–19). Reading this passage when feeling miserable and very lonely, I longed for someone who would tend and feed me, someone who cared for me. Suddenly Jesus's words had a new meaning for me, very different from my previously held opinion that this text was about Peter's leadership over the flock of sheep, depriving them of their autonomy and freedom. I realized that it is the harmful reception history of this text that has spoiled it. Until that morning in bed I was convinced that I would never want to be a sheep; after all, I am not the type of woman who enjoys being among a herd. Actually, Jesus commissions Peter to take over—after his own departure—the role of the good shepherd (see ch. 10). And was not Mary Magdalene one of his sheep, recognizing Jesus when he called her by name on Easter morning (see 20:16; 10:3)?

Since my own experience with tender and tending men I have felt differently about Peter and Mary Magdalene. Consequently, my reading of chapters 20 and 21 has changed, and a kind of paradigm shift has occurred. These two quite simple, though effective, experiences led me to revision the whole gospel. And I discovered that my readings were in fact strengthened by internal criteria and evidence in the gospel itself. In John 17, Jesus prays to his Father "that they may all be one" (17:20). Thus, he prays for the unity of all disciples, men and women alike. In John, gender boundaries are indeed transcended and role models reversed. Furthermore, overcoming hierarchies in the community of believers is clearly stressed in John's Gospel, in particular in Jesus's call to serve one another (see ch. 13). It is also very significant to note the shift of reference within the dialogue between Jesus and Peter in 21:15–17. "Do you love me more than these?" sounds like testing not only Peter's love for Jesus but also his ethical stance. Peter passed the test; his love is enough, and the second and third time Jesus just asks, "Do you love me?" (vv. 16–17). With regard to love, the question of more or less is inadequate, and hierarchies are out of place.

Based on my own experience, and supported by internal evidence in John's Gospel, patriarchal patterns in interpreting John 20–21 became obsolete. My personal voice has influenced my reading of John.

How Can This Be? The Personal Voices' Way into the Readings of John

Personal voices find their way into all our readings and interpretations, whether consciously or not, whether denied or embraced. The questions are: How can this happen? Why is it that all our readings and interpretations are personal, even those within the supposedly most objective and neutral criticism? Why is it that readings and interpretations, whether ordinary or critical, are as much a reservoir of information about the text as about the interpreter? These questions are closely linked to the questions "What is John?" and "Who am I?"

What Is John?

The debate about the genre and character of the gospels is still vividly pursued,[17] and learned answers, well argued, have been presented. My answer to the question "What are the gospels?" is a different and simple one. They are fragments, puzzles, rather a sketch than a finished picture. They actually withhold more information than they render, and more often than not they leave the readers frustrated. There are gaps and breaks in the stories, ambivalences, even contradictions, and open ends, often con-

---

17. See, e.g., Richard A. Burridge, *What Are the Gospels? A Comparison with Greco-Roman Biography*, SNTSMS 70 (Cambridge: Cambridge University Press, 1992); Detlev Dormeyer, *Evangelium als literarische und theologische Gattung*, EdF 63 (Darmstadt: Wissenschaftliche Buchgesellschaft, 1989).

See Segovia's reflection on the title *"What Is John?"* in the preface to Segovia, *Readers and Readings of the Fourth Gospel*, vii–x. He notes the intertextual play with Pilate's question "What is truth?" (John 18:38) and says that it "is meant to convey the slippery nature of the text's meaning and significance in contemporary Johannine studies" (ix).

nected with the disappearance of characters we have just got acquainted with. Over the past year or so, and especially since working on the New Orleans paper "How Can This Be?" I have become more and more aware of how strange the character of the gospels is in general and of John in particular. Taking seriously into account the rhetoric of the texts, instead of abstracting some kind of content from them, the great demand the gospels place on their readers becomes apparent.

Why has the good news come down to us in such a strange and sometimes even bewildering shape? So I have been asking myself. The author's intentions are beyond our reach. If I ever happen to meet the evangelists in heaven, for sure I will ask them this question. Meanwhile I am more concerned with the effects such fragmentary and puzzling texts have on us, generations of readers, what they do to us and how we react to them. Besides the frustrations and heated debates about the meanings, it is due to the fragmentary character of the gospel texts that our personal voices get a chance to come in. Because the texts are what they are, we get involved in the reading process, we have to become active and make decisions,[18] and we are responsible for what the text says. The gospel story fragments call for our personal answers to make them whole by informing them with our own life stories, which, for sure, are fragments, too. Within such a fragmentary encounter meaning emerges. This is part of the good news.

Personal Intertextualities

Reading a text in general and a gospel text in particular is always an intertextual event, where the text of the reader and the texture of the gospel text meet and interpret each other, respectively. To be sure, each of them is also made up of intertextualities. The gospel texts are embedded within a network of relations to other texts, of the Hebrew Bible, or, as with John, of the Synoptic Gospels. And the texts of the readers, too, are composed of various intertexts; they are multidimensional life stories. As different from the real flesh-and-blood readers in cultural studies, the "I" in personal voice criticism is more than a socially or historically shaped individual,

---

18. See Edgar V. McKnight, *Post-modern Use of the Bible: The Emergence of Reader-Oriented Criticism*, 2nd ed. (Nashville: Abingdon, 1990), 223–41; Wolfgang G. Iser, "The Reading Process: A Phenomenological Approach," in *Reader-Response Criticism: From Formalism to Post-structuralism*, ed. Jane P. Tompkins (Baltimore: Johns Hopkins University Press, 1980), 55.

defined by his or her social location, and thus as an individual member of a community or group of people. The "I" in personal voice criticism is completely unique, a text unlike any other in this world, on which different stories have been written, a person with a multiple identity and therefore many personal voices.[19] So it happens that a multidimensional text and a multipersonal reader meet. And the possible personal intertextualities are more than the world could hold.

The Truth Will Make You Free, or: Will the Truth Make You Free?

"You are rapidly moving out of the German orbit," a friend's voice came through cyberspace. The truth is, I am on my way, venturing out into unknown territory, getting into contact with my own personal voice/s and those of others who dare to utter theirs. The more honest I am to how I interpret, and why I interpret the way I do, the more I realize and unmask the ideologies and muted personal voices behind other interpretations, and the more I welcome and embrace those who are aware of their personal, fragmentary, and open-ended life stories and their impact on biblical criticism.

While this experience of encountering and uttering the personal voices of oneself and of others is for sure a liberating truth, pursuing this path might not be so liberating in terms of career and acceptance within the guild. Whether personal voice criticism turns out to be a truth that liberates or not depends, therefore, on the point of reference. But for sure personal voice criticism is a pathfinder, tracking the path of our life stories and reporting on their landing on those planets called "biblical texts" and on their surface of fragmentary rocks. Whether we bump into them or nestle up and kiss them, they are made alive in a very new and unique way, the ruins become vital again, and life is put back into them.[20] This is part of the good news.

---

19. See Susanna Morton Braund, "Personal Plurals," in Hallett and Van Nortwick, *Compromising Traditions*, 38–53.

20. The first image is taken from William A. Beardslee, though he uses it in a somewhat different sense. See "Vital Ruins: Biblical Narrative and the Story Frameworks of Our Lives," in *Margins of Belonging: Essays on the New Testament and Theology*, AARSR 58 (Atlanta: Scholars Press, 1991), 219–36. For the second image, see Wilhelm Wuellner, "Putting Life Back into the Lazarus Story and Its Reading: The Narrative Rhetoric of John 11 as the Narration of Faith," *Semeia* 53 (1991): 113–32.

Reading and Rereading the Samaritan Woman's Story: Characterization and Social Location

There he was, sitting at the well, in the heat of the day, tired and alone. "Give me a drink," he said, looking at me, with expectant eyes, deep as the well.

∞

There I was, sitting at the well, in the heat of the day, tired and thirsty, disciples gone. "Give me a drink," I said to her, who suddenly appeared, unexpectedly, "Deep is the well, and I cannot reach."

∞

A Well-Known Story?

We all know this story, don't we? The encounter at the well, between a man and a woman, a Jew and a Samaritan, one named Jesus, the other unnamed. An encounter of long ago that, nevertheless, has been discussed and reflected on by many spectators and critics. An intimate one-to-one encounter has become the object of debate by those watching and listening. The disciples are gone, but we are present. How ironic indeed. And yet, we have never been present either, in the real event. Nobody, except the two people involved, knows what happened that day in this specific place, two thousand years ago. We do not have access to the encounter

---

This chapter was originally a lecture at Vanderbilt University, Nashville, November 14, 1996. I thank Fernando F. Segovia and Daniel Patte, who kindly invited me on behalf of the Divinity School, the Department of Religious Studies, the Graduate Department of Religion, and the Office of the University Chaplain. It turned out to be a wonderful experience, in which I encountered other border crossers, faculty and students, from different parts of the world and social locations.

itself; we only have a literary version of this encounter, a narrative constructed by using certain literary devices, shaped and determined by the author's and narrator's point of view, by what he says or does not say, by the message and ideology conveyed to the readers, and the author's skills to guide them through the unfolding narrative and thus affect their reactions and responses in certain ways. Consequently, the characters in the story are also constructs, portraits, not the real persons behind the picture.

So, what is the story in John 4:1–42 all about? And who are the characters in the story; in particular, who is the Samaritan woman?

How nice and kind of Jesus, some people say, to speak to this woman, a Samaritan even, and to consider her worthy of a theological conversation.

How great of John, the evangelist, others say, to give so much attention to this woman, and to other women in his gospel; what a positive image he portrays of them, thereby reflecting the importance of women in his own community.

The Samaritan woman becomes a disciple and a missionary to her people, so some, not only explicit feminists, are convinced.

She is immoral, a sinner, a harlot, others contradict, just think of her six men! She is husband hunting, now being after Jesus, a recent voice suggested.[1]

She is quite slow in understanding, others say. Even when Jesus reveals himself to her, she does not really come to believe in him as the Christ.

It is a story about God's grace and gracious gifts, still others insist; it is about the abundance of living water welling up from the believer into eternal life and quenching the spiritual thirst forever. The woman is not really important in this context; she just functions to demonstrate this divine revelation through Jesus.

Reading and Rereading the Story: A Challenge

The readings and interpretations of this text appear to be endless, with ever new versions coming up. The meaning of this text seems to be as elusive as the Christ of the Fourth Gospel.[2]

---

1. Jo-Ann Brant, "Husband Hunting: Characterization and Narrative Art in the Gospel of John," *BibInt* 4 (1996): 205-33.

2. Mark Stibbe, "The Elusive Christ: A New Reading of the Fourth Gospel," *JSNT* 44 (1991): 20-38.

I have been reading and rereading this story many times, alone and with others—scholarly and ordinary readers—in different contexts. And my own rereadings produced different results, according to my own flowing identity and changing life situations.

Comparing different readings, by different people and also by oneself, is indeed a challenge. How is this possible? There are basically two reasons for the diversity and multiplicity of readings, in general and of the Samaritan woman's story in particular.

First, it is one of the longest and most complex gospel narratives, comparable in fact only to the narrative of Lazarus's resurrection, and his sisters Mary and Martha of Bethany, in John 11. Such narratives are, like the gospel story itself, meant for rereading. "The end is where we start from," to say it in T. S. Eliot's words. It is impossible to come to terms with these narratives in the course of just one reading, due to the complexity of the text, the gaps, ambivalences, and puzzles the readers are confronted with. In addition, rereading is adequate to the text, because of the richness and the potentials inherent in it. One reading could never do justice to this. The text is, therefore, not a fixed entity and does not present a closed world whose meaning could be excavated once and for all, if one only had the proper tools. On the contrary, reading is a process, constantly flowing like living water, never static, and irrigating various trees bearing various fruits. The diversity and multiplicity of readings is legitimized by the text itself because of its many meaning-producing dimensions, its multidimensionality.[3]

Second, "You will know them by their fruits," so Jesus concludes at the end of the Sermon on the Mount (Matt 7:20).[4] The fruits of different readings and interpretations, too, reveal something about the persons behind them. They reflect, even if unconsciously, the readers' personal voices and their social locations, that is, the specific life contexts and biographical backgrounds that have left their imprints on the "text written on the soul."[5]

Consequently, the variety of readings of the Samaritan woman's story is also due to its readers' social locations. It is obvious that a Jew or a

---

3. See Daniel Patte, *Ethics of Biblical Interpretation: A Reevaluation* (Louisville: Westminster John Knox, 1995), esp. 37–40.

4. Unless otherwise indicated, biblical quotations in this chapter are from the RSV.

5. This expression was coined by Weli Mazamisa, from South Africa, in personal email communication.

Samaritan or a Christian, a man or a woman, read this story differently. However, the interaction between text and reader is much more complex than that. Furthermore, social location does not remain static even for the same person. It can and in fact does change. Consequently, it has an impact on the reading of the text. This has become evident in my own rereadings of the Samaritan woman's story over the years.

Characterization and Social Location

We know who Jesus is, don't we? At least we think we know. We are in a privileged position. When the Samaritan woman met Jesus, she did not know who he was. She had not read the prologue of the gospel and the narratives developing Jesus's identity in chapters 2–3. When we encounter the woman's encounter with Jesus, we know much more than she does, and so we watch, listen, and wait for what happens. We are curious whether she comes to understand or not, and we make up our minds about her, often with contradicting results.

The challenging aspect about characterization is its double nature. On the one hand, characterization is the art of an author or narrator to portray a character. On the other hand, characterization is the reader's task and his or her reconstruction of a character. The author or narrator provides the bones, and the flesh-and-blood reader fills in the flesh and blood to recreate the human being, as it were; and in his or her image they are created.

In my approach to characterization, I have an open view of character, as advocated by Seymour Chatman.[6] Characters are not only evaluated by the function of their actions in relation to the plot but are treated as autonomous beings and are assessed the way we evaluate real people. Rhoads describes this approach very well when he states: "In this approach we analyze not only what characters do but also who they 'are.' The interpreter reconstructs what kind of 'persons' the characters are from the narrator's description and characterization, the characters' interactions with others, their motives, and so on, then assign them traits, noting how the traits are revealed and whether they change in the story."[7] "The interpreter reconstructs characters only from the evidence suggested within the boundaries

---

6. Seymour Chatman, *Story and Discourse: Narrative Structure in Fiction and Film* (Ithaca, NY: Cornell University Press, 1978), 107–38.

7. David Rhoads, "Narrative Criticism and the Gospel of Mark," *JAAR* 50 (1982): 411–34.

of the narrative world," so Rhoads adds. However, characters are also constructed to a great extent by the real world of the real readers, which interacts with the narrative world the text offers to its readers. Thus, the boundaries of the narrative world are opened up, and characters in the story are as much the author's construction as the reader's reconstruction. Two different worlds meet, and the boundaries become fluent.

Our social location is where we start from, and it is where we turn to again after our encounter with the text. And both, the text and we ourselves, experience transformation in the process.

The Samaritan Woman's Story—the Story of a Border Woman, or: Two Strangers Meeting in the Borderland

"I am a border woman," she says. "I grew up between two cultures, the Mexican (with heavy Indian influence) and the Anglo (as a member of a colonized people in our own territory). I have been straddling the tejas-Mexican border, and others, all my life." In her book, *Borderland/La Frontera: The New Mestiza*, Gloria Anzaldúa deals with the "actual borderland," the Texas–US Southwest/Mexican border, but she adds: "The psychological borderlands, the sexual borderlands and the spiritual borderlands are not particular to the Southwest. In fact, the borderlands are physically present wherever two or more cultures edge each other, where people of different races occupy the same territory, where under, lower and upper classes touch, where the space between two individuals shrinks with intimacy."[8]

"I am a border woman," the Samaritan says. "I am living in two different worlds and in none really. I am the daughter of a mixed race, Jewish and pagan, a bastard. I am a woman, a stranger in a men's world. Invisible but strongly felt borders separate us, women from men, Samaritans from Jews. I am an unmarried woman, not belonging to the community of 'normal women,' with husbands and children. I am an outsider, and sometimes an outcast, belonging nowhere really, living a life of multiple identities. The borderland is my home."

"To construct feminist (sub)versions of biblical narratives and to claim for women a voice denied to them by the larger story"—this is J. Cheryl

---

8. Gloria Anzaldúa, *Borderland/La Frontera: The New Mestiza* (San Francisco: Aunt Lute, 1987), preface.

Exum's aim in her book *Fragmented Women: Feminist (Sub)versions of Biblical Narratives*.⁹

"So long as we remain within the boundaries of the literary text itself … the study of women in ancient literature cannot become anything other than the study of men's views of women. Thus the first step in constructing versions of women's stories from the submerged strains of their voices in men's stories is to subvert men's stories. This can only be done … by stepping outside the androcentric ideology of the biblical text," and the task is "bringing to the surface and problematizing what is suppressed, distorted, and fragmented."¹⁰

The Samaritan woman's story in John 4 is not her story. It is a male, androcentric, and patriarchal version. The text reflects the patriarchal attitude toward women but also the Jewish attitude toward the Samaritans. It reflects a hierarchical, binary worldview, including domination and colonization. We, the readers, are taken along this track and view the woman as "the other" and the inferior. The "how nice of Jesus" attitude drastically reflects this pattern and thereby accepts the structures of suppression and injustice. A subversion, or counterreading, of the story implies stepping outside the story's framework and ideology. It is only then that the sexism and racism inherent in the story can be discovered, even though both are—at least partially—transcended in the course of the narrative. Counterreading the story implies rereading from a different perspective, the irruption of the "I," the woman's self, speaking with her own voice. Rereading is revisioning, which shatters certainties in order to release liberating potentials.

In an androcentric-patriarchal context, women are fragmented and muted, and they "are often made to speak against their own interests," so Exum found out.¹¹ "Come, see a man who told me all that I ever did. Can this be the Christ?" Thus the woman reports to her townsfolk on returning from the well (John 4:29). What did she ever do? Jesus was presented as having knowledge about her previous five men and the present sixth man in her life, but he did not make any judgment. By putting the words "that I ever did" on the woman's lips, she is made to speak against her own interests. The value judgment of an androcentric-patriarchal community—including

---

9. J. Cheryl Exum, *Fragmented Women: Feminist (Sub)versions of Biblical Narratives*, JSOTSup 163 (Sheffield: JSOT Press, 1993), 9.

10. Exum, *Fragmented Women*, 9–10.

11. Exum, *Fragmented Women*, 11.

male biblical interpreters—is thus justified by the woman's own words. And, ironically enough, it is because of these words that the people of Samaria come to believe in Jesus (v. 39). The woman is made to speak against her own interests and is thus made a stranger to herself.

This is further achieved by being portrayed as a woman who has internalized the patriarchal world view and self-understanding. "Our father Jacob," she says, "who gave us this well, and drank from it himself, and his sons, and his cattle" (v. 12). "Our fathers worshipped on this mountain," she states later on (v. 20). The woman defines herself through the ancestral line of fathers and sons; the mothers and daughters are completely missing, and nothing seems to be wrong with that. The woman agrees to and accepts her social location as "the other," the inferior—with regard to men and the Jews. "How is it that you, a Jew, ask a drink of me, a Samaritan woman?" So she is wondering at the beginning (v. 9). She is portrayed as a woman who knows where her proper place, her location, is.[12]

Furthermore, she is estranged from herself and fragmented by being reduced to her sexuality. "Come, see a man who told me all that I ever did," so the woman reports to her townspeople, with the implicit indication of her sexual immorality. Jesus's insight into her history of relationships is presented as the source of her still-hesitant belief that he is the Christ and as the source of the subsequent belief of the inhabitants of Sychar. Not a single word is mentioned of the highly theological conversation about living water from God, and about prayer and worship. Why? Because the story is about a woman, who, by her very nature, is bound to her sexuality? In the case of Nathanael in chapter 1, Jesus also shows insight. "How do you know me?" Nathanael asks Jesus, puzzled about his statement, "Behold, an Israelite indeed, in whom is no guile" (v. 47). "Before Philip called you," Jesus answers him, "when you were under the fig tree, I saw you" (v. 48). This leads to Nathanael's confession that Jesus is the Rabbi, the Son of God, King of Israel (v. 49). In the Samaritan woman's case, Jesus's insight into her sexual past and present initiates her belief in him as the Christ. There is a parallel between both stories and a difference. There is nothing wrong with sitting under a fig tree, or any other tree. But we believe, or are made to believe, that there is something wrong with a woman having had a few men in her life. This shows patriarchal double standards. The woman is

---

12. See Anne Thurston, *Knowing Her Place: Gender and the Gospels* (New York: Paulist, 1998).

defined by her sexuality and nonmarital status, whereas sexuality is no issue in men's stories. Why does the Johannine Jesus not ask Nathanael about the women in his life? Sitting under a fig tree is so innocent, isn't it? The trees in the garden of Eden in the Genesis story were more challenging and turned out to be disastrous because of the lustful first woman, the prototype of all women. After eating the forbidden fruit, the eyes of Adam and his wife "were opened, and they knew they were naked; and they sewed fig leaves together and made themselves aprons," so the story tells us (Gen 3:7). Why fig leaves? And why was Nathanael sitting under a fig tree? We do not know. Is there any intertextual meaning dimension intended? We may just guess.

Through various literary devices, the woman is portrayed as a stranger, to others and to herself. However, viewed from a different perspective, it is Jesus who is the stranger. Indeed, the woman meets Jesus on her home ground. We were blind to this fact by the prevailing view, so that this important dimension of the story went unnoticed. This can only be achieved by counterreading, reading against the grain and viewing the scene through the woman's eyes.

In Samaria, it is Jesus the Jew who is the stranger, the foreigner, the tourist, passing through this transit country on his journey from Jerusalem to Galilee (v. 4). However, he is portrayed by the author and narrator, and consequently perceived by the readers, as the master, the patron. And because it is Jesus, this seems to be all right, appropriate, and legitimate.

However, the Jesus of the Fourth Gospel is a stranger from beginning to end. "He came to his own home, and his own people received him not," so the prologue informs us programmatically (1:11). Jesus himself testifies that "a prophet has no honor in his own country" (4:44). He is not really understood and fully recognized by the people he encounters, his own brothers do not believe in him (7:5), and he remains a stranger even to his own disciples, male and female, until after his resurrection.

Like the Samaritan woman who lived a borderland existence with a mixed identity, belonging to two worlds and none at all, so Jesus, too, lived such an existence, although differently. He lived in the earthly and heavenly realms simultaneously. While walking on earth, he did not really belong there and remained a stranger.[13]

---

13. One of the border crossers I met at my Vanderbilt lecture was Leticia A. Guardiola-Sáenz, who contributed a wonderful chapter on Jesus's position in John in a later volume of mine: "Border-Crossing and Its Redemptive Power in John 7:53–8:11: A

"Living on borders and in margins," Anzaldúa says in her preface, "keeping intact one's shifting and multiple identity and integrity, is like trying to swim in a new element, an 'alien' element."

"We are always strangers or aliens, the permanent others, both where we come from and where we find ourselves." This is the social location of Hispanic Americans, as Segovia has described it.[14] "It is a continuous twofold existence," of "having two places and no place on which to stand."[15] However, by making this the starting point of an autonomous self-definition, this mixed identity and privileged knowledge can become the source of liberation, the empowerment to "swim in a new element."

My Social Location and Reading of the Samaritan Woman's Story

I am a border woman, too. I have not only lived close to geographical borders all my life, in different places, but I have also inhabited various other borderlands. As a woman, I have lived the greater part my life, both private and professional, in a men's world, belonging and not belonging, being defined as "the other," deprived of self-definition and of speaking with my own personal voice. Like the Samaritan woman, I was speaking with a man's tongue, speaking in androcentric language, and thinking in patriarchal terms. And for a long time I took it for granted that Jesus's disciples and apostles were an exclusively male community. This is what I had learned, in church and even at university. Nothing seemed to be wrong with that. Looking back now, decades later, I realize how much I was made a stranger to myself, like the Samaritan woman in the story.

"What do you want?" and "Why are you speaking with her?" So the disciples wonder when they return from the town of Sychar to the well and see Jesus engaged in conversation with the woman, but they do not say anything (v. 27).

Cultural Reading of Jesus and *the Accused*," in *Transformative Encounters: Jesus and Women Re-viewed*, ed. Ingrid Rosa Kitzberger, BibInt 43 (Leiden: Brill, 2000), 267–91.

14. Fernando F. Segovia, "The Text as Other: Toward a Hispanic American Hermeneutic," in *Text and Experience: Toward a Cultural Exegesis of the Bible*, ed. David Christopher-Smith (Sheffield: JSOT Press, 1995), 276–98, here 289; Segovia, "Two Places and No Place on Which to Stand: Mixture and Otherness in Hispanic American Theology," *Listening* 27.2 (1992): 26–40.

15. Segovia, "Text as Other," 287.

"What do you want?" That was also part of an atmosphere I experienced when I began to study theology at a time when women were just a few newcomers in a male world and profession. Border woman again, but then I began to cross borders and boundaries, however difficult this turned out to be. The experience of being confronted with the question "What do you want?" has been repeated many times along my academic path.

In addition, since 1981 I have lived in a foreign country, as an Austrian in Germany. I belong to both countries, and to none (even though I still have my Austrian passport). The borderland has become my home, and it is in my heart, where both cultures, mentalities, and languages meet.[16]

Because of my social location I have been able to realize these meaning-producing dimensions in the text that refer to borders and boundaries and to being a stranger. And during a recent stay in my home country, Austria, it dawned on me that the Samaritan woman met Jesus on her home ground. Being "at home" in Austria, also a transit country like Samaria, I imagined a German tourist coming along and treating me the way the Johannine Jesus treats the Samaritan woman, "Give me a drink!" "Go, call your husband, and come here." "If you knew the gift of God, and who it is that is saying to you, 'Give me a drink,' you would have asked him, and he would have given you living water." Receiving orders, and being blamed for not knowing something I never had a chance to learn, and now being told that it is too late for the gift—would you wish to be treated like that? I asked myself. Definitely not, was my answer. And all of a sudden the wonderful portrait of the liberating Jesus who overcomes ethnic and gender boundaries, and the portrait of the Samaritan woman as disciple, missionary, and apostle, collapsed. In addition, my fascination for the image of living water gave way to noticing the sexist and racist meaning dimensions of the story. Changing position by turning to the other side of the well, identifying with the woman and revisioning the scene through her eyes, has made this rereading possible. To be sure, the other textual dimensions are still present in this story, but no longer exclusively. By sitting with the woman, rereading her story and reconstructing the characters from my own social location, I also have gained new knowledge about myself, and I have reconstructed my own identity.

---

16. There is indeed quite a difference between Austrian German and German German, with a variety of local variations in both countries and a difference in mentalities.

Conclusions

Characterization and social location cannot be separated. Reflecting on, and being honest to our own readings and rereadings, but also being attentive to the readings of others, remains a never-ending task and challenge. Sitting at the wells of our own lives, we can meet and share our readings, respecting the otherness of readings different from our own and empowering each other to speak with our own personal voices. This is the kind of truth that can make us free, bring about transformative encounters that cross and overcome hierarchical borders and boundaries, and establish mutuality and equality. Together we can reread biblical texts, and the texts of our own lives, and envision creative and liberating alternatives.

Flowing Identities

Gone with the Wind, Reborn of the Spirit—
An Autobiographical Reading of John

Now there was a baby named Benjamin, the tiniest human creature I have ever seen. He had come by day, on September 25. But his hour had not yet come.

"Very truly, I tell you, no one can enter the kingdom of God without being born of water and Spirit. What is born of the flesh is flesh, and what is born of the Spirit is Spirit" (John 3:5).

The reading from the gospel was still echoing among the newborns and among us who stood near when, on September 27, Benjamin was baptized. He was fast asleep, due to medication, when he became a child of God and was received into the Roman Catholic Church.

"To all who received him, who believed in his name, he gave the power to become children of God, who were born, not of blood or the will of the flesh or the will of man, but of God" (John 1:13).

Benjamin's mother and father, through whose will he had been born, were sitting next to the incubator and looked tenderly at their little one, who as yet had not decided between life and death. Tears were flowing from their eyes and from ours.

"'Out of the believer's heart shall flow rivers of living water.' Now he said this about the Spirit which believers in him were to receive; for as yet there was no Spirit, because Jesus was not yet glorified" (John 7:37–39).

It was the last day of the festival of Sukkot, remembering the days when God's people lived in their temporary dwelling places during their desert wanderings.

Originally published as "Flowing Identities," in *Autobiographical Biblical Criticism: Between Text and Self*, ed. Ingrid Rosa Kitzberger (Leiden: Deo, 2002), 79–96.

"And the Word became flesh and tented among us, and we have seen his glory, the glory of a father's only son, full of grace and truth" (John 1:14).

Benjamin lay motionless, yet his tiny chest was moving up and down, up and down, assisted by a respirator; wires and tubes were fixed all around his tiny body. He had come into the world fifteen weeks before his hour would have had come. He was his parents' second son, full of grace, and the truth was still to be seen. Daniel, the four-year-old firstborn, had as yet not had a chance to see his little brother. "When will he come home?" he kept asking his parents, who went to visit Benjamin every day.

"How can anyone be born after having grown old? Can one enter a second time into his mother's womb and be born?" (John 3:4). Nicodemus, who had come to Jesus by night, wondered.

Benjamin had been expelled from his temporary dwelling place before he was ready to move on in life, and his mother's womb was a womb of no return. Three more weeks might have made the difference, the doctors said.

"Let the little children come to me, and do not stop them; for it is to such as these that the kingdom of heaven belongs" (Matt 19:14).

"No one can enter the kingdom of God without being born of water and Spirit" (John 3:5).

On October 3, seven days after his baptism, Benjamin entered the kingdom of God, and nobody could stop him. Outside, the autumnal wind was tossing about the dead leaves, still radiant with bright colors.

"The wind blows where it chooses, and you hear the sound of it, but you do not know where it comes from and where it goes. So it is with everyone who is born of the Spirit" (John 3:8).

~~~

Seven days after Benjamin had gone, Rebekka came, by night. When she entered into the world, she had already been dead in her mother's womb two days.

"After having heard that Lazarus was ill, he stayed two days longer in the place where he was.... When Jesus arrived, he found that Lazarus had already been in the tomb four days" (John 11:6, 17).

"Jesus cried with a loud voice, 'Lazarus, come out!' The dead man came out, his hands and feet bound with strips of cloth, and his face wrapped in a cloth. Jesus said to them: 'Unbind him and let him go'" (John 11:43–44).

Her mother cried with a loud voice, and Rebekka came out. They cut the umbilical cord, wrapped her in cloths, and let her go, their firstborn and only daughter.

~~~

"How can this be?" I kept asking, by day and by night, in the weeks that followed the births and deaths of these babies. "Am I a teacher of Scripture, and yet I do not understand these things?" I wondered. "Could not he who is the resurrection and the life have kept these little ones from dying?"

"After forty days and forty nights, there was a great wind, so strong that it was splitting mountains and breaking rocks in pieces, but the answers were not in the wind; and after the wind an earthquake, but the answers were not in the earthquake; and after the earthquake a fire, but the answers were not in the fire; and after the fire a sound of sheer silence. And out of the silence a voice came to me: 'I will pour out a spirit of compassion and supplication, so that you shall mourn for him, as one mourns for an only child, and weep bitterly over her, as one weeps over a firstborn'" (Zech 12:10; see 1 Kgs 19:11–13).

∞

Rereading John from Saint Francis Hospital: The Biblical Text and My Personal Plurals

Rereading John 3: Nicodemus, Benjamin, and Myself

"Now there was a Pharisee named Nicodemus, a leader of the Jews. He came to Jesus by night" (John 3:1).

Since taking up Nicodemus's question "How can this be?" for a paper at the 1996 Society of Biblical Literature Annual Meeting in New Orleans, the story of Nicodemus's nightly encounter with Jesus and their talk about rebirth in John 3 has attracted and fascinated me.[1] I have journeyed a long way with Nicodemus and have returned time and again to his story in John, from his first encounter with Jesus to the moment when he placed

---

1. See "'How Can This Be?' (John 3:9): A Feminist-Theological Rereading of the Gospel of John," in this volume.

Jesus's body into the tomb (John 19:38–42). Each time I reread the story new meaning dimensions were added both to the gospel text and my own self-text. Three recent chapters are the result of my obsession with Nicodemus.[2] And my own story with him continues.[3]

That day in September 2000 in the neonatal intensive care in Saint Francis Hospital in Münster, where I worked as chaplain, a new chapter was added. By encountering at the same time Nicodemus, a leader of the Jews, and Benjamin, the tiniest human creature I had ever seen, a transformation happened that affected the biblical text and the text of my own self in front of the text. The gospel reading at Benjamin's baptism was chosen by the priest, who had no idea whatsoever of my rereading John 3 for about four years. To me, this was one of those experiences of synchronicity, which, according to Carl Jung, is a meaningful coincidence in time, an acausal connecting principle.[4] My autobiographical reading, as presented above, resulted from this chance encounter.

The main reason why I became attracted to Nicodemus's story in the first place was the evocative juxtaposition of the old man and the subject of rebirth. Birthing is naturally related to women, not men, and here it is also closely related to aging and consequently to death. In my chapter "Aging and Birthing" I explored this latter aspect in more detail by linking Nicodemus interfigurally to Simeon and Anna in Luke 2 (vv. 21–38) and to Abraham and Sarah in the Genesis stories (Gen 15:1–21; 17:1–14; 18:1–15).[5] All of them are faced with birth, in the physical or spiritual sense, at old age, or even at the time of death, and thereby they embark on a new journey, full of God's promises.

When I encountered Benjamin, my chapter "Aging and Birthing" was in print, finished only a couple of months prior to this encounter. There-

---

2. Ingrid Rosa Kitzberger, "Synoptic Women in John: Interfigural Readings," in *Transformative Encounters: Jesus and Women Re-viewed*, ed. Kitzberger, BibInt 43 (Leiden: Brill, 2000), 77–11; Kitzberger, "Aging and Birthing: Open-Ended Stories and a Hermeneutics of Promise," in this volume; "Transcending Gender Boundaries in John," in this volume.

3. Note also my fellow traveler, Francis J. Moloney, "An Adventure with Nicodemus," in *The Personal Voice in Biblical Interpretation*, ed. Ingrid Rosa Kitzberger (London: Routledge, 1999), 97–110.

4. Carl G. Jung, *Synchronicity: An Acausal Connecting Principle*, trans. R. F. C. Hulll (London: Routledge & Kegan Paul, 1981); Jung, "Über Synchronizität," in *Archetyp und Unbewußtes*, vol. 2 of *Grundwerk* (Olten: Walter, 1990), 279–90.

5. Kitzberger, "Aging and Birthing."

fore, the close connection between birth and death was still very vividly present on my mind and deeply ingrained in my soul. When I witnessed to the baptism of this tiny newborn struggling for life, and when I learned of his death only a week later, my eyes were opened in a new way to the close relation between, if not identification of, birth and death in the Gospel of John. Consequently, I started rereading John's story in the light of Benjamin's short story. (1) As early as John 3, and significantly in the context of the dialogue between Jesus and Nicodemus about rebirth from above,[6] Jesus's own death comes to the fore when he talks about the "Son of Man," who must be lifted up, thereby referring to his own death on the cross (see 3:14). Thus, while Nicodemus is facing the chance of rebirth, Jesus is facing his forthcoming death. The juxtaposition is striking. (2) In 16:21 Jesus compares his disciples' reaction to his impending death to a woman in labor. "When a woman is in labor, she has pain, because her hour has come. But when the child is born, she no longer remembers the anguish because of the joy of having brought a human being into the world. So you have pain now; but I will see you again, and your hearts will rejoice, and no one will take your joy from you." The disciples' weeping and mourning, which will eventually turn into joy (16:20), is thus identified with the birthing process.[7] And the little while when the disciples and Jesus will not see each other (16:16–19) will be followed by a lasting reunion. (3) Jesus's death on the cross can be viewed as a birthing scene.[8] Those who stand near the cross and witness (19:25–27) are reborn of the Spirit (see 3:8) when Jesus gives[9] the Spirit (19:30). They become children of God and are born from him (see 1:12–13). Furthermore, when Jesus entrusts his mother and the Beloved Disciple to each other, a new son is born to the

---

6. The Greek ἄνωθεν can mean both "again" and "from above." I translate it as "rebirth from above" because both meanings are inherent at the same time, a common feature in Johannine terminology.

7. Note also that, in John, the process of becoming a disciple is expressed in terms of birth. See Fernando F. Segovia, *The Farewell of the Word: The Johannine Call to Abide* (Minneapolis: Fortress, 1991), 254.

8. See also Judith M. Lieu, who relates the crucifixion scene, and in particular Jesus's mother, to the parable in 16:21: "So is this a birthing or a dying? …; we meet birth here only when we encounter death. Indeed, the birth, which is not narrated in the Gospel, becomes through 16:21 a death, or is the death a birth?" See Lieu, "The Mother of the Son in the Fourth Gospel," *JBL* 117 (1998): 73.

9. The Greek is παρέδωκεν τὸ πνεῦμα. The NRSV "gave up his spirit" is inaccurate.

mother just when the other one is about to die (19:26–27).[10] Finally, blood and water flowing from Jesus's pierced side (19:34) may also be considered as reminiscent of an actual birthing[11] and the water thus be related to the amniotic fluid. In his death Jesus indeed gives life to others. (4) According to my interpretation of the burial scene in 19:38–42, Nicodemus, too, is finally reborn of the Spirit when he places Jesus's dead body into the tomb.[12] Thus, death and birth, the tomb and the womb (see 3:3–8), are closely linked together.

Benjamin's story added new significance also to "the hour" in John and vice versa. In John the expression refers to Jesus's passion, death, and resurrection.[13] It is a time appointed by the Father (12:27), and thus beyond Jesus's own control. The hour has not yet come at the Cana wedding in chapter 2 (2:4), nor at the feast of Sukkot in chapter 7 (7:6, 8, 30; 8:20). Finally, the hour comes, and Jesus speaks repeatedly about it, from chapter 12 onwards (see 12:23, 27; 13:1; 17:1; see also 16:21).

When I talked about Benjamin's birth in my autobiographical reading, I applied the Johannine term "the hour" to the appointed time of Benjamin's birth,[14] which would have been fifteen weeks later. Consequently, my reference to Jesus's hour of death interpreted Benjamin's story, because in hindsight his birth could be viewed as the onset of his death. As with Jesus, Benjamin's hour was beyond his control. He was born prematurely, and he died too early. However, since Jesus's hour in John refers not only to his death but also to his resurrection, the hour eventually became a "generator of hope" and promise:[15] that Benjamin's passion and death were not in vain and are followed by his resurrection.

---

10. This aspect is expanded in "Stabat Mater? Rebirth at the Foot of the Cross," in this volume.

11. On "birth from water and Spirit" and the references to baptism, see Craig R. Koester, *Symbolism in the Fourth Gospel: Meaning, Mystery, Community* (Minneapolis: Fortress, 1995), 163–67.

12. See Kitzberger, "Synoptic Women in John," 88–102.

13. See Raymond E. Brown, *The Gospel according to John: I–XII*, AB 29 (New York: Doubleday, 1966), 99. He says the term refers "to the period of the passion, death, resurrection and ascension." See also the appendix, 517–18.

14. See the woman's "hour" of labor in 16:21.

15. See J. Severino Croatto, "The Function of the Non-fulfilled Promises: Reading the Pentateuch from the Perspective of the Latin-American Oppressed People," in Kitzberger, *Personal Voice in Biblical Interpretation*, 50; and Kitzberger, "Aging and Birthing," with their focus on a "hermeneutics of promise."

Another aspect of how Benjamin's story and Nicodemus's story interpret each other is related to the womb. Nicodemus's question "Can one enter a second time into the mother's womb and be born?" (3:4) is generally viewed in terms of the Johannine use of irony and as a demonstration of Nicodemus's inability to understand Jesus's talk about a spiritual rebirth and not physical rebirth. Apart from that, biblical scholars have not paid much attention, if at all, to the strange idea of a return into the womb. "Sometimes the most important things—such as life—are forgotten," Croatto commented, with regard to the context of the production of the Pentateuch.[16] I have also learned from him that in a text everything is significant. Nicodemus's talk about a return into the mother's womb is, therefore, a significant text dimension in John 3. Based on my life experience with Benjamin, the perplexing idea became meaningful, because a return into his mother's womb for only three more weeks, were it possible, would have saved his life.

When I characterized our small company who was present at Benjamin's baptism as those "standing near," a hermeneutical process of the opposite kind was implied: I used the biblical text as an interpretive key for our experience. Viewing the scene in neonatal intensive care in Saint Francis Hospital in the light of the Johannine crucifixion scene at Golgotha, we became witnesses, just like Jesus's mother, his mother's sister, Mary the wife of Clopas, Mary Magdalene, and the Beloved Disciple (John 19:25–27).[17] Coincidentally, we too were four women, including Benjamin's mother, and one man.[18] But, as opposed to the crucifixion scene, the father was also present.[19] Indeed, Benjamin's situation in the incubator

---

16. Croatto, "Function of the Non-fulfilled Promises," 42.

17. The number and identity of the women at the foot of the cross has been debated. The better arguments, I find, are for four women, not three, which implies that the mother's sister, and consequently Jesus's aunt, and Mary wife of Clopas are not identical. It would be strange to have two sisters in a family named Mary. Besides, the four women parallel the four soldiers (19:23).

18. Besides Benjamin's mother and myself, two nurses were present. The man was my colleague in the chaplaincy.

19. In John, Jesus's mother is implicitly portrayed as a widow. That Jesus entrusts her and the Beloved Disciple to each other is evidence that she had no husband, and no other sons, to care for her. For the parallelism between John 19:26–27 and Luke 7:11–17 (the raising of the son of the widow of Nain), see my chapters "Synoptic Women in John," 106–7, and "Stabat Mater? Rebirth at the Foot of the Cross."

could be paralleled to Jesus's situation on the cross. And both were pierced, whether by the spear (19:34) or by the wires and tubes.

When I interpreted our tears as "rivers of living water" that flow from the believer's heart, I chose Jesus's talk on the last day of the festival of Sukkot in John 7:37–39 as another intertext in my autobiographical reading. Jesus's mention of the Spirit, which believers in him were to receive, and the narrator's comment that "as yet there was no Spirit, because Jesus was not yet glorified" (7:39), links this scene in chapter 7 to the nightly encounter between Nicodemus and Jesus and their dialogue about rebirth of water and Spirit in chapter 3, on the one hand, and to the crucifixion scene in chapter 19, where Jesus is glorified and gives the Spirit (19:30), on the other hand.

By linking Nicodemus's story, and consequently Benjamin's story, to John 7, the festival of Sukkot added a new meaning dimension to the latter's story. The feast is celebrated in remembrance of Israel's exodus from Egypt, when they lived in tents,[20] their temporary dwelling places during the desert wanderings. Like them, Benjamin had only a temporary dwelling place, within and outside his mother's womb;[21] and his short journey on earth was indeed a wandering through the desert. The time span of seven days between Benjamin's baptism and his death, and then another seven days between his death and Rebekka's death-birth, became also significant, because the feast of Sukkot is celebrated for seven days.[22] Coincidentally,

---

20. The festival of Sukkot is often termed "Feast of Tabernacles," but the tabernacle, the sanctuary the Israelites built during their desert wanderings, according to God's instruction (Exod 25–26), has no connection to this feast, which, therefore, should rather be called "Feast of Booths." The *sukkah* as a temporary shelter during the feast of Sukkot is a portable shelter, with three walls and the roof, which must be made of something natural, such as branches cut from trees. The roof must cover most of the *sukkah* but still permit viewing the stars. The tabernacle is a sanctuary, but the *sukkah* is not. My grateful thanks to Orna Teitelbaum for providing this information and sharing her own life experience of celebrating Sukkot in her family with me in private conversation and with the wo/men of my class Jesus and Women: Transformative Encounters at the Graduate Theological Union Berkeley in the fall semester 2001.

21. Talking about tabernacles, sanctuaries, and temporary dwelling places, and having read my draft of this paper, Orna Teitelbaum, a mother of two, noted that the mother's womb could be regarded as a sanctuary that God made, while the incubator is a man-made womb without this sacred quality of the sanctuary.

22. See Lev 23:39–43: "You shall live in booths for seven days; all that are citizens in Israel shall live in booths, so that your generation may know that I made the people

Benjamin's baptism and my first encounter with him occurred also seven days after I had started working in the hospital. Besides that, Sukkot is celebrated in September or October,[23] the time of the year when the stories around Benjamin and Rebekka happened. Sukkot is the last harvest festival of the year,[24] so death can be considered to be the last harvest of our lives, regardless of the number of years that are gathered into it. Thus, Benjamin's death around the time of Sukkot gained special significance. Thereby, another "generator of hope" was added to Benjamin's story: that, like the Israelites, he may see the promised land, after his desert wandering.[25] Since Sukkot is a feast of great joy, there is hope that those who wept and mourned at Benjamin's death will eventually be able to join in the joy of reunion (see John 16:16–22).

The reference to John's prologue in my autobiographical reading linked Benjamin's story to Jesus's story. For Jesus, too, the earth was only a temporary dwelling place: "the Word became flesh and tented among us, and we have seen his glory, the glory of the Father's only son, full of grace and truth" (1:14). Having been born from the Father's womb (1:13, 18),[26] Jesus returned into it a second time, when he was lifted up on the

---

of Israel live in booths when I brought them out of the land of Egypt: I am the Lord your God."

23. Sukkot is celebrated from the fifteenth to the twenty-second of Tishri. In the year 2000 (5761 in the Hebrew calendar), Sukkot started in the evening of October 13 and ended on Friday (sundown) October 21. Thanks, again, to Orna Teitelbaum for providing this information.

24. Sukkot was originally a harvest feast and later became one of the three pilgrimage feasts (Exod 23:16; 34:22–23). See Lev 23:39: "Now the fifteenth day of the seventh month, when you have gathered in the produce of the land, you shall keep the festival of the Lord, lasting seven days, and a complete rest on the eighth day." It is notable that, during harvests, farmers often lived in temporary shelters near their fields.

25. See Croatto, "Function of the Non-fulfilled Promises," 50: "The Pentateuch is an *open text*, a generator of hope. The journeys of the patriarchs and the sons and daughters of Israel through the desert, with their crises, their risks, and their suffering, indicate that the land is an objective that is to be achieved."

26. The Greek κόλπος can mean both, "bosom" and "womb." Most translations have "bosom" (RSV), or alternatively "heart" (NRSV). Obviously, it is difficult for most to imagine a father with a womb. However, normally one is born from a womb ("born of God," 1:13). This is only one instance in John's Gospel where gender boundaries are transcended. See my chapter "Transcending Gender Boundaries in John." Lieu draws attention to the tradition of the maternal God in the Hebrew Bible (Hos

cross, and he completed his return after his farewell encounter with Mary Magdalene (20:16–17). However, since Benjamin was his parents' second son, Rebekka, for that matter, can be more closely related to Jesus, the Word-become-flesh of the prologue: she was her parents' firstborn and only daughter, just as Jesus was his Father's only son (1:14). But, for sure, both babies were full of grace, and the truth was hard to accept.

Rereading John 11: Lazarus, Rebekka, and Myself

Rebekka came seven days after Benjamin had gone. Like Nicodemus, she came by night. When she was born, she had already been dead in her mother's womb two days. When I received this information, I immediately linked Rebekka's story to Lazarus's story in John 11. He had been dead in the tomb four days when Jesus, after his delay of two days, finally arrived in Bethany (11:6, 17). Lazarus's story, like Nicodemus's story, has fascinated and attracted me for many years. At the 1998 Annual Meeting of the Society of Biblical Literature in Orlando, I presented a paper on Lazarus, titled "Untying Lazarus—A Sisters' Task? Revisioning Gender and Characterization in John 11." Since then I have returned to Lazarus's tomb many times and watched him hobbling out of the tomb, still bound in the burial cloths, and have wondered about the open end of the story, as to who should, and eventually did, unbind him and let him go (11:44). Due to this open end, my reading Lazarus's story was also open-ended in September 2000. When I learned about little Rebekka's fate, the scene at the tomb in Bethany came to my mind, and it interpreted the scene in Saint Francis Hospital.

On the other hand, Rebekka's story also added a new meaning dimension to Lazarus's story. I had always wondered about the paradoxical narrative detail "the dead man came out" (11:43), because by then Lazarus was certainly already alive, regardless of his restricted mobility. Since the dead girl Rebekka came out of the womb, the fact that the dead man Lazarus came out of the tomb became meaningful and made sense to me. And like Lazarus, though in a reversed order, Rebekka was bound in cloths and let go. Furthermore, since Lazarus's coming out of the tomb was the demonstration of his resurrection, there was hope, so I gathered, also for Rebekka's

---

11:1–4; Isa 42:14; Ps 139:13, and especially Deut 32:18; see "Mother of the Son in the Fourth Gospel").

resurrection, beyond her death-birth. Thus, new meaning was added also to her life story when read in the light of Lazarus's remarkable story.

Rereading Personal Questions, Living the Answer

After the deaths of Benjamin and Rebekka, I returned to Nicodemus's story and took up his question "How can this be?" but I changed the reference point: from Nicodemus's (potential) rebirth to the deaths of these little ones. "Could not he who opened the eyes of the blind man have kept this man from dying?" some of the Jews, who had come to Mary and Martha after the death of their brother, asked (11:37). Likewise, my belief in him, who is the resurrection and the life (11:25), was tested with regard to Benjamin and Rebekka. The story of the prophet Elijah's journey from Beersheva to Mount Horeb,[27] and his final encounter with the Lord (1 Kgs 19:1–18), came to interpret my experience, and it provided the framework for an answer to my question. The Lord's personal voice came to Elijah not in spectacular events but in the silence. I, too, received an answer out of the silence. The word came from the prophet Zechariah, which is also an intertext of the Johannine crucifixion scene (19:37): "I will pour out a spirit of compassion and supplication on the house of David and the inhabitants of Jerusalem, so that, when they look on the one whom they have pierced, they shall mourn for him, as one mourns for an only child, and weep bitterly over him, as one weeps over a firstborn" (Zech 12:10). The question "Why?" with regard to the deaths of the babies may have to remain unanswered. Yet, there is an answer beyond words that is simple and existential: compassion.

My Personal Plurals and John: An Exercise in Border Crossing

My autobiographical reading of John and my reflection on, and analysis of, the reading process are due to my personal plurals.[28] At least two of

---

27. Coincidentally, Beersheva is the birth place of my friend Orna Teitelbaum, who read this paper "with me," and the location of Mayer I. Gruber, whose "The Personal Voice of the Listening Heart," in which he refers to the biblical Rebekah and to birth, was sparked by an experience in Beersheva. See Gruber, "The Personal Voice of the Listening Heart," in Kitzberger, *Personal Voice in Biblical Interpretation*, 97–104.

28. Susanna Morton Braund, "Personal Plurals," in *Compromising Traditions: The Personal Voice in Classical Scholarship*, ed. Judith P. Hallett and Thomas Van Nort-

them were influential here: my self the biblical scholar, and my self the clinic chaplain. Both selves belong to very different worlds, which I felt drastically whenever I vacillated between my desk and the hospital. And yet these different selves became intersected and formed my self-text from which a reading was born that would not have been possible with only a personal singular. However, I am more than these two persons.

My past and present have shaped a multiple "I," which is that of a very complex woman, who has lived in the borderlands and crossed many borders.[29] The border between life and death, and the border crossing that happens in the process of birthing and dying, has always held a special, awesome fascination for me.[30] As a consequence, this "I" was particularly receptive to the birthing and dying of the two babies.

On the other hand, since I have concentrated on the Gospel of John in my scholarly work for the past decade, I have also come to live by this gospel. It has become a matrix, a permanent intertext that has informed and interpreted my personal experiences. Reading my life in the light of the gospel, and reading the gospel in the light of my own life, has come naturally.

During the last years, coinciding with my starting on personal voice and in particular autobiographical criticism, my personal plurals have multiplied in the process of applying for academic positions on both sides of the Atlantic. My spinning out different selves, living and working in

---

wick (London: Routledge, 1997), 38–53. See also one of the characters in Virginia Woolf's novel *The Waves*, Bernard, who wonders about his identity: "Which of these people am I? … When I say to myself 'Bernard,' who comes?" See Woolf, *The Three Great Novels: Mrs Dalloway, To the Lighthouse, The Waves* (London: Penguin Books, 1992), 519. Robert Lee Frost (1874–1963), the famous San Francisco–born poet, best described himself as "one-half farmer, one-half teacher, and one-half poet."

29. See my chapter "Border Crossing and Meeting Jesus at the Well: An Autobiographical Re-reading of the Samaritan Woman's Story in John 4:1–44," in Kitzberger, *Personal Voice in Biblical Interpretation*, 111–27.

30. According to my birth chart, I have most planets in the eighth house, which is the house of death and (re)birth. Besides that, I am a Scorpio, whose house is the eighth house, which confirms my special attraction to death and (re)birth experiences, in my own life and in that of others. Following Norman N. Holland, I regard "birth and death" as my "identity theme," in terms of which I re-create texts, both the biblical texts and my life texts. See Norman N. Holland, "Unity Identity Text Self," in *Reader-Response Criticism: From Formalism to Post-structuralism*, ed. Jane P. Tompkins (Baltimore: Johns Hopkins University Press, 1980), 118–33, esp. 126. I owe my astrological insights to my dear friend Rosemary Brown.

different parts of the world and in very different social locations, together with the experiences that came along in the outer reality, has had a far-reaching influence on my identity. Thus, my future selves,[31] just as my past and present selves, have also shaped my rereading of the Gospel of John.

When I encountered Benjamin and Rebekka, the little border crossers, I did so with my own border-crossing and multidimensional self and with my potential of rebirth into a different life, into a different version of myself.

Flowing Identities: Methods and Ethics of the Personal Voice

I am no longer the person I was at last year's Annual Meeting when we decided on this session, and I am no longer the person who chose the title for this paper and wrote the abstract last spring. Since then, seasons have come and gone, and I have changed, like the leaves in autumn, radiating with bright colors. I have been different persons, subsequently or at the same time. My identity is fluid and shifting. And so are the biblical texts. Each time we encounter each other, we are met with surprises. We look different, and yet we recognize each other. We have changed yet have remained ourselves. Like a river flowing. *Panta rei*, as Greek philosopher Heraclitus said.

When I decided on the title "Flowing Identities" I had no idea how much the image of water would inform this paper. Then there was no baby yet to be reborn of water and Spirit and to deeply affect me and my reading of John as a consequence. Benjamin and Rebekka were still in their mothers' wombs, enjoying their swim in the amniotic fluid. And John and I were as yet unaffected by the intertexts from Saint Francis Hospital.

For about a decade, I have been rereading and reconstructing the gospel text and my own self-text, ever anew within each encounter. Transformation has happened to the text and my self. And it is an ongoing process.

Because of the fragmentary character and the open-endedness of both the biblical story text and my own story text I, was able to re-create

---

31. In his article "Getting to Know My Future Selves," *Chronicle of Higher Education,* December 10, 1999, James L. Lang describes so very well this process of projecting different versions of oneself into the future. He speaks of the "spinning out of different narratives that will lead me into each of these different selves, watching those selves unfold and develop into their separate lives."

John in my own image and likeness, and to re-create myself in John's image and likeness.

Intertextuality has been the methodological key and concept for this endeavor, in which focus text and intertext kept shifting. Apart from that, no method has been employed; or rather, the method was in the process. Often, the autobiographical readings just came to me, like a dream comes at night, activating powerful images. Memories of long ago are reclaimed from the dark, like land from the sea, painfully liberating. Disparate pieces of a jigsaw puzzle are falling into place; a picture full of meaning becomes visible to the eye and the heart. A gift from the sea left behind on the shore, when the tide is out again. Collecting the shells and listening to the ocean, I am aware of the Self that, according to Jung, comprises not only my conscious ego, but also the unconscious, both personal and collective.[32]

Recollecting what happened, I used the analytical skills that I acquired during my pre-autobiographical phase of biblical interpretation in order to explain the process of autobiographical reading and communicate it to others who want to speak with me and enter into dialogue with their own personal voices. Thereby, autobiographical reading becomes truly autobiographical criticism.

By listening to one's own voice, to the voices of others, and to the voices of the biblical texts, and by taking all of them seriously into account, autobiographical criticism becomes truly ethical. At the same time, this process sharpens the awareness of the personal voices in supposedly objective criticisms and thus becomes an exercise in ideological criticism.

At least one ethical problem remains and needs to be addressed. As Charles Martindale put it: "To write oneself is almost inevitably to write others—and does one have that right?"[33] This, for sure, is a critical issue and needs to be pondered seriously in each of our autobiographical writings. At least in one case, I believe, writing others may in fact turn out to be one of the most ethical dimensions of our writings: when we memorialize the dead and thereby reclaim them from dissolution into nothingness.

I am no longer the person I was when I presented this paper at the Society of Biblical Literature Annual Meeting in Nashville in November

---

32. C. G. Jung, "Die Beziehungen zwischen dem Ich und dem Unbewußten," in *Persönlichkeit und Übertragung*, vol. 3 of *Grundwerk*, 3rd ed. (Olten: Walter, 1990), 11–55.

33. Charles Martindale, "Proper Voices: Writing the Writer," in Hallett and Van Nortwick, *Compromising Traditions*, 94.

2000. Since then, seasons have come and gone, and I have changed, like the leaves in autumn, back home, radiating with bright colors. (I missed these leaves last fall in Berkeley.) I have been different persons, subsequently or at the same time.[34] My identity is fluid and shifting. And so are the biblical texts. Each time we encounter each other we are met with surprises. We look different, and yet we recognize each other. We have changed, and yet have remained ourselves.[35] Like a river flowing, or the waves of the sea, whether the tide is in or out. *Panta rei*, as Greek philosopher Heraclitus said.

On October 3, 2001, I hobbled out of my tomb[36] to the Franciscan School of Theology at the Graduate Theological Union Berkeley to join the celebration of the Transitus, Saint Francis's passing away. I wondered about the coincidence of Benjamin's death in Saint Francis Hospital on the anniversary of Saint Francis's death and wondered who would still remember the tiny newborn a year later. And who would remember Rebekka, who died even before her birth? Memorializing the dead and reclaiming them from dissolution into nothingness.[37]

I am rereading the stories of Benjamin and Rebekka, and their Johannine intertexts, from my room with a view of the East Bay, with San Francisco, Saint Francis's city, to the left, on the other side, and Golden Gate Bridge in front. To my right, on the bookshelf, is my Johannine literature library that has made it across the Atlantic.[38]

---

34. Since I presented my paper in Nashville, I have been spinning out many other different selves, in different countries and on different continents, as I applied for further academic positions.

35. See Stanley E. Fish's notion of literature as "kinetic art" and his recognition of the "fluidity," "the movingness" of the meaning experience. "Kinetic art does not lend itself to a static interpretation because it refuses to stay still and doesn't let you stay still either." See Stanley E. Fish, "Literature in the Reader: Affective Stylistics," in Tompkins, *Reader-Response Criticism*, 83.

36. On August 29, 2001, shortly after my arrival in Berkeley, I broke my right foot and, apart from rides to my classrooms, was totally confined to an apartment, which was not home and which became a tomb over the weeks. Hobbling out of the tomb on my crutches was my first adventure and a kind of rebirth experience, strangely as I was joining in the celebration of Saint Francis's death.

37. For the importance of telling also minor lives, see Geoffrey Wolff, "Minor Lives," in *Telling Lives: The Biographer's Art*, ed. Marc Pachter (Philadelphia: University of Pennsylvania Press, 1979), 57–72.

38. Many of my books got lost on their way from Münster to Berkeley. Strangely, most of them were the books needed to prepare this volume, *Autobiographical Biblical*

I love the sight of the water, from my window, and all around the Bay Area, living water, ever flowing. Collecting the shells and listening to the ocean, I am aware of the Self, so much greater than my self. A gift from the sea left behind on the shore, when the tide is out again.

I have come a long way since my first border crossing and meeting Jesus at the well,[39] and since encountering the little border crossers, crossing many other borders in the process, between continents, people, and worlds. Golden Gate Bridge has fascinated me, even long before I first crossed it in 1993. Bridges in general have always attracted me because of their border-crossing quality. One of Monet's famous water-lilies paintings, with the bridge over the pond, decorated the little room next to the adult intensive unit in Saint Francis Hospital, where the bodies were brought for the last farewell. The bridge had become, as opposed to its original meaning, a signifier of the border crossing that happens in death. I vividly remember my first experience of attending to the corpse and to the family of the deceased when I was on duty, with the dead man's head viewed against Monet's water-lilies pond and bridge. A lasting impression.

Attending to the terminally ill and to the dying was an essential part of my work in the hospital, which happened to be also renowned for its maternity ward. Thus, encountering newborns and the dying, birth and death, was an everyday experience during my work as chaplain in Saint Francis Hospital. Consequently, it reaffirmed my awareness of the close relation between death and birth in the Gospel of John, and of the temporary dwelling place this life on earth is.

"And the Word became flesh and tented among us, and we have seen his glory, the glory of the father's only son, full of grace and truth" (John 1:14).

Criticism, and my class Text and Self: Methods and Ethics of Personal Voice Biblical Criticism in spring semester 2002. My Johannine books, however, survived, though most of them were badly damaged.

39. See my chapter with the same title in *Personal Voice in Biblical Interpretation*, 111–27. Water is the most significant image in this chapter and came to interpret also this present one. I share this attraction to water with Jeffrey L. Staley. See his "Wu wei: Go with the Flow," in "What Is Critical about Autobiographical Biblical Criticism?," in *Autobiographical Biblical Criticism: Between Text and Self*, ed. Ingrid Rosa Kitzberger (Leiden: Deo, 2002), 20–21.

Across the water, in San Francisco's Grace Cathedral,[40] the *Smiling Saint Francis* by Benjamin Bufano stands, with arms wide outstretched, next to the baptismal fountain, welcoming whoever enters the sanctuary.

"Very truly, I tell you, no one can enter the kingdom of God without having been born of water and Spirit. What is born of flesh is flesh, and what is born of the Spirit is spirit" (John 3:6).

"The wind blows where it chooses, and you hear the sound of it, but you do not know where it comes from and where it goes. So it is with everyone who is born of the Spirit" (John 3:8).

The wind always blows in San Francisco, especially high up on top of Nob Hill. When I enter the cathedral, two blocks away from Saint Francis Memorial Hospital, I tip my fingers into the water of the baptismal fountain, make the sign of the cross on my body, smiling at Saint Francis, and imagine Benjamin and Rebekka enfolded in his arms, wide outstretched.

---

40. Two of my students named John are related to the cathedral. One has just become associate pastor there, and the other one was ordained deacon on June 1, 2002.

Part 5
Teaching Strategies

Models of Discipleship and Teaching Strategies: Learning from John

Preliminaries

"So many gathered around that there was no longer room for them, not even in front of the door; and she was speaking the word to them."

∞

"How would you teach your new approach?" he asked me, unexpectedly. "I am glad I am not teaching right now," I answered spontaneously, "so I can focus on my own process, without having to ponder over how to communicate it to my students."

∞

Teaching the crowd is a distinctive feature of Mark's portrait of Jesus. As early as chapter 2, at the very beginning of his public ministry in Galilee, the crowd follows Jesus and gathers around him inside and even outside the house, which has become his home base, in Capernaum. In spite of being a collective character in the gospel story, the crowd is made up of individuals, some of whom Jesus encounters in a transformative way. The paralytic who, because of the hindering crowd, is let down to Jesus through the roof, is just one of these individuals singled out from the crowd.

John, too, knows of the crowd following Jesus, but they do not explicitly turn up until chapter 6, when they follow him because of the signs he

---

This chapter was originally a lecture at the University of Sheffield, Department of Biblical Studies, July 8, 1999. Revised and updated for this publication. With fond memories of my two overseas companions and our lovely time together, as we joined the large community of those they did not hire.

did for the sick, and eventually he feeds the five thousand. Jesus's teaching, however, is restricted to his disciples and those gathered in the synagogue of Capernaum. The Johannine Jesus keeps withdrawing from the crowd; he does not teach them. He prefers the smaller circles, for that matter.

Teaching Practice: Between Paradigms and Ethical Responsibility

Teaching the crowd has been a distinctive feature of my own teaching career at various German universities. When I started teaching at the University of Freiburg in 1981, I attracted a great number of students right from the beginning. This was partly due to the fact that I was then the only woman teaching theology, and many—female as well as male—students wanted to see what it is like to study with a woman. Several years later, when I moved to the University of Münster in 1989, I initiated courses in feminist biblical interpretation. This was, once again, an additional reason for attracting the crowd, especially of female students. Coincidentally, however, it just happened that wherever I started a new position, or lectured temporarily (e.g., the University of Cologne), the number of students had increased drastically right then, a kind of welcome present, as it were. Thus, teaching thousands of students over the years, I have become increasingly aware of the great impact and responsibility that comes along with this challenging and wonderful job of teaching. The ethical responsibility is intensified with regard to the paradigms and methods of biblical interpretation that we offer to our students. These, in turn, inform their own approach to Scripture and what they pass on to others, teaching and preaching the Bible.

"How would you teach your new approach?" The question came from Patte after I had presented my paper " 'The Truth Will Make You Free' (John 8:32): The Power of the Personal Voice and Readings of/from the Gospel of John" at the International Research Consultation on Ideology, Power, and Interpretation at the University of Birmingham in August 1997. Then, just for a change, I was not teaching, as I had received a research grant. Indeed, while focusing on my own projects, my approach to biblical interpretation was transformed profoundly, and I was finally able to move on to a new paradigm. This would certainly not have been possible had I continued teaching the crowd, in particular in the German context, which required to teach within the historical-critical paradigm.

Now I am standing at a threshold as I am about to return to teaching, yet in a different context and with different agenda. This is an excellent opportunity for both recollection and prospect. Reflecting on my past teaching experience and envisioning my future teaching practice, I shall draw on the Gospel of John, in which I discovered some interesting models of discipleship and teaching strategies. I shall make explicit how closely related they are, how the models of discipleship, and thus the relationship between teacher and student, shape and inform the teaching strategies and pedagogical discourse.

"Come and See!" Teaching by Showing, Sharing, and Experiencing

"Rabbi, where are you staying?" the two disciples of John the Baptist ask Jesus, whom they have followed. "What are you looking for?" was Jesus's question addressed to them (see John 1:37–38).

"What are you looking for?" So we, too, could, ask the students who come to us, to our lectures and seminars, to the places where we teach.

Unlike the Synoptic Jesus, who simply and without any further debate tells his would-be-disciples to follow him and leave everything behind (see Mark 1:16–20), the Johannine Jesus extends an invitation, "Come and see!" "They came and saw where he was staying, and they remained with him that day," so the story continues (v. 39).

Our students, too, come to us and remain with us, sometimes for just one semester, sometimes for several years. "Come and see" implies three things with regard to teaching.

First, as teachers we are called to make explicit our own stance in biblical scholarship, inclusive of our own values and agenda, and thus to communicate to our students where we are "staying." Second, teaching and learning is a mutual, interpersonal process in which both parties, teacher and students, encounter each other as active and creative participants. Third, by taking the students' faculties seriously into account, we acknowledge that they can see for themselves, and consequently read and interpret the biblical texts prior to, and independent of, any "instructions" from a teacher.

"A Burning and Shining Lamp," or: Let the Student Shine!

"He was a burning and shining lamp, and you were willing to rejoice for a while in his light." Thus Jesus refers to the mission of his predecessor, John the Baptist (5:35).

"I am the light of the world. Whoever follows me will never walk in darkness but will have the light of life." This is Jesus's own claim (8:12).

Many professors, in particular in my German context, seem to think likewise and behave accordingly. This age of enlightenment is still very much present at universities, even in departments of theology and among biblical scholars, who should know better. Consequently, hierarchical and patriarchal patterns of teaching prevail. Teachers/professors are supposed to hold the key to knowledge and lead their students out of the darkness of their ignorance.

"You were willing to rejoice for a while in his light." Jesus's reference to the Baptist, on the other hand, could provide the key to a liberating model of discipleship. Eventually, students are called to step out of the "light" of their teachers, and these do well to encourage such liberating movements. Let the student shine! This imperative might become a guideline for all teachers, and in particular those teaching the New Testament. This implies to give one's students room so that they can develop their own creative potentials and talents.

No Longer Servants but Friends:
Liberating Practice and the Ethics of Teaching

"I do not call you servants any longer, because the servant does not know what the master is doing; but I have called you friends, because I have made known to you everything that I have heard from my Father" (15:15). The Johannine model of discipleship is a discipleship of friends who are entrusted with knowledge and treated in a liberating manner,[2] thereby overcoming hierarchy and oppression. Passing on knowledge without treating students in a subservient and subaltern manner is called for in a teaching that is ethically accountable.

"Rabbi, Eat!": Nourishing Students

"Rabbi, eat!" So the disciples encourage and invite Jesus, after their return from the town of Sychar to the well, where they find him in conversation with the Samaritan woman (4:31). However, Jesus declines the food they offer him (since his food is to do the will of God, v. 34). He should not have done so. Of course, we are aware of the typical Johannine style in drawing

---

2. For the prominence of friendship in John, see Sharon H. Ringe, *Wisdom's Friends: Community and Christology in the Fourth Gospel* (Louisville: Westminster John Knox, 1999). It is a "model of accompaniment" (5).

this scene, with the double meaning of food and Jesus's preference for the spiritual. However, so I have come to think, Jesus could have accepted both and thus not rejected his disciples. Why not indulge in God's food, by doing his will, *and* accept the disciples' food, so generously offered to him?

Nourishing our students by what we offer to them in our classes is one aspect. Equally important, however, and vital for our own survival and development as teachers and scholars, is what students offer to us, their own nourishing practice. Recollecting twenty years of teaching, I have learned so much from my students, often in a very concrete way. Many text dimensions or possible interpretations of a biblical text were opened to me by students. Nourishing students are more influential than many of us might recognize and admit. Teaching and learning are mutual processes, with changing roles. We should acknowledge and embrace them as such.

"Do Not Hold On to Me!": Empowered for Greater Works

Holding on to one's professor, walking in his or her footsteps, and the establishment of scholarly schools is a well-known phenomenon in our discipline and beyond. Students are quite often dependent on their teachers, in their doctoral dissertations or postdoctoral qualifications, and even long after they have become teachers/professors themselves. They keep engaging in the same kind of research, working within the same paradigm, and applying the same methods. This, however, creates a cage where many a student's creative potential has lost its wings.

"Do not hold on to me" is the advice a teacher might give to his or her students, just as the resurrected Jesus tells Mary Magdalene before she embarks on her mission (20:17). The Johannine Jesus seems to have learned in the process. Even though he claimed that "apart from me you can do nothing" (15:5), he announces to his disciples, at the end of his earthly ministry, that they will be able to do greater works than he (14:12). A student who is able to do greater works than his or her teacher/professor is the best compliment and tribute one can wish for. Empowering our students for greater works and enjoying them is a liberating teaching strategy versus creating subservient followers. Whether from the Fish Tower (Migdal Nunya) or from the Arts Tower,[3] we should encourage and

---

3. The Department of Biblical Studies at Sheffield University is located in the Arts Tower. The Fish Tower is another ancient name for Magdala. At the end of John's

empower our students to venture out into their own worlds and develop their own potentials.

Jesus, the Untrained Teacher: Unorthodox Modes of Teaching and Learning

"How does this man have such learning, when he has never been taught?" The Jews in John's story voice their astonishment about Jesus being an untrained teacher, who nevertheless is teaching, even in the temple (7:14–15). According to John, Jesus's teaching came directly from God: "My teaching is not mine but his who sent me" (7:16). According to Luke, the twelve-year-old Jesus was found by his parents in the temple, "sitting among the teachers, listening to them and asking questions. And all who heard him were amazed at his understanding and his answers" (Luke 4:46–47). Without being trained, Jesus spent his short earthly life teaching, and the crowds gathered around him and many followed him. Thus, as teachers of biblical studies and being well trained ourselves, we are confronted with a very odd situation indeed. At the same time, the validity and legitimacy of our teaching and learning may be questioned or challenged. Consequently, we are encouraged to be open to unorthodox ways of teaching and learning, besides the established academic curricula. Autodidactic learning is one such way of gaining knowledge. And blessed are those who acknowledge it.

"Can Anything Good Come Out of Nazareth?" Teaching for Postcolonialism

Nathanael, obviously from studying in the shade of the fig tree, knew exactly how things are or have to be. Therefore, he about whom Moses and the prophets wrote was definitely not to come out of Nazareth (1:45–46). In his book *Jesus and the Marginalized in John's Gospel*, Robert Karris mentions five groups: the geographically marginalized people, that is, the Galileans and Samaritans; the poor; those ignorant of the law; the physically afflicted; and the women.[4] Coming out of Nazareth is thus synonymous with belonging to

---

Gospel, Mary of Magdala is commissioned to proclaim the good news and thus, as one of Jesus's disciples, do greater works than he.

4. Robert J. Karris, *Jesus and the Marginalized in John's Gospel*, ZSNT (Collegeville, MN: Liturgical Press, 1990).

the geographically marginalized, as defined by those belonging to the center. Listening to the voices from the margin and overcoming the center-margin dichotomy and the colonialism resulting from it must be an essential dimension of our teaching strategies.[5] Recruiting undergraduates and graduates from the Two-Thirds World is the presupposition for such teaching for postcolonialism, for teaching as learning *with* them, not *about* them, and developing a listening heart in the process. Teaching for postcolonialism also implies to look out for students from underrepresented ethnicities. In so saying, I recall Mark Brett deploring the fact that our discipline has not produced a single (Australian) aboriginal biblical scholar.

Teaching for postcolonialism further implies, with regard to the interpretation of biblical texts, realizing the liberating potentials and reading against the grain of oppressive dimensions in the text.[6]

Teaching marginalized students in a marginalized faculty department, the teachers' training department, for seven years, besides having experienced marginalization myself in my scholarly career, I have become extremely sensitive to the issue but also empowered to overcome it.

Many Dwelling Places and the Miraculous Catch of Fish: Teaching for Plurality

What is true of the Father's house (14:2) should also hold true in our house of biblical scholarship. There are many different dwelling places as regards paradigms, methods, and discourse strategies, and we should welcome them as the manifestation of the richness and variety in our discipline. This implies each biblical scholar's freedom to choose her or his dwelling place, according to his or her special interests and talents. The same attitude should be applied to teaching and learning. Students have a right to be offered different approaches and paradigms, so that they have a choice as to which path they want to follow in their own work, according to their special interests and talents. The miraculous post-Easter catch of fish in the Sea of Tiberias embraces plurality, diversity, and inclusiveness. The number of fish caught after a futile night's work runs to 153, which is

---

5. R. S. Sugirtharajah, ed., *Voices from the Margin: Interpreting the Bible in the Third World* (London: SPCK, 1991).

6. See also Fernando F. Segovia, *Decolonizing Biblical Studies: A View from the Margins* (Maryknoll, NY: Orbis Books, 2000), on the postcolonial optic in biblical studies (119–42) and on racial and ethnic minorities in biblical studies (157–77).

supposed to be the number of fish known at the time, "and though there were so many, the net was not torn" (21:11). Likewise, the net of biblical scholarship, and the community of biblical teachers and students of different standing, need not be torn. "Come and have breakfast," Jesus invites his disciples (21:12). And it was a full breakfast, including fish and bread (21:9, 13). We should have full meals in our scholarship, and offer the same to our students. However, I am well aware that this is quite often impossible at our universities, due to a limited number of positions, with perhaps just one chair in New Testament or Hebrew Bible. Besides that, in many places teaching within one paradigm is still required, with no opportunity for other approaches.[7] Blessed are departments where plurality, diversity, and inclusiveness are possible.

Final Reflections: Paradigms of Interpretation and Pedagogical Discourse

In his introduction to the volume *Teaching the Bible: The Discourses and Politics of Biblical Pedagogy*, Segovia raises the question of pedagogy in relation to the main paradigms in biblical scholarship and brings to the surface the pedagogical discourse and practices within each paradigm.[8] He names six basic elements or principles operative in all paradigms: location of meaning, reading strategy, theoretical foundations, role of the reader, theological presuppositions, and pedagogical implications.

Investigating the paradigms of historical criticism, literary criticism, and cultural criticism, Segovia notes that "the question of pedagogy has rarely, if ever, been raised, much less addressed, explicitly," yet in each paradigm, pedagogical discourse and practices were presupposed. He concludes that the pedagogical models of the three paradigms are highly pyramidal, patriarchal, and authoritative. They imply "learned impartation and passive reception," and "student/readers would become teacher/critics by learning how not to read themselves," while "the teacher/critics hold

---

7. I vividly remember J. Cheryl Exum's guest lecture at the University of Münster, presenting her literary approach and claiming it as hers. I envied her for this privilege to choose her own approach in research *and* teaching, while I had to split the two for several years in my career.

8. Fernando F. Segovia, "Introduction: Pedagogical Discourse and Practices in Contemporary Biblical Criticism," in *Teaching the Bible: The Discourses and Politics of Biblical Pedagogy*, ed. Fernando F. Segovia and Mary Ann Tolbert (Maryknoll, NY: Orbis Books, 1998), 1–28. See also Segovia, *Decolonizing Biblical Studies*, 3–115.

the key to the meaning of the biblical text." Cultural studies, on the other hand, produces students who are "competent" or "responsible" students of the Bible. Emphasis is placed on the diversity of readers and contexts, as well as on the diversity of methods and readings, thereby overcoming the Eurocentrism and Western domination of our discipline.

In a similar way, Patte refers to the pedagogical goal of his volume *The Challenge of Discipleship: A Critical Study of the Sermon on the Mount as Scripture*.[9] He states that "informational pedagogy" or the "banking" model of pedagogy, which is primarily characterized by the communication of knowledge about the Bible, is, as regards adults, ethically inappropriate. It is an oppressive and alienating kind of education, in which learners are supposed to be passive receivers of knowledge bestowed on them as gifts by teachers who alone possess the "true" knowledge. Over against such a pedagogy, that of his book is aimed at transforming what students/readers already know and hence transforming their modes of being in the world. This is an "interactive pedagogy."

Paradigms and methods that rely on knowledge gained prior to the interpretation of biblical texts, which is true of the three paradigms mentioned by Segovia, establish a gap between teacher and student. While one knows, the other is ignorant to start with. And it is true, wherever knowledge is communicated, he or she who is the giver ranks higher than the receiver. While this is theoretically true, it nonetheless need not always be so in practice. Interactive, student-centered learning and teaching is also possible within the paradigms whose characteristics Segovia describes as "learned impartation" and "passive reception," though, to be sure, the degree varies compared to other paradigms, in particular that of cultural studies or autobiographical criticism. While teaching the historical-critical methods, still exclusively applied in the German-speaking countries, I nevertheless made recourse to interactive and proactive teaching and learning strategies, starting from the acknowledged competence of students to see for themselves and make meaning of the text in front of them. Providing additional information in the ensuing process is then by no means a way of silencing the subaltern. Rather, it can turn out to be the students' empowerment by sharing one's own knowledge.

---

9. Daniel Patte, *The Challenge of Discipleship: A Critical Study of the Sermon on the Mount as Scripture* (Harrisburg, PA: Trinity Press International, 1999).

To sum up, my teaching aims at the students' developing the following skills:

- trusting their own interpretations of a biblical text;
- analyzing critically their own interpretations and being responsible for them;
- understanding the interpretations of others, why they interpret the way they do, and how these interpretations are grounded in the text;
- making explicit the interface between ordinary and critical readings, and regarding both important;
- respecting other interpretations;
- raising the question of the ethics of biblical interpretation, asking about the effects of one's own interpretations, and others' interpretations, on others;
- being willing to revise one's own interpretation if it turns out to be oppressive to others;
- reading the Bible as Scripture with regard to its revelatory character and the religious experiences manifested in it, regardless of whether one views them oneself as Scripture and shares in the belief or not.

Epilogue

"How would you teach your new approach?" he had asked me. And I was glad I did not have to teach at that time. Two years later, I was ready and eager to teach again.

"Are you coming?" two Asian students, who had listened to my lecture, asked me when our paths crossed later in the staircase of the Arts Tower. Quite symbolically, they were ascending as I was descending. I informed them that the decision was not up to me but to the search committee. But, yes, I added, if I was offered the position I would accept it and look forward to seeing them again in class. However, it was not meant to be.

And so it happened that, two years later, I was able to accept an offer from the other side of the Atlantic. As visiting professor at the Jesuit School of Theology and the Graduate Theological Union in Berkeley I had the unique opportunity to work with students from across the world, very different cultural backgrounds and religious affiliations. Finally, I was in a position to "teach" my new approach, especially in the course Text and

Self: Methods and Ethics of Personal Voice Biblical Criticism in the spring semester 2002. This was exactly what I had wished for, the realization of my vision of mutuality in teaching and learning, a lively process of interaction. And, just for a change, I was not teaching the crowd but a small yet great group of students.

A Response: Where from and Where To?

Francis J. Moloney, SDB

The publication of this collection of essays by Ingrid Rosa Kitzberger is an important event for contemporary New Testament studies. Most of them appeared in the exciting years that marked the end of the second and the opening of the third millennium. All of them invite a reader into an ever-expanding interpretative experience of texts that allows an appreciation of the possibilities of narrative criticism, especially when read autobiographically. As Ingrid Rosa writes of her interpretation of the mother of Jesus at the cross: "My surprise about Jesus' mother at the cross is forever linked to my surprise about the way a biblical text can transform a believer's life and death, and thus how the horizons of the world of the text and the world of the reader in front of the text can merge."[1] Such interpretations challenged mainstream New Testament scholarship at the time. Rejecting the academy's strong focus on history as the bedrock of "correct" interpretations, especially in German-language scholarship, Ingrid Rosa's work was not always well received. She was part of a movement away from a methodology deeply committed to the interpretation of what has come to be known as "the world in the text" in the light of "the world behind the text." Her contribution focuses intensely and creatively on the world in front of the text. Across that period, such interpretations took on many forms, from a moderate use of narrative-critical readings that sought to enhance traditional Christian interpretations to more destabilizing postmodern readings that questioned the contemporary relevance of the biblical text by resisting readings, and reading against the grain.[2]

---

1. "Stabat Mater? Rebirth at the Foot of the Cross," in this volume.
2. Copious documentation of these different hermeneutical stances can be found in the notes of the essays reproduced in this volume. A single-volume indication of

Regretfully, over the past twenty years the more historically oriented interpretations have returned to center stage. Destabilizing autobiographical narrative readings have faded from the scene as history and reception dominate the agendas of a younger generation of fine scholars. In the difficult job market in today's universities, as Ingrid Rosa's own professional career has shown, scholars who pursue more reader-oriented methodologies have difficulties in finding employment. The fruits of such work are too personal and thus should be disqualified.[3] It is a delight that the Society of Biblical Literature has published this volume of essays from a courageous scholar. Its appearance reminds us of what has been largely abandoned. As she herself describes in her introduction, Ingrid Rosa's doctoral dissertation on Pauline language, completed at the University of Salzburg (Austria) and published in 1986, prepared her for a career as a historical critic. Although a generation older than her, I, along with many others, shared a journey that began in the historical-critical mode, moved from redaction criticism into a more literary approach to narrative texts, and then saw the need to reach further.[4] Strongly influenced by the emerging interest in the potential of postmodern readings, Ingrid Rosa became an active member of the seminars dedicated to this approach at the meetings of the Society for New Testament Studies and the Society of Biblical Literature. Austrian by birth, she quickly emerged as the least German critic in the German-speaking New Testament guild.

A Unique Reading of Texts and Characters

The studies found in this volume are more than narrative readings. Ingrid Rosa developed a unique approach to the biblical text, capturing the

---

the range of these so-called postmodern interpretations can be found in The Bible and Culture Collective, *The Postmodern Bible* (New Haven: Yale University Press, 1995).

3. This situation is worsened by the recent adoption of a system of judging the standing of scholarly publication by its publisher. In secular Australia, this leads to the disqualification of publications from long-standing and prestigious religious publishers, e.g., de Gruyter, Herder, Peeters, SCM Press, SPCK, Fortress, Baker Academic, Westminster John Knox, SBL Press. In this narrow world, only works published with Oxford and Cambridge University Press and their peers are considered. Academic positions and career advancement are measured by these narrow, classical criteria. Creativity is stifled.

4. See Francis J. Moloney, "From History, into Narrative, and Beyond," in *Johannine Studies 1975–2017*, WUNT 372 (Tübingen: Mohr Siebeck, 2017), 3–29.

imaginations of some readers and alienating others, as she made strikingly novel suggestions. She raises many unanswerable questions and regards it as her prerogative to do so. Several methodological stances generated her unique approach. In the first place, she associated herself with the feminist hermeneutical stances of Elisabeth Schüssler Fiorenza.[5] Second, she began to focus more and more on the Fourth Gospel. That magic pool in which an infant can paddle and an elephant swim offers endless imaginative possibilities. Crucial to her interpretation of the Gospel of John is her conviction that John knew the Gospels of Matthew, Mark, and Luke. John's knowledge of the threefold Synoptic tradition played into his own narrative. However, she never explicitly claims that John manifests a literary dependence on Mark, Matthew, or Luke—but she insists that he has a knowledge of all three.[6]

On those methodological building blocks she can construct her provocative interpretations. To offer one example, locating herself as a female first reader, a woman in the Johannine community, she adopts Wolfgang Müller's use of configuration and interfigurality in reading the message conveyed by a number of interrelated characters (largely, but not only, women).[7] The reader can make rich interpretative links between different

---

5. Especially as articulated in Elisabeth Schüssler Fiorenza, *In Memory of Her: A Feminist Theological Reconstruction of Christian Origins* (New York: Crossroad, 1983).

6. In my opinion, the Johannine tradition stands alone. No doubt there are many indications that John knew Synoptic traditions. Kitzberger's work insists on John's knowledge of Mark, Matthew, and Luke, but she never determines the *nature* of that knowledge. Whatever it was, it is impossible to claim that John's use of Mark, Matthew, and Luke has some form of literary dependence, i.e., he uses one or other, or all three (depending on one's decision on a Synoptic source theory) as a source: e.g., as Matthew and Luke had recourse to Mark, in the widely accepted two-source theory. This is *not* the case for John. On this, see the valuable study of Michael Labahn and Manfred Lang, "Johannes und die Synoptiker: Positionen und Impulse seit 1990," in *Kontexte des Johannesevangeliums: Das vierte Evangelium in religions- und traditionsgeschichtlicher Perspektive*, ed. Jörg Frey and Udo Schnelle, WUNT 175 (Tübingen: Mohr Siebeck, 2004), 443–515. I use the names Mark, Matthew, Luke, and John to refer to "authors" of the Four Gospels for ease of reference and respect for the tradition. They are most likely not indications of the names of historical authors.

7. The example comes from "Mary of Bethany and Mary of Magdala—Two Female Characters in the Johannine Passion Narrative: A Feminist, Narrative-Critical Reader Response," in this volume.

See Wolfgang G. Müller, "Interfigurality: A Study on the Interdependence of Literary Figures," in *Intertextuality*, ed. Heinrich E. Plett, RTT 15 (Berlin: de Gruyter,

Johannine characters, for example, Mary of Magdala and Mary of Bethany with the Samaritan woman, aided by the characterization of women from Mark and Matthew who anoint Jesus (see Mark 14:3–9; Matt 26:6–13), and the sinful woman who weeps on Jesus's feet, wipes them with her hair, and anoints him (Luke 7:36–50). By establishing the interplay between several characters, Ingrid Rosa claims that there can be no finished view of the nature and role of any single character in the Johannine narrative. Just as the reader's experiences are *unfinished*, so are those of the characters in the story. The reader must be free to creatively put life into the Lazarus story through the interplay between Martha, Mary, Mary Magdalene, and the women who anoint Jesus. No character is an island, a secluded entity, "but is embedded into a network of relationships—to other persons, to their own world, and to worlds and texts other than their own."[8]

Ingrid Rosa's rich interplay among characters across narratives, be they from the Synoptic or the Johannine tradition, and even from the narrative of the book of Revelation,[9] throws into relief the many possible constructions and reconstructions that open up for a perceptive reader. Read together, texts from Luke (Elizabeth and Mary, Simeon and Anna), Genesis (Abraham and Sarah), and John (Nicodemus, the mother of Jesus, the Beloved Disciple) transcend gender boundaries and promise birth, no matter what age we readers might be.[10] Read transfigurally and interfigurally, allowing all the Marian passages across the Synoptic and Johannine traditions to have an impact on one another, the mother of Jesus is not standing at the cross: "She has journeyed on, thus sharing in the flowing identity of the rivers of living waters that signify believers."[11] The theme of the never-ending possibilities of the Word of God, and the never-ending God-given possibilities of all who read the Word of God, summons them to journey on.

1991), 101–21. The processes of configuration and interfigurality play a large part in Ingrid Rosa's work.

8. "Mary of Bethany and Mary of Magdala," in this volume.

9. I refer to an essay originally published in German and thus not present in this collection. See Ingrid Rosa Kitzberger, "'Wasser und Bäume des Lebens' – eine feministisch-intertextuelle Interpretation von Apk 21/22," in *Weltgericht und Weltvollendung: Zukunftsbilder im Neuen Testament*, ed. Hans-Josef Klauck, QD 150 (Freiburg: Herder, 1994), 206–24.

10. See "Aging and Birthing: Open-Ended Stories and a Hermeneutics of Promise," in this volume.

11. See "Stabat Mater?," in this volume.

By Way of a Response

By the time my reader has worked through the above sample reading of Ingrid Rosa's work to arrive at this brief response, she or he will be familiar with the hermeneutical processes that Ingrid Rosa has developed. You will most likely have made up your own mind about the usefulness of this subtle intertextuality and the dynamic Christian conclusions it produces. For myself as a reader they are invaluable. But I was not invited to write this response as an independent and objective critic. Although not as radically as Ingrid Rosa, I have also been excited by the potential of postmodern readings. Ingrid Rosa does not deal much with the objective.

The publication of this volume of essays takes me back to the exciting days that produced them. I first met Ingrid Rosa at the General Meeting of the Society for New Testament Studies in Edinburgh in August 1994. As more reader-oriented interpretations gathered momentum, she exuded enthusiasm and energy. She had initiated her own journey into an approach to the Scriptures that is entirely hers. She adds the further resource of a knowledge and appreciation of the literature and art associated with the Christian phenomenon, obvious across the body of essays you have encountered. Ingrid Rosa moves easily across various forms of communication with an intense focus on the impact that text, read autobiographically, makes on the reader.[12]

Fundamental to Ingrid Rosa's hermeneutic, and the major lesson I have learned from her over the decades is her insistence that every interpretation of a text is a personal interpretation. For some, this disqualifies her contribution: the objective message of the text is lost in the unqualified acceptance of the priority of the personal voice. But she is correct! There is no unfolding of texts, even in the most rigid of historical-critical interpretations, that does not reflect the personal voice. Looking back, we can see that an underlying Hegelian *Weltanschauung* dominated the work of the Tübingen school, and the early form critics must be criticized for imposing a history-of-religions view in their assessment of the

---

12. On a personal and more recent note, Ingrid Rosa continues to move easily across all New Testament scholarship, especially when it deals with contemporary challenges within the life of the church. She has recently provided a sparkling German translation of my study of the New Testament eucharistic texts: Francis J. Moloney, *Gebrochenes Brot für gebrochene Menschen: Eucharistie im Neuen Testament*, trans. Ingrid Rosa Kitzberger (Freiburg im Breisgau: Herder, 2018).

relationship between form and meaning.[13] Redaction critics depended on the assured historical conclusions of the form critics as they determined the meaning of the whole utterance of a text. Narrative critics have sought to distinguish between the dialogue between an implied author and an implied reader, a heuristic device *in the text*, and a real reader, the historical person from any age who is the reader *of the text*. We claimed that tracing the communication between the implied author and the implied reader provided the possibility of an objective interpretation. Only a text in which the real reader identifies her- or himself with the implied reader bears a message that transcends the world of the text itself. As Seymour Chatman puts it: "When I enter the fictional contract I add another self: I become an implied reader."[14] But all too often, the worldview and religious sensitivities of the real reader are imposed on the implied reader. My construction of the implied reader reflects my social location, life experiences, faith perspectives, and so on.[15] My pretended objective interpretation is little more than my personal voice.

In my appreciation of Ingrid Rosa Kitzberger's copious, imaginative, and probing interpretations, this is her single most significant achievement. Her relentless insistence that she has every right to find her personal voice in her interpretation of the New Testament must be acknowledged. Its best exposition is found in the collection *The Personal Voice in Biblical Interpretation*.[16] Personally involved in a narrative-critical reading of the New Testament in the late 1990s, I was invited by Ingrid Rosa to contribute to that volume. It was a humiliating experience to go back on already-published work to analyze how my personal experience had influenced my so-called exegetical interpretations of the three appearances of Nicodemus in the Fourth Gospel (John 3:1–21; 7:50–52; 19:38–42).[17] Writing

---

13. See Horton Harris, *The Tübingen School* (Oxford: Clarendon, 1975); Francis J. Moloney, *The Gospel of Mark: A Commentary* (Grand Rapids: Baker Academic, 2012), 4–6, and the literature cited there.

14. Seymour Chatman, *Story and Discourse: Narrative Structure in Fiction and Film* (Ithaca, NY: Cornell University Press, 1978), 150.

15. On this, see Francis J. Moloney, *Belief in the Word: Reading John 1–4* (Minneapolis: Fortress, 1992), 12–14.

16. Ingrid Rosa Kitzberger, ed., *The Personal Voice in Biblical Interpretation* (London: Routledge, 1999).

17. Francis J. Moloney, "An Adventure with Nicodemus," in Kitzberger, *Personal Voice in Biblical Interpretation*, 97–110. My earlier commentary on John 3:1–21 and

today, some twenty years after writing that study, approaching my eightieth birthday, I continue to recognize myself:

> At this moment, hopefully only beginning the latter half of my biography, I recognize Jesus at the tomb and wonder where Nicodemus will lead me. But in the difficulties of this postmodern moment, which may obviously intensify, I journey on, attempting to cross the bridge constructed by the Johannine Jesus' final words: "Blessed are those who have not seen yet believe" (20:29). In this I am armed with a prayer which comes from another Gospel: "I believe, help my unbelief" (Mark 9:24).[18]

Once the interpreter accepts the inevitable presence of the personal voice, then other strategies can be adopted that may or may not endorse Ingrid Rosa's approach and conclusions. Differing understanding of exegetical details may lead the reader elsewhere. For example, my personal reading of John 11:1–12:8 focuses more intensely on the narrative priority of Mary in 11:1–2, 28–33, and 12:1–8. Mary leads the way to faith in the revelation that will take place in the Johannine passion narrative of 18:28–19:16. Martha fails to accept Jesus's self-revelation in 11:25. Her response in verse 26 reveals *her* expectations (as in vv. 21–22, 24). Jesus roundly criticizes her for this lack of faith in verse 40. The two appearances of the verb *embrimasthai* in verses 33 and 38 do not indicate Jesus's sharing in the surrounding atmosphere of sorrow. On the contrary, he manifests a high level of frustration at the universal lack of faith in the truth, articulated in Jesus's words in 11:4 that this sickness is not unto death but for the glory of God and the glorification of the Son (the disciples [see vv. 13–16], Martha, "the Jews," and in the end—Mary [v. 33: weeping with "the Jews"]).[19] The purpose of the narrative is to throw into relief the lack of belief among all the characters surrounding Jesus (see vv. 14–15; 25–26; 40, 42, 45–46). Armed with the information provided in the prologue (1:1–18), the reader's faith is called into question.

7:50–52 had appeared in Moloney, *Belief in the Word*, 106–21; Moloney, *Signs and Shadows: Reading John 5–12* (Minneapolis: Fortress, 1996), 91–93.

18. Moloney, "Adventure with Nicodemus," 106.

19. See Moloney, "The Faith of Martha and Mary: A Narrative Approach to John 11:17–40," in *Johannine Studies 1975–2017*, 385–404. See also Francis J. Moloney, "Can Everyone Be Wrong? A Reading of John 11:1–12:8," in *The Gospel of John: Text and Context*, BibInt 72 (Leiden: Brill, 2005), 214–40.

Furthermore, unconditional agreement among interpreters on which characters the interpreter might choose from across the Bible in the processes of configuration and interfigurality is an impossible dream. While some might offer themselves more obviously (e.g., the Marys in the Johannine narrative), others may seem forced. For example, in my reading of the book of Revelation I found that Ingrid Rosa's location of herself as "a woman reading in Thyatira" lacks an awareness of all the woman texts in Revelation. From her "womanly" location she finds the contrast between the prostitute in Rev 17 and the bride of the Lamb in Rev 21–22 unacceptable. She thus universalizes the promise of water and the tree of life in 22:1–2 through intertextual readings from Isaiah that overcome the displeasure of the woman in Thyatira.[20] I too would like to emerge from a reading of the book of Revelation with a positive view of "the woman." However, I would do so through a literary and theological association between the *three* appearances of "the woman" as a character: 12:1–18 (the potential of humankind lost with the resultant ambiguity, pursued by the serpent), 17:1–18 (the sinful resolution of the ambiguity by the woman's "mounting" the beast), and 21:9 (the bride's final resolution of the ambiguity through a grace-filled intimate association with the Lamb). Ingrid Rosa devotes no attention to the provocative portrait of the woman initially clothed with the sun, who finished in the desert, pursued by the ancient serpent who deceived the whole world, in 12:1–18. It may have been better to start with that portrait of "the woman" before having recourse to Isaiah.[21] But choices must be made in this novel and exciting approach to the New Testament.

Ingrid Rosa does not expect us to agree on the characters we choose for configuration and interfigurality. That choice can be an intensely personal. But she would insist that a determining factor in interpretation is always the personal voice. Such an approach is not without its challenges. As Peter Rabinowitz once warned: "Once you take seriously that readers 'construct' (even partially) the texts that they read, then the canon (any canon) is not (or not only) the product of the inherent qualities in the text; it is also (at least partially) the product of particular choices by the arbiters

---

20. See Kitzberger, "Wasser und Bäume des Lebens," esp. 213–23.

21. For a detailed development of this case, see Francis J. Moloney, *The Apocalypse of John: An Alternative Commentary* (Grand Rapids: Baker Academic, forthcoming). See also Eugenio Corsini, *Apocalisse di Gesù Cristo secondo Giovanni*, SEI Frontiere (Turin: Società Editrice Internazionale, 2002), 386–90.

of taste who create it—choices always grounded in ideological and cultural values, always enmeshed in class, race and gender."[22] Can Ingrid Rosa's work be accused of losing "the inherent qualities of the text," imposing her own "ideological and cultural values"? I suggest that this is not the case, as she is not only articulating her own voice. She is listening to another voice! Her work is permeated with a keen awareness and acceptance of two thousand years of Christian tradition. While her work may be put under the general, and vague, classification of postmodern, she is acutely aware of the inherent qualities of the voice of two thousand years of Christian tradition. There is no hint of the postmodern tendency to read against the text in order to address the wrongs that have been done by the male-dominated texts of terror. On the contrary, while a critique of such an established way of reading biblical texts can be found in her work, in the end she wishes to uncover many biblical voices in a careful listening and subsequent interplay between an original imaginative storyteller in biblical texts, and a contemporary imaginative interpreter.

Some two thousand years ago authors attempted to communicate a point of view by telling a story *in a certain way*, very often guided by the sacred Scriptures of Israel. These texts remain alive, and even appear in best-seller lists, because Christians accept that New Testament narratives continue to say something relevant in today's world. Across two thousand years many voices have responded to that original voice. Ingrid Rosa's work joins those voices as she continues and enriches the Christian tradition by insightful interplay across the many biblical voices. She accepts the Christian tradition that they always have and always will say something relevant to those who turn to the biblical Word of God for inspiration and hope.

Where from and Where To?

As I opened this response, I pointed out that the wind has gone out of the sails of the many reader-oriented interpretations that emerged and blossomed in the final decade of the second millennium and the first decade of the third. This volume seeks to put some wind back into those sails. Nowadays the increasing availability of ancient texts, readily accessible via electronic media and rapidly searched by electronic search engines, has

---

22. Peter J. Rabinowitz, "Whirl without End," in *Contemporary Literary Theory*, ed. C. Douglas Atkins and Laura Morrow (London: Macmillan, 1989), 94.

generated a return to close attention to the worlds behind our biblical texts. Equally central to much biblical research is the study of the reception of texts and their message, especially in the earlier periods, as Christianity took shape. There can be no questioning the value of a return to history and the assessment of the formative reception of the biblical traditions, although I sometimes wonder why so much detailed scholarship is devoted to trace interpretations that are clearly mistaken.[23]

But we should not disregard the contribution of the achievements of the more reader-focused interpretations, however out of fashion they may have become. This publication of Ingrid Rosa's essays is a sign that the recent history of where we came from may still have a role to play in where we are heading in our interpretation of biblical texts. Generally, in scholarly disciplines, we stand on the shoulders of those who went before us. In the seriousness of the contemporary return to the historical-critical paradigm, perhaps it may be opportune to recapture some of the joy and playfulness that comes from the rich reflections found in this volume. No doubt there were hermeneutical weaknesses and many false turns in the reader-oriented studies that formed our immediate past. No doubt some of them are found in Ingrid Rosa's work. But when has that not been the case? When will that not be the case? Might I suggest that we should continue to pursue reflection on the way "a biblical text can transform a believer's life and death, and thus how the horizons of the world of the text and the world of the reader in front of the text can merge."[24]

---

23. Only some work on reception falls into this category. Much of it is admirable. One thinks immediately of one of the founders of this approach, Ulrich Luz. The third volume of his commentary on the Gospel of Matthew (dedicated to Matt 21–28) is a masterpiece. There is something for everyone in its pages: theology, literature, art history, the history of Christian spirituality, etc. See Ulrich Luz, *Matthew*, trans. James E. Crouch, 3 vols., Hermeneia (Minneapolis: Fortress, 2001–2007).

24. "Stabat Mater?," in this volume.

Bibliography

Alcoff, Linda. "The Problem of Speaking for Others." *CC* (1991–1992): 5–32.

Alter, Robert. *The Pleasures of Reading in an Ideological Age*. New York: Simon & Schuster, 1989.

Anderson, Janice Capel, and Jeffrey L. Staley, eds. *Taking It Personally: Autobiographical Biblical Criticism*. Semeia 72 (1995).

Anzaldúa, Gloria. *Borderland/La Frontera: The New Mestiza*. San Francisco: Aunt Lute, 1987.

Bach, Alice. "Signs of the Flesh: Observations on Characterization in the Bible." *Semeia* 63 (1993): 61–79.

Ball, D. Mark. *"I Am" in John's Gospel: Literary Function, Background and Theological Implications*. JSNTSup 124. Sheffield: Sheffield Academic, 1996.

Bar-Efrat, Shimon. *Narrative Art in the Bible*. BLS 17. Sheffield: Sheffield Academic, 1989.

Baumgarten, Joseph. "Purification after Childbirth and the Sacred Garden in 4Q265 and Jubilees." Pages 3–10 in *New Qumran Texts and Studies: Proceedings of the First Meeting of the International Organization for Qumran Studies, Paris 1992*. Edited by George J. Brooke with Florentino Garcia Martinez. Leiden: Brill, 1994.

Beardslee, William A. "Vital Ruins: Biblical Narrative and the Story Frameworks of Our Lives." Pages 219–36 in *Margins of Belonging. Essays on the New Testament and Theology*. AARSR 58. Atlanta: Scholars Press, 1991.

Beck, David R. "The Narrative Function of Anonymity in Fourth Gospel Characterization." *Semeia* 63 (1993):143–58.

Bible and Culture Collective. *The Postmodern Bible*. New Haven: Yale University Press, 1995.

Black, Fiona C., Roland Boer, and Erin Runions, eds. *The Labour of Reading: Desire, Alienation, and Biblical Interpretation.* SemeiaSt 36. Atlanta: Society of Biblical Literature, 1999.

Blanchard, Paula. *Margaret Fuller: From Transcendentalism to Revelation.* New York: Dell, 1979.

Blank, Josef. "Der johanneische Wahrheitsbegriff." *BZ* 7 (1963): 164–73.

Bleich, David. *Subjective Criticism.* Baltimore: Johns Hopkins University Press, 1978.

Boer, Martinus C. de. "John 4:27—Women (and Men) in the Gospel and Community of John." Pages 208–30 in *Women in the Biblical Tradition.* Edited by George J. Brooke. SWR 31. Lewiston, NY: Mellen, 1992.

Boobyer, G. H. "The Early History of Studiorum Novi Testamenti Societas." *Bulletin of New Testament Studies* 1 (1950): 7–10.

Booth, Wayne C. *The Rhetoric of Fiction.* 2nd ed. Chicago: University of Chicago Press, 1983.

Bösen, Willibald. *Der letzte Tag des Jesus von Nazareth: Was wirklich geschah.* Freiburg im Breisgau: Herder, 1994.

Boyarin, Daniel. *Intertextuality and the Reading of Midrash.* Bloomington: Indiana University Press, 1994.

Brant, Jo-Ann. "Husband Hunting: Characterization and Narrative Art in the Gospel of John." *BibInt* 4 (1996): 205–33.

Braund, Susanna Morton. "Personal Plurals." Pages 38–53 in *Compromising Traditions: The Personal Voice in Classical Scholarship.* Edited by Judith P. Hallett and Thomas Van Nortwick. London: Routledge, 1997.

Brown, Raymond E. *The Birth of the Messiah: A Commentary on the Infancy Narratives in the Gospels of Matthew and Luke.* ABRL. New York: Doubleday, 1993.

———. *The Death of the Messiah: From Gethsemane to the Grave.* 2 vols. ABRL. New York: Doubleday, 1994.

———. *The Gospel according to John: XIII–XXI.* AB 29A. New York: Doubleday, 1970.

———. "Roles of Women in the Fourth Gospel." *TS* 36 (1975): 688–99.

Burnett, Fred W. "Characterization and Reader Construction of Characters in the Gospels." Pages 69–88 in *Listening to the Word of God: A Tribute to Boyce W. Blackwelder.* Edited by Barry L. Callen. Anderson, IN: Anderson University Press, 1990.

Burridge, Richard A. *What Are the Gospels? A Comparison with Graeco-Roman Biography.* SNTSMS 70. Cambridge: Cambridge University Press, 1992.

Calinescu, Matei. *Rereading*. New Haven: Yale University Press, 1993.
Charlesworth, James H. *The Beloved Disciple: Whose Witness Validates the Gospel of John?* Valley Forge, PA: Trinity Press International, 1995.
Chatman, Seymour. *Story and Discourse: Narrative Structure in Fiction and Film*. Ithaca, NY: Cornell University Press, 1978.
Corsini, Eugenio. *Apocalisse di Gesù Cristo secondo Giovanni*. SEI Frontiere. Turin: Società Editrice Internazionale, 2002.
Croatto, J. Severino. *Biblical Hermeneutics: Toward a Theory of Reading as the Production of Meaning*. Translated from the Spanish by Robert R. Barr. Maryknoll, NY: Orbis Books, 1987.
———. *Die Bibel gehört den Armen: Perspektiven einer befreiungstheologischen Hermeneutik*. ÖEH 5. Munich: Kaiser, 1989.
———. "The Function of the Non-fulfilled Promises: Reading the Pentateuch from the Perspective of the Latin-American Oppressed People." Pages 38–52 in *The Personal Voice in Biblical Interpretation*. Edited by Ingrid Rosa Kitzberger. London: Routledge, 1999.
Culpepper, R. Alan. *Anatomy of the Fourth Gospel: A Study in Literary Design*. FFNT. Philadelphia: Fortress, 1983.
———. "The Gospel of John as a Document of Faith in a Pluralistic Culture." Pages 107–27 in *Readers and Readings of the Fourth Gospel*. Vol. 1 of *"What Is John?"* Edited by Fernando F. Segovia. SymS 3. Atlanta: Scholars Press, 1996.
Dalman, Gustaf. *Jesus—Jeshua: Studies in the Gospels*. New York: Ktav, 1971.
Darr, John. *On Character Building: The Reader and the Rhetoric of Characterization in Luke-Acts*. Louisville: Westminster John Knox, 1992.
Davies, Margaret. *Rhetoric and Reference in the Fourth Gospel*. JSNTSup 69. Sheffield: Sheffield Academic, 1992.
Denaux, Adelbert, ed. *John and the Synoptics*. BETL 101. Leuven: Peeters, 1992.
Dewey, Joanna. "Point of View and the Disciples in Mark." Pages 97–106 in *1982 Society of Biblical Literature Seminar Papers*. Edited by K. H. Richards. SBLSP 21. Chico, CA: Scholars Press, 1982.
Dormeyer, Detlev. *Das Neue Testament im Rahmen der antiken Literaturgeschichte: Eine Einführung*. DA. Darmstadt: Wissenschaftliche Buchgesellschaft, 1993.
———. *Der Sinn des Leidens Jesu: Historisch-kritische und textpragmatische Analysen zur Markuspassion*. SBS 96. Stuttgart: Katholisches Bibelwerk, 1979.

———. "Die Familie Jesu und der Sohn der Maria im Markusevangelium (3:20f, 31–35; 6:3)." Pages 109–35 in *Vom Urchristentum zu Jesus: Für Joachim Gnilka*. Edited by Hubert Frankemölle and Karl Kertelge. Freiburg im Breisgau: Herder, 1989.

———. *Evangelium als literarische und theologische Gattung*. EdF 263. Darmstadt: Wissenschaftliche Buchgesellschaft, 1989.

———. "The Implicit and Explicit Readers and the Genre of Philippians 3:2–4:3, 8–9: Response to the Commentary of Wolfgang Schenk." *Semeia* 48 (1989): 149–59.

Draisma, Siepke, ed. *Intertextuality in Biblical Writings: Essays in Honour of Bas van Iersel*. Kampen: Kok Pharos, 1989.

Easthope, Anthony. *Literary into Cultural Studies*. London: Routledge, 1991.

Eliot, T. S. *The Complete Poems and Plays of T. S. Eliot*. London: Guild, 1986.

Exum, J. Cheryl. *Fragmented Women: Feminist (Sub)versions of Biblical Narratives*. JSOTSup 163. Sheffield: JSOT Press, 1993.

Fehribach, Adele. *The Women in the Life of the Bridegroom: A Feminist Historical-Literary Analysis of the Female Characters in the Fourth Gospel*. Collegeville, MN: Liturgical Press, 1998.

Ferguson, Thomas J. "Faith and Order Movement Turns 100." Episcopal Church. October 18, 2010. https://tinyurl.com/SBL4523d.

Fewell, Danna Nolan, and Gary A. Phillips, eds. *Ethics, Bible, Reading as If*. Semeia 77 (1998).

Fish, Stanley. "Literature in the Reader: Affective Stylistics." *NLH* 2 (1970): 123–62. Reprinted in *Reader-Response Criticism: From Formalism to Post-structuralism*. Edited by Jane P. Tompkins. Baltimore: Johns Hopkins University Press, 1980.

Fitzmyer, Joseph A. *The Gospel according to Luke I–IX*. AB 28. Garden City, NY: Doubleday, 1981.

Fowler, Robert M. "Irony and the Messianic Secret in the Gospel of Mark." *Proceedings: Eastern Great Lakes Biblical Society* 1 (1981): 26–36.

———. *Let the Reader Understand. Reader-Response Criticism and the Gospel of Mark*. Minneapolis: Fortress, 1991.

Genette, Gérard. *Narrative Discourse: An Essay in Method*. Ithaca, NY: Cornell University Press, 1980.

Gruber, Mayer I. *The Motherhood of God and Other Studies*. SFSHJ 57. Atlanta: Scholars Press, 1992.

———. "The Personal Voice of the Listening Heart." Pages 97–104 in *The Personal Voice in Biblical Interpretation*. Edited by Ingrid Rosa Kitzberger. London: Routledge, 1999.

———. "Purity and Impurity in Halakic Sources and Qumran Law." Pages 65–76 in *Wholly Woman, Holy Blood: A Feminist Critique of Purity and Impurity*. Edited by Kristin de Troyer et al. Harrisburg, PA: Trinity Press International, 2003.

Guardiola-Sáenz, Leticia A. "Border Crossing and Its Redemptive Power in John 7:53–8:11: A Cultural Reading of Jesus and the *Accused*." Pages 267–91 in *Transformative Encounters: Jesus and Women Re-viewed*. Edited by Ingrid Rosa Kitzberger. BibInt 43. Leiden: Brill, 2000.

Hallett, Judith P., and Thomas Van Nortwick, eds. *Compromising Traditions: The Personal Voice in Classical Scholarship*. London: Routledge, 1997.

Harris, Horton. *The Tübingen School*. Oxford: Clarendon, 1975.

Hengel, Martin. *The Four Gospels and the One Gospel of Jesus Christ: An Investigation of the Collection and Origin of the Canonical Gospels*. Translated by John Bowden. London: SCM, 2000.

Holland, Norman N. "Unity Identity Text Self." Pages 118–33 in *Reader-Response Criticism: From Formalism to Post-structuralism*. Edited by Jane P. Tompkins. Baltimore: Johns Hopkins University Press, 1980.

Hooker, Morna D. *Beginnings: Keys That Open the Gospels*. Harrisburg, PA: Trinity Press International, 1997.

Howard-Brook, Wes. *Becoming Children of God: John's Gospel and Radical Discipleship*. B&L. Reprint, Maryknoll, NY: Orbis Books, 2001.

Ilan, Tal. "Notes on the Distribution of Jewish Women's Names in Palestine in the Second Temple and Mishnaic Periods." *JJS* 40 (1989): 186–200.

Ingarden, Roman. *Gegenstand und Aufgaben der Literaturwissenschaft: Aufsätze und Diskussionsbeiträge (1937–1964)*. Edited by Rolf Fieguth. Tübingen: Niemeyer, 1976.

Inglis, Fred. *Ideology and the Imagination*. London: Cambridge University Press, 1975.

Iser, Wolfgang. *Der implizite Leser*. UTB 163. Munich: Fink, 1972.

———. "The Reading Process: A Phenomenological Approach." Pages 50–69 in *Reader-Response Criticism: From Formalism to Post-structuralism*. Edited by Jane P. Tompkins. Baltimore: Johns Hopkins University Press, 1980.

Jacobus, Mary. "Is There a Woman in This Text?" Pages 83–109 in *Reading Women: Essays in Feminist Criticism*. New York: Columbia University Press, 1986.
Jaroff, Leon. "Rock Festival on Mars." *Time*. July 21, 1997: 72–74.
Jasper, Alison. *The Shining Garment of the Text: Gendered Readings of John's Prologue*. JSNTSup 165. GCT 6. Sheffield: Sheffield Academic, 1998.
Jung, Carl G. "Die Beziehungen zwischen dem Ich und dem Unbewußten." Pages 11–55 in *Persönlichkeit und Übertragung*. Vol. 3 of *Grundwerk*. 3rd ed. Olten: Walter, 1990.
———. *Synchronicity. An Acausal Connecting Principle*. Translated by R. F. C. Hull. Reprint, London: Routledge & Kegan Paul, 1981.
———. "Über Synchronizität." Pages 279–90 in *Archetyp und Unbewußtes*. Vol. 2 of *Grundwerk*. 4th ed. Olten: Walter, 1990.
Karris, Robert J. *Jesus and the Marginalized in John's Gospel*. ZSNT. Collegeville, MN: Liturgical Press, 1990.
Kelber, Werner H. "Metaphysics and Marginality in John." Pages 129–54 in *Readers and Readings of the Fourth Gospel*. Vol. 1 of *"What Is John?"* Edited by Fernando F. Segovia. SymS 3. Atlanta: Scholars Press, 1996.
Kitzberger, Ingrid Rosa. "Aging and Birthing: Open-Ended Stories and a Hermeneutics of Promise." Pages 387–411 in *Los caminos inexhauribles de la Palabra: Las relecturas creativas en la Biblia y de la Biblia; Homenaje a J. Severino Croatto*. Edited by Guillermo Hansen. Buenos Aires: Lumen-ISEDET, 2000.
———, ed. *Autobiographical Biblical Criticism: Between Text and Self*. Leiden: Deo, 2002.
———. *Bau der Gemeinde: Das paulinische Wortfeld οἰκοδομή/(ἐπ)οικοδομεῖν*. Würzburg: Echter, 1986.
———. "Border Crossing and Meeting Jesus at the Well: An Autobiographical Re-reading of the Samaritan Woman's Story in John 4:1–42." Pages 111–27 in *The Personal Voice in Biblical Interpretation*. Edited by Ingrid Rosa Kitzberger. London: Routledge, 1999.
———. "Caracterization en el Cruce." *RT* 19 (2005): 50–61.
———. "Characterization at the Crossroads." Paper presented at the Annual Meeting of the Society of Biblical Literature. Denver, CO, November 20, 2001.
———. "'How Can This Be?' (John 3:9): A Feminist-Theological Re-reading of the Gospel of John." Pages 19–41 in *Literary and Social Readings of the Fourth Gospel*. Vol. 2 of *"What Is John?"* Edited by Fernando F. Segovia. SymS 7. Atlanta: Scholars Press, 1998.

———. "Love and Footwashing: John 13:1–20 and Luke 7:36–50 Read Intertextually." *BibInt* 2 (1994): 190–206.

———. "Mary and Martha." Page 121 in vol. 8 of *Religion Past & Present: Encyclopedia of Theology and Religion*. Edited by Hans Dieter Betz, Don S. Browning, Bernd Janowski, and Eberhard Jüngel. Leiden: Brill, 2010.

———. "Mary Magdalene." Page 122 in vol. 8 of *Religion Past & Present: Encyclopedia of Theology and Religion*. Edited by Hans Dieter Betz, Don S. Browning, Bernd Janowski, and Eberhard Jüngel. Leiden: Brill, 2010.

———. "Mary, Mother of Jesus." Pages 113–14 in vol. 8 of *Religion Past & Present: Encyclopedia of Theology and Religion*. Edited by Hans Dieter Betz, Don S. Browning, Bernd Janowski, and Eberhard Jüngel. Leiden: Brill, 2010.

———. "Mary of Bethany and Mary of Magdala—Two Female Characters in the Johannine Passion Narrative: A Feminist, Narrative-Critical Reader Response." *NTS* 41 (1995): 564–86.

———, ed. *The Personal Voice in Biblical Interpretation*. London: Routledge, 1999.

———. "Synoptic Women in John: Interfigural Readings." Pages 77–111 in *Transformative Encounters: Jesus and Women Re-viewed*. Edited by Kitzberger. BibInt 43. Leiden: Brill, 2000.

———, ed. *Transformative Encounters: Jesus and Women Re-viewed*. BibInt 43. Leiden: Brill, 2000.

———. "'Wasser und Bäume des Lebens'—Eine feministisch-intertextuelle Interpretation von Apk 21/22." Pages 206–24 in *Weltgericht und Weltvollendung: Zukunftsbilder im Neuen Testament*. Edited by Hans-Josef Klauck. QD 150. Freiburg im Breisgau: Herder, 1994.

Klauck, Hans-Josef. "Die erzählerische Rolle der Jünger im Markusevangelium: Eine narrative Analyse." *NovT* 24 (1982): 1–26.

Kluger, Jeffrey. "Uncovering the Secrets of Mars." *Time*. July 14, 1997: 40–41.

Koester, Craig R. "The Spectrum of Johannine Readers." Pages 5–19 in *Readers and Readings of the Fourth Gospel*. Vol. 1 of *"What Is John?"* Edited by Fernando F. Segovia. SymS 3. Atlanta: Scholars Press, 1996.

———. *Symbolism in the Fourth Gospel: Meaning, Mystery, Community*. Minneapolis: Fortress, 1995.

Kügler, Joachim. "Gold, Weihrauch und Myrrhe: Eine Notiz zu Mt 2,11." *BN* 87 (1997): 24–33.

Kysar, Robert. *John's Story of Jesus*. Philadelphia: Fortress, 1984.

———. "The Making of Metaphor: Another Reading of John 3:1–15." Pages 21–41 in *Readers and Readings of the Fourth Gospel*. Vol. 1 of *"What Is John?"* Edited by Fernando F. Segovia. SymS 3. Atlanta: Scholars Press, 1996.

Labahn, Michael, and Manfred Lang. "Johannes und die Synoptiker: Positionen und Impulse seit 1990." Pages 443–515 in *Kontexte des Johannesevangeliums: Das vierte Evangelium in religions- und traditionsgeschichtlicher Perspektive*. Edited by Jörg Frey and Udo Schnelle. WUNT 175. Tübingen: Mohr Siebeck, 2004.

Lang, James L. "Getting to Know My Future Selves." *Chronicle of Higher Education*. December 10, 1999. http://www.chronicle.com/jobs.

Lategan, Bernard C. Introduction to *Scriptura* 9 (1991): 1–6.

———. "The Truth That Sets Man Free (John 8:31–36)." *Neot* 2 (1968): 70–80.

Levine, Amy-Jill, with Marianne Blickenstaff. *A Feminist Companion to John*. 2 vols. Sheffield: Sheffield Academic, 2003.

Lieu, Judith M. "The Mother of the Son in the Fourth Gospel." *JBL* 117 (1998): 61–77.

———. "Scripture and the Feminine in John." Pages 225–40 in *A Feminist Companion to the Hebrew Bible in the New Testament*. Edited by Athalya Brenner. FCB 10. Sheffield: Sheffield Academic, 1996.

Link, Hannelore. *Rezeptionsforschung: Eine Einführung in Methoden und Probleme*. UTB 215, R 80. 2nd ed. Stuttgart: Kohlhammer, 1980.

Luz, Ulrich. *Matthew*. Translated by James E. Crouch. 3 vols. Hermeneia. Minneapolis: Fortress, 2001–2007.

Maccini, Robert G. *Her Testimony Is True: Women as Witnesses according to John*. JSNTSup 125. Sheffield: Sheffield Academic, 1996.

Malbon, Elizabeth Struthers. "Disciples/Crowds/Whoever: Markan Characters and Readers." *NovT* (1986): 104–30.

———. "Fallible Followers: Women and Men in the Gospel of Mark." *Semeia* 28 (1983): 29–48.

———. *In the Company of Jesus: Characters in Mark's Gospel*. Louisville: Westminster John Knox, 2000.

———. "The Poor Widow in Mark and Her Poor Rich Readers." *CBQ* 53 (1991): 589–604.

Malbon, Elizabeth Struthers, and Adele Berlin, eds. *Characterization in Biblical Literature. Semeia* 63 (1993).

Martindale, Charles. "Proper Voices: Writing the Writer." Pages 73–101 in *Compromising Traditions: The Personal Voice in Classical Scholarship*. Edited by Judith P. Hallett and Thomas Van Nortwick. London: Routledge, 1997.

McKinlay, Judith E. *Gendering Wisdom the Host: Biblical Invitations to Eat and Drink*. JSNTSup 216. GCT 4. Sheffield: Sheffield Academic, 1996.

McKnight, Edgar V. *The Bible and the Reader: An Introduction to Literary Criticism*. Philadelphia: Fortress, 1985.

———. *Jesus Christ in History and Scripture: A Poetic and Sectarian Perspective*. Macon, GA: Mercer University Press, 1999.

———. *Post-modern Use of the Bible: The Emergence of Reader-Oriented Criticism*. 2nd ed. Nashville: Abingdon, 1990.

Miller, Nancy K. *Getting Personal: Feminist Occasions and Other Autobiographical Acts*. London: Routledge, 1991.

Miller, Owen. "Intertextual Identity." Pages 19–40 in *Identity of the Literary Text*. Edited by Mario J. Valdes and Owen Miller. Toronto: University of Toronto Press, 1985.

Moloney, Francis J. "An Adventure with Nicodemus." Pages 97–110 in *The Personal Voice in Biblical Interpretation*. Edited by Ingrid Rosa Kitzberger. London: Routledge, 1999.

———. *The Apocalypse of John: An Alternative Commentary*. Grand Rapids: Baker Academic, forthcoming.

———. *Belief in the Word: Reading John 1–4*. Minneapolis: Fortress, 1993.

———. "Can Everyone Be Wrong? A Reading of John 11:1–12:8." Pages 214–40 in *The Gospel of John: Text and Context*. BibInt 72. Leiden: Brill, 2005.

———. "The Faith of Martha and Mary: A Narrative Approach to John 11:17–40." Pages 385–404 in *Johannine Studies 1975–2017*. WUNT 372. Tübingen: Mohr Siebeck, 2017.

———. "From History, into Narrative, and Beyond." Pages 3–29 in *Johannine Studies 1975–2017*. WUNT 372. Tübingen: Mohr Siebeck, 2017.

———. *Gebrochenes Brot für gebrochene Menschen: Eucharistie im Neuen Testament*. Translated by Ingrid Rosa Kitzberger. Freiburg im Breisgau: Herder, 2018.

———. *Glory Not Dishonor: Reading John 13–21*. Minneapolis: Fortress, 1998.

———. *The Gospel of Mark: A Commentary*. Grand Rapids: Baker Academic, 2012.

———. "John 21 and the Johannine Story." Pages 521–37 in *Johannine Studies 1975–2017*. WUNT 372. Tübingen: Mohr Siebeck, 2017.

———. *Signs and Shadows: Reading John 5–12*. Minneapolis: Fortress, 1996.

Moore, Stephen D. *Literary Criticism and the Gospels: The Theoretical Challenge*. New Haven: Yale University Press, 1989.

———. "True Confessions and Weird Obsessions: Autobiographical Interventions in Literary and Biblical Studies." *Semeia* 72 (1995): 19–50.

Müller, Wolfgang G. "Interfigurality: A Study on the Interdependence of Literary Figures." Pages 101–21 in *Intertextuality*. Edited by Heinrich E. Plett. RTT 15. Berlin: de Gruyter, 1991.

Neirynck, Frans. "ΕΙΣ ΤΑ ΙΔΙΑ: Jn 19, 26 (et 16, 32)." *ETL* 55 (1979): 357–65.

———. "John and the Synoptics." *ETL* 45 (1977): 73–106.

———. "La traduction d'un verset johannique, Jn 19, 27b." *ETL* 57 (1981): 83–106.

Nutu, Liliana M. "Opening Mouths and Legs, or Women's Talk: Can One Hear the Mother of Christ in John's Gospel and Leeloo in Luc Besson's *The Fifth Element*?" Unpublished paper.

O'Day, Gail. *Revelation in the Fourth Gospel: Narrative Mode and Theological Claim*. Minneapolis: Fortress, 1986.

Patte, Daniel. "Can One Be Critical without Being Autobiographical? The Case of Romans 1:26–27." Pages 34–59 in *Autobiographical Biblical Criticism*. Edited by Ingrid Rosa Kitzberger. Leiden: Deo, 2002.

———. *The Challenge of Discipleship: A Critical Study of the Sermon on the Mount as Scripture*. Harrisburg, PA: Trinity Press International, 1999.

———. *Discipleship according to the Sermon on the Mount: Four Legitimate Readings, Four Plausible Views of Discipleship, and Their Relative Values*. Valley Forge, PA: Trinity Press International, 1996.

———. *Ethics of Biblical Interpretation: A Reevaluation*. Louisville: Westminster John Knox, 1995.

———. "The Guarded Personal Voice of a Male European-American Biblical Scholar." Pages 12–23 in *The Personal Voice in Biblical Interpretation*. Edited by Ingrid Rosa Kitzberger. London: Routledge, 1999.

Petersen, Norman R. *The Gospel of John and the Sociology of Light: Language and Characterization in the Fourth Gospel*. Valley Forge, PA: Trinity Press International, 1993.

———. *Literary Criticism for New Testament Critics*. GBS. Philadelphia: Fortress, 1978.

———. "'Point of View' in Mark's Narrative." *Semeia* 12 (1978): 97–121.
Powell, Mark Allan. *What Is Narrative Criticism?* Minneapolis: Fortress, 1990.
Rabinowitz, Peter J. "Whirl without End." Pages 81–100 in *Contemporary Literary Theory*. Edited by C. Douglas Atkins and Laura Morrow. London: Macmillan, 1989.
Rad, Gerhard von. *Das erste Buch Mose: Genesis*. ATD 2/4. Göttingen: Vandenhoeck & Ruprecht, 1981.
Rand, Jan A. du. "The Characterization of Jesus as Depicted in the Narrative of the Fourth Gospel." *Neot* 19 (1985): 18–36.
———. "Plot and Point of View in the Gospel of John." Pages 149–69 in *A South African Perspective on the New Testament*. Edited by J. Hartin Petzer and Peter J. Martin. Leiden: Brill, 1986.
Rashkow, Ilona N. "In Our Image We Create Him, Male and Female We Create Them: The E/Affect of Biblical Characterization." *Semeia* 63 (1993): 105–13.
Reinhartz, Adele. *Befriending the Beloved Disciple: A Jewish Reading of the Gospel of John*. New York: Continuum, 2001.
———. "From Narrative to History: The Resurrection of Mary and Martha." Pages 161–84 in *"Women Like This": New Perspectives on Jewish Women in the Greco-Roman World*. Edited by Amy-Jill Levine. EJL 1. Atlanta: Scholars Press, 1991.
———. "A Nice Jewish Girl Reads the Gospel of John." *Semeia* 77 (1977): 177–93.
Rhoads, David. "Narrative Criticism and the Gospel of Mark." *JAAR* 50 (1982): 411–34.
Ringe, Sharon H. *Wisdom's Friends: Community and Christology in the Fourth Gospel*. Louisville: Westminster John Knox, 1999.
Robbins, Vernon K. *Exploring the Texture of Texts: A Guide to Socio-rhetorical Interpretation*. Valley Forge, PA: Trinity Press International, 1996.
———. "The Reversed Contextualization of Psalm 22 in the Markan Crucifixion: A Socio-rhetorical Analysis." Pages 1161–83 in vol. 2 of *The Four Gospels 1992: Festschrift Frans Neyrinck*. Edited by Frans Van Segbroeck et al. BETL 100. Leuven: University Press; Peeters, 1992.
Rodgers, Michael, and Mark Losack. *Glendalough: A Celtic Pilgrimage*. Blackrock: Columba, 1996.
Rosenblatt, Roger. "Visit to a Smaller Planet." *Time*. July 14, 1997: 47.

Ruckstuhl, Eugen. "Der Jünger, den Jesus liebte." Pages 355–95 in *Jesus im Horizont der Evangelien*. SBABNT 3. Stuttgart: Katholisches Bibelwerk, 1988.

———. *Jesus, Freund und Anwalt der Frauen: Frauenpräsenz und Frauenabwesenheit in der Geschichte Jesu*. Stuttgart: Katholisches Bibelwerk, 1996.

———. "Jesus und der geschichtliche Mutterboden im vierten Evangelium." Pages 256–86 in *Vom Urchristentum zu Jesus*. Edited by Hubert Frankemölle and Karl Kertelge. Freiburg im Breisgau: Herder, 1989.

Sabbe, Maurits. "The Anointing of Jesus in John 12, 1–8 and Its Synoptic Parallels." Pages 2051–82 in *The Four Gospels 1992*. Edited by Frans Van Segbroeck et al. BETL 100. Leuven: Peeters, 1992.

———. "The Footwashing in Jn 13 and Its Relation to the Synoptic Gospels." *ETL* 58 (1982): 279–308.

———. "The Johannine Account of the Death of Jesus and Its Synoptic Parallels (Jn 19, 16b–42)." *ETL* 70 (1994): 34–64.

Sawicki, Marianne. "Magdalenes and Tiberiennes: City Women in the Entourage of Jesus." Pages 181–202 in *Transformative Encounters: Jesus and Women Re-viewed*. Edited by Ingrid Rosa Kitzberger. BibInt 43. Leiden: Brill, 2000.

Schneiders, Sandra M. "John 20:11–18: The Encounter of the Easter Jesus with Mary Magdalene—A Transformative Feminist Reading." Pages 155–68 in *Readers and Readings of the Fourth Gospel*. Vol. 1 of *"What Is John?"* Edited by Fernando F. Segovia. SymS 3. Atlanta: Scholars Press, 1996.

———. *The Revelatory Text: Interpreting the New Testament as Sacred Scripture*. San Francisco: Harper, 1991.

———. "Women in the Fourth Gospel and the Role of Women in the Contemporary Church." *BTB* 12 (1982): 35–45.

———. *Written That You May Believe: Encountering Jesus in the Fourth Gospel*. New York: Crossroad, 1999.

Schüssler Fiorenza, Elisabeth. *Bread Not Stone: The Challenge of Feminist Biblical Interpretation*. Boston: Beacon, 1984.

———. *But She Said: Feminist Practices of Biblical Interpretation*. Boston: Beacon, 1993.

———. "The Ethics of Biblical Interpretation: Decentering Biblical Scholarship." *JBL* 107 (1988): 3–17.

———. *In Memory of Her: A Feminist-Theological Reconstruction of Christian Origins*. New York: Crossroad, 1983; London: SCM, 1988.

———. *Rhetoric and Ethic: The Politics of Biblical Studies.* Minneapolis: Fortress, 1999.
Scott, Martin. *Sophia and the Johannine Jesus.* JSNTSup 71. Sheffield: JSOT Press, 1992.
Segovia, Fernando F. "Cultural Studies and Contemporary Biblical Criticism: Ideological Criticism as a Mode of Discourse." Pages 1–17 in *Social Location and Biblical Interpretation in Global Perspective.* Vol. 2 of *Reading from This Place.* Edited by Segovia and Mary Ann Tolbert. Minneapolis: Fortress, 1995.
———. *Decolonizing Biblical Studies: A View from the Margins.* Maryknoll, NY: Orbis Books, 2000.
———. *The Farewell of the Word: The Johannine Call to Abide.* Minneapolis: Fortress, 1991.
———. "The Final Farewell of Jesus: A Reading of John 20:30–21:25." *Semeia* 53 (1991): 167–90.
———. "The Gospel at the Close of the Century: Engagement from the Diaspora." Pages 211–16 in *Readers and Readings of the Fourth Gospel.* Vol. 1 of *"What Is John?"* Edited by Fernando F. Segovia. SymS 3. Atlanta: Scholars Press, 1996.
———. "The Journey(s) of the Word of God: A Reading of the Plot of the Fourth Gospel." *Semeia* 53 (1991): 23–54.
———. "Introduction: Pedagogical Discourse and Practices in Contemporary Biblical Criticism." Pages 1–28 in *Teaching the Bible: The Discourses and Politics of Biblical Pedagogy.* Edited by Segovia and Mary Ann Tolbert. Maryknoll, NY: Orbis Books, 1998.
———, ed. *Literary and Social Readings of the Fourth Gospel.* Vol. 2 of *"What Is John?"* SymS 7. Atlanta: Scholars Press, 1998.
———. *Love Relationships in the Johannine Tradition: Agape/Agapan in 1 John and the Fourth Gospel.* SBLDS 59. Chico, CA: Scholars Press, 1982.
———, ed. *Readers and Readings of the Fourth Gospel.* Vol. 1 of *"What Is John?"* SymS 3. Atlanta: Scholars Press, 1996.
———. "Reading Readers of the Fourth Gospel and Their Readings: An Exercise in Intercultural Criticism." Pages 237–77 in *Readers and Readings of the Fourth Gospel.* Vol. 1 of *"What Is John?"* Edited by Fernando F. Segovia. SymS 3. Atlanta: Scholars Press, 1996.
———. "The Text as Other: Toward a Hispanic American Hermeneutic." Pages 276–98 in *Text and Experience: Towards a Cultural Exegesis of*

the Bible. Edited by David Christopher-Smith. Sheffield: JSOT Press, 1995.

———. "Two Places and No Place on Which to Stand: Mixture and Otherness in Hispanic American Theology." *Listening* 27.2 (1992): 26–40.

Segovia, Fernando F., and Mary Ann Tolbert, eds. *Reading from This Place*. Vol. 1, *Social Location and Biblical Interpretation in the United States*. Vol. 2, *Social Location and Biblical Interpretation in Global Perspective*. Minneapolis: Fortress, 1995.

Seim, Turid Karlsen. *The Double Message: Patterns of Gender in Luke-Acts*. SNTW. Edinburgh: T&T Clark, 1994.

———. "Roles of Women in the Gospel of John." Pages 56–73 in *Aspects of the Johannine Literature*. Edited by Lars Hartman and Birger Olsson. ConBNT 18. Uppsala: Uppsala University Press, 1987.

Smith, D. Moody. *John among the Gospels: The Relationship in Twentieth-Century Research*. Minneapolis: Fortress, 1992.

Smith-Christopher, Daniel, ed. *Text and Experience: Toward a Cultural Exegesis of the Bible*. Sheffield: JSOT Press, 1995.

Staley, Jeffrey L. *Reading with a Passion: Rhetoric, Autobiography, and the American West in the Gospel of John*. New York: Continuum, 1995.

———. "Stumbling in the Dark, Reaching for the Light: Reading Character in John 5 and 9." *Semeia* 53 (1991): 55–80.

———. "What Is Critical about Autobiographical Biblical Criticism?" Pages 12–33 in *Autobiographical Biblical Criticism: Between Text and Self*. Edited by Ingrid Rosa Kitzberger. Leiden: Deo, 2002.

Stanton, Graham N. "The Fourfold Gospel." *NTS* 43 (1997): 317–46.

Sternberg, Meir. *The Poetics of Biblical Narrative*. Bloomington: Indiana University Press, 1985.

Stibbe, Mark. "The Elusive Christ: A New Reading of the Fourth Gospel." *JSNT* 48 (1991): 20–38.

———. "A Tomb with a View: John 11.1–44 in Narrative-Critical Perspective." *NTS* 40 (1994): 38–54.

Studiorum Novi Testamenti Societas. "The Seventy-First General Meeting: Minutes." https://tinyurl.com/SBL4523e.

———. *SNTS Newsletter*. October–November 2016. https://tinyurl.com/SBL4523f.

———. *SNTS Newsletter*. October–November 2017. https://tinyurl.com/SBL4523g.

———. *SNTS Newsletter*. October–November 2018. https://tinyurl.com/SBL4523h.

Sugirtharajah, R. S., ed. *Voices from the Margin: Interpreting the Bible in the Third World*. London: SPCK, 1991.
Sylva, D. D. "Nicodemus and His Spices." *NTS* 34 (1988): 148–51.
Tannehill, Robert C. "The Disciples in Mark: The Function of a Narrative Role." *JR* 57 (1977): 386–405.
———. "The Gospel of Mark as Narrative Christology." *Semeia* 16 (1979): 57–95.
Tanner, Mary. "What Is Faith and Order?" World Council of Churches. August 1, 2009. https://tinyurl.com/SBL4523c.
Telford, William R. "SNTS, Its Origins, and Robin L. McWilson's Contribution to the Society." Address given on the occasion of the Ninetieth Birthday Celebrations for Prof. Robin L. McWilson at the University of Saint Andrews. February 18, 2006. https://tinyurl.com/SBL4523a.
Thiselton, Anthony C. "Communicative Action and Promise in Interdisciplinary, Biblical, and Theological Hermeneutics." Pages 133–39 in *The Promise of Hermeneutics*. Edited by Roger Lundin, Clarence Walhout, and Thiselton. Grand Rapids, MI: Eerdmans, 1999.
Thompson, Marianne Meye. "'God's Voice You Have Never Heard, God's Form You Have Never Seen': The Characterization of God in the Gospel of John." *Semeia* 63 (1993): 177–204.
Thurston, Anne. *Knowing Her Place: Gender and the Gospels*. New York: Paulist, 1998.
Thyen, Hartwig. "Die Erzählungen von den bethanischen Geschwistern (Joh 11,1–12,19) als 'Palimpsest' über synoptischen Texten." Pages 2021–50 in *The Four Gospels 1992: Festschrift Frans Neyrinck*. Edited by Frans Van Segbroeck et al. BETL 100. Leuven: Peeters, 1992.
Tilborg, Sjef van. *Imaginative Love in John*. BibInt 2. Leiden: Brill, 1993.
———. *Reading John in Ephesus*. NovTSup 83. Leiden: Brill, 1996.
Tompkins, Jane P., ed. *Reader-Response Criticism: From Formalism to Poststructuralism*. Baltimore: Johns Hopkins University Press, 1980.
Tovey, Derek. *Narrative Art and Act in the Fourth Gospel*. JSNTSup 151. Sheffield: Sheffield Academic, 1997.
Uspensky, Boris. *Poetics of Composition*. Berkeley: University of California Press, 1973.
Voelz, James W. "Multiple Signs and Double Texts: Elements of Intertextuality." Pages 27–34 in *Intertextuality in Biblical Writings: Essays in Honour of Bas van Iersel*. Edited by Siepke Draisma. Kampen: Kok Pharos, 1989.

Vogelsang, John D. "A Hermeneutics of Reconstruction." *Religious Education* 88 (1993): 167–77.
Watson, Francis, ed. *The Open Text*. London: SCM, 1993.
Watzlawik, Paul. *Wie wirklich ist die Wirklichkeit? Wahn—Täuschung—Verstehen*. Munich: Piper, 1976.
West, Gerald, and Musa W. Dube, eds. *"Reading With": An Exploration of the Interface between Critical and Ordinary Readings of the Bible; African Overtures*. Semeia 73.
Wiltshire, Susan Fort. "The Authority of Experience." Pages 168–81 in *Compromising Traditions: The Personal Voice in Classical Scholarship*. Edited by Judith P. Hallett and Thomas Van Nortwick. London: Routledge, 1997.
Witherington, Ben, III. *John's Wisdom: A Commentary on the Fourth Gospel*. Louisville: Westminster John Knox, 1995.
Wolff, Geoffrey. "Minor Lives." Pages 57–72 in *Telling Lives: The Biographer's Art*. Edited by Marc Pachter. Philadelphia: University of Pennsylvania Press, 1979.
Woolf, Virginia. *The Three Great Novels: Mrs Dalloway, To the Lighthouse, The Waves*. London: Penguin Books, 1992.
Wuellner, Wilhelm. "Is There an Encoded Reader Fallacy?" *Semeia* 48 (1989): 41–54.
———. "Putting Life Back into the Lazarus Story and Its Reading: The Narrative Rhetoric of John 11 as the Narration of Faith." *Semeia* 53 (1991): 113–32.
———. "Rhetorical Criticism and Its Theory in Cultural-Critical Perspective: The Narrative Rhetoric of John 11." Pages 171–85 in *Text and Interpretation: New Approaches in the Criticism of the New Testament*. Edited by Peter J. Martin and J. Hartin Petzer. NTTS 15. Leiden: Brill, 1991.
Young, Robert, ed. *Untying the Text: A Post-structuralist Reader*. London: Routledge & Kegan Paul, 1981.
Zenger, Erich. "Die Entstehung des Pentateuch." Pages 46–75 in *Einleitung in das Alte Testament*. Edited by Erich Zenger et al. KST 1.1. Stuttgart: Kohlhammer, 1995.
Zimmerman, Frank. "Origin and Significance of the Jewish Rite of Circumcision." *PR* 38 (1951): 103–12.
Zink, Jörg. *Was die Nacht hell macht: Rembrandt malt die Weihnachtsgeschichte*. Eschbach: Verlag am Eschbach, 1997.
Zumstein, Jean. "Johannes 19, 25–27." *ZTK* 94 (1997): 131–54.

Ancient Sources Index

Hebrew Bible/Old Testament		18:1–15	151, 252
		18:2	153
Genesis		18:2–5	153
2:10–14	138	18:6	153
3:7	244	18:8	153
11:27–32	154	18:9	153
15	150	18:10	153–54
15:1	151	18:11	154
15:1–6	151	18:13	154
15:1–21	151, 252	21:1–7	155
15:2–3	151		
15:5	151	Exodus	
15:7–8	151	23:16	257 n. 24
15:12	151	25–26	256
15:15	151	34:22–23	257 n. 24
15:18	151		
17	150	Leviticus	
17:1	152, 154	12	158 n. 31
17:1–14	152, 252	23:39	257 n. 24
17:1–27	151	23:39–43	256–57 n. 22
17:2–7	152		
17:5–7	152	Numbers	
17:7–10	152	22–24	209 n. 56
17:8	152	24:17	209 n. 56
17:10–14	152		
17:15	152	Deuteronomy	
17:15–16	152	32:18	115 n. 20, 201 n. 41, 258 n. 26
17:16	152		
17:17	152–54	1 Samuel	
17:19	152	1–2	160 n. 34
17:21	152		
17:23–27	152	1 Kings	
17:24	152	19:1–18	259
18	150, 153	19:11–13	251
18:1	153		

2 Kings
21:18	210 n. 59
21:26	210 n. 59

Nehemiah
3:16 LXX	210 n. 59

Psalms
22 (21 LXX)	**119–20**
22:9–10	120
22:18	120
72:10–11	209 n. 56
139:13	115 n. 20, 202 n. 41, 258 n. 26

Proverbs
8	199
8:17	199
8:12–31	199
8:35	199

Canticles
4:6	211 n. 60
4:14	211 n. 60

Isaiah
1:3 LXX	213 n. 63
7:14	134
42:14	115 n. 20, 201 n. 41, 258 n. 26
60:6	209 n. 56

Jeremiah
34:5	210 n. 59

Ezekiel
5:1–2	160 n. 38
6:8–9	160 n. 38
12:14–16	160 n. 38
14:17	121–22 n. 44
37:5	104
37:10	104

Hosea
11:1–4	115 n. 20, 202 n. 41, 257–58 n. 26

Zechariah
12:10	251, 259

Deuterocanonical Books

Wisdom of Solomon
7:4–5	212 n. 62

Sirach
24	199
24:3–6	199
24:8	199
24:9	199
24:10	199
24:16–17	199
24:19–21	199

Dead Sea Scrolls
4Q265	121 n. 43

Ancient Jewish Works and Writers

Josephus, *Jewish Antiquities*
17.198–199	210 n. 59

Jubilees
	121 n. 43

New Testament

Matthew
1–2	114
1:1–16	134
1:18–25	134
1:23	134
1:25	134
2:1	207
2:1–12	**207–11**
2:2	207–9
2:3	208
2:4	208
2:7	208
2:8	208
2:9–10	208
2:11	208, 211 n. 60

Ancient Sources Index

2:12	208	2	269
2:13–23	134	3:21	132
5:23	125 n. 52	3:21–35	115
5:24	125 n. 52	3:31–32	132
5:49	125 n. 52	3:31–35 parr.	113 n. 15
7:4	125 n. 52	3:33–35	132
7:5	125 n. 52	5:42	61, 175
7:20	239	5:43 parr.	175, 192 n. 29
9:18–26	28	6:3	120, 125
10:34–36	161 n. 39	6:1–6	120 n. 41
12:48	125 n. 52	8:27–28	128
12:50	125 n. 52	8:27–30	91
13:3–6	32	9:24	287
13:46–50	134	14:3	205
13:52	32	14:3–8	206 n. 52
13:55–56	134	14:3–9	32, 90, 101, 194 n. 35, 204, 284
18:12	125 n. 52	14:4	205
18:21	125 n. 52	14:8	90, 205
18:35	125 n. 52	15:23	211 n. 60
19:14	250	15:29–32	119
20:1–16	205 n. 49	15:34	119–20, 125
21–28	290 n. 23	15:40	125 n. 52
23:8	125 n. 52	15:40–41	55, 100, 118–19, 132
25:40	125 n. 52	15:42	202 n. 45
26:6–12	206 n. 52	15:42–47	203 n. 46
26:6–13	90, 101, 204, 284	15:47	100, 132
26:7	205	16:1	204 n. 48, 205–6, 206 n. 52
26:8	205	16:1–8 parr.	32
26:12	90, 205	16:3	100
26:56	125 n. 52, 206	16:8	120, 132
27:55–56	118 n. 33, 134		
27:57	202 n. 45	Luke	
27:57–61	203 n. 46	1–2	114, 133
27:60	203 n. 46	1:26–27	133
27:61	100, 134	1:26–38	133, 159, 213–14
28:1	134	1:34	159, 213
28:2	100	1:37	213
28:8–10	134	1:46–55	133
28:16–20	209 n. 56	2:1–5	212
28:19	209 n. 56	2:1–20	**212–14**
		2:6–7	212
Mark		2:8	213 n. 64
1:1–15	114 n. 19	2:11	212
1:16–18	56 n. 27	2:12	212
1:16–20	271	2:16	212

310 Interfigural Readings of the Gospel of John

Luke (cont.)

2:21	158 n. 32, 159 n. 33
2:21–38	122, 125, 252
2:21–40	**157–62**
2:22	159 n. 33
2:22–24	121, 158
2:22–40	160 n. 34
2:25	158, 158 n. 32
2:25–32	121
2:26	157
2:27	133, 158
2:27–32	157
2:28–32	158–59
2:29	157
2:30	157
2:30–31	162
2:33	133, 158
2:33–35	159
2:34	159 n. 33, 160 n. 38
2:34–35	121, 122 n. 45
2:35	160–61
2:36	159
2:36–37	160
2:37	121 n. 46, 159
2:38	159
2:43	133
2:48	133
2:48–50	161 n. 38
2:49	159
2:51	159
4:22	133
4:46–47	274
5:8	198
7:11–17	**123–24**, 255 n. 19
7:15	175
7:15–16	61 n. 33, 175 n. 22
7:36	195
7:36–50	32, 91, 98, 101, **194–98**, 206, 230, 284
7:37–38	91, 206 n. 52
7:38	194, 195, 197
7:39	195
7:41–42	196
7:42–43	195
7:44	195, 197
7:44–46	196
7:47	92, 196
7:48	196
7:49	196
8:1–3	207
8:2–3	133
8:3	118 n. 33
8:21	161 n. 38
10:38	98
10:38–42	97, 133, 172–73
10:39	98
10:40	98, 175
10:42	42
11:27–28 (Q)	113 n. 15, 161 n. 38
12:51–53	122, 160 n. 38, 161
15:8–9	56
23:2	100
23:49	118, 125 n. 52
23:50–55	203 n. 46
23:54	202
23:55	100, 133, 205–6
23:56	204 n. 48, 205–6, 206 n. 52
24:1	204 n. 48, 205–6, 206 n. 52
24:1–12	133
24:10	118 n. 33, 205
24:10–11	61
24:13–35	72
24:16	58
24:19	61

John

1:1–4	149
1:1–18	146, 287
1:1–19:24	49
1:2–3	199
1:4–5	199
1:5	65
1:10	199
1:11	113 n. 17, 244
1:12–13	116, 146, 153, 162, 211, 214, 253
1:13	131, 202 n. 41, 214, 249, 257, 257 n. 26
1:14	74, 110, 123 n. 48, 199, 250, 257–58, 264

ns Index

Reference	Pages
1:14–18	115
1:18	131, 202 n. 41, 214, 257
1:35–51	95, 191
1:37–38	101, 221, 271
1:38	95
1:39	46, 95, 221, 271
1:40–46	221
1:45	120 n. 42, 123
1:45–46	274
1:47	243
1:48	243
1:49	95, 243
2	59, 114, 130–31
2:1–12	48, 73, 111, 187
2:3–5	50
2:4	50, 110, 131, 187, 254
2:5	60 n. 32, 249
2:9	113 n. 15
2:11	51, 59, 61 n. 33, 111, 112 n. 10
2:12	51, 59, 111, 130
2:13–17	111
2:13–23	75
2:13–25	158
2:19–21	162
3	62 n. 38, 73, 145, 149, 150, 201, 251–58
3:1	151, 158 n. 32, 207, 251
3:1–15	63 n. 39
3:1–21	214, 286
3:3	131, 146 n. 12
3:3–8	116, 254
3:4	43, 70, 115, 146, 153, 155, 159 n. 33, 202, 250, 255
3:4–11	62, 221 n. 4
3:5	43, 146, 153, 158, 202, 213–14, 250
3:6	117 n. 29, 131, 265
3:6–9	202
3:7	146, 158
3:8	43, 66, 138, 146, 153, 158, 250, 253, 265
3:9	43, 71, 146, 148, 158, 182, 213
3:10	71, 202
3:11	147, 202
3:11–21	45
3:14	162, 253
3:14–15	51
3:17	162
3:19–21	65
3:21	147
3:22	62, 62 n. 37, 72
3:26	62, 62 n. 37
4	56, 59, 71, 93
4:1–2	62, 62 n. 37, 72
4:1–42	48, 58, **237–47**
4:4	244
4:9	58, 243
4:10	71
4:12	58, 243
4:13–14	66
4:20	58
4:20–26	58
4:25	51, 93
4:26	51, 93
4:27	58, 245
4:28	56 n. 27, 93
4:29	49, 51, 58, 93, 242
4:31	172
4:34	172
4:39	55, 566 n. 27, 58, 102, 243
4:41	58
4:42	58, 59
4:44	244
5:8	174
5:35	271
6	53, 71, 269–70
6:1–59	199–200
6:21	55
6:25	63 n. 39
6:25–26	63, 72, 221 n. 4
6:26	63 n. 39
6:35	199
6:39–40	53
6:42	120 n. 42, 123
6:51	199
7	73, 147, 200
7:3–10	123
7:5	45, 111, 244
7:6	254
7:8	254

312 Interfigural Readings of the Gospel of John

John (cont.)

7:12	123
7:13	123
7:14	123
7:14–15	274
7:15	123
7:16	274
7:16–17	123
7:30	254
7:32	147
7:35	123
7:37–38	200
7:37–39	116, 249, 256
7:38	116
7:38–39	116 n. 27
7:39	162, 200
7:45–49	147
7:50–51	202
7:50–52	286
7:51	147
7:52	202
7:53–8:11	50 n. 16
8:12	271
8:20	254
8:21–30	147
8:23	147
8:32	65, 70, 138, 222
9:1–2	198
9:3	198
9:16	197
9:24	198
9:25	198
9:31	198
10	54
10:3	192, 232
10:3–5	54, 56 n. 27
10:4	102
10:17	54
10:39–40	91
11	52, 53, 59, 88, 131, **167–77**, 192–93, 239
11:1–2	89–90, 96, 97 n. 43, 173, 287
11:1–46	**89–97**, 150, **258–59**
11:1–12:8	287
11:2	75, 91, 93, 98, 131, 175, 206 n. 52
11:3	91–92, 95, 173, 175, 189, 192
11:4	53, 92, 95–96, 98, 173, 175, 287
11:5	48, 53, 56 n. 27, 91, 95, 97, 99, 99 n. 45, 103, 131, 175, 192
11:6	91, 99, 175, 250, 258
11:7–8	99
11:7–15	173
11:8	95
11:11	175
11:13–16	287
11:14–15	287
11:15	175
11:17	91–92, 95, 113 n. 16, 174, 250, 258
11:19	92, 96, 175
11:20–28	97
11:21	93, 175
11:21–22	174, 287
11:21–27	131
11:22	93
11:23	175
11:23–24	51–52
11:24	287
11:25	259, 287
11:25–26	287
11:26	52, 287
11:27	49, 51–52, 93, 96
11:28	56 n. 27, 75, 94–95, 103
11:28–33	287
11:28–34	95
11:29	94
11:29–30	94
11:30	95
11:31	94, 100, 103
11:31–32	96
11:32	94, 174–75
11:33	131, 287
11:33–36	95
11:34	95, 102
11:35	51, 175
11:36	95, 175
11:37	95, 259
11:38	92, 95, 100, 113 n. 16, 287
11:38–39	103
11:39	59, 95, 97, 100, 175

Ancient Sources Index 313

Reference	Pages
11:40	53, 62, 62–63 n. 38, 75, 95–96, 287
11:40–42	175
11:41	96, 100, 103
11:42	287
11:43	258
11:43–44	96, 174, 250
11:44	61, 96, 174, 258
11:45	96
11:45–46	287
11:47	97
11:53	97, 170
11:55	188
11:57	97
12	53, 59, 61, 88, 131, 172, 192, 193
12:1	97, 188
12:1–2	174
12:1–8	32, 48, 51, 59, 61, **97–99**, 131, 150, 188, 192, **193–94**, 204, 287
12:1–12	75
12:2	97, 192
12:3	98, 113 n. 16, 193, 204
12:3–5	206 n. 52
12:3–8	51
12:4–6	193
12:6	193
12:7	188, 193, 203
12:8	49
12:9	174
12:9–11	61
12:10–11	174
12:12–19	61 n. 34
12:17	61 n. 34
12:23	254
12:24	188
12:25	188
12:26	188–89
12:27	254
12:27–28	188
12:32	188, 207
12:32–33	110
12:33	188
12:34	63 n. 399
12:34–35	63, 221 n. 4
12:35–36	63 n. 39
12:36	190
12:42	188
12:43	188
13	74, 146, 191–92, 194 n. 35, 226, 232
13–17	54 n. 23, 187, 192
13:1	56 n. 27, 92 n. 36, 99 n. 45, 103, 188, 191–92, 254
13:1–5	53
13:1–20	181, **187–93**, 196
13:2	189
13:2–3	189
13:4	189
13:5	189, 191
13:6	189
13:7	189
13:8	189–90
13:9	190
13:11	190
13:12	190–91
13:13	190
13:13–16	197
13:14	190
13:14–15	193, 197
13:15	190
13:16	190
13:23	191
13:33	54
13:34	191
13:34–35	197
14–17	54
14:5	191, 221
14:6	64, 64 n. 42, 221
14:7–11	200
14:12	273
14:16–17	66
14:20	275
14:31	75
15	75
15:1	200
15:5	200, 273
15:15	272
16:13	66
16:16	55
16:16–19	253

John (cont.)

16:16–22	54, 257
16:16–24	116
16:20	253
16:21	77, 116, 162 n. 43, 214 n. 67, 117 n. 28, 253, 253 n. 8, 254
17	54, 55
17:1	254
17:11	51
17:18	55
17:20	55, 232
17:24	54
18:18–38	221
18:28–19:16	287
18:33–40	211 n. 59
18:37	115 nn. 20–21, 221, 259
18:38	69
19:1–5	211 n. 59
19:14–16	211 n. 59
19:19–22	211 n. 59
19:23	161 n. 40, 255 n. 17
19:23–24	120
19:25	51, 74, 99, 122, 131
19:25–27	55, 60 n. 32, 74, **107–26**, 116 n. 27, 130, 161–62, 214, 231, 253, 255, 255 n. 19
19:25–30	51, 118 n. 34
19:26	113 n. 15
19:26–27	117, 254
19:27	113
19:30	116, 162, 200–1, 214, 253, 256
19:34	116, 116 n. 27, 117 n. 29, 200, 214 n. 67, 254
19:34–37	201
19:38	201, 210
19:38–42	71, 73, 99 n. 45, 100, 147, **201–4**, 204, 229, 252, 254, 286
19:39	148, 201, 203, 206, 211 n. 60, 213
19:40	203, 204 n. 48, 206 n. 52, 213
19:41–42	100, 148, 203
20	48–49, 55, 58, 74, 88, 114, 131
20–21	**227–33**
20:1	50, 58, 100, 114 n. 18, 228
20:1–2	114
20:1–10	74
20:1–18	**99–103**, 114 n. 18, 131, 230
20:2	100, 192, 228
20:3	101
20:3–4	114
20:3–10	228
20:4	101, 103
20:5–9	211
20:6	101
20:6–7	103
20:8	103, 228
20:10	101
20:11	55, 101, 114, 114 n. 18, 123 n. 49, 228
20:11–18	51, 141, 142, 192, 228
20:12	101
20:13	55, 101, 103, 123 n. 49
20:14	101
20:15	55, 59, 63, 63 n. 39, 72, 101–3, 123 n. 49, 221, 221 n. 4, 229
20:16	54, 566 n. 27, 102–3, 192, 221, 232
20:16–17	258
20:16–18	55
20:17	54, 102, 113, 115–16, 123, 230, 273
20:17–18	50, 56 n. 27, 230
20:18	55, 61, 74, 102, 103
20:19–23	61, 230
20:20	55
20:24–29	142
20:29	65, 228, 287
20:30	173 n. 18
20:30–31	45, 51–52, 62, 65, 125, 146, 148
20:31	65
21	49
21:7	74
21:9	276
21:11	276
21:12	276
21:12–13	192 n. 29
21:13	276
21:15–17	233
21:15–19	232

21:16–17	233
21:20–23	74
21:24	74
21:24–25	125
21:25	66, 104, 148

Acts
1:14	125

Galatians
3:28	231

Revelation
12:1–18	288
17	288
17:1–18	288
21–22	284 n. 9, 288
22:1–2	288

Greco-Roman Literature

Suetonius, *Tiberius*
61	124 n. 51

Tacitus, *Annales*
6.10	124 n. 51
6.19	124 n. 51

Early Christian Writings

Acts of Pilate
17:1	160 n. 36

Irenaeus, *Adversus haereses*
3.9.2	209 n. 55

Pseudo–Matthew
15:2	157 n. 29

Modern Authors Index

Alarcón, Edmundo 39 n. 27
Alcoff, Linda 173 n. 19
Alter, Robert 76 n. 12, 87 n. 23, 111 n. 9, 191 n. 28
Anderson, Janice Capel 111 n. 8, 143 n. 5, 171 n. 12, 224 n. 10
Anzaldúa, Gloria 241, 245
Bach, Alice 854 n. 15, 105 n. 59
Ball, D. Mark 51 n. 17
Bar-Efrat, Shimon 87 n. 22, 112 n. 13
Barr, Robert R. 125 n. 54
Baumgarten, Joseph 121 n. 43
Beardslee, William A. 235 n. 20
Beck, David R. 82 n. 4
Berlin, Adele 82 n. 4, 119 n. 35, 169 n. 6, 185 n. 13
Black, Fiona C. 76 n. 14
Blanchard, Paula 35
Blank, Josef 222 n. 5
Bleich, David 17
Blickenstaff, Marianne 36 n. 21
Boer, Martinus C. 82 n. 5, 182 n. 5
Boer, Roland 76 n. 14
Bösen, Willibald 124 n. 51
Boobyer, G.H. 3 n. 1
Booth, Wayne C. 85 n. 15, 86–87 n. 22, 112 n. 13
Bowden, John 118 n. 32
Boyarin, Daniel 38 n. 24, 135–36, 136 nn. 11–12, 138
Brant, Jo-Ann 238 n. 1
Braund, Susanna Morton 235 n. 19, 259 n. 28
Brett, Mark 275
Brien, Mary T. 129 n. 3
Brown, Raymond E. 45, 82 n. 5, 91 n. 34, 93 n. 37, 94 n. 39, 102 nn. 48–49, 102 n. 52, 104 n. 56, 110 nn. 4.7, 113 n. 12, 121–23 nn. 43–47, 124 n. 51, 157 n. 29, 158 n. 31, 160–61 nn. 34–39, 182 n. 5, 189 nn. 22–23, 200 n. 40, 202 n. 44, 205–6 nn. 50–52, 208 n. 53, 209 nn. 54–56, 210–11 n. 59, 212–12 nn. 61–63, 254 n. 13
Brown, Rosemary 260 n. 30
Burnett, Fred W. 86 n. 20, 144 n. 10, 185 n. 13
Burridge, Richard A. 70 n. 6, 233 n. 17
Calinescu, Matei 47 n. 11, 193 n. 32
Charlesworth, James H. 113 n. 15
Chatman, Seymour 83, 171, 185 n. 14, 186, 240, 286
Corsini, Eugenio 288 n. 21
Croatto, J. Severino 39, 39 nn. 25–26, 125–26 nn. 54–56, 139, 139 n. 22, 144 n. 8, 153–54 nn. 26–27, 254 n. 15, 255, 255 n. 16, 257 n. 25
Crouch, James E. 290 n. 23
Culpepper, R. Alan 44 n. 3, 49 n. 13, 52 n. 20, 62 n. 36, 81, 81 n. 1, 82 nn. 2.4.5, 85 nn. 16.18, 86 n. 21, 90 n. 32, 94 n. 39, 95 n. 41, 98 n. 44, 99–100 nn. 45–46, 102–3 nn. 47–48, 102–3 nn. 50–52, 171 n. 14, 173 n. 17, 186 n. 17, 226 n. 13
Dalman, Gustaf 124 n. 51
Darr, John 86 n. 20, 119 n. 35, 144 n. 10, 185 n. 13
Davies, Margaret 57 n. 29

Modern Authors Index

Denaux, Adelbert   117 n. 32, 186 n. 19
Dewey, Joanna   83 n. 6
Dodd, C. H.   4
Dormeyer, Detlev   8, 70 n. 6, 81, 86 n. 22, 87 n. 23, 89 n. 31, 120 n. 41, 186 n. 17, 233 n. 17
Draisma, Siepke   118 n. 35, 144 n. 7
Dube, Musa W.   168-69 n. 5, 187 n. 20
Easthope, Anthony   224 n. 9
Eliot, T. S.   125 n. 53, 164, 164 n. 46, 210 n. 58, 239
Exum, J. Cheryl   48 n. 12, 129 n. 4, 241-42, 247 nn. 9-11, 276 n. 7
Fehribach, Adele   182 n. 5
Ferguson, Thomas J.   3 n. 2
Fewell, Danna Nolan   169 n. 7, 183 n. 8
Fish, Stanley   87 n. 22, 88 n. 27, 185 n. 14, 263 n. 35
Fitzmyer, John A.   121 n. 43, 157 n. 28, 158 n. 31, 161 n. 38
Fowler, Robert M.   8, 85 n. 18, 86-87 nn. 21-22, 116 n. 5, 184 n. 12
Frost. Robert Lee   260 n. 28
Fuller, Margaret   35
Genette, Gérard   185 n. 14
Golombek, Matthew   222
Gruber, Mayer I.   107, 115 n. 20, 121 n. 43, 259 n. 27
Guardiola-Sáenz, Leticia A.   34, 110 n. 6, 150 n. 21, 244-45 n. 13
Hallett, Judith P.   10 n. 8
Harris, Horton   286 n. 13
Hengel, Martin   117-18 n. 32
Holladay, Carl R.   24
Holland, Norman N.   260 n. 30
Hooker, Morna D.   7, 114 n. 19
Howard-Brook, Wes   116 n. 24
Iersel, Bas M.E. van   8, 81
Ilan, Tal   129 n. 2
Ingarden, Roman   89 n. 31
Inglis, Fred   177 n. 25
Iser, Wolfgang   47, 87 n. 23, 93 n. 38, 105 n. 58, 111 n. 9, 185 n. 14, 191 n. 28, 234 n. 18
Jacobus, Mary   52 n. 21, 191 n. 27

Jaroff, Leon   222
Jasper, Alison   200 n. 39
Jung, Carl G.   252 n. 4, 262 n. 32
Karris, Robert J.   210 n. 59, 274
Kelber, Werner H.   62 n. 36, 226 n. 13
Klauck, Hans-Josef   83 n. 6
Kluger, Jeffrey   220 n. 2
Koester, Craig R.   52 n. 20, 146 n. 12, 203 n. 45, 254 n. 11
Kügler, Joachim   209 n. 55
Kysar, Robert   51 n. 19, 57 n. 29, 63 n. 39
Labahn, Michael   283 n. 6
Lang, James L.   261 n. 31
Lang, Manfred   283 n. 6
Lategan, Bernard C.   8, 28, 31 n. 13, 81, 87 n. 25, 222 n. 5
Levine, Amy-Jill   36, 37, 119 n. 37
Lieu, Judith M.   21-24, 115 nn. 20-21, 117 n. 28, 162 n. 43, 201 n. 41, 214 n. 67, 253 n. 8, 257-58 n. 26
Link, Hannelore   105 n. 58
Losack, Mark   133 n. 8
Luz, Ulrich   290 n. 23
Maccini, Robert G.   113 nn. 14-15, 182 n. 5
Maki, Justin   222
McKinlay, Judith E.   199 n. 38
McKnight, Edgar V.   8, 27, 30 n. 7, 31 n. 13, 32-33 n. 14, 34, 52-53 n. 22, 85 n. 18, 86 n. 23, 87 nn. 23-24, 88 nn. 26-27, 110 n. 5, 111 n. 9, 138, 144 n. 9, 184 n. 12, 191 n. 28, 234 n. 18
McWilson, Robin L.   3 n. 1
Malbon, Elizabeth Struthers   8, 30, 37 n. 22, 81, 82 n. 4, 83 n. 6, 88 n. 26, 119 n. 36, 169 n. 6, 181 n. 3, 185 n. 13
Martin, Erica   107
Martindale, Charles   262
Mazamisa, Weli   229 n. 5
Miller, Nancy K.   225 n. 12
Miller, Owen   118 n. 35, 144 n. 7
Moloney, Francis J.   vii, 28 n. 3, 57 n. 29, 113 n. 17, 115 n. 21, 146 n. 12, 148 n. 15, 149 nn. 17.20, 190 n. 26, 202 n.

Moloney, Francis J. (cont.)
  44, 252 n. 3, 282 n. 4, 285 n. 12, 286nn. 15, 286–87 nn. 17–19, 288 n. 21
Moore, Stephen D. 8, 64 n. 41, 85 n. 18, 86–87 nn. 21–22, 224 n. 10
Müller, Wolfgang G. 30, 31, 49 n. 14, 83–84, 118–19 n. 35, 144 n. 7, 18, 283–84
Neirynck, Frans 113–14 n. 17, 186 n. 19
Nutu, Liliana M. 115 n. 21
O'Day, Gail 64 nn. 41–42, 75–76 n. 10, 185 n. 15
Orton, David E. 29 n. 5
Painter, John 5 n. 3
Patte, Daniel 29, 34, 44 n. 4, 64 n. 40, 76 n. 11, 112 n. 10, 136–37 nn. 14.16, 137, 168 n. 5, 169 n. 7, 173 n. 19, 183 nn. 7–8, 187 n. 20, 225 n. 11, 227 n. 15, 237, 239, 270, 277
Peters, Vicky 33
Petersen, Norman R. 47 n. 10, 85 n. 18, 89, 200 n. 39
Phillips, Gary A. 169 n. 7, 183 n. 8
Powell, Mark Allan 82 n. 3, 85 n. 1, 87 n. 22
Rabinowitz, Peter J. 288, 289 n. 22
Rad, Gerhard von 151 n. 22, 154 n. 24
Rand, Jan A. du 82 nn. 4–5, 86 n. 19
Rashkow, Ilona N. 104 n. 53, 105 n. 59, 172 n. 15
Reinhartz, Adele 67–68, 176 n. 24
Rhoads, David 83 n. 8, 84–86, 89 n. 30, 171 n. 13, 240–41, 240 n. 7
Ringe, Sharon H. 150 n. 21, 199 n. 37, 272 n. 2
Robbins, Vernon K. 119 n. 38
Rodgers, Michael 133 n. 8
Rosenblatt, Roger 220 n. 3
Ruckstuhl, Eugen 10, 61 n. 34, 81, 114 n. 17
Runions, Erin 76 n. 14
Sabbe, Maurits 31, 90 n. 33, 125 n, 52, 193 n. 33, 194–95 n. 35, 202 n. 44, 204 nn. 47–48
Sawicki, Marianne 143 n. 4

Schenk, Wolfgang 8
Schneiders, Sandra M. 45 n. 5, 54 n. 24, 64 n. 41, 82 n. 5, 115 n. 20, 124 n. 50, 182 n. 5, 192 n. 31
Schüssler Fiorenza, Elisabeth 35, 46 nn. 6–7, 88 n. 28, 104 n. 55, 130, 169 n. 7, 182 n. 5, 183 n. 8, 205 n. 51, 283
Scott, Martin 199 n. 37
Segovia, Fernando F. vii, 33, 34, 47–48 n. 11, 54 n. 23, 55 n. 26, 36 n. 39, 64 n. 42, 65, 69, 91 n. 35, 110 n. 5, 116 n. 25, 118 n. 35, 147 n. 14, 149 n. 17, 177 n. 25, 184 n. 12, 185 n. 16, 189 n. 21, 192 n. 30, 193 n. 32, 223 n. 8, 224 n. 9, 226 n. 14, 233 n. 17, 237, 245, 245 nn. 14–15, 253, 275 n. 6, 276 n. 8, 277
Seim, Turid Karlsen 45 n. 5, 62 n. 35, 82 n. 5, 104 n. 57, 182 n. 5
Smith, D. Moody 117 n. 32, 186 n. 19
Smith-Christopher, Daniel 224 n. 9
Staley, Jeffrey L. 10 n. 8, 57 n. 29, 61 n. 33, 76 n. 13, 82 n. 4, 86 n. 21, 111 n. 8, 143 n. 5, 168 n. 4, 169 n. 6, 170–71, 172, 172 n. 16, 174–75, 177, 224, 24 n. 39
Stanton, Graham N. 117 n. 32, 13, 138 n. 18
Sternberg, Meir 111 n. 9, 191 n. 28
Stibbe, Mark 74 n. 9, 96 n. 42, 110 n. 6, 238 n. 2
Stoneman, Richard 33
Sugirtharajah, R. S. 224 n. 9, 275 n. 5
Sylva, D. D. 149 n. 18
Tannehill, Robert C. 83 nn. 6.8
Tanner, Mary 3 n. 2
Teitelbaum, Orna 107, 117 n. 30, 25–57 nn. 20–21.23, 259 n. 27
Telford, William R. 3 n. 1
The Bible and Culture Collective 282 n. 2
Thiselton, Anthony C. 164 n. 45
Thompson, Marianne Meye 82 n. 4
Thurston, Anne 243 n. 12
Thyen, Hartwig 84 n. 13

Tilborg, Sjef van   8, 45–46 n. 5, 46 n. 6,
    51 n. 18, 36 n. 27, 60 nn. 30–31, 82 n.
    5, 85 n. 15, 91 n. 35, 105 n. 59
Tolbert, Mary Ann   185 n. 16, 224 n. 9
Tompkins, Jane P.   110 n. 5, 144 n. 9, 184
    n. 12
Tovey, Derek   147 n. 13, 202 n. 43
Uspensky, Boris   85–86 n. 19
Van Nortwick, Thomas   10 n. 8
Vega, Carmen de la   109 n. 1
Viviano, Benedict T.   31 n. 13
Voelz, James W.   7 n. 4, 8, 28, 88 n. 27
Vogelsang, John D.   164 n. 45
Vorster, Willem   8
Watson, Francis   8, 81, 87 n. 24
Watzlawik, Paul   73
Wellhausen, Julius   151 n. 22
West, Gerald   168–69 n. 5, 187 n. 20
Wiltshire, Susan Fort   225 n. 12
Witherington, Ben III   199 n. 37
Wolff, Geoffrey   263 n. 37
Woolf, Virginia   260 n. 28
Wuellner, Wilhelm   61 n. 33, 81, 94
    n. 40, 96 n. 42, 104 n. 54, 105 n. 58,
    168, 173 n. 18, 235 n. 20
Young, Robert   96 n. 42
Zenger, Erich   151 n. 22
Zink, Jörg   157 n. 30
Zimmerman, Frank   121 n. 43
Zumstein, Jean   116 n. 26, 117 n. 29
Zwaan, J. de   4

Subject Index

Abram/Abraham, 150–56, 252, 284
Andrew, 95, 191. *See also* Simon Peter; disciples/discipleship; Twelve, the
androcentrism/androcentric, 52, 54, 170 n. 10, 172, 192, 242, 245
Anna/Hannah
   Hebrew Bible (Samuel's mother), 160 n. 34
   New Testament, 122, 122 n.46, **156–62, 252**, 284. *See also* temple
anointing (of Jesus), 32, 38, 51, 90–91, 93, **97–99**, 101, 188, **193–94, 204–7**, 214. *See also* Mary of Bethany, Mary of Magdala, Easter
anti-Judaism, 226
antipatriarchal, 191
apartheid/antiapartheid, 163, 183. *See also* gender
author-oriented, 31, 118. *See also* historical criticism/historical-critical
Beloved Disciple, 55, 61 n. 34, 74, 100, 101, 103, 109, 111, 114, 114 n. 17, 117, 118 n. 33, 122, 123, 125, 131, 162, 163, 179, 211, 214, 231, 232, 253, 255, 284. *See also* disciples/discipleship, crucifixion, Easter, mother of Jesus
Beersheva, 259, 259 n. 27
Bethany, 53, 90, 91, 92, 97, 99 n. 45, 99 n. 45, 150, 175, 192, 204, 258. *See also* Mary, Martha, Lazarus; Simon the leper; anointing
Bethlehem, 208, 210 n. 58, 212
Booths, Feast of, 200, 256. *See also* Sukkoth; Tabernacles, Feast of
border/s, 177, 245, 246, 260

border crossing/crosser, 30–31, 34, 38, 40, 259–61, 264
borderland/s, 241, 244, 245, 246, 250
border identity/woman, 241, 245, 246. *See also* Mexican; Samaritan woman
Cana, 48, 51, 60, 73, 74, 110, 111, 113, 123, 130, 187. *See also* mother of Jesus
Capernaum, 48, 60, 73, 111
colonial/colonized, 241, 275. *See also* decolonization, postcolonial
configuration, 37, 38, 39, 49, 50, 83–84, 100, 103, 105, 186, 187, 193, 194, 198, 288
crucifixion, 38, 55, **107–26**, 134, 161–62, 200. *See also* mother of Jesus, mother's sister, Mary of Magdala, Mary of Clopas, Beloved Disciple
cultural studies/reading, 26, 224, 227 n. 15, 276
decolonization, 32. *See also* colonial/colonized, postcolonial
deconstruct/deconstruction, 8, 37, 60, 136, 172
democracy/democratic, 12
determinacy/determinate versus indeterminacy/indeterminate, 7, 11
disciples/discipleship
   of Jesus (male/female), 46, 49, 51, 55, 55 n. 26, 56, 56 n. 27, 58, 59, 61, 71, 72, 73, 74, 75, 94, 95, 99 n. 45, 101–2, 105, 111, 113 n. 15, 116, 132, 149, 150, 189–94, 198, 200, 201, 209 n. 56, 221, 226, 228–33, 244, 245, 269–79. *See also* Andrew, Beloved Disciple, Joseph

-320-

disciples/discipleship: of Jesus (cont.)
    of Arimathea, Judas (Iscariot), Mary of Bethany, Mary of Magdala, Martha, Nathanael, Philip, Simon Peter, Thomas
    of John the Baptist, 95, 221–22, 271. *See also* Andrew
diversity, 22, 24, 32, 239, 275, 277
Easter, **99–104**, 114, **204–7**, 211, **227–33**. *See also* anointing; Beloved Disciple, Mary of Magdala, Simon Peter
Elijah, 259. *See also* Beersheva, Mount Horeb
elite/elitism, 6, 21, 22, 23, 24, 26
equality, 12, 163, 169, 176, 183, 191, 215, 226, 247
ethics
    of biblical interpretation, 11, 15, 17, 18, 19, 29, 44, 76, 169, 177, 183, 226, 262, 270–71
ethos, 1–3
Eurocentrism, 277
Euro-American, 21
European, 6, 21
exclusive versus inclusive, 23, 226
feminist criticism/feminism, 12, 12, 20, 28, 35–37, 44, 45, 62, 63, 64, 65, 88, 130, 169, 172, 176–77, 181, 196, 228, 241–42, 283, *passim. See also* postfeminist/postfeminism
footwashing, 187–93, 194–98
Galilee, 55 n. 99, 110, 134, 139, 205, 206, 244
    Sea of Galilee, 53, 139. *See also* Tiberias, Sea of
gender/genderization, 16, 22, 36, 37, 39, 40, 44, 88, 155, 163, **167–77**, 172, **179–216**, 187, 191, 199, 215, 231, 232, 246, 284, *passim*
global/globalization, 4, 15, 19, 33
Global North/Global South, 6, 7
hermeneutics. *See also* feminist criticism/feminism
    of correlation, 44
    of liberation, 64–65

hermeneutics (cont.)
    of promise, 39, 163, 164 n. 45
    of reconstruction, 164 n. 45
    of suspicion, 44, 172
Herod the Great/King Herod, 143 n. 4, 208–9. *See also* Mariamne
Hispanics/Hispanic Americans, 245
historical criticism/historical-critical, 6, 7, 21, 25, 27, 31, 32, 34, 118, 136, 223, 225, 228, 276, 282, 285, 290. *See also* author-oriented
historicism/historicist, 7, 9
identity
    of self (reader), 11, 16, 19, 26, 40, 73, 88, 235, 239, 246, 261–65
    of text, 40, 261–65
    theme, 260 n. 30
ideological criticism, 8, 9, 19, 21, 26, 177, 225, 262
ideology/ideologies, 44, 177, 235, 242
inclusive versus exclusive, 15, 19, 26, 55, 275, 276
interactive (pedagogy), 277
interpersonal, 38, 271
intratextuality, 39, **144**, 156, 163. *See also* semantic axes/axes of meaning
Jerusalem, 53, 61 n. 34, 75, 100, 110, 111, 134, 135, 150, 150, 150 n. 21, 158–59, 210 n. 58, 244, 259. *See also* temple
Jesus, 187–201, *passim*
Joanna, 118 n. 33, 205, 206
John the Baptist, 95, 114 n. 19, 271. *See also* disciples/discipleship
Joseph
    of Arimathea, 73, 73, 99 n. 45, 147, 148, 179, 201–3, 203 n. 46, 205, 213. *See also* disciples/discipleship
    Jesus's father, 123, 133, 134, 158–59, 212
Judas (Iscariot), 98–99, 189, 193, 204. *See also* disciples/discipleship; Twelve, the
justice, 12, 20, 169, 176
Lazarus, 53, 54, 57, 59–61, 61 n. 34, 75, **89–93**, 94, 95–96, 99 n. 45, 100, 102, 103, 104, 131, 150, **167–77**, 184, 188–

Lazarus (cont.)
   89, 192, 250, **258-59**, 284. *See also* Bethany, Mary, Martha
legitimacy (of readings), 29, 32, 56, 60, 87, 186
liberation/liberating, 20, 32, 34, 36, 58, 59, 60, 64, 69, 76, 155 n. 27, 163, 169, 174, 176, 177, 225, 226, 235, 242, 245, 246, 272, 273, 275
literary criticism, 8, 17, 25, 223, 276, 282
Magdala, 139, 273 n. 3. *See also* Mary
magi, 207-11
marginalization/marginalize, 7, 226 n. 13, 274-75
Mariamne, 143 n. 4. *See also* Herod the Great
Martha of Bethany, 46, 49-54, 56 n. 27, 57-61, 61 n. 34, 75, 90, **92-97**, 99 n. 45, 104, 105, 131, 150, **167-77**, 189, 192-93, 259, 287. *See also* disciples/discipleship, Martha, Lazarus
Mary
   of Bethany, 46, 48-54, 56 n. 27, 59-61, 61 n. 34, 75, **81-106, 127-39**, 150, **167-77**, 179, 181, 188-89, 192-93, **193-94**, 198, 214, 259, 284. *See also* anointing; disciples/discipleship
   of Magdala/Magdalene, 46, 48-52, 54-55, 55 n. 25, 56 n. 27, 59, 61, 63 n. 39, 72, 74, **81-106**, 109, 114, 114 n. 18, 115, 117 n. 31, 118, 118 n. 33, 119, **127-39**, 141-43, 142-43 n. 4, 161, 181, 192-93, 205, 206, 221, **227-30**, 255, 258, 273, 274 n. 3, 284. *See also* disciples/discipleship, crucifixion, Easter
   (mother) of James and Joses/Joseph, 118 n. 33, 132, 134, 205, 206
   of Nazareth, **127-39**, 159-61, 160-61 n. 38, 161, 163, 208, 211, **212-14**, 214, 284. *See also* mother of Jesus
   (wife) of Clopas, 48, 50, 51, 99, 109, 161, 161 n. 40, 255. *See also* crucifixion
Mexican-American, 241. *See also* border/s, borderland

midrash, 38, 135-36, 138
Migdal Nunya, 273. *See also* Magdala
mixture/otherness, 14, 244. *See also* border/s, borderland
mother, 231. *See also* widow of Nain
   of Jesus, 46, 48, 50, 51, 56 n. 27, 59, 60, 60 n. 32, 74, 99, 105, **107-26**, 129-31, 142-43 n. 4, 158, 159, 161, 161 n. 42, 162-63, 187, 208, 211, 213, 214, 253-54, 255, 255 n. 19, 284. *See also* Mary of Nazareth, Cana, crucifixion
   mother's sister (Jesus's aunt), 51, 99, 109, 161, 161 n. 40, 255. *See also* crucifixion
   of the sons of Zebedee, 134
Mount Horeb, 259. *See also* Elijah
Mount of Olives, 150. *See also* public versus private
multidimensional/multidimensionality, 11, 15, 37, 64, 65, 69, 76, 135, 181, 183 n. 7, 235, 239, 261
mutual/mutuality, 247, 271, 279
Nain, 175. *See also* widow
narrative criticism/narrative-critical, 8, 19, 28, 30, 32, 46, **81-106**, 184, 281, 286
narrator, 46, 53, 57, 59, 65, 85, 96, 104, 114, 116, 172, 176, 188, 201, 229, 238, 240
Nathanael, 95, 191, 243-44, 274. *See also* disciples/discipleship
Nazareth, 120, 129, 133, 139, 212, 274-75. *See also* Mary of Nazareth
Nicodemus, 43-45, 70-71, 72, 73, 75, 99 n. 45, 115-16, 139, 143, **145-50**, 153, 155-60, 162, 179-80, 184, 187, **201-15, 251-57**, 259, 284. *See also* Pharisee/s, disciples/discipleship
North Atlantic, 22, 24
objective/objectivity versus subjective/subjectivity, 7, 17, 20, 34, 225, 285, 286
oppression/oppressive, 65, 169, 272, 275, 277

paradigm/s, 28, 31–32, 40, 44, 48, 63, 118, 135–36, 223–24, 228, 232, 270–71, 275–77, 290. *See also* historical criticism/historical-critical; literary criticism; narrative criticism/narrative-critical; reader response; cultural studies
passion narrative, 38, **81–106**, 201–4, 287
Passover, 97, 187–88
patriarchal/patriarchy, 58, 59, 64, 88, 128–29, 169, 170, 172, 176, 177, 215, 226, 241–43, 272, 276
pedagogical discourse, 276–79
Pentateuch, 155, 155, 155–56 n. 27, 255
Peter, 91, 128, 232–33. *See also* Simon Peter; disciples/discipleship; Twelve, the
Pharisee/s, 96, 97, 147, 174, 195, 197–98, 201–3, 207. *See also* Nicodemus, Simon
Philip, 191. *See also* disciples/discipleship; Twelve, the
Pilate, 69, 201, 203, 219, 221
point of view, 59, 72, 85, 92, 94, 96, 101, 226, 229, 238, 289
postcolonial/postcolonialism, 275. *See also* colonial/colonized, decolonization
postfeminist/postfeminism, 35–37, 39, 177, 183. *See also* feminist criticism/feminism
postmodern, 34, 281, 282, 285, 289
public versus private, 150 n. 21
racist/racism, 58, 242, 246
reader/s, 7–20
constructs, 8, 12, 19, 30, 33 n. 14, 88 n. 26, 224
critical/ordinary, 11, 227, 227 n. 15, 239
first, 19, 25, 30, 33 n. 14, 52, 88, 223
implied (intended), 46, 63, 104–5, 223, 286
plurality of, 11, 52
real/flesh-and-blood, 8, 10, 15, 19, 21, 32, 52, 63, 110, 185, 224, 234, 240, 241, 286

reader response/reader-oriented, 10, 17, 25, 26, 30, 31, 32, 75, **100–106**, 118, 124, 144, 169, 171, 182, 185, 223, 224, 282, 285, *passim*
reading/s, 7–20
against the grain (counterreading)/with the grain, 35, 37, 44, 48, 52, 56, 57, 60, 62, 63, 68–69, 105, 169, 172, 176–77, 182, 241–44, 275, 281
first-time, 38, 47, 48, 89
rereading, 43–66, **47–48**, 56, 62, 89, 135, 138, *passim*. *See also* midrash
strategies, 30, 36, 67, 68, 69, 88 n. 26
with/in community, 187, 187 n. 20
reception (of texts), 21, 26, 290
reconstruction (of self, of texts), 7, 40, 163, 164 n. 45. *See also* hermeneutics
responsibility, 17, 18, 19, 20, 29, 66, 183
rhetoric/s, 57, 59, 60, 63, 64, 65, 185, 234
Salome, 132, 205. *See also* anointing, Easter
Samaria/Samaritans, 10, 58, 241, 274
Samaritan woman, 46, 48–49, 51, 55–57, 56 n. 27, 56–58, 60, 71, 72, 73, 75, 93, 102, 105, 181–82, 227, **237–47**, 284. *See also* Sychar
Sarai/Sarah, **150–56**, 252, 284
scholarly schools, 273. *See also* Tübingen school
semantic axes/axes of meaning, 39, 144, 156, 164, 197, 198. *See also* intratextuality
semiotics, 39
sexist/sexism, 58, 65, 242, 246
Simeon, 121–22, 125, 209 n. 56, 252, 284. *See also* temple
Simon the leper, 204–5
Simon Peter, 74, 100, 101, 103, 114, 179–80, 189–91, 197–98, 231, 232. *See also* Peter; disciples/discipleship; Twelve, the; Easter; footwashing
Simon the Pharisee, 195–97. *See also* anointing
social location, 8, 17, 32, 34, 40, 44, 65, 87, 224, 235, **237–47**, 286

sociocultural, 8, 10, 15, 19, 20, 25
Sophia/Chokmah, 199–200
subjective/subjectivity versus objective/objectivity, 17, 18, 19, 69, 118, 177
Sukkoth, 249, 254, 256–57, 256 n. 20, 257 nn. 23–24. *See also* Booths, Feast of; Tabernacles, Feast of
Susanna, 118 n. 33
Sychar, 55, 60, 73, 102, 162, 245, 272. *See also* Samaritan woman
Tabernacles, Feast of, 255 n. 256. *See also* Sukkoth; Booths, Feast of
temple, 75, 111, 121, 158, 158 n. 31, 159–62. *See also* Jerusalem; Anna, Simeon
text/s
    open(ended), 39, 60, 61, 62, 74–75, 76, 87, 96, 104, 125, 139, **155 n. 27**, 157, 158, 160, 164, 174, 216
    self as, 34, 38, 111, 135, 137, 234, 261–62, *passim*
    world in/behind/in front of, 15, 34, 36, 110–11, 136, 137, 281, 290
Thomas, 142, 191, 192, 221, 228. *See also* disciples/discipleship; Twelve, the; Easter
Tiberias, Sea of, 232, 275. *See also* Galilee, Sea of
Torah, 138. *See also* Pentateuch
transformation/transformative, 9–18, 103, 137, 163, 187, 215–16, 241, 247, 261
Tübingen school, 286. *See also* scholarly schools
Twelve, the, 226. *See also* Andrew, Judas (Iscariot), Philip, Simon Peter, Thomas; disciples/discipleship
widow
    Anna, 122
    mother of Jesus, 123–24, 255 n. 19. *See also* Joseph
    of Nain, 123–24, 125, 175, 255 n. 19